Fundamental statistics for social research

Statistics play a vital role in the description of the results of empirical research in the social sciences. Consequently, an understanding of the way in which such data have been analysed is essential to being able to evaluate those results fully and critically. This accessible introduction to statistics using the program SPSS for Windows assumes no prior knowledge of statistics or computing and explains when to apply and how to calculate a wide range of statistical procedures commonly used in the social sciences. Ranging from chi-square and the *t* test to analysis of covariance and multiple regression, Duncan Cramer covers a wide choice of statistics, including tests not found in other introductory texts, such as tests for determining whether correlations differ and the extent of agreement between observers. Important statistical points are illustrated with worked numerical examples, and exercises are provided at the ends of chapters.

Fundamental Statistics for Social Research covers the latest versions of SPSS for Windows – *Release 6* and *Release 7*. It will prove an invaluable introductory statistics text for students, and a useful resource for graduates and professionals engaged in research in the social sciences.

Duncan Cramer is Reader in Psychological Health at Loughborough University. He is author of *Basic Statistics for Social Research: Step-by-step calculations and computer techniques using Minitab* (1996); *Introducing Statistics for Social Research: Step-by-step calculations and computer techniques using SPSS* (1994); *Quantitative Data Analysis with SPSS for Windows: A guide for social scientists* (1996, with Alan Bryman); *Quantitative Data Analysis with Minitab: A guide for social scientists* (1996, with Alan Bryman); and *Quantitative Data Analysis for Social Scientists* (SPSS version) (1990, revised 1994, with Alan Bryman).

Fundamental statistics for social research

Step-by-step calculations and computer techniques using SPSS for Windows

Duncan Cramer

London and New York

First published 1998
by Routledge
11 New Fetter Lane, London EC4P 4EE

Simultaneously published in the USA and Canada
by Routledge
29 West 35th Street, New York, NY 10001

© 1998 Duncan Cramer

Typeset in Times by J&L Composition Ltd, Filey, North Yorkshire
Printed and bound in Great Britain by TJ International Ltd, Padstow, Cornwall

British Library Cataloguing in Publication Data
A catalogue record for this book is available from the British Library

Library of Congress Cataloguing in Publication Data
Cramer, Duncan, 1948–
    Fundamental statistics for social research: step-by-step calculations
    and computer techniques using SPSS for Windows / Duncan Cramer.
    p.   cm.
    Includes bibliographical references and index.
    1. Social sciences—Statistical methods—Computer programs.
    2. SPSS for Windows. I. Title.
    HA32.C68   1997
    300′.7′27—dc21   97–12951

ISBN 0–415–17203–9 (hbk)
ISBN 0–415–17204–7 (pbk)

Contents

Boxes

Figures

Tables

Preface

Statistics play a vital role in the description of the results of empirical research in the social sciences. Consequently, an understanding of the way in which such data have been analysed is essential to being able to evaluate those results fully and critically. A knowledge of statistics is also necessary for running our own statistical analyses. This book describes when to apply, how to calculate and how to interpret a comprehensive selection of statistical tests used in the social sciences, ranging from chi-square and the t test to analysis of covariance and multiple regression. It shows how to calculate these tests by hand as well as with the aid of a computer program called *SPSS for Windows*. The widespread availability of computers and programs for carrying out statistics means that statistics can now be more efficiently and accurately computed with these means. *SPSS* (which is an abbreviation of *Statistical Package for the Social Sciences*) was chosen because it was specifically written for the social sciences, has an extensive variety of statistical procedures, is considered easy to learn and, as a consequence, is widely taught and used in the social sciences.

However, in order to understand what these tests involve it is still necessary to work out the computations by hand. To make the calculations easier the examples employ small sets of data consisting of small numbers. The same set of data is often used to illustrate more than one test so that the results of different tests can be compared and less time is spent on introducing new examples. If the examples use variables which seem less relevant to your own interests, then replace them with more appropriate ones. Where possible important statistical points have been illustrated with worked numerical examples. Statistical symbols have been kept to a minimum so that there is less need to remember what these symbols represent. Exercises at the ends of chapters (together with the answers at the back of the book) enable readers to test their understanding of the computational steps involved in the tests described as well as providing additional examples of data and their statistical analysis. Once readers have learned how to operate SPSS, they can generate their own exercises and assess their knowledge by comparing their answers with those produced by SPSS. Unlike many statistical texts, references are given for when statistical procedures were first introduced, to provide a chronological context for these ideas.

The version of SPSS for Windows covered this book is the latest version which, at the time of writing, is *Release 6* and *Release 7 for Windows 95*. The Windows version requires a 386 or higher processor. SPSS terms and variable names have been printed in **bold** to distinguish them from the rest of the text. Because the differences between Releases 6 and 7 are small and Windows 95 is due to be replaced shortly, the procedures and output for this book are based on Release 6. The minor differences between the two versions are described on the Internet at http://www.routledge.com/routledge/textbooks/fssr.html.

I would like to thank Longman Group UK Ltd, on behalf of the Literary Executor of the late Sir Ronald A. Fisher, FRS, and Dr Frank Yates, FRS, for permission to reproduce Tables II, IV and VII from *Statistical Tables for Biological, Agricultural and Medical Research*, 6th edn (1974).

Duncan Cramer
Loughborough University

1 Role of statistics in social research

A major aim of the social and behavioural sciences is to develop principles which explain and provide new insights into human behaviour. One way of evaluating what appear to be sound and promising principles is to examine the extent to which they are consistent with carefully controlled observations of human behaviour. In other words, the validity of principles needs to be tested by conducting empirical research wherever possible. If the data do not agree with the principle under scrutiny, the principle may have to be modified and then re-examined. Alternatively, the way in which the controlled observations were made may have been mistaken and a new set of data may have to be collected. Suppose, for example, we tested the idea that people are likely to repeat the aggression they see in others but we found no evidence to support such a relationship. In this case, it might be necessary to make the principle more specific by proposing that individuals are likely to imitate aggression which is rewarded rather than punished, and then to test this revised proposition. On the other hand, the measure of aggression we used may have been unsuitable for the purpose and may have to be replaced with a more appropriate test.

Statistics play a vital role in collecting, summarising and interpreting data designed to empirically evaluate a principle. Consequently, an understanding of this important subject is necessary both to carry out research and to be able to critically evaluate research that has been, or is going to be, conducted. The function that statistics serves in social research can best be briefly illustrated by looking at the ways in which it is involved in testing a principle. Take, for example, the simple idea we have already introduced that people tend to imitate what they have observed. If this is the case, then individuals who, say, have watched a violent incident shown on television should be more likely to behave in this way than those who have not seen this incident. One approach to testing this idea would be to select two groups of people and to show one group (known as the *experimental group*, *condition* or *treatment*) a film or video containing a violent incident and the other group (the *control* group) a similar film not containing the violent sequence. After viewing the film, the aggression displayed by both groups of people would be observed to see if the groups differed as expected.

Suppose that the people who had watched the violent incident showed more aggression subsequently than those who had not been exposed to this violence. Before it could be concluded that these results confirm the principle that individuals tend to imitate what they have observed, at least three essential and related statistical considerations need to have been met. The first is that participants should have been *randomly sampled* from the population (e.g. Bowley 1913). A random sample is one in which each member of the population has an equal chance of being selected for the sample. The second is that the sampled participants should have been *randomly assigned* to the two groups (Fisher 1925b, 1935). Random assignment means that individuals have an equal probability of being assigned to each group. The third is that the difference in observed aggression between the two groups should be *statistically significant* (Fisher 1926, 1935), which means that the difference has a one in twenty probability or less of occurring simply by chance.

RANDOM SAMPLING

When testing a principle, we usually want to know how valid it is of people in general. Since it is not possible to test everyone when examining a particular generalisation, we carry out our study on a *sample* or subset of people. The idea of a sample implies that there is a larger *population* from which it is drawn. This population is often not specified because we assume the principle to be generally true. For example, when we postulate that watching violence on television causes aggression, we presumably believe that this holds true for all people where watching television is part of their cultural experience and that this principle does not simply apply to the people we have tested. In other words, we want to be able to generalise the findings from our sample to the population as a whole.

There are two main ways in which we can select a sample of objects or cases, which need not be people, of course. The first method is to draw a *simple random* sample where every object in a given population has an equal probability of being chosen. To do this, the population of objects needs to be specified and known and some random procedure employed for selecting objects. To give a simple example, suppose we wanted to draw a small sample of five people from a class of twenty which was the population of interest. We could assign a number from 1 to 20 to each of the individuals in the class. We could then go to a table of random numbers and select the first five numbers which fell between 1 and 20, which may be 13, 9, 17, 18 and 5. The five people who had those numbers would constitute our sample. In this method, everybody would have a one in four probability of being selected.

The second method of sampling is to generate a *non-random* sample where the probability of choosing an object from a specified population is not known. An example of this approach would be if we selected the first five people according to whether their surname started with letters closest to the beginning of the alphabet. This method would be non-random because people whose surname began with these letters would have the highest probability of being chosen.

Because of the difficulty of obtaining a random sample, many studies in the social sciences use non-random samples and assume that the sample can be thought of as random. If, however, we believed that the principle we were investigating only applied to people with certain characteristics, then we could see if this assumption was true by testing this principle on people with and without those characteristics. For example, if we thought that watching violence only made males more aggressive and did not affect females, then we could test this idea on a sample of males and females. If, on the other hand, we wanted to know how common a particular behaviour was in a specified population, we would require a random sample to answer this question. For example, we would need a random sample to find out how many adults living in Britain viewed violent programmes on television. How accurate our estimate was would partly depend on the size of that sample. If we had used a non-random sample, we would not be able to estimate this figure because we would not know how representative that non-random sample was of the population.

RANDOM ASSIGNMENT

Having obtained our sample, we then need to randomly assign them to the two conditions. One way of trying to do this is to flip an unbiased coin. The two faces of the coin are used to represent the two groups. For example, it can be agreed before hand that if the coin lands with the side showing the head ('heads up'), then the first of two people will be assigned to the group that will see the violent episode. The second person will be allocated to the group that will not be shown the violent incident. If, on the other hand, the coin lands with the side which does not display the head ('tails up'), then the first person will be assigned to the group which will not see the violent sequence, while the second participant will be allocated to the group which will be shown the violent episode. This procedure of assigning two people at a time with one coin throw will ensure that the number of people in both groups will be similar, although a similar number of people in each group is not itself a statistical requirement.

The reason for random assignment of participants to conditions is to try and ensure that there is no bias in the way that people are allocated to the two groups and that every person has an equal chance of being in either group. If random assignment is not used, then there is the possibility that one group will contain individuals who may be more prone to show aggression. If this happened, the results obtained could not be explained in terms of which films the participants had seen. Because this is a very important point to grasp, it will be further elaborated.

There are potentially a very large number of factors which may predispose individuals to be aggressive, some of which we may not readily recall or even be aware of. For example, participants who had had a poor night's sleep or gone without breakfast may be more irritable than those who had slept well or had had a hearty breakfast. Men may be more inclined to show their aggression than women, and so on. Now, it is possible to control for some of these factors by holding them constant, such as restricting participation to men or to women. Alternatively, the role of these factors may themselves be investigated by including both women and men in the study. However, because we are not necessarily aware of all the factors that might influence aggressiveness and because it would be difficult to study or to hold constant all those variables that we were conscious of, it is better to try to control for these extraneous factors through random assignment. By randomly assigning participants to treatments, it is more likely that the people in both groups will be similar in terms of a whole host of other characteristics. For example, random assignment will make it more probable that the two groups will contain the same number of people who had a disturbed night's sleep, missed breakfast or were male.

However, when only a small number of participants are involved in a study and are randomly assigned to conditions, there is a greater probability that the number or proportion of people who have the same characteristic will differ in the two conditions. This point can be illustrated by looking at the possible results of tossing a varying number of coins. The two sides of the coin can be thought of as denoting any variable which can take on two equiprobable values such as being a woman or man. If we tossed the coin once, then the probability of it turning up heads would be one of two possibilities (a head or a tail), which can be represented as the proportion 0.5 (i.e. $1/2 = 0.5$).

If we tossed two coins once, there are four possible or theoretical outcomes as shown in Table 1.1: (1) a head on the first coin and a tail on the second; (2) a tail on the first coin and a head on the second; (3) two heads on both coins; and (4) two tails on both coins. The probability of obtaining both a head and a tail (regardless of the coin) would be two out of four possibilities or 0.5 ($2/4 = 0.5$). The probability (or p value) of obtaining two

Table 1.1 Four possible outcomes of tossing two coins once and their probability

	Coin 1	Coin 2	Probability (p)
1	Head	Tail	0.25 } = 0.5
2	Tail	Head	0.25
3	Head	Head	0.25
4	Tail	Tail	0.25

heads would be one out of four possibilities or 0.25 (1/4 = 0.25). Similarly, the probability of having two tails would also be one out of four possibilities or 0.25.

If we assume that we are randomly assigning only two participants to one of the two conditions, then we can see that the probability of having all women or all men in this condition is 0.5. We can calculate the probability of any particular outcome from any number of coins by simply multiplying the probability of the two outcomes of each of the coins being used. So this probability would be 0.25 for two coins as we have already noted (0.5 × 0.5 = 0.25), 0.125 for three coins (0.5 × 0.5 × 0.5 = 0.125) and 0.0625 for four coins (0.5 × 0.5 × 0.5 × 0.5 = 0.0625). For any number of coins, there can only be one outcome which contains all heads and only one which consists of all tails. To work out the probability of obtaining both these outcomes, we simply add up their separate probabilities, which is 0.5 for two coins (0.25 + 0.25 = 0.5) as we have already calculated, 0.25 for three coins (0.125 + 0.125 = 0.25) and 0.125 for four coins (0.0625 + 0.0625 = 0.125). It should be clear then that as the number of participants increases, the probability that random assignment will lead to participants in any one group having all of one characteristic should decrease.

Of course, it is possible to check whether random assignment has resulted in the participants in the two conditions being similar in various ways before being shown the two films. However, in order not to overtax the participants' good will, it is preferable to limit this *pre-testing* to those variables of most direct interest, which in this case would be their aggressiveness before seeing the film. A pre-test is a measure taken before the experimental manipulation is carried out as opposed to a *post-test* which is taken after the manipulation has been carried out. This pre-test information can be used in three ways. First, participants with similar pre-test aggressiveness can be *matched*, *blocked* or *paired* in terms of their scores and then randomly assigned to one of the two conditions. This matching procedure will ensure that the participants in the two conditions will be similar in terms of their initial aggressiveness.

Second, without resorting to matching, the pre-test aggressiveness scores of the participants in the two conditions can be compared after all the data have been collected. If the scores in the two conditions differ, then random assignment has not been effective so far as the key variable of aggressiveness is concerned. The way of determining whether two groups of scores differ is itself a statistical issue which will be introduced below. If the pre-test scores differ, then there are statistical procedures, such as *analysis of covariance*, which take these differences into consideration. This particular procedure will be described in Chapter 10.

Third, if the pre-test scores do not differ, then they may be compared with the post-test aggressiveness scores of the participants after they have seen the film to determine the nature and statistical significance of any change that has occurred.

STATISTICAL SIGNIFICANCE

Having tested our participants, we then need to determine how likely it is that the results of our study are due to chance. Findings which have a one in twenty probability or less of occurring by chance are considered to be statistically significant in the sense that they are not thought to be due to chance. This level of significance is usually expressed as the proportion 0.05 (1/20 = 0.05). There are numerous tests for assessing the statistical significance of a finding. Indeed, most of this book is devoted to describing the more commonly used tests. However, the general principle which underlies significance testing can be simply illustrated as follows.

Assume that people's behaviour in this study is rated as being either aggressive or non-aggressive. If watching the violent film had no effect and if the probability of being aggressive was the same as being non-aggressive (i.e. 0.5), then the proportion of people who were rated as being aggressive after viewing the film should differ by chance between the two conditions. This situation is like tossing two sets of coins once, where heads depict being aggressive and tails being non-aggressive. The two sets of coins represent the people who have been randomly assigned to watching either the violent or non-violent film. If we toss two coins once (representing one person from each of the two conditions), then there are four possible outcomes as shown in Table 1.1: (1) a head and a tail; (2) a tail and a head; (3) two heads; and (4) two tails. If the first coin represents people viewing the violent film and the second coin those watching the non-violent film, then the probability is 0.25 of finding the person watching the violent film being aggressive (heads on coin 1) and the person viewing the non-violent film being non-aggressive (tails on coin 2). If we obtained this result and if we use the conventional criterion that for a difference to be statistically significant it has to have a probability of 0.05 or less, then we would have to conclude that there was no statistically significant difference in aggressiveness between the two conditions.

We can now extend this idea to the theoretical outcomes of tossing two sets of two coins once, which are shown in Table 1.2. There is one outcome (outcome 2 in Table 1.2) in which two heads were obtained with the two coins in the first set and two tails were found with the two coins in the second set. This outcome represents the situation in which the two people watching the violent film were both rated as being aggressive subsequently while the two people watching the non-violent film were both described as being non-aggressive. The probability of this outcome is 0.0625. If we obtained this result from our study, then we could conclude that this difference just failed to reach statistical significance at the 0.05 level.

Suppose, however, we had found that only one of the two people watching the violent film had been rated as being aggressive subsequently and that, as before, neither of the two people viewing the non-violent film had been described as being aggressive. From Table 1.2, we can see that there

Table 1.2 Probability of same outcome from tossing two sets of two coins once

Outcome	Set 1 (Violent film)	Set 2 (Non-violent film)	Probability (p)
1	HH	HH	0.0625
2	HH	TT	0.0625
3	HH	HT	0.0625
4	HH	TH	0.0625
5	TT	HH	0.0625
6	TT	TT	0.0625
7	TT	HT	0.0625
8	TT	TH	0.0625
9	HT	HH	0.0625
10	HT	TT	0.0625
11	HT	HT	0.0625
12	HT	TH	0.0625
13	TH	HH	0.0625
14	TH	TT	0.0625
15	TH	HT	0.0625
16	TH	TH	0.0625

are two outcomes (outcomes 10 and 14) which reflect this situation. Consequently, the probability of finding that only one of the two people watching the violent film was rated as being aggressive (and neither of the other two in the non-violent condition) is the combined probability of these two outcomes which is 0.125 (0.0625 + 0.0625 = 0.125). If we obtained this result, then this difference is clearly not significant at the 0.05 level.

The basic aim of many statistical tests is to determine the probability of obtaining a particular finding by chance. Which test to use depends on a number of considerations which are outlined in Chapter 4.

TRUE EXPERIMENTAL DESIGNS

The design of the study which has so far been used to illustrate the role of statistics in social research has been referred to as a *true experimental* design (Campbell and Stanley 1966). There are two essential features to such a design. First, only the presence of the factor (or factors) whose effects are of interest should be varied or manipulated. Everything else should be kept as similar and as constant as possible. Second, participants should be randomly assigned to the conditions which represent these variations, or to the order in which these conditions are run if participants take part in more than one condition. An example of the latter procedure would be where participants saw both the film with the violence and the one without it.

A design in which different participants (or *subjects* as they were traditionally called in psychology) are randomly assigned to different conditions has been referred to as a *between-subjects* design or one involving *independent, unrelated* or *uncorrelated* groups or samples. On the other hand, a design in which the same participants are randomly allocated to more than one condition has been described as a *within-subjects* design or one involving *repeated measures* or *dependent, related* or *correlated* groups or samples.

The advantage of a within-subjects design, apart from requiring fewer participants, is that it holds constant all those factors which are unique to any one person (such as their genetic makeup and previous personal experiences) and which may affect the way they respond to the manipulation. However, since the order in which conditions are run may alter the responses to them, it is essential to control for any potential *order effect* by making sure that the different orders are conducted the same number of times. Suppose, for instance, that watching violent films does not increase aggression but that the more often people see a film (no matter what its content), the less aggressive they feel. If the violent film is shown first more often, then it will appear that seeing violence produces aggression. Random assignment of participants to different orders, on the other hand, is necessary to determine if the order of the conditions has an effect. With non-random assignment, it is more likely that people who are prone to aggression will be allocated to one or other of the two orders. If aggressive people are more frequently assigned to seeing the violent film first, then there may appear to be an order effect (such that seeing violence first makes people more aggressive) when there is none.

Within-subjects designs (where it is possible in principle to use them) have two potential drawbacks which may outweigh their advantages. The first disadvantage is that there may be a *carryover* or *asymmetrical transfer effect* where a change induced by the first condition will carry over to the second. For instance, watching the violent film first may increase a person's tendency to be aggressive so that they are more likely to act aggressively after seeing the non-violent film. If this happens, then the difference in aggressiveness between the two conditions will be less in a within- than a between-subjects design and consequently may not be statistically significant. The second potential disadvantage of the within-subjects design is that participants will have more information about the experiment as a result of being exposed to more than one condition. This knowledge may affect what they think the experiment is about which in turn may influence their subsequent behaviour.

The great strength of a true experimental design is that by virtue of trying to hold all other extraneous variables constant and to vary only those factors of interest, it enables us to determine with more certainty whether the effects we observe are due to the factors that have been manipulated. For example, suppose we find that, with everything else held constant, participants who watched the violent film behaved more aggressively than those who saw the non-violent film. Then, provided that this effect occurred more frequently than is likely to have happened just by chance, it seems reasonable to conclude that the greater aggression shown resulted from watching the violent film.

NON-EXPERIMENTAL DESIGNS

Experimental designs which do not entail the random assignment of participants to the systematic manipulation of one or more variables have been called *non-*, *pre-* or *quasi-experimental* designs (Campbell and Stanley 1966). Perhaps the most common of these designs is one in which two or more variables are measured at one moment in time. This kind of design is very similar to what Campbell and Stanley (1966) term the *static-group comparison* and often takes the form of a survey. Suppose, for example, we wanted to find out whether people who watched more violence on television also behaved more aggressively. In other words, we wished to determine if the amount of violence seen on television was related to the level of aggression displayed. The simplest way of examining whether there is such a relationship between these two characteristics is to ask a number of individuals how much violence they watched on television and how aggressively they behaved and to work out what the association is between these two variables.

There are two main statistical approaches for determining whether there is a statistically significant association between these two factors. The first approach is essentially a test of difference. It examines whether there is a statistical difference in aggression between the two groups of people and is the same as that previously used in the true experiment described above to find out if there was a significant difference between those participants who saw the violent film and those who did not. In the static-group comparison we could divide the participants into two groups according to how much violence they watched on television. Individuals in one group will have watched little or no violence on television, while those in the other group will have seen more violence on television. The exact criterion we use to form the two groups need not concern us here. We can then compare the amount of aggression reported by the people in the two groups.

As before, any difference we find between the two groups may be due to chance and so we would have to work out what the statistical probability was of coming up with any such difference by chance. Suppose we noted that those who watched more violence on television also reported being more aggressive than those who saw less violence. If the probability of finding this difference was calculated to be 0.05 or less, we could conclude that those who watched more violence on television behaved significantly more aggressively than those who saw less violence. If the probability of obtaining this difference was greater than 0.05, we would have to conclude that there was no significant difference between these two groups of individuals.

The second statistical approach for calculating whether there is a significant association between two factors (such as watching violence on television and aggression) is essentially a test of the strength of that association. We are interested in estimating how strong the relationship is between two factors. To illustrate the principle behind this test, suppose that of four people questioned about their television viewing habits and aggressive behaviour, two are classified as watching little or no violence on television while the other two are categorised as viewing violence on television. Furthermore, the two who did not watch violence on television did not behave aggressively, while the two who viewed violence on television did act aggressively. We could summarise these results in the form of a simple table as shown in Table 1.3.

To work out the strength of the relationship between watching violence on television and being aggressive, we can count the number of people who watch violence and are aggressive (which is 2) and the number of people who do not watch violence and are not aggressive (which is also 2). We can then calculate the proportion of people who fall into either of these two categories by adding these two figures together and dividing by the total number of people in the sample. This proportion is 1.00 [(2 + 2)/4 = 1.00]. In other words, since both the persons who watch violence on televison are aggressive while both those who do not watch violence on television are not aggressive, we have a perfect relationship between watching violence on television and being aggressive.

It should be noted that an index of association can also be worked out for the results of a true experiment between the manipulated variable (e.g. watching the violent or non-violent film) and the measured variable (e.g. aggression). However, this is done less often with data from true experimental designs. The important point to remember is that statistical tests of difference and association can be used with either true or non-experimental designs and that the choice of which test to use depends primarily on the purpose of the analysis.

The static-group comparison design includes the following three advantages. First, it is relatively simple and inexpensive to carry out. Second, information on a large number of potentially relevant factors can be assessed which is useful in exploring which factors are likely to be the most influential. And third, these factors can be studied in the natural, everyday context in which they occur.

Table 1.3 Results showing a perfect relationship between watching violence on television and aggression

		Aggression	
		No	*Yes*
Violence watched	No	2	0
	Yes	0	2

The main drawback of this design, however, is that it does not enable us to determine the causal nature of the relationship between any two variables. Suppose, for instance, we found that people who watched violence on television also behaved more aggressively in general. The causal connection between these two variables can be explained in four possible ways. First, as originally suggested, watching violence on television may produce aggression.

1 Watching violence ⟶ Aggression

But, this is by no means the only possible explanation. Indeed, the causal direction of this association may be reversed, with aggression resulting in watching violence on television. In other words, aggressive people may like to view violence on television.

2 Watching violence ⟵ Aggression

In both these explanations, only one variable affects the other. Consequently, these causal directions are sometimes referred to as *one-way, unidirectional, unilateral, non-reciprocal* or *recursive*.

However, it is also possible that both variables affect each other. Watching violence on television may encourage aggression while aggression itself may lead to viewing violence on television.

3 Watching violence ⟷ Aggression

Relationships in which both variables influence each other are sometimes described as *two-way, bidirectional, bilateral, reciprocal* or *non-recursive*.

Finally, two variables may appear to be related when in reality they are not because they are both associated with a third variable. For example, adolescents may both watch more violence on television and be more aggressive than adults. In other words, if age is strongly related to both these variables, then the two variables will themselves appear to be directly associated when they are not.

4 Watching violence ⟶ Aggression
                    ↖   ↗
                       Age

This kind of relationship is described as *spurious* because it is due to other factors. Note, however, that although age may be a *confounding* variable in this case, an alternative possibility is that aggression is an *intervening* or *mediating* variable through which age acts to affect watching violence.

Age ⟶ Aggression ⟶ Watching violence

Whether age is better seen as a confounding variable or aggression as an intervening variable depends partly on the size of the associations between the variables and partly on theoretical argument.

On the other hand, if we find no relationship between watching violence on television and aggression, then it is still possible that there is an association between these two variables but that it has been suppressed by some other factor(s). For instance, if the more physically active watched less violence on television and behaved more aggressively, then the relationship between these two variables may be hidden by the fact that the less physically active watched more violence on television but behaved less aggressively. Where we believe that the relationship between two variables may be either spurious or suppressed, we should try to measure the factor(s) that are bringing this about and to remove or control the influence of these factor(s) statistically. Statistical tests for doing this are described in Chapters 6 and 13.

It is important to realise that making claims about the causal relationship between two (or more) variables depends primarily on the experimental design used to examine the relationship and not on the statistical analysis of the results. True experimental designs enable causality to be ascertained with more confidence because an attempt is made to hold constant all other variables except the ones of interest which are systematically varied. Non-experimental designs, such as the static-group comparison, do not allow causality to be inferred because they do not systematically manipulate the variables of concern. The same statistical tests can be used to analyse the appropriate results of both non- and true experimental designs. What these tests generally do is to provide us with an estimate of the size of any relationship and the probability of finding that relationship by chance.

Factors whose effects we are interested in are often called *independent variables* while the effects themselves are usually referred to as the *dependent variables* because it is assumed that these effects *depend* on the independent variables. Consequently, if we believed that watching violence on television increased aggressiveness, we would call the degree to which violence was watched on television the independent variable and the level of aggressiveness displayed the dependent variable. If we thought that the direction of causality was the other way round, we would call the level of aggressiveness the independent variable and the degree to which violence was watched on television the dependent variable. Strictly speaking, however, the terms independent variable and dependent variable should be respectively reserved for the manipulated variable and the measured effect in a true experimental design. In such a design the independent variable should be manipulated independently of other features of the design so that any observed effect is more likely to be due to this manipulated variable than to the other features of the study. Factors in a true experimental design which cannot be independently manipulated, such as the age and gender of the participants, are sometimes more appropriately referred to as *subject variables* since they cannot be separated from the individual. Often, however, these factors are also described as independent variables.

MEASURING CONCEPTS

Finally, an understanding of statistics is required for making decisions about how a concept or variable should be measured and for assessing how reliable and valid that measure is. For example, we have to decide how we should quantify or score how aggressive someone is. Do we simply categorise people as being aggressive or non-aggressive? Do we order them in terms of how aggressive they are from the most to the least aggressive? Or do we rate them in some way in terms of how aggressive they are? Various ways of quantifying concepts are outlined in Chapter 2. When comparing levels of aggressiveness in two or more groups, we have to summarise or aggregate the scores of the individuals in the groups being compared. Different procedures for doing this are also covered in the next chapter. Statistics for describing sets of scores or the relationship between them are called *descriptive statistics* while statistics which make inferences from these sets of scores to the population from which they are drawn are known as *inferential statistics*.

Whatever method we use for assessing aggressiveness, we also need to know how reliable and valid our measures are. By reliable, we mean how similar the scores of aggressiveness are for a particular individual when measured on more than one occasion not too far apart, or by more than one person or item. A valid measure of aggressiveness, on the other hand, is one that behaves in a way which indicates that it seems to be assessing aggressiveness. For example, we would expect a measure of aggressiveness to be more highly related to other measures of aggressiveness than to measures of dissimilar constructs such as self-esteem or anxiety. The reliability and validity of a measure are usually assessed statistically. Statistical procedures for assessing validity are the same as those used for determining relationships between variables or differences between groups. Some specific statistical tests, however, have been devised for measuring reliability and agreement between observers. These tests are covered in Chapter 14.

DATA SET

To show how various statistical tests can be applied to analyse data from the same study and to avoid having to introduce new examples, different aspects of the set of data presented in Table 1.4 will be used as far as possible to illustrate the statistics described in this book.

For the purpose of demonstrating the statistics it does not matter whether the design of the study is a true experimental or non-experimental one. We will say that the design is non-experimental. Its main aim was to find out whether those having tutorials would show improved coursework marks. There were three conditions: (1) no tutorials; (2) one-to-one or individual tutorials; and (3) small group tutorials. In this case we are evaluating a

Table 1.4 Data set

Sex	Condition	Subject	Pre-test interest	Pre-test preparation	Pre-test mark	Post-test preparation	Post-test mark	Follow-up mark
Women	No tutorial	Psychology	3	2	3	3	4	5
		Education	3	3	1	2	6	3
	Individual tutorial	Sociology	4	4	5	4	7	7
		Psychology	3	4	3	3	8	5
		Education	4	3	7	4	9	9
	Group tutorial	Management	2	2	1	3	4	4
		Sociology	1	1	1	2	4	6
		Psychology	2	3	2	2	5	7
		Management	3	3	3	3	6	5
		Education	4	3	3	2	6	8
Men	No tutorial	Management	1	0	1	1	1	2
		Education	1	1	3	2	1	4
		Psychology	2	1	4	2	1	6
		Management	3	2	4	3	5	4
	Individual tutorial	Psychology	1	1	2	2	2	3
		Management	3	1	3	2	5	4
		Education	3	2	4	2	5	8
	Group tutorial	Management	4	3	1	3	5	5
		Management	4	4	2	4	5	7
		Sociology	4	2	3	3	8	9
?		?	?	?	2	2	1	2

procedure rather than a principle as such. The sample consisted of ten women and ten men studying one of four subjects: psychology; sociology; education; and management. To illustrate how missing data may be handled, an additional person was added whose sex is unknown and who has missing information on four other variables. Coursework was given at three points in time: (1) prior to tutorials being given (i.e. pre-test); (2) immediately after the tutorials had ended (i.e. post-test); and (3) some time later (i.e. at follow-up). Coursework was marked out of a maximum score of 9. In addition, students rated the extent of both their preparation for coursework and their interest in the course at pre-test and their preparation at post-test. Coursework preparation and course interest was rated on a five-point scale with 0 indicating 'no', 1 'slight', 2 'some', 3 'moderate' and 4 'much' preparation or interest. Data from the table has been excluded which would normally be collected (such as the age of participants, interest at post-test and preparation and interest at follow-up) since they would complicate the presentation and are not necessary for illustrating statistical procedures.

SUMMARY

Statistics play a vital role in collecting, summarising and interpreting data in quantitative social science research. Random assignment of participants to experimental conditions is essential for increasing the likelihood that participants assigned to different treatments will be similar and that, as a consequence, any observed differences between conditions will be more likely due to the experimental manipulation. Random selection of participants from a population, on the other hand, is necessary when a sample is used to gather information about that population. The reliability and validity of the measures employed have to be ascertained. The data collected need to be summarised in order to determine the nature of the results. The size of the association between variables and of the difference between groups indicates how important a variable might be in relationship to one or more other variables. The statistical significance of a finding estimates the likelihood of that result occurring simply by chance in the population.

2 Measurement and univariate analysis

MEASUREMENT

Statistical analysis depends on being able to measure or to quantify those aspects of objects which interest us. Measurement involves assigning numbers to observations according to certain rules. Since the type of statistical procedure used to describe and to draw inferences from empirical observations partly rests on the way in which an attribute or variable is measured, it is important to be familiar with the kinds of measurement that have been distinguished. Stevens (1946) suggested four levels or scales of measurement which are frequently referred to in discussions on the types of statistical procedures to be followed with different kinds of measurement. Although each level has its own characteristics, the levels are hierarchical. The higher levels have more sophisticated properties than the lower levels but they also include the more basic features of the lower levels.

Nominal level

The nominal level is the lowest and crudest form of measurement. Numbers are simply used to identify or to 'name' the attribute or category being described, hence the term 'nominal'. For example, the sex or gender of participants may be coded as numbers, with 1 for women and 2 for men. Similarly, the conditions in a study may be given a number. Students receiving no tutorials may be categorised as 1, those receiving individual tutorials as 2 and those receiving group tutorials as 3. The assignment of numbers is arbitrary. So, men may be coded 5 and women 9. Since the numbers have no quantitative meaning, it makes no sense to carry out mathematical operations on them such as addition, subtraction, multiplication and division. The only mathematical operation that can be performed on them is to count the frequency of each number. For instance, there may be four 1's and six 2's, denoting four women and six men respectively. Data which correspond to this level of measurement are sometimes referred to as *categorical* or *frequency* data. Numbers are often used to consecutively label and identify people or objects, such as the participants in a study. Some writers include this use of numbers as being nominal.

Ordinal level

The next higher level of measurement is the ordinal one in which the numbers indicate increasing amounts of a particular attribute. As the term 'ordinal' implies, individuals (objects or events) can be rank 'ordered' from the smallest to the largest in terms of the characteristic being evaluated. For example, ten participants can be rank ordered in terms of how interested they are in the course with 1 indicating the least interested person and 10 the most. The intervals between the numbers do not represent equal amounts of the quality being measured. For instance, the difference in interest between someone ranked 2 and someone ranked 4 need not be the same as the difference between someone ranked 6 and someone ranked 8. Furthermore, the numbers do not indicate absolute quantities, so that someone ranked 8 is not necessarily twice as interested as someone ranked 4. In some instances, it is not possible to distinguish between cases and no attempt is made to order these cases. In this situation a *tie* is said to exist and the tied cases receive the same number.

Interval level

With interval level measurement, the intervals between numbers denote equal amounts of the attribute being assessed, hence the term 'interval'. A clear example of a measure having an interval scale is a Celcius thermometer. The difference in temperature between the two readings of 5°C and 10°C is said to be the same as that between the two readings of 15°C and 20°C. However, because interval scales have no absolute zero point, we cannot say that a value which is twice as big as another value denotes twice the amount of the quality being assessed. Although a Celcius thermometer has a zero point, this point does not represent absolute zero since the scale registers temperatures below zero. Consequently, while we can say that 20°C is hotter than 10°C, we cannot claim that it is twice as hot as 10°C. This point will be easier to demonstrate when we consider the highest level of measurement.

Ratio level

The ratio scale represents the highest level of measurement and so has all the properties of the lower measurement levels in that it has equal intervals and it also categorises and rank orders scores. Unlike the other levels, however, it also includes an absolute zero point which means that a value which is twice as large as another reflects twice the amount of the attribute being measured. In other words, we can express two values on such a scale as a ratio. Age is an example of a ratio measure. Someone who is 20 is twice as old as someone of 10. In other words, these two ages can be expressed as a ratio of 2(0):1(0). If age was made to be an interval scale in which zero was arbitrarily set at 5 years, 10 would become 15 (5 + 10 = 15) and 20 would become 25 (5 + 20 = 25) in which case the interval scale value of 25 is not twice that of 15.

As we shall see, many social scientists treat what appear to be ordinal scales as if they were interval or ratio ones. In the study briefly outlined at the end of Chapter 1 a simple rating scale was developed for participants to report how interested they were in a course. The rating scale has five points which represent the following degrees of interest: 0 = no interest; 1 = slight interest; 2 = some interest; 3 = moderate interest; and 4 = much interest. Participants have to select the number which best describes their level of interest. Although this scale has a zero point, it is neither an interval nor a ratio scale since it cannot be argued that the interval or difference in interest between, say, points 0 and 1 is the same as that between 2 and 3. In effect, this scale is a simple ordinal one in which the numbers indicate increasing degrees of interest and nothing more.

None the less, many social scientists will interpret ordinal scales as interval or ratio ones. Perhaps, the main reason for this is that in many cases the main concern is not with the level of measurement as such but with whether two (or more) conditions differ or whether two (or more) variables are related. Since the statistical tests themselves only apply to numbers and not to what they mean (Lord 1953), no attention has to be paid to the measurement scales when undertaking the statistical analysis. Furthermore, there is no need to be primarily concerned with measurement levels should we, for example, find that those receiving tutorials also rate themselves as more interested. However, the failure to find a difference between the two conditions may result from using a relatively crude (i.e. ordinal level) measure of interest. Consequently, the absence of a difference or association may be due to the low level of the measure employed.

UNIVARIATE ANALYSIS

Once we have collected the data for our study, we usually need to carry out one or more *univariate* analyses in which the data for a single variable are looked at on their own. For example, we may begin by wanting to know how many participants study psychology or what the average mark is for the pre-test coursework. In describing such data, we are primarily concerned with differentiating between nominal variables (such as subject studied) and non-nominal variables (such as coursework marks). Since at this stage we are simply describing the numerical characteristics of the distribution of scores in our study and are not concerned with making any inferences from them about their distribution in the population, these kinds of statistics are known as descriptive statistics.

Proportions, percentages and ratios

With nominal variables, all we can do is to count the number or frequency of participants within each category and to report either the total number for each category or that total number as a *proportion* (or *percentage*) of the total sample. For example, if we look at the categorical variable of subject read in our study we see that 5 people read psychology, 3 sociology, 5 education and 7 management.

Rather than simply presenting the total numbers in each group, the numbers in any one category can be expressed as a proportion or percentage of the whole sample. A proportion is the frequency of cases within a category divided by the total number of cases. Since it is often easier to grasp a statistical concept in terms of a formula, we will provide formulae for such concepts wherever possible. So the formula for a proportion can be expressed as follows:

$$\text{proportion} = \frac{\text{frequency of cases in one category}}{\text{total number of cases}}$$

In our example, the proportion of people studying psychology is 0.25, rounded to two decimal places (5/20 = 0.250). The sum of proportions always equal one (5/20 + 3/20 + 5/20 + 7/20 = 1), so that the largest proportion can never be bigger than one.

A percentage is simply a proportion multiplied by 100. So the formula for a percentage is:

$$\text{percentage } (\%) = \frac{\text{frequency of cases in one category}}{\text{total number of cases}} \times 100$$

In our example, the percentage of participants reading psychology is 25 (0.25 × 100 = 25).

Comparing the frequency of one category against the frequency of another is called a *ratio* and gives an index of the relative frequency of two categories.

ratio = frequency of one category : frequency of another category

So, the ratio of people studying psychology rather than sociology is 5:3.

Describing frequencies in proportions or percentages is particularly helpful when comparing some variable across samples of different sizes. For example, suppose we want to compare the number of individuals studying psychology in two samples. The number of people doing so is 7 in one sample of 70 and 6 in another sample of 30. It is easier to grasp and to compare these figures when they are converted into one of these two indices.

Frequencies	Proportions	Percentages
7 of 70	7/70 = 0.10	7/70 × 100 = 10
6 of 30	6/30 = 0.20	6/30 × 100 = 20

For example, the percentage of people studying psychology in the first sample is 10 compared with 20 in the second.

Note that percentages can be misleading when the total number of cases is small. For example, if we had a sample of only seven people, 14 per cent of them represents only one person. Similarly, if we expanded the size of our sample by one person from seven to eight people, then this is an increase of 14 per cent which seems large although it is an increase of only one person. Consequently, attention should be paid to what the numbers represent rather than to their absolute size.

Rounding numbers and number of decimals

When dividing one number by another we frequently obtain more numbers than the original one. To take an extreme example, if we divide one by three, the resulting number is 0.3333 recurring. When this happens two questions arise. The first is how many decimals in the number should we present and the second is how do we go about reducing or rounding the decimals. Some writers have suggested that generally we should have only one or two digits more than the original number. If we restricted ourselves to having two more digits than the original number, then dividing one by three would become 0.33. We would now have three digits instead of the original one.

The general rule for rounding numbers to the nearest whole number or to the specified decimal place is that if the digit (reading from left to right) following the one to be rounded is less than five, it is dropped. So, in our example, the three in (0.33<u>3</u>) following the three to be rounded (0.3<u>3</u>3) is dropped since it is less than five. If the following digit is more than five (as in 0.33<u>6</u>, say), then the digit to be rounded (0.3<u>3</u>6) is rounded up or increased by one (to 0.3<u>4</u>).

The only complication arises when the following digit is five as in (0.33<u>5</u>) for example. The simple rule for handling this situation is to round up numbers that are equal to or greater than five and to drop numbers that are less than five. So, rounding to two decimal places, 0.3<u>3</u>5 becomes 0.34 while 0.3<u>3</u>4 becomes 0.33. Because of its simplicity and because this rule is employed by the statistical program we will be using, we shall adopt this method.

Different procedures for rounding numbers will lead to different results. One way of avoiding these differences (which may be large) is to follow the further rule that each number in a series of computations is rounded to one more decimal place than the number of places used in the final answer. The rules described in this section will generally be applied to the examples worked out by hand throughout this book to ensure that a consistent practice is adopted.

Measures of central tendency

When dealing with non-nominal variables which can have a large number of different values, it is useful to be able to summarise these scores in some way. One way of doing this is to describe these scores in terms of their typical or central value. These indices are known as *measures of central tendency*, of which the three most commonly discussed are the *mode*, the *median* and the *mean* or *arithmetic mean* (to distinguish it from other means such as the *geometric* and *harmonic* mean).

Mode

The least used and simplest of these three measures is the mode (Pearson 1895), which is the score that occurs most frequently.

mode = most frequent score

For example, take the ten pre-test marks of the women in our study:

3   1   5   3   7   1   1   2   3   3

The most common score is 3, of which there are four. Consequently, the mode is 3. Note that the mode is the most commonly occurring value (3) and not the frequency (4) of that value. If a number of the scores had the same frequency, then there would be more than one mode. For example, if there was another score of 1, then this set of scores would have two modes (3 and 1).

Median

The median is that point or number in a set of scores, arranged in ascending order of size from lowest to highest, which divides those scores into two equal parts. In some cases, it is relatively easy to determine the median as in the following example of seven scores:

6   3   5   7   1   3   4

To obtain the median, arrange the scores in ascending order of size from smallest to largest as follows:

1   3   3   4   5   6   7
            ↑

The median is 4 since the number of scores above it (3) is equal to the number below it (3). When the set of scores is an odd number, as it is here, the position of the median is the number of scores plus 1 and divided by 2 $[(7 + 1)/2 = 4]$ since this is the position of the score that divides the sample into two equal halves.

When the set of scores is an even number as in the following group of eight ordered scores

1 3 3 4 5 6 7 7
          ↑

the position of the median lies midway between the two middle scores (4 and 5) and is the average of those two scores, i.e. 4.5 [(4 + 5)/2 = 4.5].

Calculating the median, however, becomes more complicated where there is an even number of scores and where the middle scores have the same values as in the pre-test marks for women. The ascending order for these marks is:

1 1 1 2 3 3 3 3 5 7

Here the median lies between the first and second 3 but there are two other 3's to take into account.

In calculating the median in these cases, the following procedure may be undertaken which can be used to work out any *percentile* point for cutting off a specified percentage of the distribution below it, including the median (the 50th percentile point). Although it appears complicated, we have presented it because it is the procedure used by SPSS to calculate percentile points including the median and quartiles. We will illustrate the procedure by working out the 50th percentile point for this set of ten numbers.

Step 1   To find out the percentage point immediately above the required percentile point, add 1 to the number of values, multiply this sum by the desired percentile point and divide this product by the number of values. This value is 55.5 for our example.

$$\frac{(10 + 1) \times 50}{10} = \frac{550}{10} = 55.0$$

We shall call this point the cut-off percentage point.

Step 2   Work out the cumulative frequency and the cumulative percent for the values just above and below the cut-off percentage point. For our example these are

Values	Frequency	Cumulative frequency	Cumulative per cent
3	1	5	50.0
3	1	6	60.0

Step 3   From the cut-off percentage point, subtract the cumulative percent for the value immediately below it. This difference is 5.5 (55.5 − 50.0 = 5.5) for our example.

Step 4 If this difference is equal to or greater than 100 divided by the number of values, use the following formula to calculate the percentile point

$$\left(\left(1 - \left[\frac{(N+1) \times p}{100} - cc_1\right]\right) \times x_2\right) + \left(\left[\frac{(N+1) \times p}{100} - cc_1\right] \times x_2\right)$$

If this difference is less than 100 divided by the number of values, use the formula below to work out the percentile point

$$\left(\left(1 - \left[\frac{(N+1) \times p}{100} - cc_1\right]\right) \times x_1\right) + \left(\left[\frac{(N+1) \times p}{100} - cc_1\right] \times x_2\right)$$

N stands for the number of values (i.e. 10 in this example), p the desired percentile point (i.e. 50), cc_1 the cumulative frequency below the cut-off percentage point (i.e. 5), x_1 the value corresponding to the cumulative frequency below the cut-off percentage point (i.e. 3) and x_2 the value corresponding to the cumulative frequency above the cut-off percentage point (i.e. 3).

Since the difference of 5.5 is less than 10.0 (100/10 = 10.0), we use the second formula. Inserting the appropriate figures into this formula we see that the 50th percentile point is 3.00.

$$\left(\left(1 - \left[\frac{(10+1) \times 50}{100} - 5\right]\right) \times 3\right) + \left(\left[\frac{(10+1) \times 50}{100} - 5\right] \times 3\right) =$$

$$\left(\left(1 - \left[\frac{550}{100} - 5\right]\right) \times 3\right) + \left(\left[\frac{550}{100} - 5\right] \times 3\right) =$$

$$((1 - (5.5 - 5)) \times 3) + ((5.5 - 5) \times 3) =$$
$$((1 - 0.5) \times 3) + (0.5 \times 3) = (0.5 \times 3) + 1.5 = 1.5 + 1.5 = 3.00$$

Note that when following the calculations shown in this book, pay particular attention to the order in which the computations are done. Calculations in the inner brackets are carried out before those in the outer ones. To check the order of the calculations, repeat them yourself and see if you come up with the same results. If you find it easier to do this, use a cheap electronic calculator. Hopefully, there are no computational errors in this book. Although these sometimes slip through, they should be easy to spot and to correct.

Mean

The mean is the most commonly used measure of central tendency. To obtain it, add together or sum all the scores in a series and divide this sum by the number of scores. So, the formula for the mean is:

$$\text{mean} = \frac{\text{sum of scores}}{\text{number of scores}}$$

To illustrate its calculation, we will work out the mean for pre-test marks for women:

3 1 5 3 7 1 1 2 3 3

To calculate the mean, carry out the following steps.

Step 1   Add the scores together to give the sum or total score, which is 29.

3 1 5 3 7 1 1 2 3 3 = 29

Step 2   Count the number of scores, which is 10.

Step 3   Divide the sum of scores by the number of scores to give the mean, which is 2.90.

29/10 = 2.90

Comparison of mode, median and mean

Which of these three measures of central tendency we should use to describe the typical value of a set of scores depends partly on the distribution of those scores when ordered according to size. When the distribution is *unimodal* (i.e. has one mode) and symmetrical, the mode, median and mean will have very similar values. Take the following set of seven scores whose distribution is unimodal and symmetrical:

1 2 3 3 3 4 5

The mode or most frequent score is 3, of which there are 3. The median or middle score is also 3 with two scores lower and two scores higher than it. The mean is also 3 [(1 + 2 + 3 + 3 + 3 + 4 + 5)/7 = 21/7 = 3]. What this implies in practice is that when the distribution of scores has one mode and is approximately symmetrical, the mode, median and mean will have roughly the same value so that it matters less which measure we use to describe the central tendency of the array of scores.

When the distribution of scores is symmetrical but *bimodal* (i.e. has two modes), then the median and the mean will have very similar values which will obviously differ from the modes since there are two of them. For example, in the following symmetrical and bimodal distribution of seven scores

1 2 2 4 5 5 6

the two modes are 2 and 5 while the median is 4 and the mean is 3.57 (25/7 = 3.57).

When the distribution of scores is asymmetrical, then all three measures of central tendency will differ. Examine the following asymmetrical distribution of seven scores:

1 2 2 3 7 8 9

The mode is 2, the median is 3 and the mean is 4.57 (32/7 = 4.57). When most of the scores in a set are relatively low, the mode will generally have the lowest value, the median the next lowest and the mean the highest.

Conversely, when most of the scores are relatively high, the mode will have the highest value, the median the next highest and the mean the lowest, as in the following example:

1 2 3 7 8 8 9

Here the mode is 8, the median is 7 and the mean is 5.43 (38/7 = 5.43).

Further complications arise when the data contain a few extreme scores (sometimes called *outliers*) since the mean is more strongly affected by such scores than either the mode or the median. We can see this if we substitute 90 for 9 in the preceding set of numbers. The mode and the median will remain the same (at 8 and 7 respectively) while the mean will be increased from 5.43 to 17 (119/7 = 17). In such situations, it may be more appropriate to use the median than the mean. Alternatively, the mean can be employed but calculated by either omitting the extreme values or making them less extreme. In this example, the mean would be 4.83 (29/6 = 4.83) if 90 was excluded or 5.43 if it was reduced to, say, the next highest score after 8 (i.e. 9).

Another possibility is to transform all the scores so that the differences between the extreme values and the other values are less. The two most common methods of doing this is to take either the square root or the (base 10) logarithm of the scores. These transformations are given below (to one decimal place) for the following set of scores which was previously used to illustrate the influence of an extreme value.

	1	2	3	7	8	8	90
Square root	1.0	1.4	1.7	2.6	2.8	2.8	9.5
Logarithm	0.0	0.3	0.5	0.8	0.9	0.9	2.0

For the untransformed scores, the difference between 8 and 90 (i.e. 82) is at least eleven times (82/7 = 11.7) as great as that between 1 and 8 (i.e. 7). For the square root transformations of the same scores, however, the difference between 2.8 and 9.5 (i.e. 6.7) is less than four times (6.7/1.8 = 3.7) as big as that between 1 and 2.8 (i.e. 1.8). While for the logarithm transformations, the difference between 0.9 and 2.0 (i.e. 1.1) is about the same size (1.1/0.9 = 1.2) as that between 0.0 and 0.9 (i.e. 0.9).

Measures of dispersion

Measures of central tendency only describe the typical value of a distribution of scores and do not indicate the spread or variation in those scores. Two distributions may have exactly the same mean but very different spreads of scores as the following two sets of scores illustrate.

    3   3   4   4   4   5   5
    1   2   3   4   5   6   7

The mean of both sets of scores is 4 but the spread of the first set is more restricted than the second. Indices of spread are called *measures of dispersion*, of which the three most often described are the *range*, the *interquartile range* and the *standard deviation*.

Range

The range is the simplest measure of dispersion and is simply the difference between the highest and the lowest value in a set of scores.

   range = highest score − lowest score

So, the range for the first set of scores above is 2 (5 − 3 = 2) while for the second set it is 6 (7 − 1 = 6). One disadvantage of the range is that, since it is only based on the two extreme scores, it gives little indication of what the distribution of the other scores is like. If either or both of these extreme scores differs greatly from the other scores, the range will simply reflect the difference between the extreme scores. So, if in the following set of scores

    1   2   3   4   5   6   7

the 7 is replaced with 17, then the range is 16 (17 − 1 = 16) rather than 6 (7 − 1 = 6).

Interquartile range

A measure of dispersion which is less dependent than the range on the two extreme scores is the interquartile range. To calculate it, the scores have to be arranged in ascending order and divided into four quarters (i.e. quartiles) containing equal numbers of scores. The *first quartile* is the value below which the lowest quarter of scores fall. The *second quartile* is the value below which half (or two quarters) of the lowest scores lie and corresponds to the median, while the *third quartile* is the value below which three quarters of the lowest values congregate. The interquartile range is the difference between the third and first quartile.

   interquartile range = third quartile − first quartile

To work out the number of scores which fall within the first quartile of a set of scores, we add one to the total number of scores and divide by four. Similarly, to calculate the number of scores which lie within the third quartile, we add one to the total number of scores and multiply by three-quarters. So, for the following set of seven scores

1 2 3 4 5 6 7
 ↑   ↑

the first quartile lies at the second score $[(7 + 1)/4 = 2]$ which is 2. The third quartile falls on the sixth score $[(7 + 1) \times 3/4 = 6]$ which is 6. Consequently, the interquartile range of this set of scores is 4 $(6 - 2 = 4)$.

Note that the interquartile range of the following set of scores (which includes the more extreme score of 17)

1 2 3 4 5 6 17
 ↑   ↑

is also 4 since the third quartile is still 6 $[(7 + 1) \times 3/4 = 6]$.

Sometimes the *semi-interquartile range* or *quartile deviation* is used instead of the interquartile range. This measure is simply the interquartile range divided by 2

$$\text{semi-interquartile range} = \frac{\text{third quartile} - \text{first quartile}}{2}$$

In this example the semi-interquartile range is 2 $[(6 - 2)/2 = 2]$.

Calculating the first and third quartile is slightly more complicated where the quartiles fall between existing scores. Take the pre-test marks for the women, arranged in ascending order:

1 1 1 2 3 3 3 3 5 7

The first quartile falls at the 2.75th score $[(10 + 1)/4 = 2.75]$ while the third quartile lies at the 8.25th score $[(10 + 1) \times 3/4 = 8.25]$. To work out these two quartiles we apply the general procedure used to calculate the median. With this procedure we find that the first quartile or 25th percentile point is 1.00.

$$\left(\left(1 - \left[\frac{(10 + 1) \times 25}{100} - 2\right]\right) \times 1\right) + \left(\left[\frac{(10 + 1) \times 25}{100} - 2\right] \times 1\right) =$$

$$\left(\left(1 - \left[\frac{275}{100} - 2\right]\right) \times 1\right) + \left(\left[\frac{275}{100} - 2\right] \times 1\right) =$$

$$((1 - (2.75 - 2)) \times 1) + ((2.75 - 2) \times 1) =$$
$$((1 - 0.75) \times 1) + (0.75 \times 1) = (0.25 \times 1) + 0.75 = 0.25 + 0.75 = 1.00$$

Standard deviation

The most frequently used measure of dispersion is the standard deviation (Pearson 1894) which is based on all the scores in a set. The standard deviation is the square root of the *variance* (Fisher 1918),

standard deviation = $\sqrt{\text{variance}}$

The variance and hence the standard deviation of a population is calculated in a slightly different way from that of a sample. The *population* variance is derived by subtracting each score of the population from its mean, squaring these differences or deviations, adding these squared deviations together and dividing this sum by the total number of scores

$$\text{population variance} = \frac{\text{sum of (mean score} - \text{each score)}^2}{\text{total number of scores}}$$

The *sample* variance is calculated in the same way except that the sum of the squared deviations is divided by 1 subtracted from the total number of scores

$$\text{sample variance} = \frac{\text{sum of (mean score} - \text{each score)}^2}{\text{total number of scores} - 1}$$

The sum of squared deviations is usually called the *sum of squares*.

The reason for using 1 less the total number of scores in calculating the sample variance is to provide a less biased or *unbiased estimate* of the population variance and standard deviation. Consequently, the sample variance and standard deviation are sometimes respectively called the *estimated population variance* and the *estimated population standard deviation*. Because the sample variance of small samples in particular is less than that of the population, dividing the sum of squares by the total number of cases gives an underestimate of the population variance. Dividing the sum of squares by the total number of cases minus 1 provides a less biased estimate of the population variance. With large samples, the adjusted and unadjusted sample variance differ little since subtracting 1 from a large number will, proportionately, reduce that number only slightly. As we shall see the notion of variance is important since it forms the basis of the parametric tests described in this book. The sample variance is more commonly used than the population variance since we rarely have access to complete populations and are often primarily concerned with estimating the population variance from a sample.

We will begin by showing how to calculate the sum of squares, the variance and the standard deviation for the ten pre-test marks of the women in our study:

3   1   5   3   7   1   1   2   3   3

To calculate the sum of squares, we carry out the following steps.

Step 1 Find the mean score by adding the scores together and dividing by the total number of scores. The mean score for these ten scores is 2.90.

$$(3 + 1 + 5 + 3 + 7 + 1 + 1 + 2 + 3 + 3)/10 = 29/10 = 2.90$$

Step 2 Subtract each score from the mean score, square the differences and sum the squared differences to form the sum of squares. The sum of squares for these ten scores is 32.9.

$$(2.9 - 3)^2 + (2.9 - 1)^2 + (2.9 - 5)^2 + (2.9 - 3)^2 + (2.9 - 7)^2 +$$
$$(2.9 - 1)^2 + (2.9 - 1)^2 + (2.9 - 2)^2 + (2.9 - 3)^2 + (2.9 - 3)^2 =$$
$$(-0.1^2) + 1.9^2 + (-2.1^2) + (-0.1^2) + (-4.1^2) + 1.9^2 + 1.9^2 +$$
$$0.9^2 + (-0.1^2) + (-0.1^2) =$$
$$0.01 + 3.61 + 4.41 + 0.01 + 16.81 + 3.61 + 3.61 + 0.81 + 0.01 + 0.01 = 32.9$$

Note that if we simply added the differences together rather than squaring them first, we would have a sum of zero which would give no indication of the distribution of scores

$$(-0.1) + 1.9 + (-2.1) + (-0.1) + (-4.1) + 1.9 + 1.9 + 0.9 +$$
$$(-0.1) + (-0.1) = 0$$

We could, of course, have simply ignored the negative signs to give the sum of *absolute* deviations which for this set of ten scores is 13. There are various reasons why squared rather than absolute deviations are used but in general it is because they are easier to work with mathematically.

Note also that it does not matter whether we subtract each score from the mean score (mean score − each score), as shown above, or we subtract the mean score from each score (each score − mean score), as illustrated below, provided we use the same order for all scores.

$$(3 - 2.9)^2 + (1 - 2.9)^2 + (5 - 2.9)^2 + (3 - 2.9)^2 + (7 - 2.9)^2 +$$
$$(1 - 2.9)^2 + (1 - 2.9)^2 + (2 - 2.9)^2 + (3 - 2.9)^2 + (3 - 2.9)^2 =$$
$$0.1^2 + (-1.9^2) + 2.1^2 + 0.1^2 + 4.1^2 + (-1.9^2) + (-1.9^2) +$$
$$(-0.9^2) + 0.1^2 + 0.1^2 =$$
$$0.01 + 3.61 + 4.41 + 0.01 + 16.81 + 3.61 + 3.61 + 0.81 + 0.01 + 0.01 = 32.9$$

Step 3 To calculate the sample variance or *mean square* (i.e. mean squared deviations), we divide the sum of squares by the total number of scores minus 1. The sample variance for our eight scores is 3.66.

$$32.9/(10 - 1) = 32.9/9 = 3.655$$

Step 4 To calculate the standard deviation, take the square root of the variance. The standard deviation for our ten scores is 1.91.

$$\sqrt{3.66} = 1.91$$

Note that the variance is expressed in mean squared units, which are not directly comparable to the original values. So, for example, as the ten scores represent marks, the variance refers to 'mean squared marks'. The square root of the variance is used to convert the squared units into the original ones. The square root of the variance (3.66) of the ten scores above is 1.91, which describes more closely than the variance the *mean deviation* of the ten scores (13/9 = 1.44).

Because the standard deviation, like the mean, is based on all the scores in a sample, it is strongly affected by extreme scores. This point can be demonstrated with the following set of ten scores where 68 replaces the value of 7 in the previous example.

$$3 \quad 1 \quad 5 \quad 3 \quad 68 \quad 1 \quad 1 \quad 2 \quad 3 \quad 3$$

The mean of this set of scores is now 9 (90/10 = 9) instead of 2.9. The sum of squares is 3882 instead of 32.9.

$$(9 - 3)^2 + (9 - 1)^2 + (9 - 5)^2 + (9 - 3)^2 + (9 - 68)^2 + (9 - 1)^2 +$$
$$(9 - 1)^2 + (9 - 2)^2 + (9 - 3)^2 + (9 - 3)^2 =$$
$$6^2 + 8^2 + 4^2 + 6^2 + (-59^2) + 8^2 + 8^2 + 7^2 + 6^2 + 6^2 =$$
$$36 + 64 + 16 + 36 + 3481 + 64 + 64 + 49 + 36 + 36 = 3882$$

Consequently, the variance is 431.33 (3882/9) instead of 3.66 and the standard deviation is 20.77 ($\sqrt{431.33}$ = 20.77) instead of 1.91. Once again, we can see that the standard deviation (20.77) is closer than the variance (431.33) to the mean deviation, which is 13.11.

$$[6 + 8 + 4 + 6 + (-59) + 8 + 8 + 7 + 6 + 6]/9 = 118/9 = 13.11$$

Because the above procedure for calculating the variance initially involves the arithmetic operation of division in arriving at the mean, it can result in greater rounding error than a process in which adding, subtracting and multiplying is done before dividing and taking the square root. Consequently, there is an alternative computational procedure which is generally used in deriving the variance where the division occurs at a later stage. This alternative computational formula for the variance is

$$\text{variance} = \frac{\text{sum of squared scores} - \dfrac{\text{squared sum of scores}}{\text{number of scores}}}{\text{number of scores} - 1}$$

This procedure consists of the following steps which will be illustrated with the same set of numbers previously used to calculate the sample variance, i.e.

$$3 \quad 1 \quad 5 \quad 3 \quad 7 \quad 1 \quad 1 \quad 2 \quad 3 \quad 3$$

Step 1 Sum the scores and square the sum. The sum of scores for these numbers is 29

$3 + 1 + 5 + 3 + 7 + 1 + 1 + 2 + 3 + 3 = 29$

which squared is 841.

Step 2 Divide the squared sum of scores by the number of scores. Dividing 841 by 10 gives 84.1.

Step 3 Square each of the original scores and sum them. For our example the sum of squared scores is 117.

$3^2 + 1^2 + 5^2 + 3^2 + 7^2 + 1^2 + 1^2 + 2^2 + 3^2 + 3^2 = 9 + 1 + 25 + 9 + 49 + 1 + 1 + 4 + 9 + 9 = 117$

Step 4 To give the sum of squares, subtract the sum of squared scores (i.e. the results of Step 3) from the squared sum of scores divided by the number of scores (i.e. the results of Step 2). The sum of squares for our example is 32.9.

$117 - 84.1 = 32.9$

Step 5 To calculate the variance, divide the sum of squares by the number of scores minus 1. So, the variance for our example is 3.66 as previously calculated.

$32.9/(10 - 1) = 3.655$

Because the mean score in this example had only one decimal place (i.e. 2.9), both formulae gave the same result for the variance. However, when the mean score has a large number of decimal places which have been rounded to a few places, the results from the two formulae will differ. Take, for example, the following set of seven scores

4 4 5 5 6 7 8

The mean of these seven scores is 5.6 rounded to one decimal place ($39/7 = 5.571$).

Using the first computational formula, the variance is 2.33.

$[(5.6 - 4)^2 + (5.6 - 4)^2 + (5.6 - 5)^2 + (5.6 - 5)^2 + (5.6 - 6)^2 + (5.6 - 7)^2 + (5.6 - 8)^2]/(7 - 1) =$
$[1.6^2 + 1.6^2 + 0.6^2 + 0.6^2 + (-0.4)^2 + (-1.4)^2 + (-2.4)^2]/6 =$
$(2.6 + 2.6 + 0.4 + 0.4 + 0.2 + 2.0 + 5.8)/6 = 14.0/6 = 2.33$

With the second computational formula, the variance is 2.29.

$$\frac{231 - \dfrac{39^2}{7}}{7 - 1} = \frac{231 - \dfrac{1521}{7}}{6} = \frac{231 - 217.29}{6} = \frac{13.71}{6} = 2.29$$

As can be seen from these two examples the numbers involved in the intermediate stages of the second more accurate computational procedure become large. Furthermore, the way in which this procedure is related to the idea of variance is less obvious. Consequently, this second computational procedure for calculating variance will not be followed in the book. If greater accuracy is required, use either the second procedure, or the first procedure with more decimal places in the calculations.

One advantage of the standard deviation as a measure of dispersion is that if the scores of a sample are normally distributed, then the percentage of scores which fall between, say one standard deviation above and below the mean, is known and is about 68.26. In other words, if the mean and standard deviation of a sample of normally distributed scores is known, then it is possible to work out what percentage of the scores lie within any set of two values. In such cases, the mean and standard deviation give a detailed summary of the distribution of scores and are, therefore, often used. The procedure for determining whether a set of scores is normally distributed and for working out what percentage of values lies between any two values of a normal distributed variable is described in Chapter 4.

Now that we have shown how to calculate the sum of squares and the variance, let us return to the issue of demonstrating that dividing the sum of squares by the number of cases minus 1 rather than simply the number of cases gives a less biased estimate of the population variance. Let us assume that the population consists of the following three scores

0   1   2

The population mean of these three scores is 1 [(0 + 1 + 2)/3 = 3/3 = 1] and the population variance is 0.667.

$$[(1 - 0)^2 + (1 - 1)^2 + (1 - 2)^2]/3 = [1^2 + 0^2 + (-1)^2]/3 = 2/3 = 0.667$$

If we drew a sample of two scores from this population of three scores, the maximum number of different samples that could be drawn is the nine shown in Table 2.1. Also presented in this table are the population and sample variances for the nine samples on their own and averaged across the nine samples. We can see that the sample variance averaged for the nine samples of two cases is 0.667 which is the same as the population variance for all three cases. However, the population variance averaged for the nine samples of two cases is 0.333 which is less than the population variance of the three cases. In other words, the population variance (i.e. dividing by the number of cases rather than the number of cases minus 1) for the two cases underestimates that for the three cases.

In calculating the estimated population variance, we divide the sum of

Table 2.1 Population and sample variances for two cases

No	Two cases		Mean	Population variance (SS/2)	Sample variance (SS/1)
1	0	0	0.0	0.00	0.00
2	0	1	0.5	0.25	0.50
3	1	0	0.5	0.25	0.50
4	0	2	1.0	1.00	2.00
5	2	0	1.0	1.00	2.00
6	1	1	1.0	0.00	0.00
7	1	2	1.5	0.25	0.50
8	2	1	1.5	0.25	0.50
9	2	2	2.0	0.00	0.00
Sum				3.00	6.00
N				9	9
Average				0.333	0.667

squares by the number of cases minus 1 or what is known as the *degrees of freedom* (*df*) (Fisher 1915, 1925a). This concept is an important and complex one which is explained more fully elsewhere (Walker 1940). The degrees of freedom are the number of independent observations, which is the number of original observations minus the number of *parameters* estimated from them. A parameter is a measure which describes the distribution of the variable in the population such as its mean or variance.

Suppose we want to estimate the variance of a population of three scores from a sample of two scores, consisting of 0 and 2. To do this we need to estimate the mean of the population. Now the best estimate of the population mean is the sample mean which is 1 [(0 + 2)/2 = 1]. Once we have estimated the population mean, we have fixed it for estimating the population variance and so we have lost one degree of freedom. Since, in this case, we have two original observations and the one parameter of the population mean, we are left with one degree of freedom (2 − 1 = 1). If we had three original observations, we would have two degrees of freedom (3 − 1 = 2).

We can show that if we know the mean of a number of observations, the value of one of those observations must be fixed and is not free to vary. Take the example of two observations. If the mean is 1 and one of the two observations is 0, we know that the other observation must be 2 since 0 added to 2 makes 2 which divided by 2 is 1 [(0 + 2)/2 = 2/2 = 1]. One of these two observations is free to vary. So, for example, with the mean fixed at 1, 0 could be changed to, say, −10 in which case the other observation would become 8 since −10 added to 8 and then divided by 2 is 1 [(−10 + 8)/2 = 2/2 = 1]. Similarly, if the mean is known for three observations, one of the observations on which that mean is based must be fixed while the other two observations are free to vary. For instance, if the mean is 4 and two of the three observations are 2 and 3, the third observation must be

fixed at 7 since 7 added to 2 and 3 makes 12 which divided by 3 gives 4
$[(7 + 2 + 3)/3 = 12/3 = 4]$.

SUMMARY

Four levels or scales of measurement have been distinguished, called
nominal (or categorical), ordinal, interval and ratio. Ordinal scales are
often treated as interval or ratio scales in the social sciences. The distribution of nominal or categorical data can only be quantified in terms of
the frequency of each category, which can be further summarised as a
proportion, percentage or ratio. The distribution of non-nominal or non-
categorical data, on the other hand, can be described in terms of measures
of central tendency (such as the mode, median and arithmetic mean) and
dispersion (such as the range, interquartile range and standard deviation).
The sum of squared deviations from the mean (i.e. the sum of squares) and
the mean of that sum of squares (i.e. the mean square or variance) provides
the basis of parametric tests of association and difference. Extreme scores
can disproportionately affect the mean and standard deviation of a sample.

EXERCISES

1 Which is the highest level of measurement that socio-economic status represents?
2 Which is the highest level of measurement that number of persons in a household
represents?
3 For this set of scores

   7 2 5 3 8 6 1 4 3 4

provide the following statistics: (a) mode; (b) range; (c) median; (d) interquartile
range; (e) mean; (f) sum of squares; (g) sample variance; and (h) sample
standard deviation (to two decimal places).

3 Introducing SPSS for Windows

To understand the way in which statistical values are arrived at, it is preferable to work through the calculations ourselves since this practice will check our grasp of the steps involved. These calculations are relatively easily and quickly carried out by hand when the data consist of a small set of low whole numbers and when the statistics are comparatively straightforward like those presented in the previous chapter. However, with larger sets of numbers, the manual calculation of even these simple statistics is time-consuming and may result in elementary mistakes being made. These two drawbacks become more serious when we need to employ more complicated statistics and/or when we want to examine the data in different ways, as is often the case. The advent of computers has led to the development of various computer programs for calculating statistics. These programs are not difficult to operate and carry out the required computations very quickly. With the ready accessibility of these packages, calculating statistics by computer is generally more efficient than doing so by hand, once the principles underlying the statistical tests have been grasped.

Knowing how to work one of these programs has three further advantages. First, our understanding and ability to carry out these tests by hand on new sets of numerical data can be simply checked against the results given by the program. If our calculations differ from those of the program, the reason for this discrepancy needs to be determined. Since the error may lie in either our calculations or the way in which we ran the program, this procedure will test our comprehension of both these processes. In other words, these programs can be used to assess the accuracy of our own efforts in conducting these tests by hand as well as by computer. Moreover, we can explore our knowledge of various statistical principles by generating and running examples of data which either confirm or disconfirm our expectations about what should happen. In this way we can try out our understanding of statistics on as many problems as we like, knowing that we can easily verify whether our work is correct.

Second, these programs can be employed for other aspects of data analysis such as selecting subsets of individuals for further investigation or creating new variables. For example, we may wish to examine the scores for females and males separately as well as together. Or, we may want to create a new variable which we can routinely work out from information we possess. For example, we may wish to calculate the age of each person in a sample from their year of birth.

And third, we can write our own programs to perform tests we need to use repeatedly but which are not part of the package. In addition, provided that the necessary information is reported, we can construct programs which enable us to conduct tests on other people's data which have not been carried out or we can check the accuracy of what has been done by repeating the analyses. For example, if we know the mean and standard deviation of two groups of participants, we can work out whether these measures differ significantly between the two groups. Needless to say, in order to do this we have to know how to run the test as well as the program.

Consequently, there are considerable advantages in learning how to use a computer program for performing statistical tests. The aim of this chapter is to introduce you to one of the most widely used, comprehensive and flexible statistical programs in the social sciences, which is aptly called the *Statistical Package for the Social Sciences* and which is usually referred to as SPSS for short. The development of SPSS began in 1965 at Stanford University and continued in 1970 at the National Opinion Research Centre at Chicago University. It became a commercial organisation based in Chicago in 1975. SPSS is readily available on both *mainframe* and *personal* computers. As the software is continuously being revised and the revisions take time to be implemented in different institutions, various versions of it may be accessible at any one time and these versions may be periodically replaced with new ones when these become available.

At present, there are two main kinds of *operating system* for computers. The traditional system requires *commands* and names to be typed in. The more recent system uses *menus* (for an example see Box 3.2) and *dialog boxes* (for an example see Box 3.4) from which commands can be selected by *keys* or a *mouse*, although commands can also be typed in (for an example see Box 3.15). The menu system was originally developed for Macintosh personal computers and is now available as a Windows environment on IBM-compatible personal computers having a 386 or higher processor. The use of two earlier versions of SPSS, *SPSS Release 4.0* (Norusis/SPSS 1990a, 1990b) and *SPSS/PC+ Version 4.0* (Norusis/SPSS 1990c, 1990d), have been outlined in an earlier book (Cramer 1994). This volume describes the use of a Windows version of SPSS called *SPSS for Windows*. At the time of writing, the latest revision of this version is *Release 6* (Norusis/SPSS 1993b, 1994a, 1994b) and *Release 7 for Windows 95* (SPSS Inc. 1997a, 1997b, 1997c). An earlier version is available for UNIX on mainframe computers (Norusis/SPSS 1993a). Because it is generally easier to use, the menu procedure is usually presented. The command or syntax procedure is given for procedures which are not available with the menu system. A list of the main commands is presented in Appendix 1.

SPSS commands and names will be printed in bold type to distinguish them from the rest of the text. Because the differences between Release 6 and 7 are small and Windows 95 is due to be replaced shortly, the procedures and output for this book are based on Release 6. The minor differences between the two versions are described on the Internet at http://www.routledge.com/routledge/textbooks/fssr.html.

To use SPSS for Windows, it is necessary to have access to it via a personal computer (or PC for short). A personal computer consists of five major parts: (1) a television-like *screen* (also called a monitor or visual display unit) to display information; (2) a *keyboard* for typing in instructions; (3) a small hand-held *mouse* which provides an alternative way of moving about the screen and selecting instructions; (4) a *system unit* which houses the computer itself and a *drive* for inserting a *floppy disk*; and usually (5) a *printer* for printing out information stored in the computer including a record of what you have done. While the amount of information shown at any one moment on the screen is necessarily limited, further information can be brought into view with the appropriate use of the keys or mouse. Keyboards are used to type or put in (hence the term *input*) the data that you want to analyse, the names of variables and files you have created, and commands.

The Windows system allows commands to be selected from words presented in a menu or dialog box in a window on the screen. Commands can be selected by moving a pointer called a *cursor* onto them with either the keys or, more usually, the mouse, and then pressing the Return key or the left button on the mouse (or in Windows 95 by simply selecting the next option). Choosing options is generally easier with the mouse than the keys since it simply involves moving the mouse appropriately. With keys, however, some options are chosen by pressing the relevant cursor keys while others are selected by pressing up to two keys other than the cursor keys. The cursor keys are usually on the right hand side of the keyboard and have arrows on them pointing in the direction in which the cursor is to be moved. You may prefer to use the mouse for some operations and the keys for others.

To invoke SPSS in the windows environment, select the appropriate **SPSS icon** which produces three overlapping windows as shown in Box 3.1. The front window is entitled **Newdata**, the one immediately behind it **!Output1**, and the one behind that **SPSS for Windows** but which is referred to by SPSS as **Applications**. Data can be entered directly into the **Newdata** window using the Data Editor. SPSS output is displayed in the **!Output1** window. The **Applications** window lists various procedures under such names as **File**, **Edit** and so on.

To see what applications there are, we simply move the cursor to a particular option and press the left button on the mouse once when a *drop-down* menu will appear as shown in Box 3.2 where the **Data** option

Applications   Output   Newdata   Maximize
window   window   window   buttons

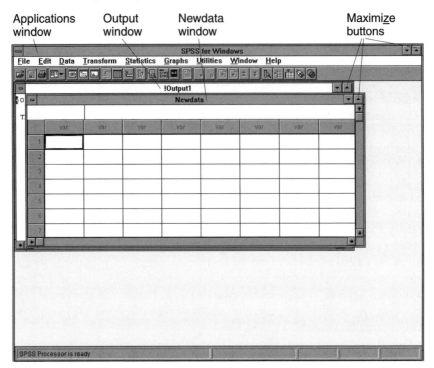

Box 3.1 Opening sequence of SPSS for Windows (Release 6.1)

has been chosen. To cancel a drop-down menu, place the cursor anywhere outside the option and press the left button.

The ellipse or three dots after an option term (**. . .**) on a drop-down menu, such as on the **Define Variable . . .** option, signifies a dialog box will appear when this option is chosen. If we select this option, for example, the **Define Variable** dialog box displayed in Box 3.4 will appear. To cancel a dialog box, select the **Cancel** button in the dialog box. A right facing arrowhead ▶ after an option term, such as on the **Merge Files** option, indicates that a further submenu will appear to the right of the drop-down menu. An option with neither of these signs means that there are no further drop-down menus to select.

Note that the form of the cursor varies according to the window it is in. In the **Newdata** window it is a thin upright cross (sometimes called a *cross-hair* or *wire*), in the **Output** window it is a flashing vertical line while in the **Applications** window it is a pointer. To increase the size of a window with the mouse, place the cursor on the upward-pointing triangle (the **Maximize** button) in the right-hand corner of the window (see Box 3.1) and press the left button. To return the window to its original size, place the pointer on the square in the right-hand corner containing the upward and

Click Syntax
button

| File | Edit | Data | Transform | Statistics | Graphs | Utilities | Window | Help |

Define Variable...
Define Dates...
Templates...
Insert Variable
Insert Case
Go to Case...

Sort Cases...
Transpose...
Merge Files
Aggregate...
Orthogonal Design

Split File...
Select Cases...
Weight Cases...

!Output1
Newdata

var   var   var   var   var   var

SPSS Processor is ready

Box 3.2 **Data** drop-down menu (Release 6.1)

downward facing triangle (the **Restore** button – see Box 3.3) and press the left button.

TABULATING DATA

When carrying out research, we normally collect data on more than one variable. For example, in the study briefly described at the end of Chapter 1, we have data on nine variables: (1) sex of participant; (2) presence of tutorials; (3) subject studied; (4) interest in course prior to tutorial period; (5) coursework preparation prior to tutorial period; (6) coursework mark prior to tutorial period; (7) coursework preparation during tutorial period; (8) coursework mark during tutorial period; and (9) coursework mark after tutorial period.

Before analysing data, we usually arrange it in the form of a table, such as Table 1.4, where the values for each variable are placed in the same column and the value for each person or *case* is placed in a separate row. Cases are often people but can be any entity such as newspapers, schools or years.

In many situations, the way in which the cases are ordered does not matter as in this instance and they could have been entered as the information became available. Although the cases do not have to be numbered, enumerating them is advantageous when we want to refer to any of them. Missing data should also be unambiguously coded. The sex of the 21st participant is missing. If women are coded as 1 and men as 2, then we could use any other number to code sex which is missing. In this case we will code it as 0. In addition, the rating for pre-test course interest and coursework preparation is missing. Since these rating scales include 0, we will code the missing ratings as −1.

ENTERING AND EDITING DATA IN Newdata

When using SPSS for Windows, however, it may not be necessary to tabulate the data first since this will, in effect, be done when the data are entered into the computer. When we have a large amount of data, this task is very time-consuming. If your institution employs people for this purpose, then this job is best left to them since they will do it more efficiently and accurately than you can. The examples of data in this book have been kept deliberately small so that you should be able to quickly type in the data yourself. Although these are not physically displayed on the screen, the space into which the data are put consists of a potentially very large number of rows. Each row, however, is made up of a much more limited number of columns which should be restricted to about 4,5000.

If we want to analyse a small set of data, like that shown in Table 1.4, it is convenient to enter these data ourselves using SPSS for Windows. In doing this, names need to be turned into numbers so that, for example, women are coded as 1 and men as 2.

Initially the cursor is in the *cell* in the first row of the first column. The *frame* of this cell is shown in bold to denote that it is the *active* cell. To enter a value in any one cell, make that cell active by moving to it with either the cursor keys or the mouse, type in the value and then move to the next cell into which you want to put a value. Columns are consecutively numbered once you enter a value. So if you enter a value in the fifth column the first five columns will be labelled **var00001** to **var00005**. To change any value already entered, move to the cell containing that value, type in the new value and move to another cell. If you want to leave a cell empty delete the entry with the Backspace or Delete key and move to another cell, when a full stop (**.**) will be left denoting a missing value. Type in the data in Table 1.4 in **Newdata** as shown in Box 3.3. Note that the variables (and the file) have been named and decimal places have been dropped. The procedures for doing this are described below.

Moving within a window with the mouse

Not all the information in this window can be seen even when it is expanded. To move or to *scroll* vertically or horizontally through a window use the *vertical* or *horizontal scroll bar* respectively (see Box 3.3). The

Vertical scroll arrows

Restore button

Vertical scroll button

Vertical scroll bar

SPSS for Windows - [c:\windows\issr2\eg.sav]

File   Edit   Data   Transform   Statistics   Graphs   Utilities   Window   Help

1:sex   1

	sex	cond	subject	intpre	prepre	markpre	prepos	markpos	markfol	var
1	1	1	1	3	2	3	3	4	5	
2	1	1	3	3	3	1	2	6	3	
3	1	2	2	4	4	5	4	7	7	
4	1	2	1	3	4	3	3	8	5	
5	1	2	3	4	3	7	4	9	9	
6	1	3	4	2	2	1	3	4	4	
7	1	3	2	1	1	1	2	4	6	
8	1	3	1	2	3	2	2	5	7	
9	1	3	4	3	3	3	3	6	5	
10	1	3	3	4	3	3	2	6	8	
11	2	1	4	1	0	1	1	1	2	
12	2	1	3	1	1	3	2	1	4	
13	2	1	1	2	1	4	2	2	6	
14	2	1	4	3	2	4	3	4	4	
15	2	2	1	1	1	2	2	2	3	

SPSS Processor is ready

Horizontal scroll button   Horizontal scroll arrows   Horizontal scroll bar

Box 3.3 Expanded **Newdata** window with data (Release 6.1)

position of the *scroll button* or *box* indicates your relative position in the window. For example, if the scroll box is at the top of the scroll bar (as it is in Box 3.3), you are at the top of the window. If the scroll box is in the middle of the scroll bar you are in the middle of the window.

To scroll one screenful at a time place the cursor on the *scroll arrow* pointing in the direction you want to go and press the left mouse button once. For example, to move down a screenful at a time place the cursor on the downward pointing arrow (or below the scroll box) and press the left mouse button. You can also *drag* the scroll box to the position in the window you want by placing the cursor on it, pressing the left mouse button without releasing it, moving the cursor to the desired position, and then releasing the button. You will particularly need to scroll when looking at information in the **Output** window.

Naming variables in Newdata

To name a variable in **Newdata** place the cursor anywhere in the column containing that variable. Select the **Data** option in the **Applications** window followed by the **Define Variable . . .** option to open the **Define Variable** dialog box shown in Box 3.4. Type in your own variable name [e.g. **sex**] which deletes the default highlighted name [e.g **var00001**] in the box beside **Variable Name:**. Select the **OK** button to complete the procedure.

A particular notation is generally used throughout this book as shorthand to describe the steps involved in any application. The selection of a step or option is indicated with a right facing arrow → pointing to the term(s) on the menu or dialog box to be chosen. Any explanations are placed in square parentheses after the option shown. The first step in a dialog box begins on a new line. The whole sequence is indented. Thus, the notation for naming a variable in **Newdata** is

→column to be named [e.g. **var00001**] →**Data** →**Define Variable . . .** [opens **Define Variable** dialog box as in Box 3.4]
→in box beside **Variable Name:** type in own variable name [e.g. **sex** which deletes default name **var00001**] →**OK**

SPSS names

Variable and file names in SPSS have to meet certain specifications. They must be no longer than eight characters and must begin with an alphabetic

---

Define Variable

Variable Name: `VAR00001`

OK

Variable Description
Type: Numeric8.2
Variable Label:
Missing Values: None
Alignment: Right

Cancel

Help

Change Settings

| Type... | Missing Values... |
| Labels.. | Column Format... |

Box 3.4 **Define Variable** dialog box

character (A–Z). The remaining characters can be any letter, number, period, @ (at), $ (dollar) or _ (underscore). Blank spaces are not allowed. Names cannot end with a period and preferably not with an underscore. In addition certain words, known as *keywords*, cannot be used because they can only be interpreted as commands by SPSS. They include words such as **add**, **and**, **any**, **or**, and **to**, to give but a few examples. If you accidentally use a prohibited keyword as a name, you will be told this is invalid when you try to run this procedure with the **OK** button. No keyword contains numbers so you can be certain that names which include numbers will always be recognised as such. It is important to remember that the same name cannot be used for different variables or files. We will call our nine variables **sex**, **cond** (**cond**ition), **subject**, **intpre** (**pre**-test course **int**erest), **prepre** (**pre**-test coursework **pre**paration), **markpre** (**pre**-test coursework **mark**), **prepos** (**pos**t-test coursework **pre**paration), **markpos** (**pos**t-test coursework **mark**) and **markfol** (**fol**low-up coursework **mark**).

Defining other aspects of variables in Newdata

We can define four other aspects of variables when naming them. In the **Define Variable** dialog box there is a box entitled **Variable Description** which lists the four aspects of (1) **Type:**, (2) **Variable Label:**, (3) **Missing Values:** and (4) **Alignment:**. The default setting of these four aspects is **Numeric8.2** for variable type, a blank space for variable label, **None** for missing values and **Right** for alignment. To change any of these settings, we select the appropriate button in the box below entitled **Change Settings**. In general and for our purposes the most important of these is **Missing Values** and the least important is **Alignment**.

Defining Missing Values

In our example, we have missing values for sex, subject, pre-test course interest and pre-test coursework preparation for the 21st person. So we have to specify the appropriate missing values for these variables which is **0** for **sex** and **subject**, and **−1** for **intpre** and **prepre**. We do this as follows:

> →appropriate column [e.g. **sex**] →**Data** →**Define Variable . . .** [opens **Define Variable** dialog box as in Box 3.4]
> →**Missing Values . . .** [opens **Missing Values** dialog box as in Box 3.5]
> →**Discrete missing values** →in first box below type missing value [e.g. 0] →**Continue** →**OK**

If the data are being entered by others we need to let them know how missing data for any of the variables are to be coded.

```
┌─────────────────────────────────────────────────────────────┐
│ ▬       Define Missing Values: sex                            │
├─────────────────────────────────────────────────────────────┤
│                                                               │
│  ○ No missing values                    ┌──────────────┐      │
│                                         │   Continue   │      │
│  ● Discrete missing values              └──────────────┘      │
│    ┌──────────┐ ┌──────────┐ ┌────────┐ ┌──────────────┐      │
│    │ 0│       │ │          │ │        │ │    Cancel    │      │
│    └──────────┘ └──────────┘ └────────┘ └──────────────┘      │
│                                         ┌──────────────┐      │
│  ○ Range of missing values              │     Help     │      │
│                                         └──────────────┘      │
│    Low: ┌──────────┐   High: ┌──────────┐                     │
│         └──────────┘         └──────────┘                     │
│                                                               │
│  ○ Range plus one discrete missing value                      │
│                                                               │
│    Low: ┌──────────┐   High: ┌──────────┐                     │
│         └──────────┘         └──────────┘                     │
│                                                               │
│    Discrete value: ┌──────────┐                               │
│                    └──────────┘                               │
│                                                               │
└─────────────────────────────────────────────────────────────┘
```

Box 3.5 **Missing Values** dialog box

Defining Variable Type

The default variable type is **Numeric8.2** which means that the variable is a number which consists of eight digits, two of which are decimal places. For most purposes it is easier to code all variables as numbers which we have done for our example. Since all our values are whole numbers which consist of a maximum of two digits (−1 for **intpre** and **prepre**), this default value would apply to all our variables. However, if we wished we could change it to drop the two decimal places. To define a number of variables in the same way, we could use the **Templates** option as follows:

→appropriate columns [e.g. **sex** to **markfol** by putting cursor in **sex**, pressing and holding down left button on mouse, moving cursor to **markfol** and releasing button] →**Data** →**Templates . . .** [opens **Template** dialog box as in Box 3.6]
→**Type** in **Apply** section →**Define** >> [opens more of **Template** dialog box]
→**Type . . .** [opens **Define Variable Type** dialog box as in Box 3.7]
→highlight **2** beside **Decimal Places:** and type **0** →**Continue** [closes **Define Variable Type** dialog box]
→**OK** [closes **Template** dialog box]
→**OK** [closes **SPSS for Windows** warning box]

```
┌─────────────────────────────────────────────────────────┐
│ ─ │                    Template                          │
├─────────────────────────────────────────────────────────┤
│                                                          │
│     Template: DEFAULT              ±    ┌──────────┐      │
│                                         │    OK    │      │
│   ┌Template Description┐ ┌Apply┐        └──────────┘      │
│   │ Name:   DEFAULT    │ │ □ Type        ┌──────────┐     │
│   │                    │ │               │  Cancel  │     │
│   │ Type:  Numeric8.2  │ │ □ Value labels └─────────┘     │
│   │                    │ │               ┌──────────┐     │
│   │ Missing Values: None│ │ □ Missing values│ Help │      │
│   │                    │ │                └─────────┘     │
│   │ Alignment:  Right  │ │ ⊠ Column format ┌─────────┐    │
│   └────────────────────┘ └─────┘         │ Define >>│     │
│                                          └─────────┘      │
└─────────────────────────────────────────────────────────┘
```

Box 3.6 **Template** dialog box

```
┌─────────────────────────────────────────────────────────┐
│ ─ │         Define Variable Type: DEFAULT                │
├─────────────────────────────────────────────────────────┤
│  ◉ Numeric                              ┌──────────┐      │
│  ○ Comma                                │ Continue │      │
│  ○ Dot                  Width: 8        └──────────┘      │
│  ○ Scientific Notation  Decimal Places: 2  ┌────────┐    │
│  ○ Date                                  │ Cancel │      │
│  ○ Dollar                                └────────┘      │
│  ○ Custom Currency                       ┌────────┐      │
│  ○ String                                │  Help  │      │
│                                          └────────┘      │
└─────────────────────────────────────────────────────────┘
```

Box 3.7 **Define Variable Type** dialog box

Defining Variable and Value Labels

SPSS variable names are limited to eight characters which usually means that they have to be abbreviated making their meaning less clear. Using this option, variable labels can be created which will be displayed on the output. These variable labels can be up to 120 characters long, although most output will not present labels this long (see Table 3.1). The SPSS variable name **intpre**, for example, could be labelled **pre-test course interest**. At the same time, we could label the values of the variable such as the pre-test course interest ratings (**0** = **none**, **1** = **slight**, **2** = **some**, **3** = **moderate** and **4** = **much**). Value labels can be up to 60 characters long, although most output will not show labels this long. To label variables and values, execute the following procedure:

→column to be named [e.g. **intpre**] →**Data** →**Define Variable . . .**
[opens **Define Variable** dialog box as in Box 3.4]
→**Variable Name:** box and type in own variable name [e.g. **pre-test
course interest**] →**Labels . .** [opens **Define Labels** dialog box as in
Box 3.8]
→**Value:** and type first value [e.g. **0**] →**Value Label:** and type label
[e.g. **none**] →**Add** →**Value:** and type second value [e.g. **1**] →**Value
Label:** and type label [e.g. **slight**] →**Add** [and so on] →**Continue**
[closes **Define Labels** dialog box]
→**OK**

To remove a label we first select it and then **Remove**. To change a label, we
first select it, make the desired changes and then select **Change**.

Defining Column Format and Alignment

It is unlikely that you would wish to change the width of the column in
Newdata or the alignment of data within a column but if you do, select
Column Format to open the **Define Column Format** dialog box shown in
Box 3.9 and make the desired changes.

SAVING DATA IN Newdata

When we want to leave SPSS for Windows or work on another data set in
the same session, these data will be lost unless we save them as a file. We
could save this file onto the hard disk of the computer. However, the
computer may be used by others who may delete our files. Even if no
one else is likely to use the computer, it is good practice to make a *back-up*

Define Labels: intpre		
Variable Label: [ ]		**Continue**
Value Labels		**Cancel**
Value: [ ]		**Help**
Value Label: [ ]		
Add **Change** **Remove**		

Box 3.8 **Define Labels** dialog box

Define Column Format: intpre

Column Width: 8

Text Alignment
○ Left   ○ Center   ● Right

Continue

Cancel

Help

Box 3.9 **Define Column Format** dialog box

copy of our files on one or more *floppy disks* in case we should lose them. The floppy disk is inserted into a slot called a *drive* and needs to be formatted if new. One way of formatting a floppy disk in Windows is to select a program called **File Manager**, select **Disk** from the program menu bar to open the **Format Disk** dialog box shown in Box 3.10, insert the floppy disk into the drive and select **OK**.

To be able to retrieve a file, we need to give it a name. This name can consist of a prefix or *stem* of up to eight characters followed by a full stop and a suffix or *extension* of three characters. The stem name usually refers to the content of the file (such as **eg** in the case of our data example) while the extension name refers to the type of file. The default extension name for files in **Newdata** is **sav**. Thus, we could call our data file **eg.sav**.

Format Disk

Disk In: Drive A:

Capacity: 1.44 MB

Options
Label:

☐ Make System Disk

☐ Quick Format

OK

Cancel

Help

Box 3.10 **Format Disk** dialog box

To save this file on a floppy disk, we carry out the following sequence:

→**File** →**Save As** . . . [opens **Newdata: Save Data As** dialog box as in Box 3.11]
→box under **Drives:** →drive [e.g. **a**] from options listed →box under **File Name:**, delete asterisk and type file stem name [e.g. **eg**] →**OK**

An asterisk or *wildcard* denotes any name which in this case is any stem name.

Retrieving a saved Newdata file

To retrieve this file at a later stage when it is no longer the current file, use the following procedure:

→**File** →**Open** →**Data** . . . [opens **Open Data File** dialog box as in Box 3.12]
→box under **Drives:** →drive [e.g. **a**] from options listed →box under **File Name:** →file name [e.g. **eg.sav**] →press left button once and select **OK** or press left button twice

Help SYSTEM

SPSS has a **Help** system which you may like to use to avoid referring to a book like this one or to find out more about the software. As the system is meant to be self-explanatory you should be able to learn to use it yourself with a little experience. There are various ways of navigating around the

```
┌─────────────────────────────────────────────────────────────┐
│ ─              c:\windows\issr2\eg.sav: Save Data As          │
├─────────────────────────────────────────────────────────────┤
│                                                               │
│  File Name:              Directories:          ┌───────────┐  │
│  ┌──────────────────┐    c:\windows\issr2      │    OK     │  │
│  │ *.sav            │                          └───────────┘  │
│  └──────────────────┘                          ┌───────────┐  │
│  ┌────────────────┬─┐   ┌────────────────┬─┐   │   Paste   │  │
│  │ eg.sav         │▲│   │ 🗁 c:\          │▲│   └───────────┘  │
│  │                │ │   │  🗁 windows     │ │   ┌───────────┐  │
│  │                │ │   │   🗀 issr2      │ │   │  Cancel   │  │
│  │                │ │   │                │ │   └───────────┘  │
│  │                │ │   │                │ │   ┌───────────┐  │
│  │                │ │   │                │ │   │   Help    │  │
│  │                │▼│   │                │▼│   └───────────┘  │
│  └────────────────┴─┘   └────────────────┴─┘   ┌───────────┐  │
│                                                │ Network...│  │
│  Save File as Type:      Drives:               └───────────┘  │
│  ┌────────────────┬─┐   ┌────────────────────┬─┐              │
│  │ SPSS [*.sav]   │▼│   │ ▤ c: ms-dos_6_2    │▼│              │
│  └────────────────┴─┘   └────────────────────┴─┘              │
│                                                               │
│  ☒ Compress SPSS data                                         │
│  ☒ Write variable names to spreadsheet                        │
│                                                               │
└─────────────────────────────────────────────────────────────┘
```

Box 3.11 **Newdata: Save Data As** dialog box

```
┌─────────────────────────────────────────────────────────────┐
│ ──              Open Data File                                │
├─────────────────────────────────────────────────────────────┤
│                                                               │
│ File Name:              Directories:        ┌─────────────┐   │
│ ┌───────────────┐       c:\windows\issr2    │     OK      │   │
│ │ eg.sav        │                           └─────────────┘   │
│ └───────────────┘                                             │
│ ┌───────────────┐▲      ┌───────────────┐▲  ┌─────────────┐   │
│ │ eg.sav        │       │ 📁 c:\         │   │    Paste    │   │
│ │               │       │ 📂 windows     │   └─────────────┘   │
│ │               │       │   📁 issr2     │   ┌─────────────┐   │
│ │               │       │               │   │   Cancel    │   │
│ │               │       │               │   └─────────────┘   │
│ │               │▼      │               │▼  ┌─────────────┐   │
│ └───────────────┘       └───────────────┘   │    Help     │   │
│                                              └─────────────┘   │
│ File Type:              Drives:              ┌─────────────┐   │
│ ┌──────────────┬─┐      ┌──────────────────┬─┐ │ Network...│  │
│ │ SPSS (*.sav) │▼│      │ 💻 c: ms-dos_6_2 │▼│ └─────────────┘ │
│ └──────────────┴─┘      └──────────────────┴─┘                │
│ ┌─ Options ───────────────────────────────────────────────┐  │
│ │ □ Read variable names     Range: ┌──────────────┐        │  │
│ │                                  └──────────────┘        │  │
│ └──────────────────────────────────────────────────────────┘ │
└─────────────────────────────────────────────────────────────┘
```

Box 3.12 **Open Data File** dialog box

system. You should experiment with them to find out your preference. There are two main ways of obtaining the information on a topic such as **file**.

The first consists of the following steps:

→**Help** →**Contents** →**SPSS commands** →**File menu** →choose from list

The second involves the following procedure:

→**Help** →**Contents** →**Search** [from menu bar] [opens **Search** dialog box as in Box 3.13]
→in first box type in term or select it from list below [a quick way to scroll through this list is to put the cursor on the button in the vertical scroll bar, hold down the left button on the mouse, pull the mouse to where you want to be and then release the left button on the mouse]
→**Show Topics** →appropriate or closest term →**Go To** →if appropriate select term highlighted or select more appropriate term

If you want help while in a dialog box, select the **Help** option in the dialog box.

Leaving SPSS

To leave SPSS,

→**File** →**Exit** [if a window has been opened in a session, you will be asked if you wish to save the contents in it: if you don't, →**No**; if you do, →**Yes** and name it if you have not already done so].

```
┌─────────────────────────────────────────────────────────────┐
│ ┌───┐                    Search                              │
│ │ ─ │                                                        │
│ Type a word, or select one from the list.    ┌─────────────┐ │
│ Then choose Show Topics.                     │   Cancel    │ │
│                                              └─────────────┘ │
│ ┌──────────────────────────────────────────┐┌─────────────┐ │
│ ││                                          ││ Show Topics │ │
│ └──────────────────────────────────────────┘└─────────────┘ │
│    ┌───────────────────────────────────────────────────┬──┐ │
│    │ 1-sample tests                                     │▲ │ │
│    │ 2 independent samples                              │──│ │
│    │ 2 related samples                                  │  │ │
│    │ 2SLS command                                       │  │ │
│    │ 3-D rotation                                       │  │ │
│    │ 3-D scatterplots                                   │▼ │ │
│    └───────────────────────────────────────────────────┴──┘ │
│ ─────────────────────────────────────────────────────────── │
│                                              ┌─────────────┐ │
│ Select a topic, then choose Go To.           │   Go To     │ │
│                                              └─────────────┘ │
│ ┌──────────────────────────────────────────────────────────┐│
│ │                                                          ││
│ │                                                          ││
│ │                                                          ││
│ └──────────────────────────────────────────────────────────┘│
└─────────────────────────────────────────────────────────────┘
```

Box 3.13 **Search** dialog box

STATISTICAL ANALYSIS WITH SPSS FOR WINDOWS

To carry out a statistical analysis of the data in Table 1.4 we need to use the appropriate SPSS procedure. So far, we have only described the relatively simple descriptive statistical measures of central tendency and dispersion. One SPSS procedure which calculates the mean together with some other descriptive statistics is the **Descriptives** option. We use this option as follows to calculate the mean for pre-test course interest ratings (**intpre**) for the whole sample:

→**Statistics** →**Summarize** →**Descriptives** . . . [opens **Descriptives** dialog box as in Box 3.14]
→variable [e.g. **intpre**] →▶ button [puts selected variable in box under **Variable[s]:**] →**OK**

The output for this procedure is displayed in Table 3.1. The mean rating is **2.75** which is based on 20 cases as the datum for the last one is missing. Note also that the full variable name is not given. The other descriptive statistics provided by default are the standard deviation and the minimum and maximum values. We can check the accuracy of these descriptive statistics by calculating them by hand. Conversely, SPSS procedures can

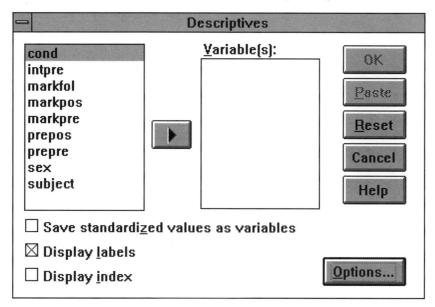

Box 3.14 **Descriptives** dialog box

Table 3.1 SPSS output for the **Descriptives** procedure for pre-test course interest for women and men

Number of valid observations (listwise) = 20.00

Variable	Mean	Std Dev	Minimum	Maximum	Valid N	Label
INTPRE	2.75	1.12	1	4	20	pre-test course inter

be used to check the manual calculations in the previous and subsequent chapters.

To show the syntax commands for carrying out this procedure we select **Paste** in the dialog box which produces the output presented in the **!Syntax1** window in Box 3.15. To run this syntax command put the cursor anywhere inside it and select the **Click Syntax** button in SPSS Release 6.1 (see Box 3.2) or the **Run** button in SPSS Release 6.0 (see Box 3.16) depending on which is available.

If we wanted other descriptive statistics available on this option we select **Options . . .** in the **Descriptives** dialog box to open the **Descriptives: Options** dialog box shown in Box 3.17. We then select or de-select the appropriate ones by moving the cursor onto them and pressing the left button. The statistics chosen deliberately or by default are indicated by the box beside them being marked with a tick or cross.

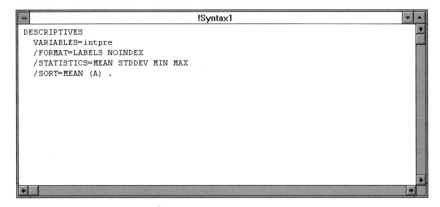

Box 3.15 **!Syntax1** window (Release 6.1)

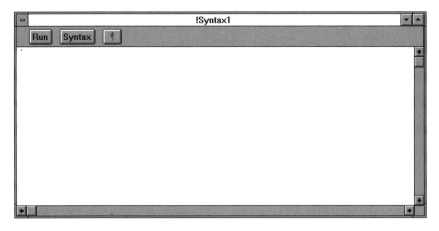

Box 3.16 **Run** button (Release 6.0)

Saving and printing output

To print the contents of any window on a printer directly connected to your PC, enter that window and then execute the following sequence:

→**File** →**Print** . . . →**OK**

If you want to store the contents of any window on a floppy disk, then carry out the following steps:

→**File** →**Open** →window [e.g. **SPSS Output** . . . which opens the ***.LST: Save SPSS Output As** dialog box as in Box 3.18]
→box under **Drives:** →drive [e.g. **a**] from options listed →box under **File Name:** →file name [e.g. **jsr.lst**] →press left button once and select **OK** or press left button twice

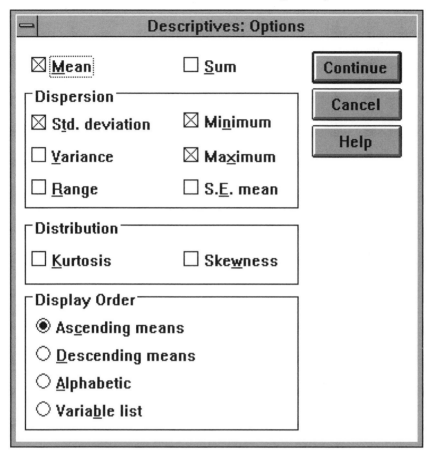

Box 3.17 **Descriptives: Options** dialog box

Box 3.18 ***.LST: Save SPSS Output As** dialog box

The default extension name for output files is **lst** which is short for **listing** file. You can edit output files before saving them. For example, you may wish to delete certain analyses or type in some further explanation.

Selecting subgroups of cases

To select a subgroup of cases to work on such as the women in Table 1.4, we carry out the following procedure:

→**Data** →**Select** **Cases** . . . [opens **Select Cases** dialog box as in Box 3.19]
→**If** **condition is satisfied** →**If** . . . [opens **Select Cases: If** dialog box as in Box 3.20]
Either
→type in box **sex = 1**
Or
→first selector variable [e.g. **sex**] →▶button [puts selected variable in empty box] →= →value of variable [e.g. **1**]
→**Continue** [closes **Select Cases: If** dialog box]
→**OK**

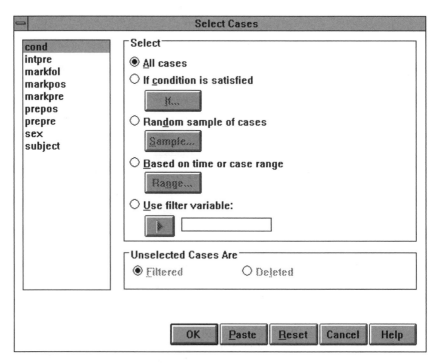

Box 3.19 **Select Cases** dialog box

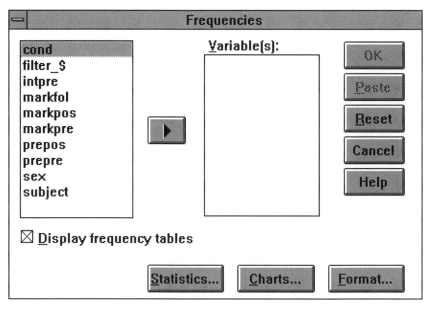

Box 3.20 **Select Cases: If** dialog box

To obtain the mode, median, mean, first quartile, sample variance and sample standard deviation for the ten pre-test coursework marks for women in our data we could run the **Frequencies** procedure as follows:

→**Statistics** →**Summarize** →**Frequencies** . . . [opens **Frequencies** dialog box as in Box 3.21]
→variable(s) [e.g. **markpre**] →▶button [puts selected variable(s) in **Variable[s]:** text box] →**Statistics** . . . [opens **Frequencies: Statistics** dialog box as in Box 3.22]

Box 3.21 **Frequencies** dialog box

—	Frequencies: Statistics		

Percentile Values
- ☐ Quartiles
- ☐ Cut points for [10] equal groups
- ☐ Percentile(s): [ ]
  - [Add]
  - [Change]
  - [Remove]

Central Tendency
- ☐ Mean
- ☐ Median
- ☐ Mode
- ☐ Sum

[Continue] [Cancel] [Help]

☐ Values are group midpoints

Dispersion
- ☐ Std. deviation   ☐ Minimum
- ☐ Variance   ☐ Maximum
- ☐ Range   ☐ S.E. mean

Distribution
- ☐ Skewness
- ☐ Kurtosis

Box 3.22 **Frequencies: Statistics** dialog box

Table 3.2 SPSS output for the **Frequencies** procedure for pre-test coursework marks for women

MARKPRE

Value Label		Value	Frequency	Percent	Valid Percent	Cum Percent
		1	3	30.0	30.0	30.0
		2	1	10.0	10.0	40.0
		3	4	40.0	40.0	80.0
		5	1	10.0	10.0	90.0
		7	1	10.0	10.0	100.0
		Total	10	100.0	100.0	

Mean	2.900	Median	3.000	Mode	3.000
Std dev	1.912	Variance	3.656		

Percentile	Value	Percentile	Value	Percentile	Value
25.00	1.000	50.00	3.000	75.00	3.500

Valid cases   10   Missing cases   0

→**Quartiles** →**Mean** →**Median** →**Mode** →**Std deviation** →**Variance**
→**Continue** [closes **Frequencies: Statistics** dialog box]
→**OK**

The output for this sequence is shown in Table 3.2 where we can see that the mode is **3.000** the median **3.000**, the mean **2.900**, the first quartile (or **25.00 Percentile**) **1.000**, the (sample) variance **3.656** and the (sample) standard deviation (**Std deviation**) **1.912** as calculated in Chapter 2.

DATA TRANSFORMATIONS

In addition to carrying out statistical tests, SPSS for Windows has procedures for transforming variables (i.e. those within a row) by changing their value (e.g. taking their square root) and for combining two or more variables (e.g. adding the value of one variable to that of another). These data transformation procedures will be used to show how to carry out some of the computations needed to calculate a particular statistic.

The procedure for carrying out these kinds of arithmetic operations is **Compute**. For example, to add the three coursework marks we could use the following procedure:

→**Transform** →**Compute** . . . [opens **Compute Variable** dialog box as in Box 3.23]
→**Target Variable:** box and type new variable name [e.g. **marktot**]
→select or type in appropriate expression in **Numeric Expression:** box [e.g. **markpre + markpos + markfol**] →**OK** [closes **Compute Variable** dialog box]

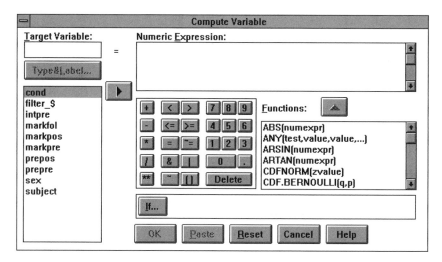

Box 3.23 **Compute Variable** dialog box

The total marks will be displayed in the last column of data in **Newdata** and is **12.00** for the first row (**3 + 4 + 5**). If we wanted the mean coursework mark we could add the three marks and divide the total by 3 [(**markpre + markpos + markfol)/3**]. We have to enclose the addition operation in brackets, otherwise only **markfol** is divided by **3**. Without parentheses, certain arithmetic operations are done before others. The operation of raising to a power (******) is performed before that of multiplication (*****) and division (**/**), which are both executed before that of addition (**+**) and subtraction (**−**). Operations in parentheses [**( )**] are performed before those outside them.

Recoding values

We may wish to recode the values of a variable such as collapsing the coursework marks into the two categories of those who have passed (3 to 9) and those who have failed (0 to 2). To do this, we use the **Recode** procedure as follows:

→**Transform** →**Recode** →**Into Different Variables . . .** [opens **Recode Into Different Variables** dialog box as in Box 3.24]
→first variable to be recoded [e.g. **markpre**] →▶ button [puts first variable in **Numeric Variable → Output Variable:** box →**Name:** box and type name for recoded variable [e.g. **pmarkpre**] →**Change** →**Old and New Values . . .** [opens **Recode into Different Variables: Old and New Values** dialog box as in Box 3.25] Repeat for similarly recoded variables [e.g. **markpos markfol**]
→**Range:** in **Old Value** section →type lowest value in range [e.g. **0**] →box after **through** and type highest value in range [e.g. **2**] →**Value:** box in **New Value** section and type value for range [e.g. **0**] →**Add** Repeat for other values [e.g. **3 → 9**]
→**Continue** [closes **Recode into Different Variables: Old and New Values** dialog box]
→**OK**

The new values are displayed in the last three data columns of **Newdata**.

SUMMARY

Statistical programs enable statistics to be calculated quickly and accurately. One of the most widely used and comprehensive statistical packages in the social sciences is SPSS for Windows, which is available for UNIX on mainframe computers and for personal computers with a 386 or higher processor. Procedures are also available for selecting particular subsets of data and for creating new variables. Data are entered into the **Newdata** window which has a very large capacity. The values of each variable are listed in the same column and the data for each case or unit are put into the

Box 3.24 **Recode Into Different Variables** dialog box

Box 3.25 **Recode Into Different Variables: Old and New Values** dialog box

same row. Values which are missing should be defined with an unambiguous numerical code. Procedures can be selected from menus and dialog boxes or can be entered as syntax commands in the **Syntax** window. The statistical results are displayed visually in the **Output** window and can be edited before being printed.

EXERCISES

1 How would you numerically code the variable of marital status which has the following five categories: single and never married; married; separated; divorced; and widowed?

2 How would you code someone who had said they were both single and widowed?

3 In your data file you have information on the year of birth of your respondents. What SPSS procedure would you use to calculate their age in the year 2000?

4 For 10 respondents you have collected information on their responses to 10 dichotomous questions measuring course interest. What SPSS procedures would you use to do the following:

(a) input this information in your SPSS data file;

(b) reverse the dichotomous scores for the even numbered items;

(c) add up the scores of the 10 questions to give a total score for each person;

(d) find the mean score for each person;

(e) find the mean of the total score for the whole sample of 10 individuals?

5 If some of the responses were missing what effect would this have on the total score?

4 Statistical significance and choice of test

As outlined in the first chapter, one of the main uses of statistics in the social sciences is to determine the probability of three different kinds of events or outcomes happening. The first kind is estimating whether a sample drawn from a population is representative of that population in terms of a specified characteristic. Suppose, for example, we know that the population of interest consists of an equal number of women and men and we draw a sample of five women and seven men. How likely are we to obtain this particular number of women and men by chance? The second kind is deciding whether one sample differs from another in terms of a particular variable. Assume, for instance, that ten people are randomly assigned to either having tutorials or not having tutorials. Three of the five having tutorials receive higher coursework marks than three of the five not having tutorials, while there is no difference between the other two. What is the likelihood of finding this difference by chance? The third kind is estimating the probability of two events being associated by chance. Imagine, for example, that three of four people having tutorials do well in their coursework compared with three of six people who do not have tutorials. How likely are we to come across such a relationship by chance?

The probability of obtaining any particular event by chance on any occasion is one divided by the total number of possible events. So, the probability of randomly selecting a woman or man from a population containing an equal number of women and men is 0.5 (1/2 = 0.5). The probability of finding a person randomly assigned to having tutorials doing better than another randomly assigned to not having tutorials is 0.33 (1/3 = 0.33) since that individual can do better than, worse than or the same as the other, while the probability of someone by chance both doing better and having tutorials is 0.25 (1/4 = 0.25). If the probability of doing better is independent of having tutorials, then the probability of both events occurring is the product of their separate probability (0.5 × 0.5 = 0.25).

The probability of obtaining a particular sequence of independent events is the product of their separate probabilities. So, the probability of randomly choosing two women from a population consisting of the same number of women and men is 0.25 (0.5 × 0.5 = 0.25). The probability of finding two people randomly allocated to having tutorials doing better than two individuals randomly assigned to not having tutorials is 0.11 (0.33 × 0.33 = 0.11), whereas the probability of two people by chance both doing better and having tutorials is 0.06 (0.25 × 0.25 = 0.06).

Since the procedure for determining the probability of independent events is the same for the three kinds of situations described above, we will use the simplest case of randomly selecting women and men from a population containing an equal proportion of women and men. This situation is the same as tossing a number of unbiased coins once. If we select one person at random, then there are only two possible outcomes since that person can only be a woman or a man. Consequently, the probability of selecting a woman or a man is 0.5 (1/2 = 0.5). If we pick two people, there are four possible outcomes: (1) two women; (2) two men; (3) a woman followed by a man; and (4) a man followed by a woman. If these four outcomes are equiprobable, then the probability of any one of them occurring is 0.25 (1/4 = 0.25). Since there are two different orders in which a woman and a man can be selected, the probability of obtaining a woman and a man is the sum of the probability of these two orders which is 0.5 (0.25 + 0.25 = 0.5).

We can plot the distribution of the probability of choosing these three different numbers of women and men in terms of a *polygon* as shown in Figure 4.1. On the horizontal *axis* the varying proportions of women to men are ordered, ranging from two women and no men to no women and two men. The probabilities of these proportions are depicted on the vertical axis, ranging from zero to 0.75. Points are placed on the figure where the appropriate values on the horizontal and vertical axes meet. So we place a point, for example, where the vertical line drawn from the position on the horizontal axis representing the proportion of two women and no men meets the horizontal line drawn from the position on the vertical axis denoting a probability of 0.25. The points on the figure are then connected by straight lines. If we do this, we see that this distribution of proportions takes the form of an upturned 'V'.

If we select four people, there are sixteen possible outcomes as presented in Table 4.1. If these sixteen outcomes are equiprobable, then the probability of any one of them happening by chance is 0.0625 (0.5 × 0.5 × 0.5 × 0.5 = 0.0625). As there are four different ways in which either three women and one man or one woman and three men can be selected, the probability of obtaining either of these two outcomes is 0.25 (0.0625 + 0.0625 + 0.0625 + 0.0625 = 0.25). Similarly, as there are six different orders containing two women and two men, the probability of finding this outcome is 0.375 (0.0625 + 0.0625 + 0.0625 + 0.0625 + 0.0625 + 0.0625 = 0.375). If we plot the distribution of the probability of selecting these five different numbers of women and men, then this distribution takes the shape of an inverted 'V' once more, as drawn in Figure 4.2.

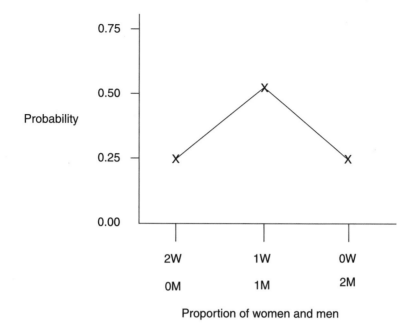

Figure 4.1 Two-case example of a probability distribution

Table 4.1 Four-case example of equiprobable gender outcomes

Possible outcomes	Probability
1 WWWW	0.0625
2 WWWM 3 WWMW 4 WMWW 5 MWWW	0.2500
6 WWMM 7 WMWM 8 WMMW 9 MWWM 10 MWMW 11 MMWW	0.3750
12 MMMW 13 MMWM 14 MWMM 15 WMMM	0.2500
16 MMMM	0.0625

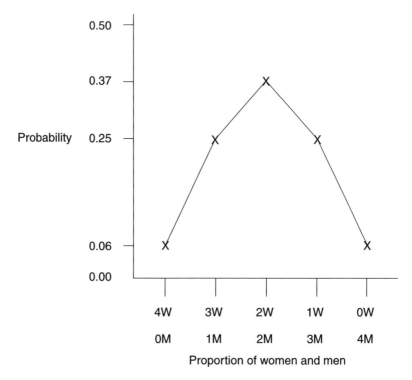

Figure 4.2 Four-case example of a probability distribution

The distribution of the probability of only two outcomes (e.g. a woman and a man) occurring by chance on a specified number of occasions (e.g. for four people) is called a *binomial* distribution. The binomial distributions shown in Figures 4.1 and 4.2 are for two and four occasions respectively. The distribution of the probability of two outcomes occurring by chance on an infinite number of occasions takes the form of an inverted U or bell-shaped distribution usually called a *normal* or *z* distribution but also known as *DeMoivre's* or a *Gaussian* distribution. Such a distribution is illustrated in Figure 4.3. We can see that the binomial distribution approximates a normal one if we produce the binomial distribution for ten occasions as shown in Figure 4.4.

As can be worked out, the larger the number of people selected from a population, the less likely it is that the sample will consist of all women or men. For example, the probability of obtaining all five women from a population consisting of equal numbers of women and men is 0.031 (0.5 $\times$ 0.5 $\times$ 0.5 $\times$ 0.5 $\times$ 0.5 or $0.5^5 = 0.031$), while the probability of obtaining all six women is 0.016 ($0.5^6 = 0.016$). However, even with very large samples of people, there is always a very small probability that the sample will contain all women or all men. Consequently, the

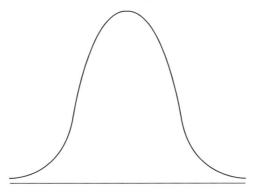

Figure 4.3 A normal distribution

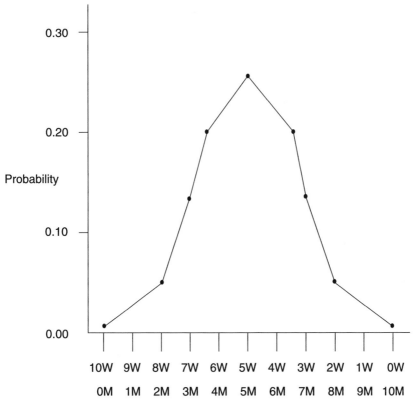

Figure 4.4 Ten-case example of binomial probability distribution

question arises as to when we decide that a sample is or is not representative of the population from which it is drawn. The same issue, of course, is also raised when determining whether there is or is not a difference in the scores (e.g. marks) between two groups (e.g. those having or not having tutorials) or whether there is or is not a relationship between two variables (e.g. doing well and having tutorials).

The conventional probability or *p* value for deciding that a result is not due to chance has been set as equal to or less than 0.05 or five times out of a hundred. If the probability level of an outcome is at or below 0.05, then the result is *statistically significant* in that it is thought unlikely to have been due to chance. If, on the other hand, the probability level of an outcome is above 0.05, then that result is *statistically non-significant* in the sense that it is considered likely that it could have been due to chance. Note that this result is *non*-significant and not *in*significant.

When analysing the probability of an outcome, we can either specify the direction of the results we expect to obtain or we can leave the direction unstated. In terms of the three kinds of situation outlined at the beginning of this chapter, we could predict the direction of the results by stating that the sample will contain a greater proportion of women than that in the population, that the people randomly assigned to having tutorials will do better than those randomly assigned to not having tutorials, and that people who do better will have attended tutorials. Take the case of expecting that the sample will consist of a greater proportion of women than that in the population. Suppose we obtain a sample of four women and no men. Since the probability of selecting such a sample is 0.0625 which is greater than 0.05, we would conclude that the sample does not differ significantly from the population. If, on the other hand, we had a sample of five women and no men, we would assume that the sample varied significantly from the population since the probability of finding such a sample is 0.031 which is below the 0.05 level. When the hypothesis is *directional*, we adopt the *one-tailed* probability level since only one end or tail of the probability distribution is used.

When, however, the hypothesis is *non-directional* in the sense that we do not predict what the results will be, we employ the *two-tailed* probability level which takes account of both ends or tails of the probability distribution. Suppose, for instance, we wanted to know whether the proportion of women in the sample differed from that in the population but did not have any expectations about the way in which it differed. Since the sample may contain either proportionately more or proportionately less women than that in the population, both these probabilities have to be included. Consequently, the criterion value of 0.05 for deciding whether the sample differs significantly from the population is made up of the 0.025 probability that the sample will contain proportionately more women than the population and the 0.025 probability that the sample will comprise proportionately less women than the population.

For example, if a sample of five women was obtained from a population containing equal numbers of women and men, then this sample could be interpreted as not differing from the population since the probability of obtaining five women (0.031) combined with the probability of obtaining five men (0.031) is 0.062 (0.031 + 0.031 = 0.062) which is greater than 0.05. If, on the other hand, a sample of six women was selected from the same population, then this sample could be said to differ from the population since the probability of selecting six women (0.016) added to the probability of selecting six men (0.016) is 0.032 (0.016 + 0.016 = 0.032) which is less than 0.05. Since the one-tailed probability level is half that of the two-tailed probability level, statistical significance is more likely to be obtained when the direction of the hypothesis is stated. However, the one-tailed probability level can only be used when the direction the results will take has been specified before the data are analysed. If the direction of the results are not predicted before the data are examined, the two-tailed probability level has to be employed.

The convention of adopting the 0.05 probability level as the cut-off point for determining the statistical significance of a finding is arbitrary since there is always the probability that any result is due to chance. For example, although we assume that a sample containing only six women differs significantly from a population known to consist of an equal number of women and men, there is a two-tailed probability of 0.032 that this result could have occurred by chance.

Because we can never be certain about whether a sample differs from its population, whether two groups differ from each other or whether a relationship exists between two variables, we can make one of two types of error as shown in Table 4.2. The first type of error, known as *Type I error* or *alpha error*, is when we accept that there is a difference or relationship when in reality there is none. For example, we may assume that the sample differs from its population when it does not. A *Type II* or *beta error* is when we accept there is no difference or relationship when in actuality there is one. These two types of error are illustrated in Figure 4.5.

We may reduce the possibility of making a Type I error by lowering the significance level from 0.05 to say, 0.01 (one in a hundred) or less. If, for example, we adopt the 0.01 probability level, then a sample of only six

Table 4.2 Type I and Type II errors

		Real difference or relationship	
		Yes	No
Accept difference or relationship	Yes	Correct decision	Type I error (α)
	No	Type II error (β)	Correct decision

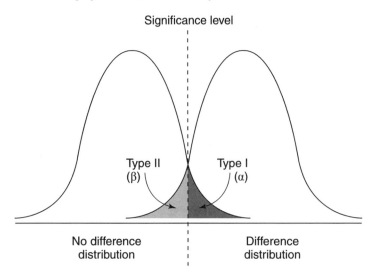

Figure 4.5 The probability of Type I and Type II errors

women would not differ significantly from a population containing equal numbers of women and men since the two-tailed probability of obtaining this result (0.032) is greater than 0.01. However, employing a more con- servative probability level has the effect of increasing a Type II error. One way of decreasing the probability of making this kind of error is to increase the size of the sample. For instance, the two-tailed probability of finding that a sample contains all women is 0.062 for a sample of five but 0.032 for a sample of six.

DIFFERENT KINDS OF STATISTICAL TESTS

What particular statistical test we use for deciding whether a result is statistically significant depends on five main considerations. First, are we interested in determining whether two variables are related or whether one or more groups differ on some variable? Tests of association assess the size and often the direction of a relationship between two variables, whereas tests of difference ascertain whether one or more groups differ on some variable. Second, are the data categorical or non-categorical? With cate- gorical data, the number or frequency of cases in each category is simply counted whereas with non-categorical data, the data can be described in terms of measures of central tendency and dispersion. Third, do we need to make assumptions about the way the values of the variables are distribu- ted? *Non-parametric* tests generally depend less than *parametric* tests on the distribution of variables in the population and are, therefore, sometimes known as *distribution-free* tests. Fourth, when two or more groups are being compared, do they consist of different (*unrelated*) cases or ones which are the same or have been matched (*related*)? And fifth, are there one, two or more groups being compared? *Omnibus* tests for comparing three or more groups are listed in Table 4.3 which determine whether a difference exists between the groups but do not tell which groups differ. To find this out we need to compare two groups at a time. When we have predicted before hand where the differences lie, we determine whether any differences are significant with what is called an *a priori* or *planned* test. Whereas when we have not previously predicted any differences, we test for what appear to be differences using what has been variously called an *a posteriori*, *post hoc* or *unplanned* test.

The major tests of difference and association covered in this book are presented in Tables 4.3 and 4.4 respectively, together with the considerations for their application. Each of these tests have their own test statistic (such as *t* and *r*) and the probability of that statistic arising by chance. In other words, the way in which a particular test calculates the probability of a certain outcome occurring by chance depends on the five considerations outlined above. The test for determining, for example, whether people having tutorials do better than those not having tutorials will be different from the test that assesses whether, say, there is a statistically significant association between doing better and tutorial attendance. Many of these tests use the same test statistic for determining the statistical significance of the result. The five most common distributions are the binomial, *z*, chi-square, *t* and *F*. Table 4.5 lists the tests in Tables 4.3 and 4.4 which use these distributions.

PARAMETRIC AND NON-PARAMETRIC TESTS

One of the unresolved issues in statistics is the question of when parametric rather than non-parametric tests should be used. Some writers have argued that parametric tests should only be applied when the data fulfil the following three conditions: (1) the variables are measured with an equal interval or ratio scale; (2) the samples are drawn from populations whose variances are equal or *homogeneous*; and (3) whose distributions are normal. A normal distribution is a theoretical or idealised one which is based on a population of an infinite number of cases and which takes the form of a bell or an inverted-U as shown in Figure 4.3. The extent to which a normal distribution looks like a bell depends upon the values of its parameters. Greater variances will create flatter distributions. The term *parameter* refers to a measure which describes the distribution of the variable in the population such as its mean or variance. Parametric tests are so called because they are based on assumptions about the parameters of the population from which the sample has been drawn (i.e. that the variances should be equal and that the distributions should be normal).

Whether these three conditions have to be satisfied before parametric tests can be employed has been seriously questioned. Concerning the first

Table 4.3 Tests of difference

Nature of variable	Type of test	Kind of data	Number of groups	Name of test	Page numbers
Categorical (nominal or frequency)	Non-parametric	Unrelated	1	Binomial	281–285
			1	Chi-square	287–294
			2	Fisher's exact	303–306
			2+	Chi square	298–303 306–309
		Related	2	McNemar	316–319
			3+	Cochran Q	319–323
Non-categorical	Non-parametric	Unrelated	1	Kolmogorov–Smirnov	325–327
			2	Kolmogorov–Smirnov	327–331
			2	Mann–Whitney U	333–339
			2+	Median	331–333
			3+	Kruskal–Wallis H	339–342
		Related	2	Sign	342–343
			2	Wilcoxon	343–346
			3+	Friedman	346–349
	Parametric	Unrelated	1	t	103–108
			2	t	108–117
			2+	One-way and two-way analysis of variance	117–133 220–233
		Related	2	t	205–208
			3+	Single factor repeated measures	209–216
		Related and un-related	2+	Two-way analysis of unrelated variance with repeated measures on one factor	247–254
				One-way analysis of covariance	258–278

condition, it has been suggested that parametric tests can also be used with ordinal variables since tests apply to numbers and not to what those numbers refer to (Lord 1953). Suppose, for example, we compare the number of hours reading for a course during the last week by three individuals who are performing well and three people who are not doing so well. The number of hours worked by the three more successful individuals is 5, 7 and 8 respectively and is 1, 3 and 6 for the three less successful ones as

Table 4.4 Tests of association

Nature of variable	Type of test	Name of test	Page numbers
Categorical (nominal or frequency)	Non-parametric	Phi coefficient	353–354
		Contingency coefficient	354–357
		Cramér's *V*	357–358
		Goodman and Kruskal's lambda	358–359
		Goodman and Kruskal's tau	359–361
Non-categorical	Non-parametric	Kendall's tau *a*	363–364
		Kendall's tau *b*	364–366
		Kendall's tau *c*	366–368
		Goodman and Kruskal's gamma	368–369
		Somers' *d*	369–371
		Spearman's rank-order correlation	371–373
		Mantel–Haenszel's chi-square	373–374
		Kendall's partial rank-order correlation	375–376
		Partial gamma	376–377
	Parametric	Pearson's product moment correlation	137–144 152–154
		Pearson's partial correlation	156–162
		Eta	154–156
		Unstandardised regression coefficient	169
		Standardised regression coefficient	174
		Part correlation	185–187

shown in Table 4.6. Consequently, the more successful group has worked 20 hours in all while the less successful group has worked 10. The variable of the number of hours worked is a ratio scale since it has a zero point and the numbers indicate equal intervals. Indeed, the more successful group has worked twice as many hours as the less successful group.

Now, assume that instead of asking people how many hours they had worked, we had them rate on a 4-point scale how much time they worked where 1 signifies 'no time', 2 'a little time', 3 'some time' and 4 'much time'. This measure would be an ordinal scale since someone scoring 4 would not necessarily have spent twice as many hours working as someone scoring 2. As indicated in Table 4.6, the three more successful individuals rated themselves as 3, 3 and 4 and the three less successful ones as 1, 2 and 2. Therefore, the total score is 10 for the more successful group and 5 for the less successful one. Since, the measure is an ordinal one, we cannot say that the more successful group worked twice as long as the less successful

Table 4.5 Tests of difference and association arranged according to the statistical significance test used

Binomial	Binomial ($n < 26$, p of outcome = 0.5)
	Sign (< 26 differences)
Chi-square	Chi-square
	Contingency coefficient
	Friedman
	Kolmogorov-Smirnov one-tailed (n1 + n2 < 60)
	Kruskal-Wallis
	McNemar (cells indicating change)
	Mood's median
	Phi coefficient
F	Analysis of variance and covariance
	2+ homogeneous variances
	Multiple correlation
	Multiple regression
t	Bivariate regression
	2 means
	Pearson's correlation
	Spearman's rho
z	Binomial test ($n > 25$, p of outcome = 0.5)
	Kendall's tau c
	Kurtosis
	Mann-Whitney ($n1 + n2 < 20$)
	Sign (> 25 differences)
	Skewness
	Wilcoxon (> 25 differences)

one. However, we can state that the more successful group spent more time working than the less successful group. Since a parametric test applied to these two measures simply determines whether the mean scores of the two groups differ, the measure can be ordinal, equal interval or ratio.

With respect to the second and third conditions, a number of studies have been conducted to see what effect samples drawn from populations with non-normal distributions and unequal variances have on the values of parametric tests. Some authors have suggested that violation of these two

Table 4.6 Ratio and ordinal measures of number of hours worked by three more and three less successful individuals

	More		Less	
	Ratio	*Ordinal*	*Ratio*	*Ordinal*
	5	3	1	1
	7	3	3	2
	8	4	6	2
Total	20	10	10	5

assumptions generally has little effect on the values of these tests (e.g. Boneau 1960). One exception to this general finding was where both the size of the samples and the variances were unequal although some have argued that this exception applies even with equal sample sizes (Wilcox 1987). Another exception was where both distributions of scores were non-normal. In such circumstances, it may be prudent to compare the results of a non-parametric test with those of a parametric test. Where the distributions of scores are not normal, it may also be worth running a parametric test on the scores as they are and after they have been transformed closer to normality. For more details on transforming scores to normality, see Mosteller and Tukey (1977). Tests for determining a normal distribution and equal variances are described next.

Non-parametric tests are less powerful than parametric tests in the sense that the result is less likely to be statistically significant when there is a relationship between two or more variables. The exact probability levels of a number of parametric and non-parametric tests are shown in Table 4.7 for the marks of women in the two or three conditions. The probability levels are higher for the non-parametric than for the parametric tests.

SKEWNESS

The extent to which a set of scores deviates from a normal or bell-shaped distribution is estimated by two statistics called *skewness* and *kurtosis*. Skewness is a measure of the extent to which the distribution is not

Table 4.7 Significance levels of parametric and non-parametric tests of marks in women for two or three of the conditions

	Parametric		Non-parametric	
Two unrelated groups (Post-test marks in groups 2 and 3)	Unrelated *t*	0.006	Kolmogorov-Smirnov Mann-Whitney Median	0.047 0.0236 0.0179
Three unrelated groups (Post-test marks in groups 1, 2 and 3)	*F*	0.0143	Kruskal-Wallis	0.0493
Two related groups (Pre- and post-test marks for group 2)	Related *t*	0.095	Sign Wilcoxon	0.2500 0.1008
Three related groups (Pre-, post- and follow-up marks for group 2)	*F*	0.049	Friedman	0.0970
Post-test and follow-up marks	Pearson	0.195	Kendall's tau *b* Spearman	0.222 0.255

symmetrical while kurtosis is an index of the degree to which there are either too many or too few cases in the middle of the distribution.

The formula for skewness (Bliss 1967) is:

$$\text{skewness} = \frac{[\text{sum of (each score} - \text{mean) cubed}] \times N}{\text{standard deviation cubed} \times (N - 1) \times (N - 2)}$$

where N is the total number of cases.

We will demonstrate the steps involved in using this formula to calculate skewness with the following four follow-up coursemarks for men in the no tutorial group which are symmetrically distributed.

   2   4   4   6

Step 1   Compute the mean, which for these four scores is 4 [(2 + 4 + 4 + 6)/4 = 16/4 = 4].

Step 2   Subtract the mean from each score, which give the following differences: -2 0 0 2.

Step 3   Cube these differences, which become -8 0 0 8.

Step 4   Sum the cubed differences for each of the scores, which is 0 ($-8 + 0 + 0 + 8 = 0$).

Step 5   Multiply this sum by the number of cases, which is also 0 (0 × 4 = 0).

Step 6 Compute the standard deviation. To compute the standard deviation of the four scores, the mean is first subtracted from each score to give -2 0 0 2 which are then squared to give 4 0 0 4.

These squared differences are summed and divided by one less than the number of cases to give a variance of 2.66 [(4 + 0 + 0 + 4)/(4 − 1) = 8/3 = 2.66]. The square root of the variance is the standard deviation which is 1.63 ($\sqrt{2.66} = 1.63$).

Step 7   Cube the standard deviation and multiply it by the number of cases less one and the number of cases less two. The standard deviation cubed ($1.63^3 = 4.33$) and multiplied by the number of cases less one (4 − 1 = 3) and the number of cases less two (4 − 2 = 2) is 25.98 (4.33 × 3 × 2 = 25.98).

Step 8 Divide the result of Step 5 by that of Step 7 to give the value for skewness, which is 0 (0/25.98 = 0).

The value of skewness is zero when a set of scores is symmetrically distributed because the sum of the cubed differences below the mean is equal to the sum of the cubed differences above the mean. The need to cube the differences will become apparent when the two examples of asymmetrical distributions are presented. When most of the scores are to the left of the mean and therefore smaller than the mean, the distribution is said to be *positively skewed* as the value of the differences and therefore of skewness is positive. This point can be illustrated with the following four post-test coursemarks for men in the no tutorial group which are positively skewed:

1   1   1   5

To show the steps involved in the calculation of skewness for this set of scores, the scores will be arranged in a column as displayed in Table 4.8. The sum of these scores is given at the bottom of this column followed by the mean. The difference (d) between these scores and their mean is presented in a second column while the differences squared (d^2) and cubed (d^3) are displayed in a third and fourth column. The result for Step 5 of the calculation, which involves multiplying the sum of the cubed differences (24) by the number of cases (4), gives 96 ($24 \times 4 = 96$). The variance is 4.0 [$12/(4 - 1) = 4.0$] which yields a standard deviation of 2.0 ($\sqrt{4} = 2.0$). Consequently, the value for Step 7 is 48 ($2^3 \times 3 \times 2 = 48$). Dividing the result for Step 5 by that for Step 7 gives a skewness value of 2 ($96/48 = 2$).

The reasons for cubing the difference between each score and the mean should be clearer from this example. First, since the mean is the central point in any distribution, the sum of differences below the mean is equal to the sum of differences above the mean regardless of the shape of the distribution. Second, as negative signs become positive when squared but remain negative when cubed, cubing the difference indicates the direction of any asymmetry in the distribution.

When most of the scores are clustered to the right of the mean, the distribution is *negatively skewed* and skewness takes on a negative value as shown by the following four pre-test coursemarks for men in the no tutorial group which are negatively skewed:

1   3   4   4

Table 4.8 Positively skewed scores: Initial computations

	Scores	d	d^2	d^3
	1	−1	1	−1
	1	−1	1	−1
	1	−1	1	−1
	5	3	9	27
Sum	8	0	12	24
N	4			
Mean	2			

Once again, to make it easier to follow the steps in calculating skewness, the scores and the three indices of their difference from the mean are displayed in columns as shown in Table 4.9. Multiplying the sum of the cubed differences by the number of cases gives -24 ($-6 \times 4 = -24$) for Step 5. The square root of the variance is 1.414 ($\sqrt{6/3} = 1.4142$) which when cubed (1.4142^3) and multiplied by the number of cases less one ($4 - 1$) and the number of cases less two ($4 - 2$) becomes 16.97 in Step 7 ($1.4142^3 \times 3 \times 2 = 16.97$). Consequently, skewness equals -1.414 ($-24/16.97 = -1.414$).

To determine whether the distribution is significantly asymmetrical, the value of skewness is divided by the *standard error of skewness* and the resulting value looked up in the table of the *standard normal distribution* in Appendix 2 (Bliss 1967). The standard error of skewness is a measure of the extent to which skewness may vary as a function of the size of the sample. It is most conveniently described in terms of the following formula where N is the total number of cases:

$$\text{Standard error of skewness} = \sqrt{\frac{6 \times N \times (N - 1)}{(N - 2) \times (N + 1) \times (N + 3)}}$$

To calculate the standard error of skewness for a sample containing four cases, we substitute 4 for N in the formula:

$$\sqrt{\frac{6 \times 4 \times (4 - 1)}{(4 - 2) \times (4 + 1) \times (4 + 3)}} = \sqrt{\frac{6 \times 4 \times 3}{2 \times 5 \times 7}} = \sqrt{\frac{72}{70}} =$$

$$\sqrt{1.028} = 1.01$$

To find out, for example, whether a skewness value of -1.41 for a sample of 4 differs significantly from a normal curve, we divide this value by 1.01 which gives a figure of -1.40 ($-1.41/1.01 = -1.40$). We look up this figure in the table in Appendix 2. To use this table, we need to know what the standard normal distribution or curve is.

The standard normal distribution is a theoretical distribution which has a

Table 4.9 Negatively skewed scores: Initial computations

	Scores	d	d^2	d^3
	1	-2	4	-8
	3	0	0	0
	4	1	1	1
	4	1	1	1
Sum	12	0	6	-6
N	4			
Mean	3			

mean of 0 and a standard deviation of 1. Since the distribution is perfectly symmetrical, 50 per cent or 0.50 of the values lie at or above the mean and 0.50 of the values fall at or below it. Furthermore, because the shape of the distribution is fixed and known, the proportion of values falling between any two points on its base can be easily calculated. For example, the proportion of values lying between the mean and one, two and three standard deviations on one side of the distribution is about 0.341, 0.477 and 0.499 respectively. The values given in the table represent that proportion of the distribution which lies between the mean and a cut-off point called z on the horizontal axis. In the left-hand margin of the table are the z values to one decimal place which range from 0.0 to 3.9. Along the top row of the table are the z values given to the second decimal place which vary from 0.00 to 0.09. In the extreme case where the z value is zero (0.00), the proportion of the area between z and the mean is zero which makes the proportion beyond z 0.5 ($0.5 - 0.0 = 0.5$). The value of z becomes larger as it moves away from the centre of the distribution towards either tail. As it does so, the proportion of the area between it and the mean increases while the proportion beyond it decreases. For example, the proportion of area between a z value of 3.0 (which corresponds to a standard deviation of 3) and the mean is 0.4987 while the proportion at or beyond it is 0.0013 ($0.5000 - 0.4987 = 0.0013$). Since the tails of the standard normal curve never touch the horizontal axis (i.e. the distribution is *asymptotic*), z increases to infinity.

In effect, dividing skewness by its standard error provides a statistic which can be seen to be comparable to z. When this statistic has a value of 0, the distribution is perfectly symmetrical. The further this statistic departs from zero, the more asymmetrical the distribution is. To look up how far a z value of -1.40 is from the midpoint of a distribution, we ignore its negative sign since the z values describe either the left- or the right-hand side of the distribution. In the table of Appendix 2, the relevant portion of which has been reproduced in Table 4.10, we see that the proportion of the area between a z value of 1.40 and the mean is 0.4192 of the distribution.

Table 4.10 Part of the table of the standard normal distribution

z	0.00	0.01	0.02	. . .
.				
.				
.				
1.3	0.4032	0.4049	0.4066	
1.4	0.4192	0.4207	0.4222	
1.5	0.4332	0.4345	0.4357	
.				
.				
.				

This indicates that the proportion of the area at or beyond z is 0.0808 (0.5000 − 0.4192 = 0.0808).

Now, the proportion of the area at or beyond z can be interpreted as representing the probability of an outcome occurring at the one-tailed level so that a z of −1.40 indicates a one-tailed probability of 0.0808. However, to determine whether a distribution is asymmetrical, we have to use a two-tailed probability level since the asymmetry can be either positive or negative. As the two-tailed probability level reflects the possibility that the value of 1.40 may have been either positive or negative, it is simply twice the one-tailed level which makes it 0.1616 (2 × 0.0808 = 0.1616). Since this figure is larger than 0.05, we would conclude that this distribution was not significantly asymmetrical. On the other hand, the z value for the example of the positively skewed distribution is 1.98 (2.00/1.01 = 1.98). From the table in Appendix 2, it can be seen that this value has a one-tailed probability of 0.0239 which may be converted into a two-tailed one of 0.0478 (0.0239 × 2 = 0.0478) by doubling it. As the two-tailed probability level of this value is less than 0.05, we would assume that this distribution is significantly asymmetrical. Note that the larger the value of z is, the further away it is from the centre of the distribution and, so, the more likely it is to be statistically significant. A z value of 1.96 or more is statistically significant at the 0.05 two-tailed level.

To obtain skewness and its standard error for, say pre-test marks for men in the no tutorial group, first select this group using **Select Cases (sex = 2 & cond = 1)** and then execute the following procedure:

→**Statistics** →**Summarize** →**Descriptives** . . . [opens **Descriptives** dialog box as in Box 3.14]
→variable [e.g. **markpre**] →▶button [puts variable in box under **Variable[s]:**] →**Options** . . . [opens **Descriptives: Options** dialog box as in Box 3.17]
→**Skewness** →**Continue** →**OK**

Table 4.11 displays the output for this procedure. As SPSS does not give the probability level for skewness this has to be worked out as described above.

Table 4.11 SPSS output for skewness and its standard error for pre-test marks for men in the no tutorial group

Number of valid observations (listwise) =					4.00		
							Valid
Variable	Mean	Std Dev	Skewness	S.E. Skew	Minimum	Maximum	N
MARKPRE	3.00	1.41	-1.41	1.01	1	4	4

KURTOSIS

Distributions can be symmetrical but not normal if there are either too many or too few cases in the middle of the distribution. A normal distribution may be called *mesokurtic* (derived from the Greek of 'meso' meaning middle and 'kurtic' meaning curve) and has a kurtosis value of 0. A distribution with too many cases in the centre of the distribution is known as *leptokurtic* ('lepto' meaning narrow) and has a positive kurtosis value while a distribution with too few cases at its centre is referred to as *platykurtic* ('platy' meaning flat) and has a negative kurtosis value. The formula for kurtosis (Bliss 1967) is:

$$\text{kurtosis} = \frac{[(d^4 \text{ summed})(N)(N+1)] - [(d^2 \text{ summed})(d^2 \text{ summed})(3)(N-1)]}{(SD^4)(N-1)(N-2)(N-3)}$$

where d is the difference of each score from the mean, SD is the standard deviation, N is the total number of cases, and values in adjacent parentheses are multiplied by each other [e.g. $(3)(N-1) = (3) \times (N-1)$].

We will illustrate the steps involved in using this formula to work out kurtosis for the following six pre-test marks for men in the two tutorial groups which approximate a mesokurtic distribution

1   2   2   3   3   4

Step 1   Calculate the mean, which for these six scores is 2.5 [$(1 + 2 + 2 + 3 + 3 + 4)/6 = 15/6 = 2.5$].

Step 2   Subtract the mean from each score, which give the following differences:

−1.5   −0.5   −0.5   0.5   0.5   1.5

Step 3   Square each of these differences, which become:

2.25   0.25   0.25   0.25   0.25   2.25

Then sum these squared differences (d^2 summed), which give 5.5 (2.25 + 0.25 + 0.25 + 0.25 + 0.25 + 2.25 = 5.5).

Step 4   Raise each of these differences to the power of 4 (i.e. multiply them by themselves four times), giving

5.06   0.06   0.06   0.06   0.06   5.06

Then sum these differences to the power of 4 (d^4 summed), making 10.36 (5.06 + 0.06 + 0.06 + 0.06 + 0.06 + 5.06 = 10.36).

Step 5   Calculate the standard deviation by dividing the sum of squared differences in Step 3 by one less the number of cases and then take the square root of the result, which is 1.05

$$[\sqrt{(2.25 + 0.25 + 0.25 + 0.25 + 0.25 + 2.25)/(6 - 1)} = \sqrt{5.5/5} = 1.05].$$

Step 6 Multiply the standard deviation by itself four times (SD^4), giving 1.22 ($1.05^4 = 1.216$).

Step 7 Multiply the sum of differences to the power of 4 (d^4 summed) in Step 4 by the number of cases (N) and the number of cases plus one ($N + 1$). This is 435.12 [$10.36 \times 6 \times (6 + 1) = 435.12$].

Step 8 Multiply the sum of squared differences (d^2 summed) in Step 3 by itself, by 3 and by the number of cases minus one ($N - 1$). This becomes 453.75 [$5.5 \times 5.5 \times 3 \times (6 - 1) = 453.75$].

Step 9 Multiply the standard deviation to the power of 4 (SD^4) in Step 6 by the number of cases minus one ($N - 1$), the number of cases minus two ($N - 2$) and the number of cases minus three ($N - 3$). This becomes 73.2 [$1.22 \times (6 - 1) \times (6 - 2) \times (6 - 3) = 73.2$].

Step 10 Subtract the result of Step 8 from that of Step 7 and divide the difference by the result of Step 9 to give kurtosis. This is -0.25 [$(435.12 - 453.75)/73.2 = -18.63/73.2 = -0.25$]. In other words, kurtosis for this set of scores is slightly negative.

To clarify the computations for this last example, we will arrange these scores in a column with the relevant difference indices in adjacent columns as presented in Table 4.12. The standard deviation is 1.05 ($\sqrt{5.5/5} = 1.05$). Substituting the appropriate figures in the above formula, we obtain a kurtosis of -0.25:

$$\frac{[(10.36)(6)(6+1)] - [(5.5)(5.5)(3)(6-1)]}{(1.05^4)(6-1)(6-2)(6-3)} = \frac{435.12 - 453.75}{73.2}$$

$$= \frac{-18.63}{73.2} = -0.25$$

We will illustrate the calculation of kurtosis for a leptokurtic distribution represented by the six post-test marks for men in the two tutorial groups shown in the first column of Table 4.13. The standard deviation of these scores is 1.9 ($\sqrt{18/5} = 1.9$). Placing the relevant numbers in the formula produces a kurtosis of 2.5:

$$\frac{[(162)(6)(7)] - [(18)(18)(3)(5)]}{(1.9^4)(5)(4)(3)} = \frac{6804 - 4860}{781.93} = \frac{1944}{781.93} = 2.486$$

Kurtosis for this group of scores is positive, indicating a leptokurtic curve.

Table 4.12 A mesokurtic distribution: Initial computations

	Scores	d	d^2	d^4
	1	−1.5	2.25	5.06
	2	−0.5	0.25	0.06
	2	−0.5	0.25	0.06
	3	0.5	0.25	0.06
	3	0.5	0.25	0.06
	4	1.5	2.25	5.06
Sum	15	0.0	5.50	10.36
N	6			
Mean	2.5			

Table 4.13 A leptokurtic distribution: Initial computations

	Scores	d	d^2	d^4
	2	−3	9	81
	5	0	0	0
	5	0	0	0
	5	0	0	0
	5	0	0	0
	8	3	9	81
Sum	30	0	18	162
N	6			
Mean	5			

Finally, we will show the calculation of kurtosis for a platykurtic distribution exemplified by the six follow-up marks for men in the two tutorial groups presented in the first column of Table 4.14. The standard deviation of these scores is 2.37 ($\sqrt{28/5} = 2.37$). Inserting the pertinent values in the same formula gives a kurtosis of −1.86:

$$\frac{[(196)(6)(7)] - [(28)(28)(3)(5)]}{(2.37^4)(5)(4)(3)} = \frac{8232 - 11760}{1892.97} = \frac{-3528}{1892.97} = -1.864$$

The negative value for kurtosis signifies that the distribution is platykurtic.

To determine whether a distribution differs significantly from a mesokurtic curve, we divide the kurtosis value by its standard error and look up in the table of the standard normal distribution in Appendix 2 how probable the resulting figure is (Bliss 1967). The standard error of kurtosis is most conveniently described in terms of the following formula:

$$\text{standard error of kurtosis} = \sqrt{\frac{(\text{variance of skewness})(4)(N^2 - 1)}{(N-3)(N+5)}}$$

The use of this formula can be illustrated by calculating the standard error of kurtosis for the example of the mesokurtic distribution.

Table 4.14 A platykurtic distribution: Initial computations

	Scores	d	d^2	d^4
	3	−3	9	81
	4	−2	4	16
	5	−1	1	1
	7	1	1	1
	8	2	4	16
	9	3	9	81
Sum	36	0	28	196
N	6			
Mean	6			

First, we need to work out the variance of skewness according to the following formula:

$$\text{variance of skewness} = \frac{6 \times N \times (N - 1)}{(N - 2) \times (N + 1) \times (N + 3)}$$

Inserting the appropriate figures in this formula, variance of skewness is found to be 0.71

$$\frac{(6)(6)(6 - 1)}{(6 - 2)(6 + 1)(6 + 3)} = \frac{(6)(6)(5)}{(4)(7)(9)} = \frac{180}{252} = 0.71$$

Putting the variance of skewness in the formula for calculating the standard error of kurtosis gives a standard error of 1.74:

$$\sqrt{\frac{(0.71)(4)(6^2 - 1)}{(6 - 3)(6 + 5)}} = \sqrt{\frac{(0.71)(4)(35)}{(3)(11)}} = \sqrt{\frac{99.4}{33}} = \sqrt{3.01} = 1.74$$

Dividing the kurtosis by its standard error results in a value of −0.14 (−0.25/1.74 = −0.144) which, looked up in the table in Appendix 2, has a one-tailed probability of 0.4443 and a two-tailed one of 0.8886 (2 × 0.4443). As this level is not statistically significant, we would conclude that the distribution is mesokurtic.

To compute kurtosis and its standard error for, say pre-test marks for men in the two tutorial groups, first select these two groups using **Select Cases** (sex = 2 & cond ~= 1) and then perform the following procedure:

→**Statistics** →**Summarize** →**Descriptives** . . . [opens **Descriptives** dialog box as in Box 3.14]
→variable [e.g. **markpre**] →▶button [puts variable in box under **Variable[s]:**] →**Options** . . . [opens **Descriptives: Options** dialog box as in Box 3.17]
→**Kurtosis** →**Continue** →**OK**

Table 4.15 displays the output for this procedure. The probability level for kurtosis needs to be worked out as described above since SPSS does not provide it.

Table 4.15 SPSS output for kurtosis and its standard error for pre-test marks for men in the two tutorial groups

Number of valid observations (listwise) =				6.00			

Variable	Mean	Std Dev	Kurtosis S.E.	Kurt	Minimum	Maximum	Valid N
MARKPRE	2.50	1.05	-.25	1.74	1	4	6

NORMAL AND STANDARD NORMAL DISTRIBUTION

If we know that the data for a variable are normally distributed, then we can work out what proportion or percentage of scores lies between any two values of that variable and also what the probability is of obtaining a score between those two values. To do this, we first need to transform the original or *raw* scores into *standard* or *z* scores by subtracting from the individual score the mean score and then dividing this *deviation* score by the standard deviation of the scores.

$$\text{standard score} = \frac{\text{individual score} - \text{mean score}}{\text{standard deviation of scores}}$$

Take, for instance, the following data which are normally distributed:

1   2   3   3   4   5

Subtracting the mean score of 3 from each of these values gives deviation scores of:

−2   −1   0   0   1   2

The standard deviation of these scores is 1.41:

$$\sqrt{[(-2^2)+(-1^2)+(0^2)+(0^2)+1^2+2^2]/(6-1)} = \sqrt{(4+1+0+0+1+4)/5} =$$

$$\sqrt{10/5} = \sqrt{2} = 1.41$$

Dividing by the standard deviation of 1.41 produces standard scores of:

−1.42   −0.71   0   0   0.71   1.42

Note that dividing the standard deviation of the raw scores (1.41) by itself (1.41) gives 1 (1.41/1.41 = 1) which is why the standard deviation of the standard normal distribution is always 1. The mean of the standard normal distribution is always 0 since the sum of the negative standard scores below it ($-1.42 + -0.71 = -2.13$) equals the sum of the positive standard scores above it ($1.42 + 0.71 = 2.13$). So, a standard normal distribution always has a mean of 0 and a standard deviation of 1.

To obtain the standard scores for these numbers, type them into **Newdata** and then carry out the following procedure:

→**Statistics** →**Summarize** →**Descriptives** . . . [opens **Descriptives** dialog box as in Box 3.14]
→variable [e.g. **var00001**] →▶button [puts variable in box under **Variable[s]:**] →**Save standardized values as variables** →**OK**

The standardised values will appear in the next column in **Newdata**.

A standard score is a score measured in standard deviation units. So, a standard score of -1.42 is a score that is 1.42 standard deviation units below the mean while a standard score of 1.42 is 1.42 standard deviation units above the mean. We can illustrate how these standard scores can be used to work out what proportion of them lie between certain values. Because the number of scores is small, we will look up in the table in Appendix 2 the z values of the two non-zero scores (1.42 and 0.71) which, rounded to two decimal places, are 0.42 and 0.26 respectively. Below we have ordered the distribution of the raw scores, their standard scores and the z values they represent.

			3		
Raw scores	1	2	3	4	5
Standard scores	-1.42	-0.71	0	0.71	1.42
z values	-0.42	-0.26	0	0.26	0.42

If we take the raw score of 3 which is the midpoint of the distribution, we see that it has a z value of 0. This means that half or 0.50 of the scores lie at or below the midpoint and 0.50 lie at or above it. In other words, there will be three scores ($6 \times 0.50 = 3$) at or below the standard score of 0 (i.e. 1, 2 and 3) and three scores at or above it (i.e. 3, 4 and 5). If we turn to the raw score of 1, we see that it has a z value of -0.42. This means that 0.42 of the scores lie between it and 0 inclusive, 0.08 ($0.50 - 0.42 = 0.08$) lie at or below it and 0.92 ($1.00 - 0.08$ or $0.42 + 0.50 = 0.92$) lie at or above it. Since there is only one score of 1, half of this score lies at and below the z value of -0.42 while the other half lies at and above it. We can see that, of the six scores, half a score represents a proportion of 0.08 ($0.5/6 = 0.083$) while the remaining five and a half scores reflect a proportion of 0.92 ($5.5/6 = 0.916$). We can also work out that two and a half scores ($0.42 \times 6 = 2.5$) lie between the z values of -0.42 and 0 inclusive. In the same way, we can calculate the proportion of scores that fall between any two standard scores.

Proportions of scores falling between any two standard scores can also be thought of as the probability of obtaining a score between those two standard scores. So, the probability of obtaining a standard score between

−1.42 and 0 is 0.42. The probability of getting a standard score between −1.42 and −0.71 is 0.16 (0.42 − 0.26 = 0.16).

It may also be worth pointing out here that it is possible to compare the relative standing of an individual or case on two or more normally distributed measures when the values on these measures differ widely. Suppose, for example, we wanted to compare the performance of Ann on an English and Maths test in relation to that of other people who also took these tests. The marks (out of 10) for these people are shown in Table 4.16. The mean score for the English test (1) is considerably lower than that for the Maths test (8). In effect, the mean mark of 1 on the English test is the equivalent of the mean mark of 8 on the Maths test. Because of the different range of marks used in these two tests, it is difficult to compare the relative performance of Ann. To do so, we need to convert her raw scores into standard ones which are shown in Table 4.17 together with those for the other people. We can see that Ann's mark in English was 1.22 standard deviation units above the mean $[(2 − 1)/0.82 = 1.22]$ while her mark in Maths was 0.71 standard deviation units below the mean $[(7 − 8)/1.41 = −0.71]$.

Table 4.16 Raw scores on an English and a Maths test

People	English	Maths
Ann	2	7
Mary	0	8
Jane	1	9
Susan	1	8
Helen		6
Emily		10
Sum	4	48
N	4	6
Mean	1	8

Table 4.17 Deviation and standard scores on an English and a Maths test

People	Deviation scores		Standard scores	
	English	Maths	English	Maths
Ann	1	−1	1.22	−0.71
Mary	−1	0	−1.22	0
Jane	0	1	0	0.71
Susan	0	0	0	0
Helen		−2		−1.41
Emily		2		1.41
SD	0.82	1.41		

PLOTTING FREQUENCY DISTRIBUTIONS

The shape of a distribution can be visualised more clearly if it is displayed graphically as either a *histogram* or *polygon*. A histogram contains a horizontal line (called the *x* axis or *abscissa*) and a vertical line (called the *y* axis or *ordinate*) (Pearson 1895). The values of the distribution are shown on the horizontal axis while the frequencies of the values are depicted on the vertical axis. The frequency of each value is represented by a vertical bar or box which is centred on the midpoint of the value. The height of the box corresponds to the frequency of the value. A histogram of the above example of a normal distribution is shown in Figure 4.6. In a polygon, on the other hand, the frequency of each value is represented by a point which lies directly above its value and whose height corresponds to its frequency. Adjacent points are connected by straight lines. The line extends to meet the horizontal axis where the frequency of the adjacent value is zero so that the whole area of the distribution is bounded by straight lines. Figure 4.7 presents this normal distribution as a polygon. One advantage of the polygon over the histogram is that it is easier to read when two distributions are plotted along the same axis for comparison. For instance, in Figure 4.8 the polygon for a mesokurtic and a leptokurtic distribution is shown. In both histograms and polygons the frequency of each value can also be plotted as a percentage or proportion of the total number of values. This has the advantage that, where the size of two samples differs, the area covered by the two distributions is the same.

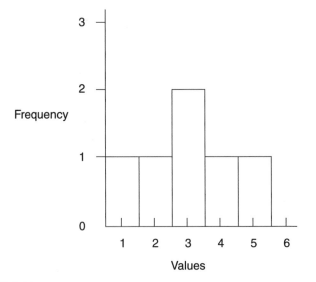

Figure 4.6 A histogram

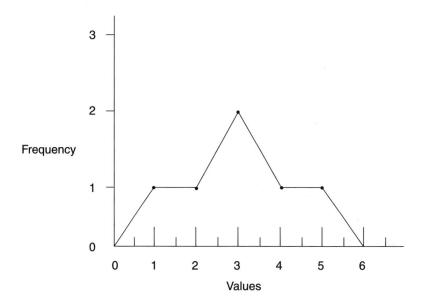

Figure 4.7 A polygon

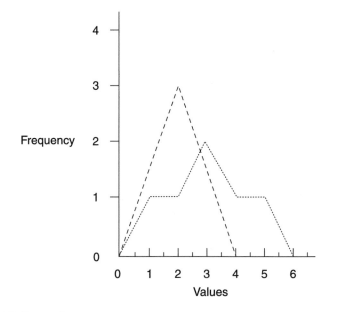

Figure 4.8 Two polygons

To produce a histogram of this normal distribution, enter the data in **Newdata** and then execute the following procedure:

→**Graphs** →**Histogram . . .** [opens **Histogram** dialog box as in Box 4.1] →variable [e.g. **var00001**] → ► button [puts variable in box under **Variable:**] →**Display normal curve** [superimposes a normal curve on histogram] →**OK**

The output for this procedure is displayed in the **Chart Carousel** window as shown in Box 4.2.

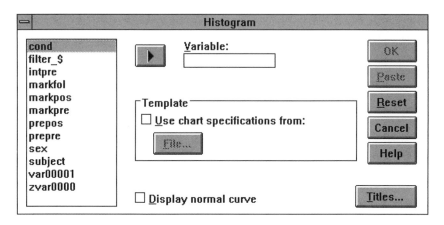

Box 4.1 **Histogram** dialog box

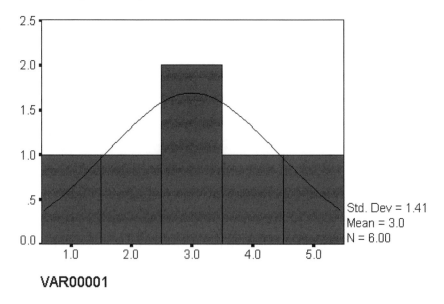

Box 4.2 Histogram in **Chart Carousel** window

F TEST FOR EQUAL VARIANCES IN UNRELATED SAMPLES

One test for determining whether the variances of two groups of scores differ is the *F* test or ratio (Snedecor 1934), named in honour of Sir Ronald Fisher who was primarily responsible for developing analysis of variance (Fisher and MacKenzie 1923). Since this test is affected by non-normality of data (Box 1953), it should only be used when the data are normally distributed. As described in Chapter 2, the sample variance or estimated population variance is calculated by subtracting each score from the mean score for the group, squaring these differences, adding the squared differences together and dividing this total by the number of scores minus one. The *F* test for two groups is simply the greater variance of one group divided by the smaller variance of the other:

$$F = \frac{\text{greater variance}}{\text{smaller variance}}$$

In other words, it compares the greater variance against the lesser variance. Since the greater variance is always divided by the smaller variance, *F* values cannot be smaller than 1. To find out if the two variances differ significantly, we look up the statistical significance of the *F* value in a table like that in Appendix 3. Note that the minimum value of *F* in this table (in the bottom right-hand corner) is 1.000. The larger the value of *F* is, the bigger the greater variance is in relation to the smaller variance and, therefore, the more likely it is to be statistically significant.

Take, for example, the pre-test marks for women in the two tutorial groups which are reproduced in Table 4.18 together with the computations for the *F* ratio. To calculate this *F* ratio, we carry out the following steps.

Table 4.18 Computations for the *F* ratio comparing the variance of pre-test marks between the two tutorial groups in women

	Individual tutorial			Group tutorial		
	Marks	*d*	*d²*	*Marks*	*d*	*d²*
	5	0	0	1	−1	1
	3	−2	4	1	−1	1
	7	2	4	2	0	0
				3	1	1
				3	1	1
Sum	15		8	10		4
N	3			5		
Mean	5			2		
df			2			4
Variance			4			1

$$F = \frac{4}{1} = 4.0$$

Step 1   Calculate the variances for each group by subtracting the mean from the individual scores in that group, squaring the differences, adding the squared differences together and dividing by the degrees of freedom which are the number of scores for that group minus 1.

The variance for the individual tutorial group is 4

$$[(5 - 5)^2 + (3 - 5)^2 + (7 - 5)^2]/(3 - 1) = [0^2 + (-2)^2 + 2^2]/2 = (0 + 4 + 4)/2 = 8/2 = 4$$

while the variance for the group tutorial is 1

$$[(1 - 2)^2 + (1 - 2)^2 + (2 - 2)^2 + (3 - 2)^2 + (3 - 2)^2]/(5 - 1) =$$
$$[(-1)^2 + (-1)^2 + 0^2 + 1^2 + 1^2]/4 = (1 + 1 + 0 + 1 + 1)/4 = 4/4 = 1$$

Step 2   Divide the larger variance by the smaller variance to give the *F* ratio which in this case is 4 (4/1).

Step 3   Look up the statistical significance of this ratio in the table of *F* values in Appendix 3, the relevant portion of which has been reproduced in Table 4.19. In this example, the number of people in the group with the larger variance (the *numerator*) is 3 while the number in the group with the smaller variance (the *denominator*) is 5. The *degrees of freedom* (*df*) for each group are the number of people in that group minus one which is 2 for the individual tutorial condition and 4 for the group tutorial condition.

According to this table, for an *F* ratio to be significant at the 0.05 two-tailed probability level with 2 degrees of freedom for the numerator and 4 degrees of freedom for the denominator, the *F* ratio must be equal to or larger than the *critical* value of 6.9443. In other words, the larger variance has to be about seven times (6.9443 rounded up to 7.000) as big as the smaller variance to be statistically significant at the 0.05 two-tailed level. The critical value of a test statistic is that value on its distribution which represents the cut-off point at and beyond which a result is considered to be statistically significant. Since an *F* ratio of 4 is smaller than 6.9443, we can

Table 4.19 Part of the table of two-tailed 0.05 critical values of *F*

df_1	1	2	3	. . .
df_2				
.				
.				
.				
3	10.128	9.5521	9.2766	
4	7.7086	6.9443	6.5914	
5	6.6079	5.7861	5.4095	
.				
.				
.				

assume that the variances of the two groups are equal. If the F ratio had been greater than the critical value of 6.9443, then we would have inferred that the variances of the two groups were not equal.

The F distribution table, like many of the tables for the other test statistics described in this book, differs from the table for the standard normal distribution. It would be possible to present a table similar to the standard normal distribution for these other test statistics. However, since these distributions vary according to their degrees of freedom, we would have to present separate tables for different degrees of freedom. As we often need to look up the test statistic for various degrees of freedom, we would have to include a large number of such tables. However, since we are usually only interested in the critical values of a test statistic, most of this information would not be used. Consequently, to conserve space, we have only provided tables of certain critical values for these other test statistics. Note that if we had wanted to have a table containing only the 0.05 two-tailed critical value of z, then this table would have consisted of the sole value of 1.96 since a z of 1.96 cuts off a proportion of 0.025 (0.5 − 0.4750 = 0.025) at either end of the distribution, representing a two-tailed probability of 0.05 (0.025 × 2 = 0.05).

The F test statistic represents the probability of obtaining that statistic by chance for a specified pair of degrees of freedom. All distributions of F are skewed to the right but as the degrees of freedom increase, they begin to approximate the shape of the normal distribution. With 1 degree of freedom in the numerator (i.e. two groups) and infinite degrees of freedom in the denominator (i.e. an infinite number of cases), F is equal to z^2. We can illustrate this by selecting a z value of 1.96 which denotes a two-tailed probability of 0.05. The square of this value is 3.8416 (1.96 × 1.96 = 3.8416) which is virtually identical to that of 3.8415 shown in the table in Appendix 3 for a two-tailed 0.05 critical value of F with 1 degree of freedom in the numerator and infinite (∞) degrees of freedom in the denominator.

SPSS no longer gives the F ratio when comparing two unrelated means but the variances for two or more groups can be obtained with the following procedure after first selecting the women (**sex = 1**):

→**Statistics** →**Compare Means** →**Means** . . . [opens **Means** dialog box as in Box 4.3]
→variable [e.g. **markpre**] →▶button beside **Dependent List:** [puts variable in this box] →**cond** →▶button beside **Independent List:** [puts variable in this box] →**Options** . . . [opens **Means: Options** dialog box as in Box 4.4]
→**Variances** →**Continue** →**OK**

Table 4.20 shows the output for this procedure. The greater variance needs to be divided by the smaller variance and the statistical significance

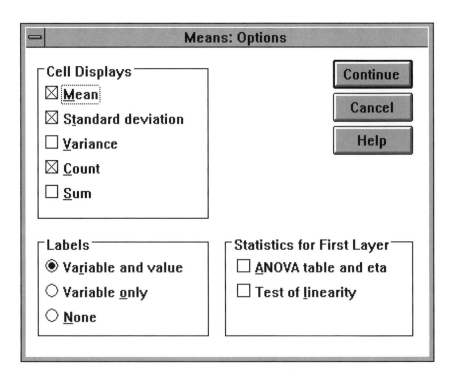

Box 4.3 **Means** dialog box

Box 4.4 **Means: Options** dialog box

Table 4.20 SPSS output of the **Means** procedure for pre-test marks for women

- - Description of Subpopulations - -

Summaries of   MARKPRE

By levels of   COND

Variable	Value	Label	Mean	Std Dev	Variance	Cases
For Entire Population			2.9000	1.9120	3.6556	10
COND	1	notut	2.0000	1.4142	2.0000	2
COND	2	indivtut	5.0000	2.0000	4.0000	3
COND	3	grouptut	2.0000	1.0000	1.0000	5
Total Cases = 10						

of the resulting F ratio looked up against the appropriate degrees of free-dom in a table of critical F values as described above.

LEVENE'S TEST FOR EQUAL VARIANCES

When the data are not normally distributed, a more appropriate test for equality of variances is Levene's (1960) test. Levene's test is the F test of a *one-way analysis of variance* of the absolute deviation scores rather than the raw scores. Analysis of variance, often referred to by its abbreviated name ANOVA (*an*alysis *of va*riance), is used to compare the means of two or more groups and is essentially an F test in which estimates of variance are compared (Fisher and MacKenzie 1923; Gosset 1923). In a one-way analysis of variance the F test compares the estimate of the variance between the groups (i.e. the *between-groups* estimated variance) against the estimate of the variance within the groups (i.e. the *within-groups* estimated variance) by dividing the former by the latter:

$$F = \frac{\text{between-groups estimated variance}}{\text{within-groups estimated variance}}$$

The between-groups estimated variance is based on the difference between the overall or *grand* mean of the groups and the means of the groups weighted by group size, while the within-groups estimated variance reflects the degree to which the scores within each group vary from the mean of that group summed across all the groups. The between-groups estimated variance is often referred to as the *explained* variance since it is more likely to reflect the variance of the variable being investigated. The within-groups estimated variance, on the other hand, is often called the *error* variance (or sometimes the *residual* variance) as it is more likely to correspond to the variance of other factors which have not been measured or controlled. Consequently, if the between-groups variance is considerably greater than the within-groups variance, then this implies that the differences between the means are less likely to be due to chance error or variation. Note that this *F* ratio may also have values between 1 and 0 because the between-groups variance may be less than the within-groups variance. If the means of two or more groups were identical, then the *F* ratio would be zero.

We will begin by showing how to compute a one-way analysis of variance. We will then demonstrate how to calculate Levene's test. The steps in both procedures will be illustrated with the data in Table 4.18 which consist of the pre-test marks for women in the individual tutorial and group tutorial groups.

One-way analysis of variance

A one-way analysis of variance may be computed with the following steps.

Step 1   Compute the between-groups estimated variance.

Step 1.1   Calculate the mean of each group, which is 5 for the individual tutorial group and 2 for the group tutorial group.

Step 1.2   Calculate the overall or grand mean by adding the sum for each group and dividing by the total number of scores. Adding the sum for the individual tutorial group (15) to that for the group tutorial group (10) gives a grand sum of 25 (15 + 10 = 25), which divided by the total number of scores (3 + 5 = 8) is 3.13 (25/8 = 3.125).

Step 1.3   Subtract the grand mean from each of the group means, square this difference, multiply this squared difference by the number of cases within that group and sum these products for all the groups (giving what is known as the between-groups *sum of squares* or *SS*). For our example, doing this gives a between-groups sum of squares of 16.90.

$$[(5 - 3.13)^2 \times 3] + [(2 - 3.13)^2 \times 5] = (1.87^2 \times 3) + (-1.13^2 \times 5) =$$
$$(3.50 \times 3) + (1.28 \times 5) = 10.50 + 6.40 = 16.90$$

When we multiply the squared difference by the number of cases in that group we are saying this is what the overall variation in that group would be if everyone in that group had that group's mean score. The group's mean is used since it is the best estimate of the effect that group represents.

Step 1.4   Work out the between-groups degrees of freedom which are the number of groups minus 1. In the case of two groups there is only one degree of freedom (2 − 1). That is to say, if we know the grand mean, then only one of the two group means is free to vary.

Step 1.5 Divide the between-groups sum of squares by its degrees of freedom to form the between-groups *mean square* or *MS*. Since the between-groups degrees of freedom is 1, the between-groups mean square remains 16.90 (16.90/1 = 16.90).

Step 2 Compute the within-groups mean square.

Step 2.1 To calculate the within-groups sum of squares, subtract the group mean from the individual score in the group, square this difference and add these squared differences across all the groups. Doing this for our data gives a within-groups sum of squares of 12.00.

$$(5-5)^2+(3-5)^2+(7-5)^2+(1-2)^2+(1-2)^2+(2-2)^2+(3-2)^2+(3-2)^2 =$$
$$0^2+(-2^2)+2^2+(-1^2)+(-1^2)+0^2+1^2+1^2 =$$
$$0+4+4+1+1+0+1+1 = 12.00$$

Step 2.2 Calculate the within-groups degrees of freedom which are the number of cases for a group minus 1 summed across all groups. In this case the within-groups degrees of freedom are 6.

$$(3 - 1) + (5 - 1) = 2 + 4 = 6$$

In other words, if we know the group mean for any group then all but one of the individual scores are free to vary.

Step 2.3 Divide the within-groups sum of squares by its degrees of freedom, which gives a within-groups mean square of 2.00 (12.00/6 = 2.00).

Step 3 Compute the F ratio by dividing the between-groups mean square by the within-groups mean square, which gives an F ratio of 8.45 (16.90/2.00 = 8.45).

Step 4 Look up the statistical significance of this F ratio in the table in Appendix 3. As already mentioned, the degrees of freedom for the between-groups mean square are the number of groups minus 1 while for the within-groups mean square they are the number of cases within each group minus 1 summed across all groups. The degrees of freedom are 1 for the between-groups mean square (or the numerator of the F ratio) and 6 for the within-groups mean square (or the denominator of the F ratio). With these degrees of freedom the F value has to be 5.9874 or greater to be significant at the 0.05 level, which it is. Consequently, we would conclude in this case that there was a statistically significant difference in the mean pre-test mark of the two groups and that the mean mark for the individual tutorial group was significantly greater than that of the group tutorial group.

The results of this one-way analysis of variance can be summarised in the table shown in Table 4.21. The total degrees of freedom and total sum of squares can be obtained by simply adding those for the between-groups and within-groups sources of variance. Alternatively, we can calculate them as follows. The total degrees of freedom are the number of cases in the sample minus 1, which is 7 ($8 - 1 = 7$). In other words, if we know the grand mean, then all but one of the other individual scores are free to vary. The total sum of squares is the result of subtracting the grand mean from each score, squaring the difference and adding the squared differences together, which makes about 28.92.

$$(5-3.13)^2+(3-3.13)^2+(7-3.13)^2+(1-3.13)^2+(1-3.13)^2+(2-3.13)^2+$$
$$(3-3.13)^2+(3-3.13)^2 =$$
$$1.87^2+(-0.13^2)+3.87^2+(-2.13^2)+(-2.13^2)+(-1.13^2)+(-0.13^2)+$$
$$(-0.13^2) =$$
$$3.50+0.02+15.00+4.54+4.54+1.28+0.02+0.02 = 28.92$$

To carry out this one-way analysis of variance with SPSS first select the women (**sex = 1**) and then proceed as follows:

→**Statistics** →**Compare Means** →**One-Way ANOVA** . . . [opens **One-Way ANOVA** dialog box as in Box 4.5]
→dependent variable [e.g. **markpre**] →▶ button beside **Dependent List:** [puts variable in this box] →factor or independent variable [e.g. **cond**] →▶ button beside **Factor:** [puts variable in this box] →**Define Range** . . . [opens **Define Range** dialog box as in Box 4.6]
→in box beside **Minimum:** type lower group value [e.g. **2**] →box beside **Maximum:** and type higher group value [e.g. **3**] →**Continue** [closes **Define Range** dialog box]
→**OK**

Table 4.22 displays the output for this procedure.

Levene's test

Levene's test is simply an analysis of variance of the absolute deviation of individual scores from their group mean rather than of the individual scores

Table 4.21 One-way analysis of variance table

Sources of variance	SS	df	MS	F	p
Between-groups	16.90	1	16.90	8.45	< .05
Within-groups	12.0	6	2.00		
Total	28.90	7			

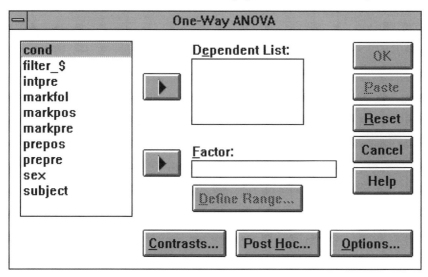

Box 4.5 **One-Way ANOVA** dialog box

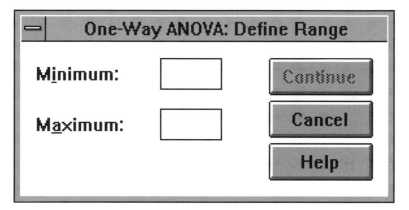

Box 4.6 **One-Way ANOVA: Define Range** dialog box

themselves. So, we first find the absolute deviation of scores by subtracting the group mean from the individual scores in that group. We then perform a one-way analysis of variance on these absolute deviations. We will illustrate the calculation of Levene's test with the data on the pre-test marks of women in the two tutorial groups previously used. The raw scores, absolute deviations and some of the computations needed for calculating a one-way analysis of variance are shown in Table 4.23.

Step 1 Compute the between-groups estimated variance.

Step 1.1 Calculate the mean of the absolute deviations in each group,

Table 4.22 SPSS output of a one-way analysis of variance comparing pre-test marks for the two tutorial groups in women

- - - - O N E W A Y - - - -

Variable   MARKPRE

By Variable   COND

Analysis of Variance

Source	D.F.	Sum of Squares	Mean Squares	F Ratio	F Prob.
Between Groups	1	16.8750	16.8750	8.4375	.0272
Within Groups	6	12.0000	2.0000		
Total	7	28.8750			

Table 4.23 Computations for Levene's test

	Individual tutorial group				Group tutorial group			
	Scores	d	dd	dd^2	Scores	d	dd	dd^2
	5	0	0.0	0.00	1	1	0.2	0.04
	3	2	0.7	0.49	1	1	0.2	0.04
	7	2	0.7	0.49	2	0	0.0	0.00
					3	1	0.2	0.04
					3	1	0.2	0.04
Sum	15	4			10	4		
N	3	3			5	5		
Mean	5	1.3			2	0.8		
df				2				4

d is the absolute deviation of the individual score from the group mean (e.g. $3 - 5 = 2$); *dd* is the deviation of the absolute deviation from the group mean absolute deviation (e.g. $2 - 1.3 = 0.7$)

which is 1.33 for the individual tutorial group and 0.80 for the group tutorial group.

Step 1.2   Calculate the grand mean by adding the sum of absolute deviations for each group and dividing by the total number of scores. Adding the sum for the individual tutorial group (4) to that for the group tutorial group (4) gives a grand sum of 8 ($4 + 4 = 8$), which divided by the total number of scores ($3 + 5 = 8$) is 1.0 ($8/8 = 1.0$).

Step 1.3 Subtract the grand mean from each of the group means, square this difference, multiply this squared difference by the number of cases within that group and sum these products for all the groups to give the between-groups sum of squares, which is 0.53 in this case.

$$[(1.33 - 1.00)^2 \times 3] + [(0.80 - 1.00)^2 \times 5)] =$$
$$(0.33^2 \times 3) + (-0.20^2 \times 5) = (0.11 \times 3) + (0.04 \times 5) =$$
$$0.33 + 0.20 = 0.53$$

Step 1.4 Work out the between-groups degrees of freedom which are the number of groups minus 1. In this case it is 1 $(2 - 1)$.

Step 1.5 Divide the between-groups sum of squares by its degrees of freedom to give the between-groups mean square, which is 0.53 $(0.53/1 = 0.53)$.

Step 2 Compute the within-groups mean square.

Step 2.1 To calculate the within-groups sum of squares, subtract the mean absolute deviation of the group from each individual absolute deviation (dd) within this group, square this difference (dd^2) and add these squared differences across all the groups. Doing this for our data gives a within-groups sum of squares of 3.47.

$$(0 - 1.33)^2 + (2 - 1.33)^2 + (2 - 1.33)^2 + (1 - 0.80)^2 + (1 - 0.80)^2 +$$
$$(0 - 0.80)^2 + (1 - 0.80)^2 + (1 - 0.80)^2 =$$
$$(-1.33^2) + 0.67^2 + 0.67^2 + 0.20^2 + 0.20^2 + (-0.80^2) + 0.20^2 + 0.20^2 =$$
$$1.77 + 0.45 + 0.45 + 0.04 + 0.04 + 0.64 + 0.04 + 0.04 = 3.47$$

Step 2.2 Calculate the within-groups degrees of freedom, which are the number of cases for a group minus 1 summed across all groups. In this case the within-groups degrees of freedom are 6.

$$(3 - 1) + (5 - 1) = 2 + 4 = 6$$

Step 2.3 Divide the within-groups sum of squares by its degrees of freedom, which gives a within-groups mean square of 0.58 $(3.47/6 = 0.578)$.

Step 3 Compute the *F* ratio by dividing the between-groups mean square by the within-groups mean square, which gives an *F* ratio of 0.91 $(0.53/0.58 = 0.914)$.

Step 4 Look up the statistical significance of this *F* ratio in the table in Appendix 3. As already mentioned, the degrees of freedom for the between-groups mean square are the number of groups minus 1 while for the within-groups mean square they are the number of cases within each group minus 1 summed across all groups. The degrees of freedom are 1 for the between-groups mean square (or the numerator of the F ratio) and 6 for the within-groups mean square (or the denominator of the F ratio). With these degrees of freedom the F value has to be 5.9874 or greater to be significant at the 0.05 level, which it is not. Consequently, we would conclude that the variances of the two groups were equal since they were not significantly different.

Table 4.24 summarises the results of this Levene's test.

Table 4.24 One-way analysis of variance table for Levene's test

Sources of variance	SS	df	MS	F	p
Between-groups	0.53	1	0.53	0.91	*ns*
Within-groups	3.47	6	0.58		
Total	3.98	7			

Levene's test is provided as an option with the SPSS one-way analysis of variance procedure. So to obtain it, we proceed as before, after selecting the women (**sex = 1**):

→**Statistics** →**Compare Means** →**One-Way ANOVA** . . . [opens **One-Way ANOVA** dialog box as in Box 4.5]
→dependent variable [e.g. **markpre**] →▶ button beside **Dependent List:** [puts variable in this box] →factor or independent variable [e.g. **cond**] →▶ button beside **Factor:** [puts variable in this box] →**Define Range** . . . [opens **One-Way ANOVA: Define Range** dialog box as in Box 4.6] →in box beside **Minimum:** type lower group value [e.g 2] →box beside **Maximum:** and type higher group value [e.g. **3**] →**Continue** [closes **One-Way ANOVA: Define Range** dialog box]
→**Options** . . . [opens **One-Way ANOVA: Options** dialog box as in Box 4.7] →**Homogeneity-of-variance** →**Continue** [closes **One-Way ANOVA: Options** dialog box]
→**OK**

Table 4.25 shows the output for this option.

A test for comparing homogeneity of variance in two related samples is described in Chapter 8.

Table 4.25 SPSS output for Levene's test in a one-way analysis of variance comparing pre-test marks for the two tutorial groups in women

Levene Test for Homogeneity of Variances

	Statistic	df1	df2	2-tail Sig.
	.9231	1	6	.374

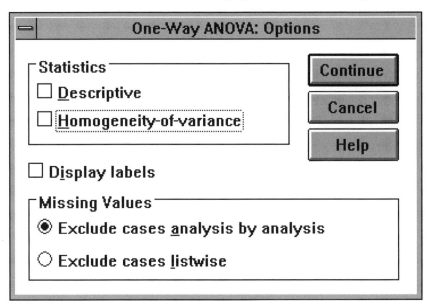

Box 4.7 **One-Way ANOVA: Options** dialog box

SUMMARY

One of the principal uses of statistics in the social sciences is to determine the probability of a finding occurring by chance. Results having a probability of happening at or less than 0.05 (i.e. 1 out of 20) are considered to be statistically significant and are thought to be unlikely due to chance. Where the direction of the results has been predicted before the data have been analysed, a one-tailed probability level is used. Where the direction of the results has not been predicted before hand a two-tailed probability level is employed. A number of different statistical tests exist for determining the size and often the probability of an association between two or more variables and the probability of a difference between two or more groups. Which test to use depends primarily on whether the data are categorical or not, and if the data are not categorical whether their variances are equal and their distributions normal. Non-parametric or distribution-free tests are used for analysing categorical data or non-categorical data whose variances are unequal and whose distributions are non-normal. Parametric tests are applied to non-categorical data whose variances are equal and whose distributions are normal. Tests of skewness and kurtosis assess whether distributions are normal. To find out whether variances are equal, the F test should be used with normal distributions and Levene's test with non-normal distributions. The F test is the greater variance of one group divided by the smaller variance of the other. Levene's test is the F test of a one-way analysis of variance of the absolute deviation scores.

EXERCISES

1　Toss a coin six times. What is the probability of finding the particular outcome obtained?

2　There are 10 women and 10 men in a room. The first 3 people selected are women. What is the probability of this outcome if each person selected is replaced before the next selection?

3　There are 15 women and 5 men in a room. The first 3 people selected are women. What is the probability of this outcome if each person selected is replaced before the next selection?

4　A test of general knowledge consists of 50 statements, half of which are true and half of which are false. One point is awarded for each correct answer. What is the most likely score on this test for someone with no general knowledge?

5　The probability value of a finding is 0.15. Is the finding statistically significant?

6　It is predicted that two groups in a study will differ significantly. Should a one- or a two-tailed probability level be used?

7　Does the skewness and kurtosis of this distribution of scores differ from normality?

　　5 3 1 2 1 2 3 4 2

(a) What is the value of its skewness (to three decimal places)?
(b) What is the standard error of it skewness (to three decimal places)?
(c) What is its z value?
(d) What is the one-tailed probability of this value?
(e) What is the two-tailed probability of this value?
(f) Is the distribution symmetrical, positively skewed or negatively skewed?
(g) What is the value of its kurtosis?
(h) What is the standard error of its kurtosis?
(i) What is its z value?
(j) What is the one-tailed probability of this value?
(k) What is the two-tailed probability of this value?
(l) Is the kurtosis mesokurtic, leptokurtic or platykurtic?

8　Determine for these two groups of scores whether their variances differ significantly using the F test and Levene's test.

Group A	Group B
2	1
3	9
2	2
2	8
3	

(a) What is the F ratio (to two decimal places)?
(b) What are the degrees of freedom for the numerator?
(c) What are the degrees of freedom for the denominator?
(d) What is its probability level?
(e) Do the two variances differ significantly?
(f) What is the F value of Levene's test?
(g) What is its probability level?
(h) Do the two variances differ significantly?

5 Tests of difference for interval/ratio data on unrelated samples for one factor

The statistical tests covered in this chapter determine whether the means of interval or ratio measures differ between a sample and the population and between two or more unrelated samples of cases on one variable or factor. In terms of the first situation, we may be interested in finding out whether the pre-test course marks for the women in our study are similar to the population from which they were drawn which may be all the students studying those subjects in that college at the time of the study. In terms of the second situation, we may want to determine whether the mean of the pre-test marks for women differs across two or three of the tutorial conditions.

t TEST FOR ONE SAMPLE

This test is used to determine if the mean of a sample is similar to that of the population (Gosset 1908). As just mentioned, we could use this test to find out whether the mean of the pre-test marks for the ten women in our study differed from that of their peers studying the same disciplines. Suppose we knew that the overall mean mark for this coursework for the students as a whole was 2.00. The formula for the *t* test is the difference between the population and the sample mean, divided by the *standard error of the mean*

$$t = \frac{\text{population mean } - \text{ sample mean}}{\text{standard error of the mean}}$$

It is important to outline what the standard error of the mean is since this important idea also forms the basis of other parametric tests such as the analysis of variance. One of the assumptions of many parametric tests is that the population of the scores of the variable to be analysed is normally distributed. The errors of most distributions are known to take this form. For example, if a large group of people were asked to guess the mean height of an adult woman in Britain, the distribution of their guesses would approximate that of a normal distribution, even if the height of individual women did not represent a normal distribution.

If we draw sufficiently large samples of the same size from a population of values (which need not be normally distributed), the means of those samples will also be normally distributed. In other words, most of the means will be very similar to that of the population, although some of them will vary quite considerably. This proposition is known as the *central limit theorem* (LaPlace 1814/1951). The standard error of the mean represents the standard deviation of the means of samples of that size divided by the square root of the number of cases in the sample

$$\text{standard error of the mean} = \frac{\text{standard deviation of the sample means}}{\sqrt{\text{number of cases in the sample}}}$$

However, it may be more convenient to re-express this formula as the square root of the division of the variance of the sample means by the number of cases in the sample

$$\text{standard error of the mean} = \sqrt{\frac{\text{variance of the sample means}}{\text{number of cases in the sample}}}$$

This formula is the same as the previous one. What we have done is simply to square the two terms in the first formula

$$\frac{(\text{standard deviation of the sample means})^2}{\sqrt{(\text{number of cases in the sample})^2}} = \frac{\text{variance of the sample means}}{\text{number of cases in the sample}}$$

and then taken the square root of the result.

We can check this using 1 as the standard deviation of the sample means and 4 as the number of cases in the sample. The standard deviation of the sample means divided by the square root of the number of cases in the sample is 0.5 ($1/\sqrt{4} = 1/2 = 0.5$) which is the same as the square root of the division of the variance of the sample means ($\sqrt{1} = 1$) by the number of cases in the sample ($\sqrt{1/4} = 0.5$).

Finally, in order to compare the formula for the standard error of the mean with the formula for the standard error of the difference in means used in the *t* test for two samples outlined below, we should note that the formula can be re-written as

$$\text{standard error of the mean} = \sqrt{\text{variance of the sample means} \times \frac{1}{\text{number of cases in the sample}}}$$

It is also worth pointing out the difference between the standard error of the means and the population standard deviation. The standard deviation of the individual scores in a population is the square root of the variance of those scores. The standard error of the means, however, is the standard deviation of the variance of the means of samples of a particular size. Since we do not know what the variance of the means of samples of that size is, we assume that it is the same as the variance of the sample. However, in order to calculate the standard deviation of the means we have to take account of the size of that sample by dividing the sample variance by the size of the sample (or, what amounts to the same thing, by multiplying by 1 over the size of the sample).

The bigger the sample is, the closer the sample mean will be to the population mean. If, for example, the number of cases in the sample is 100 and its variance is 1, then the standard error of the mean will be 0.10 ($\sqrt{1/100} = \sqrt{0.01} = 0.10$). Note, however, that if you quadruple the size of the sample, the standard error of the mean is a half ($\sqrt{1/400} = \sqrt{0.0025} = 0.05$) and not a quarter of its original size. In other words, very large samples are often unnecessary since they do not produce a sufficient decrease in standard error to be worthwhile.

The one-sample t test compares the mean of a sample with that of the population in terms of how likely that difference has arisen by chance. The smaller this difference is, the more likely it is to have resulted from chance.

To work out a one-sample t test for, say, comparing the mean pre-test mark of the ten women in our example, we carry out the following six steps.

Step 1   Work out the mean of the sample which is 2.9

$(3 + 1 + 5 + 3 + 7 + 1 + 1 + 2 + 3 + 3)/10 = 29/10 = 2.9$

Step 2   Calculate the variance of the sample which is 3.66

$[(3 - 2.9)^2 + (1 - 2.9)^2 + (5 - 2.9)^2 + (3 - 2.9)^2 + (7 - 2.9)^2 +$
$(1 - 2.9)^2 + (1 - 2.9)^2 + (2 - 2.9)^2 + (3 - 2.9)^2 + (3 - 2.9)^2]/(10 - 1) =$
$[0.1^2 + (-1.9)^2 + 2.1^2 + 0.1^2 + 4.1^2 + (-1.9)^2 + (-1.9)^2 + (-0.9)^2 +$
$0.1^2 + 0.1^2]/9 =$
$(0.01 + 3.61 + 4.41 + 0.01 + 16.81 + 3.61 + 3.61 + 0.81 + 0.01 + 0.01)/9$
$= 32.90/9 = 3.66$

Step 3   Work out the standard error of the mean which is the square root of the division of the variance of the sample by the number of cases in the sample. The standard error of the mean for this example is 0.61 ($\sqrt{3.66/10} = \sqrt{0.366} = 0.61$).

Step 4   Work out the t value by subtracting the sample mean from the population mean and dividing the difference by the standard error of the mean. The t value for this example is -1.48 [$(2.0 - 2.9)/0.61 = -0.9/0.61 = -1.475$].

Step 5   The degrees of freedom for this test are the number of cases minus 1 since, if we know the sample mean, one of the sample scores will be fixed while the rest will be free to vary.

Step 6   Look up the significance of the *t* value in the table in Appendix 4. With 9 degrees of freedom *t* has to be 2.262 or bigger to be significant at the two-tailed 0.05 level, which it is not. Consequently, we would conclude that the sample mean does not differ significantly from the population mean.

The distribution of *t* values is symmetrical like the normal or *z* distribution except it is flatter. As the number of cases increases, the *t* distribution begins to approximate the normal distribution. We can see this if we compare the one-tailed *t* values in the table in Appendix 4 with the one-tailed *z* values in the table in Appendix 2. The one-tailed 0.05 *z* value is 1.65 which, rounded up, is the same as the one-tailed 0.05 critical *t* value of 1.645 with infinite degrees of freedom. As the degrees of freedom decrease from infinity to 1 so the one-tailed 0.05 critical *t* value increases from 1.645 to 6.314.

To compare the population mean with the sample mean for our example, we first provide the population mean using the **Compute Variable** procedure. So we could call **pmean** the **Target Variable** and make **2** the **Numeric Expression**. We then select the women (**sex = 1**) and carry out a related *t* test comparing the population mean with the sample mean using the following procedure:

→**Statistics** →**Compare Means** →**Paired-Samples T Test** . . . [opens **Paired-Samples T Test** dialog box as in Box 5.1]
→**pmean** [puts **pmean** beside **Variable 1:** in **Current Selections** section] →variable [e.g. **markpre**] [puts variable beside **Variable 2:** in **Current Selections** section] → ▶ button [puts these variables under **Paired Variables:**] →**OK**

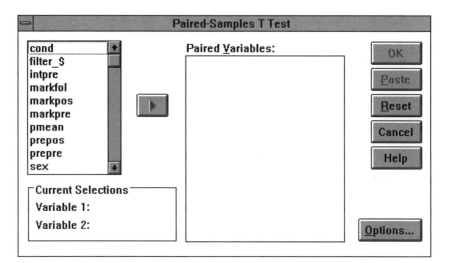

Box 5.1 **Paired-Samples T Test** dialog box

Table 5.1 SPSS output of a one sample *t* test comparing pre-test marks for women with the population mean

t-tests for Paired Samples

Variable	Number of pairs	Corr	2-tail Sig	Mean	SD	SE of Mean
MARKPRE				2.9000	1.912	.605
	10	.	.			
PMEAN				2.0000	.000	.000

Paired Differences				t-value	df	2-tail Sig
Mean	SD	SE of Mean				
.9000	1.912	.605		1.49	9	.171
95% CI (-.468, 2.268)						

Table 5.1 shows the output for this procedure. The sample mean is **2.9000**. We see that the sample mean is not significantly different from the population mean of 2.0 since, with a *t* value of **1.49**, the two-tailed probability level (**.171**) is greater than 0.05.

It should be pointed out that since we often do not know the population mean, the one-sample test is more likely to be used to estimate the population mean from the sample. The formula for the estimated population mean is

estimated population mean = sample mean ± sampling error

This formula does not tell us what the population mean is but tells us within what range of values the population mean will fall. The population mean can fall either above, below or at the sample mean. The difference between the sample mean and the estimated population mean is known as the *sampling error* while the range of values within which the population mean can fall is known as the *confidence interval*. The formula for calculating the sampling error is

sampling error = standard error of the mean × *t*

The lower confidence limit is the sample mean minus the sampling error

lower confidence limit = sample mean − sampling error

while the upper confidence limit is the sample mean plus the sampling error

upper confidence limit = sample mean + sampling error

What *t* value we choose to calculate the sampling error depends on how confident we want to be about the range within which the population mean is likely to fall. If we want to be 95 per cent confident that the population mean will fall within a certain range we would use the two-tailed 0.05 critical *t* value whereas if we wanted to be 99 per cent confident we would use the two-tailed 0.01 critical *t* value. We need to use the two-tailed rather than the one-tailed level since the population mean can fall either side of the sample mean. The *t* value and therefore the sampling error depends on the size of our sample. The bigger the sample, the smaller the *t* value and, therefore, the smaller the sampling error.

To calculate the estimated population mean we carry out the following steps.

Step 1   Calculate the standard error of the mean by taking the square root of the division of the variance of the sample by the number of cases. As we have worked out above, the standard error of the mean for our example is 0.61 ($\sqrt{3.66/10} = \sqrt{0.366} = 0.61$).

Step 2   Look up in the table in Appendix 4 the critical value of *t* we need to use for the size of our sample and for the degree of confidence we want. With a sample of 10 and to be 95 per cent confident of the range within which the population mean is likely to fall, we would choose the critical *t* value that corresponds to the two-tailed 0.05 level with 9 degrees of freedom, which is 2.262.

Step 3   Work out the sampling error by multiplying the standard error of the mean by the appropriate *t* value. For our example, the sampling error is 1.38 ($0.61 \times 2.262 = 1.380$).

Step 4   The lower confidence interval is the sample mean minus the sampling error while the upper confidence interval is the sample mean plus the sampling error. For our example, the lower confidence limit is 1.52 ($2.90 - 1.38 = 1.52$) while the upper confidence limit is 4.28 ($2.90 + 1.38 = 4.28$). In other words, we can be 95 per cent confident that the population mean of the pre-test marks in women lies between 1.52 and 4.28.

Note that in Table 5.1 SPSS gives the confidence interval (**95% CI**) for the difference between the population and sample mean (**.9000**) and not for the population mean itself. It is easy enough, however, to work out the confidence interval for the population mean by subtracting and adding the appropriate sampling error from the sample mean (**2.9000**).

t TEST FOR TWO UNRELATED SAMPLES

The *t* test for unrelated or independent samples determines if the means of two such samples differ. For example, we may wish to find out if the mean mark for women at pre-test is significantly higher in the individual tutorial condition than in the group tutorial one. The *t* test compares the difference between the means of the two samples with the probability of those two means differing by chance. To determine the probability of two means differing by chance, we would draw a large number of samples of a certain size from some given population, subtract the means of these samples from each other and plot the distribution of these differences. If we did this, these differences would be normally distributed. Since the means of most of the samples will be close to the mean of the population and therefore similar to one another, most of the differences will be close to zero. The *t* test compares the means of the two samples with what is known as the *standard error of the difference in means* which is the standard deviation of the sampling distribution of differences between pairs of means:

$$t = \frac{\text{mean of one sample } - \text{ mean of other sample}}{\text{standard error of the difference in means}}$$

Before applying the *t* test, we need to know whether the variances of the two samples differ significantly since the way in which the standard error of the difference in means is calculated varies slightly according to whether the variances are equal or not.

If the variances are unequal, they are treated separately according to the following formula:

$$\text{standard error of the difference in means} = \sqrt{\frac{\text{variance}_1}{n_1} + \frac{\text{variance}_2}{n_2}}$$

where variance$_1$ and variance$_2$ are the variances of the two samples 1 and 2 and where n_1 and n_2 are the numbers of cases in each sample.

This formula can be re-expressed in the same way as the last formula we gave for the standard error of the means which then becomes

$$\text{standard error of the difference in means} = \sqrt{(\text{variance}_1 \times 1/n_1) + (\text{variance}_2 \times 1/n_2)}$$

If, on the other hand, the variances are equal, they are averaged or *pooled* together to take account of their differing degrees of freedom according to the following formula:

$$\sqrt{\left[\frac{((\text{variance}_1 \times (n_1-1)) + ((\text{variance}_2 \times (n_2-1))}{n_1 + n_2 - 2}\right] \times \left[\frac{1}{n_1} + \frac{1}{n_2}\right]}$$

Note that this formula gives the same result as the previous one when the size of the samples is equal.

The pooled variance is calculated by multiplying the variance of one group by its degrees of freedom, doing the same for the other group, adding the two products together and dividing the result by the total degrees of freedom. This is like working out the mean of two groups of differing size from the group means. For example, suppose the mean of one group of three people is 5 while the mean of a second group of five people is 2. To calculate the mean of the two groups we multiply the first mean by the number of people in that group (3) which gives 15 ($5 \times 3 = 15$). We multiply the second mean by the number of people in that group (5) which gives 10 ($2 \times 5 = 10$). We add these two products together to give 25 ($15 + 10 = 25$) and divide this result by the total number of people in both groups (8) to give 3.13 ($25/8 = 3.125$). In effect, the standard error of the difference in means for unequal variances is the square root of the product of the pooled variance and the sum of one over the number of cases in one sample and one over the number of cases in the other group.

standard error of the difference in means $= \sqrt{\text{pooled variance} \times (1/n_1 + 1/n_2)}$

To determine whether the variances of two samples differ, we apply the *F* test if the distributions are normal and Levene's test if they are not, as described in Chapter 4.

To apply the *t* test to determine whether the mean pre-test mark for women is significantly higher in the individual tutorial condition than in the group tutorial condition we carry out the following steps:

Step 1   Calculate the means of the two samples by adding the scores for each sample and dividing by the number of cases in that sample. The individual pre-test marks for women in the two conditions as well as their means are shown in Table 5.2.

Step 2   Calculate the variance for each of the samples by subtracting each score from the mean score for the sample, squaring these differences, adding the squared differences together and dividing this total by the number of scores minus one.

Table 5.2 Pre-test marks for women in the two tutorial conditions and initial computations for the unrelated *t* test

	Individual tutorial			*Group tutorial*		
	Original	*Difference*	*Squared*	*Original*	*Difference*	*Squared*
	5	0	0	1	−1	1
	3	−2	4	1	−1	1
	7	2	4	2	0	0
				3	1	1
				3	1	1
Total	15		8	10		4
No of cases	3			5		
Mean	5			2		
df			2			4
Variance			4.0			1.0

If we do this, we obtain a variance of 4.0 for the individual tutorial condition and 1.0 for the group tutorial condition.

Step 3 To apply the *F* test, we divide the larger by the smaller variance and look up the significance of the resulting *F* value in the table in Appendix 3.

Dividing 4.0 by 1.0 gives an *F* value of 4.0 which, with 2 degrees of freedom for the numerator and 4 degrees of freedom for the denominator, needs to be greater than 6.9443 to be statistically significant at the 0.05 level, which it is not. Consequently, the variances of the two samples in this instance do not differ significantly and the variances need to be pooled.

Step 4 for pooled variances Substitute the appropriate values in the formula for calculating the standard error of the difference in the means for pooled variances, which in our example is 1.03:

$$\sqrt{\left[\frac{[4.0 \times (3 - 1) + [1.0 \times (5 - 1)]}{3 + 5 - 2}\right] \times \left[\frac{1}{3} + \frac{1}{5}\right]} =$$

$$\sqrt{\frac{8.0 + 4.0}{6}} \times 0.533 = \sqrt{2.0 \times 0.533} = \sqrt{1.066} = 1.032$$

Step 5 for pooled variances To calculate *t*, subtract the mean of one sample from that of the other and divide by the standard error of the difference in the means. Substituting the relevant values from our example, *t* is 2.91:

$$\frac{5 - 2}{1.03} = \frac{3}{1.03} = 2.913$$

Step 6 for pooled variances The degrees of freedom are found by using the following formula:

$$df = (n_1 - 1) + (n_2 - 1) = n_1 + n_2 - 2$$

Consequently, the degrees of freedom for this example are 6 (3 + 5 − 2 = 6).

Step 7 for pooled variances To determine the significance of this *t* value, look it up in the table in Appendix 4. Since we specified the direction of the difference in marks between the two groups, we use a one-tailed test. With 6 degrees of freedom, the *t* value has to be 2.132 or greater to be statistically significant at the 0.05 one-tailed level. As a *t* value of 2.91 is larger than 2.132, we would conclude that there was a significant difference in pre-test marks between the two conditions.

Step 4 for separate variances   Substitute the appropriate values in the formula for calculating the standard error of the difference in means for separate variances, which for our example would be 1.24:

$$\sqrt{\frac{4.0}{3} + \frac{1.0}{5}} = \sqrt{1.333 + 0.2000} = \sqrt{1.533} = 1.238$$

Step 5 for separate variances   To calculate t, subtract the mean of one sample from that of the other and divide by the standard error of the difference in the means. Substituting the relevant values from our example, t is 2.42:

$$\frac{5 - 2}{1.24} = \frac{3}{1.24} = 2.419$$

Step 6 for separate variances   The degrees of freedom are calculated using the following formula:

$$df = \frac{[(\text{variance}_1/n_1) + (\text{variance}_2/n_2)]^2}{\dfrac{(\text{variance}_1/n_1)^2}{(n_1 - 1)} + \dfrac{(\text{variance}_2/n_2)^2}{(n_2 - 1)}}$$

Substituting the appropriate figures from our example, the degrees of freedom are 2.64:

$$\frac{[(4.0/3) + (1.0/5)]^2}{\dfrac{(4.0/3)^2}{3 - 1} + \dfrac{(1.0/5)^2}{5 - 1}} = \frac{(1.333 + 0.200)^2}{\dfrac{1.333^2}{2} + \dfrac{0.200^2}{4}} = \frac{1.533^2}{\dfrac{1.777}{2} + \dfrac{0.040}{4}} =$$

$$\frac{2.350}{0.889 + 0.010} = \frac{2.350}{0.899} = 2.643$$

Step 7 for separate variances   Look up the significance of the t value in the table in Appendix 4. With 2 degrees of freedom, a t value of 2.42 has to be 4.303 or greater to be statistically significant at the 0.05 one-tailed level, which it is not.

It should be clear that if we know the means, standard deviations (the square root of the variances) and numbers of cases of any two samples, we are able to compute t tests by inserting the relevant information in the appropriate formulae.

To compare the means of two such samples with an unrelated t test, we use the following SPSS procedure:

→**Statistics** →**Compare** **M**eans →**Independent-Samples** **T** **Test** . . .
[opens **Independent-Samples T Test** dialog box as in Box 5.2]

→dependent variable [e.g. **markpre**] →▶button [puts variable under **Test Variable[s]:**] →independent variable [e.g. **cond**] [puts variable under **Grouping Variable:**] →**Define Groups ...** [opens **Define Groups** dialog box as in Box 5.3]

→**Group 1:** box and type lower group value [e.g. **2**] →**Group 2:** box and type higher group value [e.g. **3**] →**Continue** [closes **Define Groups** dialog box]

→**OK**

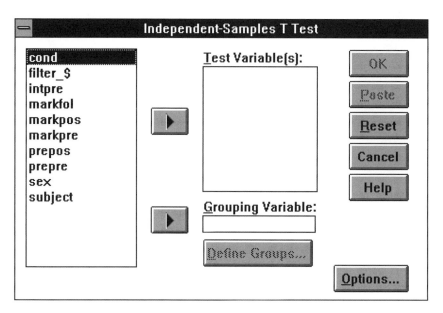

Box 5.2 **Independent-Samples T Test** dialog box

Box 5.3 **Define Groups** dialog box

Table 5.3 SPSS output of an unrelated *t* test comparing pre-test marks for women in the two tutorial conditions

t-tests for Independent Samples of COND

Variable	Number of Cases	Mean	SD	SE of Mean
MARKPRE				
indivtut	3	5.0000	2.000	1.155
grouptut	5	2.0000	1.000	.447

Mean Difference = 3.0000

Levene's Test for Equality of Variances: F= .923 P= .374

t-test for Equality of Means   95%

Variances	t-value	df	2-Tail Sig	SE of Diff	CI for Diff
Equal	2.90	6	.027	1.033	(.473, 5.527)
Unequal	2.42	2.62	.107	1.238	(-1.290, 7.290)

Table 5.3 displays the output for this procedure. For each group, the number of cases, mean, standard deviation and standard error are shown, followed by Levene's *F* test and the *t* test for equal and unequal variances. The *F* value for Levene's test is **.923** as we saw in Chapter 4. One-tailed probabilities are obtained by dividing the two-tailed levels by 2 so that the one-tailed levels for the equal and unequal tests would be 0.014 (**.027**/2 = 0.014) and 0.054 (**.107**/2 = 0.054) respectively.

SPSS COMMAND FILE FOR UNRELATED *t* TEST USING MEANS AND STANDARD DEVIATIONS

Means, standard deviations and numbers of cases are often presented in social science papers. Having this information enables you to determine whether the means and variances differ. SPSS, however, does not compute *t* tests with these descriptive statistics as data. However, if you wish to carry out a number of these tests, you might find it quicker to write a program using SPSS commands which will allow you to do this.

First, we open the **Syntax** window by selecting **File**, **New** and **SPSS Syntax**. Then, we need to define and enter the data, which we do with the following SPSS commands:

data list free/ cf m1 s1 n1 m2 s2 n2.
begin data.
1 5.000 2.000 3 2.000 1.000 5
end data.

The **data list** command specifies the names of the variables and the order they are in. **Free** means that we are using free format in which we do not have to specify the columns the data are in provided that we separate each value by a blank space or comma. The mean, standard deviation and number of cases for the group entered first have been called **m1**, **s1** and **n1** respectively and **m2**, **s2** and **n2** for the group entered second. If we wished to carry out a number of *t* tests, it may be useful to identify the test by giving it a number. This we have done with a variable called **cf** which is the abbreviation for comparison.

Since we have to know whether we need to use pooled or separate variances, the next step will be to compute the *F* test which involves dividing the greater variance by the smaller variance. Consequently, we calculate the variance by squaring the standard deviation using the following commands where the symbols ****** refer to exponentiation which in this case is to the power of **2**:

compute v1=s1**2.
compute v2=s2**2.

To ensure that the larger variance is always divided by the smaller variance, we will use the following **if** command which specifies that if the first variance (**v1**) is greater than or equal to (**ge**) the second variance (**v2**), the value of **f** will be **v1** divided by **v2** whereas if the second variance (**v2**) is greater than (**gt**) the first variance (**v1**), the value of **f** will be **v2** divided by **v1**:

if (v1 ge v2) f=v1/v2.
if (v2 gt v1) f=v2/v1.

To display the results of this computation, we need to use the **list** command, specifying the variables we want to see which in this case will be **cf**, **v1**, **v2** and **f**.

list cf v1 v2 f.

If we do this, SPSS presents the following output:

CF	V1	V2	F
1.00	4.00	1.00	4.00

We need to look up the statistical significance of this *F* value in the appropriate tables. Where the number of cases in each group differs, it would be useful if we also calculated and listed the degrees of freedom, which can be done with the following SPSS commands:

```
if (v1 ge v2) df1=n1-1.
if (v1 ge v2) df2=n2-1.
if (v2 gt v1) df1=n2-1.
if (v2 gt v1) df2=n1-1.
list cf v1 v2 df1 df2 f.
```

When writing a command for a fairly complex computation such as the pooled variances *t* test, it might be advisable to begin by breaking down the computation into a series of simpler steps to ensure that the correct sequence of calculations is carried out. Each step in the calculation can be checked by listing the relevant values. Without any further information, SPSS will perform the following mathematical operations in order of priority: (1) square root (**sqrt**); (2) exponentiation (******); (3) multiplication (*****) and division (**/**); and (4) addition (**+**) and subtraction (**-**). However, you can control the order in which operations are carried out by enclosing in brackets the operation you first want to perform. So, for example, if you want to add or subtract two variables before multiplying or dividing them by another variable, you would bracket the first operation.

Since the calculation for the separate variance *t* test is simpler than that for the pooled variance one, we will begin by showing the commands that can be used for working out this test. The computation can be broken down into two steps, the first which calculates the standard error for separate variances (**ses**) and the second which gives the *t* value for separate variances (**ts**):

```
compute ses=sqrt((v1/n1)+(v2/n2)).
compute ts=(m1-m2)/ses.
```

The operations in brackets will be performed before those outside them so, for example, **m2** will be subtracted from **m1** before being divided by **ses**. These two commands could be collapsed into one as follows:

```
compute ts=(m1-m2)/(sqrt((v1/n1)+(v2/n2))).
```

To calculate the appropriate degrees of freedom for separate variances (**dfs**), we could use the following two commands where the first command computes the denominator of the formula:

```
compute dfs=(((v1/n1)**2)/(n1-1))+(((v2/n2)**2)/(n2-1)).
compute dfs=(((v1/n1)+(v2/n2))**2)/dfs.
```

These two commands could be reduced to one as follows:

```
compute dfs=(((v1/n1)+(v2/n2))**2)/((((v1/n1)**2)/(n1-1))+
(((v2/n2)**2)/(n2-1))).
```

The obvious disadvantage of doing this is that the command is difficult to read.

If we run these commands and list **cf**, **ts** and **dfs**, SPSS produces the following output:

CF	TS	DFS
1.00	**2.42**	**2.62**

For the pooled variance test, we could break down the computation into the following five steps:

```
compute sep=(v1*(n1-1))+(v2*(n2-1)).
compute sep=sep/(n1+n2-2).
compute sep=sep*(1/n1+1/n2).
compute sep=sqrt(sep).
compute tp=(m1-m2)/sep.
```

If we wished, we could collapse these steps into a single one as follows:

```
compute tp=(m1-m2)/(sqrt(((((v1*(n1-1))+(v2*(n2-1))))/
(n1+n2-2))*(1/n1+1/n2))).
```

Calculating the degrees of freedom for the pooled variance *t* test can be done with this simple command:

```
compute dfp=n1+n2-2.
```

SPSS displays the following output if we run these commands and list **cf**, **dfp** and **tp**:

CF	DFP	TP
1.00	**6.00**	**2.90**

Once we have checked that this set of commands for calculating the *F* test, *t* test and degrees of freedom for pooled and separate variances from means, standard deviations and number of cases is accurate, we can store it as a file for future use with a name such as **t.sps**. The extension **sps** denotes that it is an SPSS command file.

ONE-WAY ANALYSIS OF VARIANCE FOR TWO OR MORE UNRELATED SAMPLES

One-way analysis of variance compares the means of two or more unrelated samples such as the mean pre-test mark of the women for the three conditions in our example. As mentioned in Chapter 4, analysis of variance is essentially an *F* test in which an estimate of the variance between the groups (i.e. the between-groups estimated variance usually known as the *between-groups* or *between-treatments mean-square*) is compared with an estimate of the variance within the groups (i.e. the within-groups estimated variance known as the *within-groups* or *within-treatments mean-square*) by dividing the former with the latter:

$$F = \frac{\text{between-groups estimated variance or mean-square}}{\text{within-groups estimated variance or mean-square}}$$

The mean-square refers to the mean of the squared deviations which is the sum of squared deviations divided by the appropriate degrees of freedom.

The between-groups mean square is based on the difference between the overall or total mean of the groups and the means of the groups weighted by group size, while the within-groups mean square reflects the degree to which the scores within each group vary from the mean of that group combined across all the groups. If the variance between the groups is considerably greater than the overall variance within the groups, then this implies that the differences between the means are less likely to be due to chance. This situation is illustrated in Figure 5.1 where the means of the three groups (M_1, M_2, and M_3) are quite widely separated causing a greater spread of between-groups variance (V_B) while the variance within the groups (V_1, V_2, and V_3) is considerably less when combined (V_W). The between-groups mean square is often referred to as the *explained* variance and the within-groups mean square as the *error* or *residual* variance since

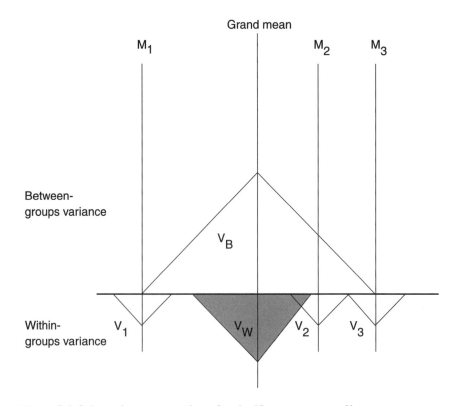

Figure 5.1 Schematic representation of a significant one-way effect

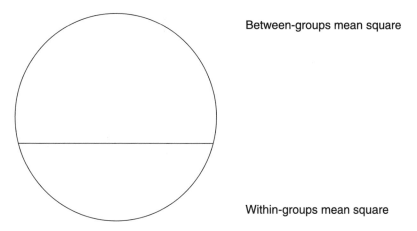

Between-groups mean square

Within-groups mean square

Figure 5.2 Venn diagram illustrating the F ratio

the between-groups mean square is more likely to represent the variance of the variable being investigated whereas the within-groups mean square is more likely to correspond to the variance of other factors which have not been measured or controlled.

Another way of visualising the F ratio is in terms of a Venn (1888) diagram as illustrated in Figure 5.2 where the circle encompasses the between- and within-groups mean square. The between-groups mean square has to be larger than the within-groups mean square for the F ratio to be statistically significant.

The procedures described in this book for calculating analysis of variance will be based on the *fixed model* where the results apply only to the particular categories of the variables chosen by the investigator. The fixed model is distinguished from the *random model* where the categories of the variables have been randomly selected to be representative of those variables and where, therefore, the results can be generalised to the variables as a whole.

To compute a one-way analysis of variance we first need to work out the between- and within-groups sum of squares (*SS*) and their respective degrees of freedom (*df*) from which we can calculate the between- and within-groups mean-squares (*MS*) and F ratio. It is helpful to display these statistics in an analysis of variance table as shown in Table 5.4. Note that the total sum of squares equals the sum of the between- and within-groups sum of squares. In other words, the total sum of squares can be broken down into a between-groups sum of squares and a within-groups sum of squares. Similarly, the total degrees of freedom equal the sum of the between- and within-groups degrees of freedom. The total sum of squares is the sum of the squared differences between each score and the overall or grand mean of all the scores. The between-groups sum of squares is the sum of the squared differences between the grand mean and the group mean for each case. In other words, the group mean is used as the best

Table 5.4 A one-way analysis of variance table

Source of variance	Sum of squares SS	Degrees of freedom df	Mean square MS	F ratio	F probability
Between-groups					
Within-groups/Error					
Total					

estimate of the treatment effect for that group. The within-groups sum of squares is the sum of the squared differences between the group mean and the individual score for each group. The degrees of freedom for the between-groups sum of squares are the number of groups minus one. The degrees of freedom for three groups will be 2 (3 − 1 = 2) because if we know the grand mean of the three groups, the group means of two of the groups will be free to vary. The degrees of freedom for the within-groups sum of squares is the number of cases in a group minus one summed across all groups. If we know the group mean of the three cases in a group, the individual scores of two of the cases will be free to vary. Consequently, if there are three groups of three cases each, the within-groups degrees of freedom are 6 [(3 − 1) + (3 − 1) + (3 − 1) = 2 + 2 + 2 = 6]. The degrees of freedom for the total sum of squares are the total number of cases minus 1. If we know the grand mean of the scores of nine cases, then eight of the individual scores will be free to vary (9 − 1 = 8).

We will illustrate the calculation of a one-way analysis of variance using the pre-test marks of the women in the three conditions.

Step 1   To compute the between-groups mean square: (1) calculate the mean of each group; (2) subtract the overall (or *grand*) mean from the group mean; (3) square this difference; (4) multiply this squared deviation by the number of cases in that group; (5) sum these products for all the groups (giving what is known as the between-groups *sum of squares*); and (6) divide by the degrees of freedom which are the number of groups minus 1 (forming what is known as the between-groups *mean square*).

$$\text{between-groups mean square} = \frac{\text{sum of } [(\text{group mean} - \text{grand mean})^2 \times \text{number of cases in group}] \text{ for all groups}}{\text{number of groups} - 1}$$

When we multiply the squared deviation (of the grand mean from the group mean) by the number of cases in that group we are saying this is what the overall variation in that group would be if everyone in that group had that group's mean score. The group's mean is used since it is the best estimate of the effect for that group.

The individual pre-test marks for the women in the three conditions are shown in Table 5.5 together with the group and overall (or grand) sum and mean. Therefore, the between-groups sum of squares is 18.90:

$[(2 - 2.9)^2 \times 2] + [(5 - 2.9)^2 \times 3] + [(2 - 2.9)^2 \times 5] =$
$[(-0.9)^2 \times 2] + (2.1^2 \times 3) + [(-0.9)^2 \times 5)] =$
$(0.81 \times 2) + (4.41 \times 3) + (0.81 \times 5) =$
$1.62 + 13.23 + 4.05 = 18.90$

The between-groups sum of squares divided by the between-groups degrees of freedom $(3 - 1 = 2)$ gives a between-groups mean-square of 9.45 $(18.90/2 = 9.45)$.

Step 2 We can calculate the within-groups mean square either directly, or indirectly by computing the total sum of squares, subtracting from it the between-groups sum of squares and dividing the result by the within-groups degrees of freedom. To compute the within-groups degrees of freedom subtract 1 from the number of cases in each group and sum the results across all the groups:

$$\text{within-groups mean square} = \frac{\text{total sum of squares} - \text{between-groups sum of squares}}{\text{within-groups } df}$$

To calculate the total sum of squares subtract each score from the grand mean, square them, and add them together. The total sum of squares is 32.90:

$(3 - 2.9)^2 + (1 - 2.9)^2 + (5 - 2.9)^2 + (3 - 2.9)^2 + (7 - 2.9)^2 +$
$(1 - 2.9)^2 + (1 - 2.9)^2 + (2 - 2.9)^2 + (3 - 2.9)^2 + (3 - 2.9)^2 =$
$0.1^2 + (-1.9)^2 + 2.1^2 + 0.1^2 + 4.1^2 + (-1.9)^2 + (-1.9)^2 +$
$(-0.9)^2 + 0.1^2 + 0.1^2 =$
$0.01 + 3.61 + 4.41 + 0.01 + 16.81 + 3.61 + 3.61 + 0.81 + 0.01 +$
$0.01 = 32.90$

Table 5.5 Pre-test marks for women in the three conditions and initial computations

	No			Individual			Group				
	O	D	D²	O	D	D²	O	D	D²		
	3	1	1	5	0	0	1	-1	1		
	1	-1	1	3	-2	4	1	-1	1		
				7	2	4	2	0	0		
							3	1	1		
							3	1	1		
Sum	4		2	15		8	10		4	Grand sum	29
N	2			3			5				10
Mean	2.0			5			2			Grand mean	2.9
df			1			2			4		
Variance			2.0			4.0			1.0		

To work out the within-groups mean square subtract the between-groups sum of squares from the total sum of squares and divide by the within-groups degrees of freedom. For our example, the within-groups mean square is 2.00:

$$\frac{32.90 - 18.90}{(2-1)+(3-1)+(5-1)} = \frac{14}{1+2+4} = \frac{14}{7} = 2.00$$

To compute the within-groups mean square directly, add together the sum of squares for each group and divide this sum by the within-groups degrees of freedom. Calculated this way, the within-groups mean square is 2.00:

$$[(3-2)^2 + (1-2)^2 + (5-5)^2 + (3-5)^2 + (7-5)^2 + (1-2)^2 + (1-2)^2 +$$
$$(2-2)^2 + (3-2)^2 + (3-2)^2]/[(2-1)+(3-1)+(5-1)] =$$
$$[1^2 + (-1)^2 + 0^2 + (-2)^2 + 2^2 + (-1)^2 + (-1)^2 + 0^2 + 1^2 + 1^2)]/(1+2+4) =$$
$$(1+1+0+4+4+1+1+0+1+1)/7 = 14/7 = 2.00$$

Step 3   To calculate the F ratio, simply divide the between-groups mean square by the within-groups mean square. In this case the F ratio is 4.73 ($9.45/2.0 = 4.725$).

Step 4   Look up the statistical significance of this F ratio in the table in Appendix 3. The degrees of freedom for the between-groups mean square are the number of groups minus 1 while for the within-groups mean square they are the sum of the number of cases within each group minus 1. So, the degrees of freedom are 2 for the between-groups mean square (or the numerator of the F ratio) and 7 for the within-groups mean square (or the denominator of the F ratio). With these degrees of freedom the F value has to be 4.7374 or greater to be significant at the 0.05 level, which it just fails to reach. Consequently, we would conclude that there was almost a significant difference in pre-test marks in women between the three conditions. These results are summarised in the one-way analysis of variance table shown in Table 5.6.

However, before we can draw such a conclusion we need to know whether the variances are homogeneous. Levene's test should be used to test this if the data are not normally distributed and the F ratio when the

Table 5.6 A one-way analysis of variance table for pre-test marks in women

Source of variance	SS	df	MS	F	p
Between-groups	18.90	2	9.45	4.73	ns
Within-groups/Error	14.00	7	2.00		
Total	32.90	9			

data are normally distributed. If the variances are unequal, then depending on the exact conditions there is a greater or lesser possibility that the F ratio will be significant. When the number of cases in each group is the same or nearly the same, there is a greater tendency for F to be significant. In these circumstances *Hartley's* and *Cochran's* test can be used for comparing variances.

Hartley's test (F_{max}) is simply the largest of the group variances divided by the smallest (Hartley 1940). In our example the individual tutorial group has the largest variance (4.0) and the group tutorial condition the smallest (1.0). So F_{max} is 4.0 (4.0/1.0 = 4.0). We check the significance of F_{max} in the table in Appendix 5 where the parameters of the distribution are the number of conditions in the numerator and the number of cases in a group minus 1 in the denominator (or where the number of cases in each group varies slightly, the number of cases in the largest group minus 1). The parameters for our example are 3 and 4 respectively. With these degrees of freedom, for the variances to be significantly different at the 0.05 level, F_{max} has to be 15.5 or larger, which it is not. Consequently, we would conclude that the variances were equal.

In Cochran's C test the largest variance is divided by the sum of the variances (Cochran 1941). In this case, C is 0.57 [4.0/(2.0 + 4.0 + 1.0) = 4.0/7.0 = 0.57]. We look up the C value in the table in Appendix 6 where the parameters of the distribution are the number of groups in the numerator and the number of cases in a group minus 1 in the denominator (or where the number of cases in each group varies slightly, the number of cases in the largest group minus 1). For the variances to be significantly different at the 0.05 level, C has to be 0.7457 or bigger, which it is not. Therefore, we would conclude that the variances were homogeneous.

Where the number of cases varies considerably and where no group is smaller than 3 and most groups are larger than 5, the *Bartlett-Box F* test can be used for comparing variances (Bartlett 1937). The procedure for computing this test will be illustrated with our example and is as follows:

Step 1   Calculate the value called M based on the following formula:

$$M = \{(N - \text{no. of groups}) \times \log \text{ of } \{\{[(n_1 - 1) \times \text{variance}_1] + [(n_2 - 1) \times \text{variance}_2] + \ldots \}/(N - \text{no. of groups})\}\} - \{[(n_1 - 1) \times \log \text{ of variance}_1] + [(n_2 - 1) \times \log \text{ of variance}_2] + \ldots \}$$

where log is the natural logarithm, N is the total number of cases, n_1, n_2 and so on are the number of cases in each of the groups in the analysis and variance$_1$, variance$_2$ the variances.

For our example, M is 1.36:

$\{(10 - 3) \times \log \text{ of } \{\{[(2 - 1) \times 2.0] + [(3 - 1) \times 4.0] + [(5 - 1) \times 1.0]\}/(10 - 3)\}\} - \{[(2 - 1) \times \log \text{ of } 2.0] + [(3 - 1) \times \log \text{ of } 4.0] + [(5 - 1) \times \log \text{ of } 1.0]\} =$

$\{7 \times \log \text{ of } \{[(1 \times 2.0) + (2 \times 4.0) + (4 \times 1.0)]/7\} - [(1 \times 0.69) + (2 \times 1.39) + (4 \times 0.00)] =$

$\{7 \times \log \text{ of } [(2.0 + 8.0 + 4.0)/7]\} - (0.69 + 2.78 + 0.00) =$

$(7 \times \log \text{ of } 14/7) - 3.47 = (7 \times \log \text{ of } 2.0) - 3.47 =$

$(7 \times 0.69) - 3.47 = 4.83 - 3.47 = 1.36$

Step 2   Calculate the value called A based on the following formula:

$$A = \frac{1}{3 \times (\text{no. of groups} - 1)} \times \left[\frac{1}{n_1 - 1} + \frac{1}{n_2 - 1} + \cdots - \frac{1}{N - \text{no. of groups}} \right]$$

where n_1, n_2 and so on are the number of cases in each of the groups in the analysis.

For our example, A is 0.27:

$$\frac{1}{3 \times (3 - 1)} \times \left[\frac{1}{2 - 1} + \frac{1}{3 - 1} + \frac{1}{5 - 1} - \frac{1}{10 - 3} \right] =$$

$$\frac{1}{6} \times \left[\frac{1}{1} + \frac{1}{2} + \frac{1}{4} - \frac{1}{7} \right] = 0.167 \times (1.00 + 0.50 + 0.25 - 0.143) =$$

$$0.167 \times 1.607 = 0.268$$

Step 3   Calculate the value of f_2 from the following formula:

$f_2 = (\text{no. of groups} + 1)/A^2$

For our example, f_2 is 57.14:

$(3 + 1)/0.27^2 = 4/0.07 = 57.14$

Step 4   Calculate the value of f_1 from the following formula:

$f_1 = 1 - A + (2/f_2)$

For our example, f_1 is 0.70:

$1 - 0.27 + (2/57.14) = 1 - 0.27 + 0.035 = 0.695$

Step 5   Calculate the Bartlett-Box F from the following formula:

$$F = \frac{f_2 \times M}{(\text{no. of groups} - 1) \times (f_2/f_1 - M)}$$

For our example, F is 0.48:

$$\frac{57.14 \times 1.36}{(3-1) \times (57.14/0.70 - 1.36)} = \frac{77.71}{2 \times (81.63 - 1.36)} =$$

$$\frac{77.71}{2 \times 80.27} = \frac{77.71}{160.54} = 0.484$$

Step 6 We look up the significance of this F value in the table in Appendix 3 where the degrees of freedom are the number of groups minus 1 in the numerator and f_2 in the denominator which are 2 and 57 degrees of freedom respectively. Since the nearest highest degrees of freedom in the denominator is 60, we choose this level and see that F has to be 3.1504 or larger to be statistically significant, which it is not. Consequently, we would conclude that the variances did not differ significantly among the three groups. If the variances were found to be unequal, it may be possible to make them similar through transforming the scores by, for example, taking their log or square root. Alternatively, a non-parametric test could be used for analysing the data.

Note that as the F test or ratio is a proportion, its minimum value is zero indicating no variation in the data. Since it cannot take on a negative value, the F test is non-directional. Therefore, the critical values for F are two-tailed in the sense that the test is non-directional. However, when comparing the variances of two groups or in an analysis of variance with two conditions, it is possible to determine whether the difference obtained is in the predicted direction. Consequently, in these cases, it is possible to use a one-tailed level by dividing the two-tailed critical value by 2.

To carry out with SPSS a one-way analysis of variance on pre-test marks for women in the three conditions, we would first select the women (**sex = 1**) and then execute the following procedure:

→**Statistics** →**Compare Means** →**One-Way ANOVA** . . . [opens **One-Way ANOVA** dialog box as in Box 4.5]
→dependent variable [e.g. **markpre**] →▶ button beside **Dependent List:** [puts variable in this box] →factor or independent variable [e.g. **cond**] →▶ button beside **Factor:** [puts variable in this box] →**Define Range** . . . [opens **Define Range** dialog box as in Box 4.6]
→in box beside **Minimum:** type lower group value [e.g. **1**] →box beside **Maximum:** and type higher group value [e.g. **3**] →**Continue** [closes **Define Range** dialog box]
→**Options** . . . [opens **One-Way ANOVA: Options** dialog box as in Box 4.7]
→**Descriptive** →**Homogeneity-of-variance** →**Continue** [closes **One-Way ANOVA: Options** dialog box]
→**OK**

Table 5.7 displays the output for this procedure. The F ratio of **4.7250** has an exact two-tailed probability of **.0503** and so just fails to be statistically significant at the 0.05 level. SPSS no longer provides Hartley's, Cochran's and the Bartlett-Box F tests but gives Levene's test which is also non-significant.

INTERPETING A SIGNIFICANT ANALYSIS OF VARIANCE F RATIO

The F ratio in the analysis of variance only tells us whether there is a significant difference between one or more of the means. It does not let us

Table 5.7 SPSS output of a one-way analysis of variance for pre-test marks in women

```
- - - - - O N E W A Y - - - - -
```

Variable   MARKPRE
By Variable   COND

Analysis of Variance

Source	D.F.	Sum of Squares	Mean Squares	F Ratio	F Prob.
Between Groups	2	18.9000	9.4500	4.7250	.0503
Within Groups	7	14.0000	2.0000		
Total	9	32.9000			

Group	Count	Mean	Standard Deviation	Standard Error	95 Pct Conf	Int for Mean
Grp 1	2	2.0000	1.4142	1.0000	-10.7062 TO	14.7062
Grp 2	3	5.0000	2.0000	1.1547	.0317 TO	9.9683
Grp 3	5	2.0000	1.0000	.4472	.7584 TO	3.2416
Total	10	2.9000	1.9120	.6046	1.5323 TO	4.2677

GROUP	MINIMUM	MAXIMUM
Grp 1	1.0000	3.0000
Grp 2	3.0000	7.0000
Grp 3	1.0000	3.0000
TOTAL	1.0000	7.0000

Levene Test for Homogeneity of Variances

Statistic	df1	df2	2-tail Sig.
.5385	2	7	.606

know where that difference lies. To find this out, we have to carry out further statistical tests. Some authors argue that these tests should be carried out even if the *F* ratio is not significant. Which tests we use depends on whether we predicted where the differences would be. If we had predicted, for example, that the mean pre-test mark would be higher in the individual tutorial condition than in either of the other two conditions and had the *F* ratio been significant, we would employ unrelated *t* tests to determine whether these predictions were confirmed (Fisher 1935). If, on the other hand, we had not anticipated any differences but discovered that the *F* ratio was significant, we could use one of a number of *post hoc* or *a posteriori* tests to find out where any differences lay. These tests take into account the fact that the more comparisons we make, the more likely we are to find that some of these comparisons will differ significantly by chance. For example, at the 5 per cent level of significance, one of 20 comparisons would be expected to differ significantly by chance while this figure would rise to five if a 100 comparisons had been made. One such test is the *Bonferroni inequality* test. This test is based on the unrelated *t* test but modifies the significance level to take account of the fact that more than one comparison is being made (Fisher 1935). To calculate this level, work out the total number of possible comparisons between any two groups, divide the chosen significance level (which is usually 0.05) by this number, and treat the result as the appropriate significance level for comparing more than three groups. In the case of three groups, the total number of possible comparisons is 3 which means the appropriate significance level is 0.017 (0.05/3 = 0.0167). Another test is the *Scheffé* (1953, 1959) test which provides an exact value for groups of unequal size and is more conservative in the sense that the probability of a Type I error is less (i.e. accepting a difference when there is no difference).

SCHEFFÉ TEST

The Scheffé test is an *F* ratio in which the difference between the means of two groups is compared against an appropriately weighted within-groups mean square. The formula for this *F* ratio is:

$$F = \frac{(\text{one group mean} - \text{another group mean})^2}{\text{within-groups mean square} \times (N_1 + N_2)/(N_1 \times N_2)}$$

So, for example, the Scheffé *F* ratio comparing the mean of the individual and the group tutorial condition is 8.44:

$$\frac{(5.0 - 2.0)^2}{2.0 \times (5 + 3)/(5 \times 3)} = \frac{3^2}{2.0 \times 8/15} = \frac{9}{1.067} = 8.435$$

We compare the significance of this F ratio with the 0.05 F ratio with 2 and 7 *df* multiplied by 1 less the number of groups i.e. $4.73 \times (3 - 1) = 9.46$. Since 8.44 is less than 9.46, we would conclude that there was no significant difference between these two means according to a Scheffé test.

The results of a Scheffé test are presented in two other ways. One is in terms of how big the difference has to be between two group means in order to be significant at a specified level such as 0.05. The other is in terms of the confidence interval within which a difference can lie. If the confidence interval includes zero, then the difference is not significant since this means that the difference could be zero.

The formula for determining the first method is:

$$\text{Scheffé test} = \sqrt{\text{within-groups mean square} \times (\text{no. of gps} - 1) \times F \times \left(\frac{1}{n_1} + \frac{1}{n_2}\right)}$$

where n_1 and n_2 is the number of cases in the two groups being compared and where F refers to the desired probability level (e.g. 0.05) with the appropriate degrees of freedom (i.e. those for the between-groups variance as the numerator and those for the within-groups variance as the denominator).

If the difference between the two means being compared is greater than the value given by the Scheffé test, then the two means differ significantly at the specified probability level.

We will calculate Scheffé test for comparing the pre-test mean mark of women in the individual and the group tutorial conditions. Substituting into the formula the following values, the value of the Scheffé test is 3.18:

$$\sqrt{2.0 \times (3 - 1) \times 4.7374 \times (1/3 + 1/5)} =$$
$$\sqrt{2.0 \times 2 \times 4.7374 \times 0.5333} = \sqrt{10.11} = 3.18$$

The difference in means between these two groups is 3.0 ($5.0 - 2.0 = 3.0$). Since this difference is smaller than the Scheffé test value of 3.18, these two means do not differ significantly from each other.

The second method is to compute the confidence interval. The lower limit is calculated as:

$$\text{difference between two means} - \sqrt{\text{within-groups mean square} \times (\text{no. of gps} - 1) \times F \times \left(\frac{1}{n_1} + \frac{1}{n_2}\right)}$$

and the upper limit as:

$$\text{difference between two means} + \sqrt{\text{within-groups mean square} \times (\text{no. of gps} - 1) \times F \times \left(\frac{1}{n_1} + \frac{1}{n_2}\right)}$$

Consequently, for our example the lower limit is -0.18:

$$3.0 - \sqrt{2.0 \times (3 - 1) \times 4.7374 \times (1/3 + 1/5)} =$$

$$3.0 - \sqrt{2.0 \times 2 \times 4.7374 \times 0.5333} = 3.0 - \sqrt{10.11} =$$

$$3.0 - 3.18 = -0.18$$

and the upper limit is 6.18:

$$3.0 + \sqrt{2.0 \times (3 - 1) \times 4.7374 \times (1/3 + 1/5)} =$$

$$3.0 + \sqrt{2.0 \times 2 \times 4.7374 \times 0.5333} = 3.0 + \sqrt{10.11} =$$

$$3.0 + 3.18 = 6.18$$

Since this interval includes zero the difference is not significant.

To compute the Bonferroni and Scheffé test with SPSS for our example, we need to first select the women (**sex = 1**) and then execute the following procedure:

→**Statistics** →**Compare Means** →**One-Way ANOVA** . . . [opens **One-Way ANOVA** dialog box as in Box 4.5]
→dependent variable [e.g. **markpre**] →▶button beside **Dependent List:** [puts variable in this box] →factor or independent variable [e.g. **cond**] →▶button beside **Factor:** [puts variable in this box] →**Define Range** . . . [opens **Define Range** dialog box as in Box 4.6]
→in box beside **Minimum:** type lower group value [e.g. **1**] →box beside **Maximum:** and type higher group value [e.g. **3**] →**Continue** [closes **Define Range** dialog box]
→**Post Hoc** [opens **One-Way ANOVA: Post Hoc Multiple Comparisons** dialog box]
→**Bonferroni** →**Scheffé** →**Continue** [closes **One-Way ANOVA: Post Hoc Multiple Comparisons** dialog box as in Box 5.4]
→**OK**

Table 5.8 presents the output for the Scheffé test. The table ranges are calculated by taking the square root of the product of 2, the number of groups minus 1 and the appropriate F value:

$$\sqrt{2 \times (\text{no. of grps} - 1) \times F}$$

Its value in this case is **4.35**:

$$\sqrt{2 \times (3 - 1) \times 4.73} = \sqrt{18.92} = 4.3497$$

The value of **1.0000** is derived by taking the square root of the within-groups mean square divided by 2 (i.e. multiplied by 0.5):

$$\sqrt{2.0 \times 0.5} = \sqrt{1.0} = \mathbf{1.0000}$$

The range for comparing the two means of the individual and group tutorial conditions [**Mean(J)** and **Mean(I)**] is worked out as follows and is 3.18:

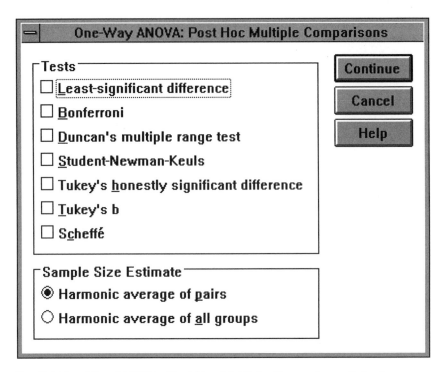

Box 5.4 **One-Way ANOVA: Post Hoc Multiple Comparisons** dialog box

Table 5.8 SPSS output for a Scheffé test comparing pre-test marks for women across three conditions

- - - - - O N E W A Y - - - - -

    Variable   MARKPRE
  By Variable   COND

Multiple Range Tests: Scheffe test with significance level .05

The difference between two means is significant if
  MEAN(J)-MEAN(I) >= 1.0000 * RANGE * SQRT(1/N(I) + 1/N(J))
  with the following value(s) for RANGE: 4.35

- No two groups are significantly different at the .050 level

Table 5.9 SPSS output for a Bonferroni test comparing pre-test marks for women across three conditions

- - - - - O N E W A Y - - - - -

    Variable   MARKPRE   pre-test marks
  By Variable COND

Multiple Range Tests: Modified LSD (Bonferroni) test with significance
                        level .05

The difference between two means is significant if
    MEAN(J)-MEAN(I) >= 1.0000 * RANGE * SQRT(1/N(I) + 1/N(J))
    with the following value(s) for RANGE: 4.42

- No two groups are significantly different at the .050 level

---

1.0000 × **4.35** × $\sqrt{(1/3 + 1/5)}$ = 4.35 × 0.73 = 3.176

None of the three means differs from each other so they are arranged in a single subset of increasing values.

The output for the Bonferroni test takes the same form as that for the Scheffé test and is reproduced in Table 5.9. The table ranges are calculated by taking the square root of the product of 2 and the appropriate F value at the 0.0167 level (0.05/3 = 0.01667) for 1 degree of freedom in the numerator and 7 degrees of freedom in the denominator:

$$\sqrt{2 \times F}$$

As this F value is 9.7817, the range is **4.42**:

$$\sqrt{2 \times 9.7817} = \sqrt{19.5634} = 4.4231$$

The value of **1.0000** is derived by taking the square root of the within-groups mean square divided by 2 (i.e. multiplied by 0.5):

$$\sqrt{2.0 \times 0.5} = \sqrt{1.0} = \textbf{1.0000}$$

The range for comparing the two means of the individual and group tutorial conditions [**Mean(J)** and **Mean(I)**] is calculated as follows and is 3.23:

1.0000 × **4.42** × $\sqrt{(1/3 + 1/5)}$ = 4.42 × 0.73 = 3.227

None of the three means differs from each other so they are arranged in a single subset of increasing values.

To illustrate the output produced when some of the means do differ, the Scheffé test for post-test marks for women across the three conditions is presented in Table 5.10. The only means that differ significantly are those for the individual (group 2) and the group (group 3) tutorial condition as indicated by the asterisk. To determine how big the difference between these two means must be for them to differ significantly, we work out the value for the following expression:

.7559 $\times$ **4.35** $\times$ sqrt[1/N(I)+1/N(J)]

which is 2.40:

.7559 $\times$ **4.35** $\times$ sqrt(1/3+1/5) = 3.29 $\times$ 0.73 = 2.402

The means of the two groups differ because their difference (8.0 $-$ 5.0 = 3.0) is bigger than this value (2.40). Note that for the means of the no tutorial (group 1) and the individual tutorial (group 2) conditions to differ their difference must be greater than 3.002, which it just fails to be.

.7559 $\times$ **4.35** $\times$ sqrt(1/2+1/3) = 3.288 $\times$ 0.913 = 3.002

Table 5.10 SPSS output for a Scheffé test comparing post-test marks for women across three conditions

- - - - - O N E W A Y - - - - -

      Variable   MARKPOS

   By Variable   COND

Multiple Range Tests: Scheffe test with significance level .05

The difference between two means is significant if

   MEAN(J)-MEAN(I) >= .7559 * RANGE * SQRT(1/N(I) + 1/N(J))

   with the following value(s) for RANGE: 4.35

   (*) Indicates significant differences which are shown in the lower triangle

		G	G	G
		r	r	r
		p	p	p
		1	3	2
Mean	COND			
5.0000	Grp 1			
5.0000	Grp 3			
8.0000	Grp 2	*		

Table 5.11 shows the output for the Bonferroni test. To calculate how large the difference between these two means must be for them to differ significantly, we work out the value for the following expression:

.7559 $\times$ **4.42** $\times$ sqrt[1/N(I)+1/N(J)]

which is 2.44:

.7559 $\times$ **4.42** $\times$ sqrt(1/3+1/5) = 3.34 $\times$ 0.73 = 2.438

The means of the two groups differ because their difference (8.0 − 5.0 = 3.0) is larger than this value (2.44).

ANALYSIS OF VARIANCE AND THE *t* TEST

It is worth noting that an unrelated analysis of variance for two conditions gives the same results as an unrelated *t* test since F is equal to t^2 (Fisher

Table 5.11 SPSS output for a Bonferroni test comparing post-test marks for women across three conditions

- - - - - O N E W A Y - - - - -

Variable   MARKPOS   post-test marks
By Variable   COND

Multiple Range Tests: Modified LSD (Bonferroni) test with significance
                        level .05

The difference between two means is significant if
   MEAN(J)-MEAN(I) >= .7559 * RANGE * SQRT(1/N(I) + 1/N(J))
   with the following value(s) for RANGE: 4.42

(*) Indicates significant differences which are shown in the lower triangle

		G	G	G
		r	r	r
		p	p	p
		1	3	2
Mean	COND			
5.0000	Grp 1			
5.0000	Grp 3			
8.0000	Grp 2	*		

1924/1950). We can readily see this if we compare the two-tailed 0.05 critical t values in the table in Appendix 4 with the two-tailed 0.05 critical F values with 1 degree of freedom in both the numerator and denominator in the table in Appendix 3. For example, with 1 degree of freedom the critical t value is 12.706 which squared is 161.44 and which (within rounding error) is the same as the critical F value of 161.45 ($12.70629^2 = 161.4498$).

Furthermore, the t-test comparing the mean pre-test marks for the individual and group condition in this chapter was 2.91 which when squared is essentially the same as the F ratio of 8.45 previously calculated for these two groups in Chapter 4.

SUMMARY

The computation of parametric tests for assessing whether the means of interval or ratio measures differ between a sample and the population and between two or more unrelated samples of cases on one factor is described. The one-sample t test compares a sample mean with the population mean and is more commonly used to estimate within what range the mean of an unknown population is likely to fall. The unrelated t test compares the difference between the means of two samples with the standard error of the difference in means which takes into account the variances of the two samples. The variances are pooled if they are equal and treated separately if they are unequal. The F test, which is the greater variance of one group divided by the smaller variance of the other, is used to determine whether the variances differ when the data are normally distributed; Levene's test is applied when the data are not normally distributed. The two means differ significantly if their difference is substantially larger than the standard error of the difference in means.

One-way analysis of variance compares the means of two or more unrelated samples and is essentially an F test in which the between-groups mean square is divided by the within-groups mean square. Differences between means are less likely to be due to chance when the between-groups variance is considerably greater than the within-groups variance provided that the variances are equal. The Hartley, Cochran C and Bartlett-Box F tests assess whether the variances differ when the data are normally distributed and Levene's test when they are not. To test for significant differences between pairs of means, the unrelated t test should be employed when differences are predicted, otherwise a range test such as the Scheffé test should be performed.

EXERCISES

The data presented in Table 5.12 are used for the exercises in Chapters 5 to 13. The data consist of type of school (with single-sex schools coded as 1 and mixed-sex

Table 5.12 Type of school, gender, socio-economic status and educational interest at 9, 12 and 15

Case	School	Gender	SES	Age 9	Age 12	Age 15
1	1	1	1	2	3	4
2	1	1	2	2	3	4
3	1	1	3	2	4	3
4	1	2	1	3	4	2
5	1	2	2	1	2	3
6	1	2	3	1	2	2
7	2	1	1	3	3	4
8	2	1	2	2	2	3
9	2	1	3	2	1	3
10	2	2	1	3	2	3
11	2	2	2	2	2	1
12	2	2	3	2	1	1

schools as 2), gender of pupil (with girls coded as 1 and boys as 2), socio-economic status (with high status coded as 1, middle as 2 and low as 3) and educational interest rated on a 4-point scale (with 1 for 'not interested', 2 for 'slightly interested', 3 for 'fairly interested' and 4 for 'very interested') at ages 9, 12 and 15 for the same pupils.

1 Use the unrelated *t* test to compare educational interest at 12 between single- and mixed-sex schools.
  (a) What is the value of the *F* test?
  (b) What are its degrees of freedom?
  (c) What is its probability level?
  (d) Do the variances differ significantly?
  (e) Should the variances be pooled?
  (f) What is the value of the *t* test?
  (g) What are its degrees of freedom?
  (h) What is its two-tailed probability level?
  (i) Is educational interest at 12 significantly greater in single- than in mixed-sex schools?
2 Use a one-way analysis of variance to compare educational interest at 12 between single- and mixed-sex schools.
  (a) What is the value of this test?
  (b) What are the degrees of freedom?
  (c) What is the two-tailed probability level?
  (d) Is educational interest at 12 significantly greater in single- than in mixed-sex schools?
3 Use a one-way analysis of variance to compare educational interest at 12 for pupils of different socio-economic status.
  (a) What is the value of this test?
  (b) What are the degrees of freedom?
  (c) What is the probability level?

(d) Does educational interest at 12 differ significantly between pupils of different socio-economic status?
(e) What is the Scheffé range which the means of the three socio-economic status groups have to exceed to be significantly different?
(f) Which group means differ according to this range?

6 Tests of association for interval/ratio data

This chapter describes Pearson's (1896) *product moment correlation* which assesses the strength, direction and probability of the linear association between two interval or ratio variables. Tests for determining whether Pearson's correlations differ for variables which come from the same or different samples are also discussed. We would use these tests to find out, for example, whether the correlation between the pre-test and post-test marks is similar to that between the post-test and follow-up marks for the sample, or whether the correlation between pre-test and post-test marks is similar for women and men. In addition, Pearson's *partial correlation* which covaries out the effects of one or more variables that may be related to the two variables of interest is covered, as is *eta* which provides an index of the non-linear association between an interval/ratio variable and a categorical/ordinal one.

PEARSON'S PRODUCT MOMENT CORRELATION OR *r*

Pearson's product moment correlation or *r* is a measure of the linear association between two interval or ratio variables and varies between -1 and $+1$. It is the same as the point-biserial correlation which is a measure of the association between a dichotomous and an interval/ratio variable and the phi coefficient which is a measure of the association between two dichotomous variables. As we shall see, the statistical significance level of the point-biserial correlation is the same as that for the unrelated *t* test.

One way of visualising a correlation is in terms of the two Venn diagrams in Figure 6.1. The two circles represent the amount of variance of each variable. In the first case the two circles do not overlap at all, indicating that there is no correlation between the two variables. In the second case the two circles overlap to some extent, the size of the correlation being reflected by the degree of overlap between the two circles. A perfect positive ($+1$) or negative (-1) correlation is indicated when the two circles overlap each other completely.

Pearson's correlation is the ratio of the variance shared by two variables

No correlation

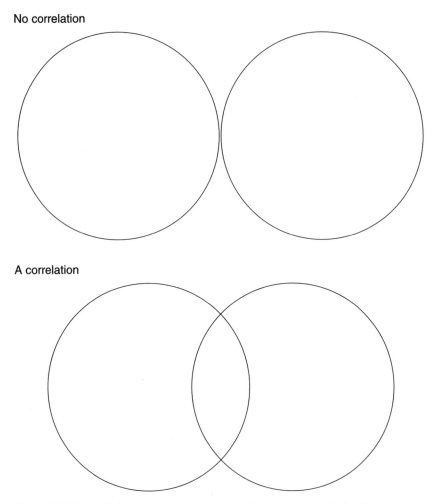

A correlation

Figure 6.1 Venn diagrams showing no correlation and a correlation between two variables

compared to the overall variance of the two variables. If the shared variance is high, this variance will be similar to the overall variance and so the correlation will come close to −1 or +1. If there is no shared variance (i.e. zero shared variance), the correlation will be zero. Variance is based on the extent to which scores differ from the mean. If high scores on one variable are associated with high scores on the other variable, the differences will be in the same direction. A positive difference on one variable will tend to go together with a positive difference on the other variable. Similarly, a negative difference on one variable will tend to be associated with a negative difference on the other. If we multiply these differences, the product of these differences will largely be positive in direction since a negative value multiplied by another negative value gives a positive value (e.g. $-2 \times -3 = 6$). On the other hand, if high scores on one variable are associated with low scores on the other variable, then a positive difference is likely to go together with a negative difference. If we multiply these differences, the product of these differences will be predominantly negative since a positive value multiplied by a negative value forms a negative value (e.g. $2 \times -3 = -6$).

The formula for computing Pearson's r may be expressed in a number of ways. One formula is the covariance of the two variables divided by the product of the square root of the separate variances of those variables:

$$r = \frac{\text{covariance of variable } A \text{ and } B}{\sqrt{(\text{variance of variable } A) \times (\text{variance of variable } B)}}$$

$$= \frac{\text{covariance of variable } A \text{ and } B}{\sqrt{(\text{variance of variable } A)} \times \sqrt{(\text{variance of variable } B)}}$$

Since the square root of the variance is the standard deviation this formula may be written as

$$r = \frac{\text{covariance of variable } A \text{ and } B}{(\text{standard deviation of variable } A) \times (\text{standard deviation of variable } B)}$$

The larger the covariance is, the stronger the relationship. The covariance can never be bigger than the product of the standard deviation of the two variables. If it is the same size as the product, the correlation is either $+1$ or -1 depending on the sign of the covariance.

Covariance is the *sum of products* of the deviation of the score of one variable (A) from its mean multiplied by the deviation of the corresponding score of the other variable (B) for all pairs of scores, which is then divided by the number of cases or pairs minus 1:

$$\text{covariance} = \frac{\text{Sum of } [(\text{mean } A - \text{each } A \text{ score}) \times (\text{mean } B - \text{each } B \text{ score})]}{\text{no. of cases} - 1}$$

Variance is the sum of squares of the deviation of each score from its mean, which is then divided by the total number of cases minus one:

$$\text{variance} = \frac{\text{sum of } (\text{mean} - \text{each score})^2}{\text{no. of cases} - 1}$$

If we replace the covariance and variance terms in the original formula with these expressions then the correlation formula becomes

$$r = \frac{\text{sum of products of } A \text{ and } B/(N-1)}{\sqrt{\text{sum of squares of } A/(N-1)} \times \sqrt{\text{sum of squares of } B/(N-1)}}$$

Since the product of $\sqrt{N-1}$ and $\sqrt{N-1}$ is $N-1$ (e.g $\sqrt{4} \times \sqrt{4} = 2 \times 2 = 4$), $N-1$ appears as a divisor on both the numerator and the denominator and so can be removed leaving this more simple formula

$$r = \frac{\text{sum of products of } A \text{ and } B}{\sqrt{\text{sum of squares of } A \times \text{sum of squares of } B}}$$

Deviations are multiplied rather than added to indicate the direction of the relationship. If the deviations were added, then the sum of these deviations would be zero. This can be illustrated with the data in Table 6.1 which are the pre-test and post-test marks for women in the no and individual tutorial groups. Table 6.1 shows the sum (19 and 34) and mean score (3.8 and 6.8) for the two variables (A and B), the difference of each score from their respective means (D_A and D_B), the squares ($D_A{}^2$ and $D_B{}^2$) and sum of squares of these differences (20.80 and 14.80), the cross product of these differences for the two variables (D_{AB}) together with their sum (10.8), and the cross sum of these differences for the two variables (D_{A+B}) together with their sum (0). Note that if we add together rather than multiply the deviations the sum of these additions is 0. Pearson's correlation is 0.62 [$10.8/\sqrt{20.8 \times 14.8} = 0.615$]. The square root of the product of the sum of squares for the two variables needs to be taken to make the units of the denominator the same as those in the numerator.

The significance level of r can be computed by converting it into t using the following formula

$$t = r \times \sqrt{\frac{N-2}{1-r^2}}$$

Table 6.1 Data and computations for Pearson's correlation showing a positive relationship between pre-test (A) and post-test (B) marks for women in the no and individual tutorial conditions

	A	B	D_A	$D_A{}^2$	D_B	$D_B{}^2$	D_{AB}	D_{A+B}
	3	4	−0.8	0.64	−2.8	7.84	2.24	−3.6
	1	6	−2.8	7.84	−0.8	0.64	2.24	−3.6
	5	7	1.2	1.44	0.2	0.04	0.24	1.4
	3	8	−0.8	0.64	1.2	1.44	−0.96	0.4
	7	9	3.2	10.24	2.2	4.84	7.04	5.4
Sum	19	34		20.80		14.80	10.80	0
N	5	5						
Mean	3.8	6.8						

Note: $r = \dfrac{10.8}{\sqrt{20.8 \times 14.8}} = \dfrac{10.8}{17.55} = 0.615$

The degrees of freedom are the number of cases (N) minus 2. Substituting the values of our example into this formula we find that t is 1.36.

$$0.62 \times \sqrt{\frac{5-2}{1-0.62^2}} = 0.62 \times \sqrt{\frac{3}{0.62}} = 0.62 \times \sqrt{4.84} =$$

$$0.62 \times 2.2 = 1.364$$

We look up the statistical significance of t in the table in Appendix 4 where we see that with three degrees of freedom t has to be 2.353 or bigger to be significant at the 0.05 one-tailed level. So if we had anticipated that the two sets of values would be positively correlated, we could conclude that the correlation was not significantly positive. Alternatively we could look up the statistical significance of r in the table in Appendix 7 where we see that with three degrees of freedom r has to be 0.8054 or larger to be significant at the 0.05 one-tailed level. If we carry out a number of correlations without predicting which of the correlations will be statistically significant, we should make a Bonferroni adjustment to the significance level by dividing the chosen probability level (which is usually 0.05) by the number of correlations undertaken. For example, if we had performed five correlations, then our significance level should be 0.01 (0.05/5 = 0.01).

The percentage of variance that is shared between two variables can be calculated by squaring Pearson's r to give what is known as the *coefficient of determination*. So, the percentage of shared variance represented by a correlation of 0.62 is 38.44. It should be noted that the amount of shared variance is not a straight function of the size of a correlation since, for example, although a correlation of 0.4 is twice the size of a correlation of 0.2, the amount of shared variance denoted by a correlation of 0.4 (16 per cent) is four times that of a correlation of 0.2 (4 per cent). The size of a correlation is usually described verbally in terms of its amount of shared variance so that correlations in the range of 0.1 to 0.3 (reflecting 1 to 9 per cent of shared variance) are often described as small, weak or low; correlations in the range 0.4 to 0.6 (16 to 36 per cent) as moderate or modest; and correlations in the range 0.7 to 0.9 (49 to 81 per cent) as large, strong or high.

To calculate Pearson's correlation with SPSS for this example we first have to select the women in these two groups (i.e. **sex = 1 & cond ~= 3**) and then carry out the following procedure:

→**Statistics** →**Correlate** →**Bivariate . . .** [opens **Bivariate Correlations** dialog box as in Box 6.1]
→variables [e.g. **markpre** and **markpos**] →▶button [puts variables in **Variables:** text box] →**OK**

Table 6.2 displays the output for this procedure. Pearson's correlation is **.6155** and is not significant since even the one-tailed p (**.269**/2 = 0.135) is

Box 6.1 **Bivariate Correlations** dialog box

Table 6.2 SPSS output for Pearson's correlation between pre- and post-test marks for women in the no and individual tutorial conditions

---

- - Correlation Coefficients - -

	MARKPRE	MARKPOS
MARKPRE	1.0000	.6155
	(5)	(5)
	P= .	P= .269
MARKPOS	.6155	1.0000
	(5)	(5)
	P= .269	P= .

(Coefficient / (Cases) / 2-tailed Significance)

" . " is printed if a coefficient cannot be computed

---

greater than 0.05. Note that the two-tailed level is presented by default and that the one-tailed level can be selected instead.

Pearson's *r* is a measure of linear association in that it assesses the extent to which higher scores on one variable are related to higher scores on another variable. However, if there is a *curvilinear* relationship between the two variables such that up to a certain point the higher scores on one variable are associated with higher scores on the other variable but after that point the higher scores are associated with lower scores, then *r* may be zero. For example, people who are not afraid or too afraid of failure may do less well in their coursework than those who are moderately afraid.

The most convenient way of determining whether there is a curvilinear relationship between two variables is to plot the position of the two variables on a graph as shown in Figure 6.2. Such a diagram is known as a *scatterplot* or *scattergram*. The scatter of the points in this plot or diagram takes the shape of an inverted-U curve. The data for this graph are taken from Table 6.3 which presents the coursework marks and fear of failure ratings for seven cases. The marks are plotted along the vertical axis, *y*-axis or *ordinate* while the fear ratings are arranged along the horizontal axis, *x*-axis or *abscissa*. The point on the graph of the mark and fear rating for the first case is where the horizontal line drawn from 1 on the vertical axis intersects with the vertical line drawn from 1 on the horizontal axis. The two scores for each of the seven cases are plotted in this way. When the relationship between two variables is curvilinear as in this case, a more appropriate measure of the relationship is *eta* which is described at the end of this chapter.

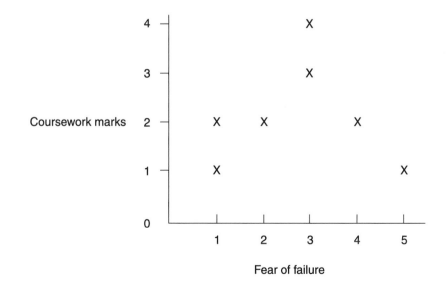

Figure 6.2 A scatterplot of coursework marks and fear of failure

Table 6.3 Data and computations for Pearson's correlation showing a curvilinear relationship between coursework marks (A) and fear of failure (B)

	A	B	D_A	$D_A{}^2$	D_B	$D_B{}^2$	D_{AB}
	1	1	1.1	1.2	1.7	2.9	1.9
	2	1	0.1	0.0	1.7	2.9	0.2
	2	2	0.1	0.0	0.7	0.5	0.1
	3	3	−0.9	0.8	−0.3	0.1	0.3
	4	3	−1.9	3.6	−0.3	0.1	0.6
	2	4	0.1	0.0	−1.3	1.7	−0.1
	1	5	1.1	1.2	−2.3	5.3	−2.5
Sum	15	19		6.8		13.5	0.5
N	7	7					
Mean	2.1	2.7					

Note: $r = \dfrac{0.5}{\sqrt{6.8 \times 13.5}} = \dfrac{0.5}{9.58} = 0.05$

The following SPSS procedure can be used to produce this scatter diagram:

→**Graphs** →**Scatter** . . . [opens **Scatterplot** dialog box as in Box 6.2]
→**Define** [opens **Simple Scatterplot** dialog box as in Box 6.3]
→dependent variable [e.g. **A**] →▶button beside **Y Axis:** box [puts variable in this box] →independent variable [e.g. **B**] →▶button beside **X Axis:** box [puts variable in this box] →**OK** [displays scattergram in **Chart Carousel** window as in Box 6.4]

The size of Pearson's r is affected by the variance of one or both variables as well as the presence of extreme scores or *outliers* which will affect the variance. Take, for example, the data in Table 6.1 which represent a positive correlation. Now, we will introduce an extreme score in these data by replacing the 1 of the second case by 12. When we do this, the Pearson's r is reduced from 0.62 to 0.07 as can be seen from the calculations in Table 6.4. Note that outliers may increase as well as decrease the size of a correlation.

If we reduced the variance in the original data by excluding the last two cases, Pearson's r decreases from 0.62 to 0.33 as shown in the calculations in Table 6.5.

TESTS OF DIFFERENCE FOR UNRELATED PEARSON'S CORRELATIONS

If we wanted to determine whether the size of a correlation differed between two unrelated samples we could carry out a z test where the difference between the two correlations converted into z correlations (z_1

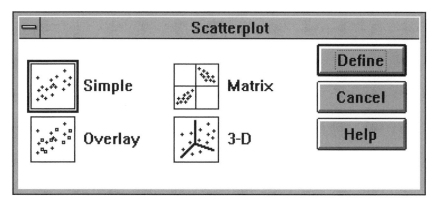

Box 6.2 **Scatterplot** dialog box

Box 6.3 **Simple Scatterplot** dialog box

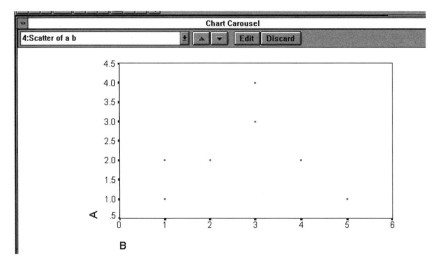

Box 6.4 Scattergram in **Chart Carousel** window

Table 6.4 Data and computations for Pearson's correlation with one extreme score

	A	B	D_A	D_A^2	D_B	D_B^2	D_{AB}
	3	4	−3.0	9.0	−2.8	7.84	8.4
	12	6	6.0	36.0	−0.8	0.64	−4.8
	5	7	−1.0	1.0	0.2	0.04	−0.2
	3	8	−3.0	9.0	1.2	1.44	−3.6
	7	9	1.0	1.0	2.2	4.84	2.2
Sum	30	34		56.0		14.80	2.0
N	5	5					
Mean	6.0	6.8					

Note: $r = \dfrac{2.0}{\sqrt{56.0 \times 14.8}} = \dfrac{2.0}{28.79} = 0.069$

Table 6.5 Data and computations for Pearson's correlation with reduced variance

	A	B	D_A	D_A^2	D_B	D_B^2	D_{AB}
	3	4	0.0	0.0	−1.7	2.89	0.00
	1	6	−2.0	4.0	0.3	0.09	−0.60
	5	7	2.0	4.0	1.3	1.69	2.60
Sum	9	17		8.0		4.67	2.00
N	3	3					
Mean	3.0	5.7					

Note: $r = \dfrac{2.0}{\sqrt{8.0 \times 4.67}} = \dfrac{2.0}{6.11} = 0.327$

and z_2) is divided by the the standard error of the difference between the transformed correlations of the two samples (N_1 and N_2):

$$z = \frac{z_1 - z_2}{\sqrt{[1/(N_1 - 3)] + [1/(N_2 - 3)]}}$$

Because the z and not the t distribution is being used, the sample size should be reasonable, say, at least above 20.

Suppose, for example, we wished to find out whether the correlation of 0.45 between coursework marks and coursework preparation for a sample of 30 women was different from that of 0.30 for a sample of 40 men. Using the table in Appendix 8 we first convert these two correlations into their respective z correlations which are 0.485 and 0.310. Inserting the appropriate values into the above formula, z is 0.69:

$$\frac{0.485 - 0.310}{\sqrt{[1/(30 - 3)] + [1/(40 - 3)]}} = \frac{0.175}{0.253} = 0.69$$

Looking up the significance of this value in the table in Appendix 2, we see that for z to be significant it would have to be 1.96 or more at the 0.05 two-tailed level and 1.65 or more at the 0.05 one-tailed level, which it is not. Consequently, we would conclude that there was no significant difference in the size of these two correlations. Note that it does not matter which way round into the formula we put the two z correlations or the two sample sizes.

If we had a large number of such correlations to compare it might be more convenient to write a few SPSS commands to do this for us. To save us looking up the appropriate z correlations, we could compute these ourselves using the following formula:

$$z_r = 0.5 \times \log_e (1 + r) - 0.5 \times \log_e (1 - r)$$

Our command file for carrying out this z test on these data could be as follows:

```
data list free/no r1 n1 r2 n2.
begin data.
1 .45 30 .30   40
end data.
compute zr1=0.5 * ln(1+r1) − 0.5 * ln(1−r1).
compute zr2=0.5 * ln(1+r2) − 0.5 * ln(1−r2).
compute dif=zr1−zr2.
compute se=sqrt(1/(n1−3)+1/(n2−3)).
compute z=dif/se.
format r1 zr1 n1 r2 zr2 n2 dif se z (f5.3).
list.
```

We first list the variable names and column locations (**data list**). We then include the data (**begin . . . end data**). We compute the two z correlations (**zr1** and **zr2**), the difference (**dif**) between them, the standard error of the difference (**se**) and the z value (**z**). If we want the numbers to be displayed to three decimal places we need to add the **format** command otherwise only two decimal places will be shown. The output of the listing of these variables is:

NO	R1	N1	R2	N2	ZR1	ZR2	DIF	SE	Z
1.00	.450	30.00	.300	40.00	.485	.310	.175	.253	.692

If we are not interested in the values of the difference between the two z correlations and the standard error of the difference, we could compute the z value with this single command:

compute z=(zr1−zr2)/sqrt(1/(n1−3)+1/(n2−3)).

A TEST OF DIFFERENCE FOR RELATED PEARSON'S CORRELATIONS WITH A SHARED VARIABLE

The tests for comparing the size of two correlations from related data are more complicated and depend on whether the two correlations include the same variable (Steiger 1980). One test for comparing two related correlations (r_{12} and r_{13}) which have a variable in common is Williams' (1959) modification of Hotelling's T_1 which is called T_2. The formula for T_2 is:

$$T_2 = (r_{12} - r_{13}) \times \sqrt{\frac{(N - 1) \times (1 + r_{23})}{[2 \times (N - 1)/(N - 3) \times A] + [B^2 \times (1 - r_{23})^3]}}$$

where

$$A = (1 - r_{12}^2 - r_{13}^2 - r_{23}^2) + (2 \times r_{12} \times r_{13} \times r_{23})$$

and

$$B = 0.5 \times (r_{12} + r_{13})$$

Suppose that for a very small sample of seven cases we found that the correlation between coursework marks and coursework preparation (r_{12}) was 0.78 while that between coursework marks and coursework interest (r_{13}) was 0.49. We wished to find out whether the correlation between coursework marks and coursework preparation was significantly bigger than that between coursework marks and coursework interest. Since these two correlations were from the same sample of cases and had the variable of coursework marks in common we could use T_2 to determine whether the two correlations differed. To do this we also need to know the correlation between coursework preparation and coursework interest (r_{23}) which was 0.85. These correlations are shown in Table 6.6.

Substituting the appropriate values in the above formula, we see that T_2 is 1.97:

Table 6.6 Correlation matrix of coursework marks, preparation and interest

	1	2
1 Marks		
2 Preparation	0.78	
3 Interest	0.49	0.85

$$A = (1 - 0.78^2 - 0.49^2 - 0.85^2) + (2 \times 0.78 \times 0.49 \times 0.85)$$

$$= (1 - 0.61 - 0.24 - 0.72) + 0.65 = 0.08$$

and

$$B = 0.5 \times (0.78 + 0.49) = 0.635$$

$$T_2 = (0.78 - 0.49) \times \sqrt{\frac{(7 - 1) \times (1 + 0.85)}{[2 \times (7 - 1)/(7 - 3) \times A] + [B^2 \times (1 - 0.85)^3]}}$$

$$= 0.29 \times \sqrt{\frac{11.10}{(3 \times 0.08) + (0.40 \times 0.003)}} = 0.29 \times \sqrt{\frac{11.10}{0.24 + 0.001}}$$

$$= 0.29 \times \sqrt{\frac{11.10}{0.24}} = 0.29 \times 6.80 = 1.97$$

We look up the value of T_2, whose degrees of freedom are the number of cases minus 3, in the table in Appendix 4. With 4 degrees of freedom, t has to be 2.132 or larger to be significant at the 0.05 one-tailed level, which it is not. Thus, we would conclude that the correlation between coursework marks and coursework preparation was not significantly more positive than that between coursework marks and coursework interest.

The following SPSS commands could be employed to compute T_2:

```
data list free/ no n r12 r13 r23.
begin data.
1 7 .78 .49 .85
end data.
compute a=(1−r12**2−r13**2−r23**2)+(2*r12*r13*r23).
compute b=0.5*(r12+r13).
compute num=(n−1)*(1+r23).
compute den=2*(n−1)/(n−3)*a+b**2*((1−r23)**3).
compute t2=(r12−r13)*sqrt(num/den).
format r12 r13 r23 (f3.2).
list.
```

The relevant output for these commands is:

NO	N	R12	R13	R23	A	B	NUM	DEN	T2
1.00	7.00	.78	.49	.85	.08	.64	11.10	.24	1.98

A TEST OF DIFFERENCE FOR RELATED PEARSON'S CORRELATIONS WITH NO SHARED VARIABLE

A test which compares two correlations from the same sample having no variable in common is Z_2* (Dunn and Clark 1969). This test has the following formula:

$$Z_2* = \sqrt{(N - 3)} \times (z_{r12} - z_{r34}) \times 1/\sqrt{2 - (2 \times A/B)}$$

where

$$A = 0.5 \times \{\{[r_{13} - (r_{12} \times r_{23})] \times [r_{24} - (r_{23} \times r_{34})]\} +$$
$$\{[r_{14} - (r_{13} \times r_{34})] \times [r_{23} - (r_{12} \times r_{13})]\} +$$
$$\{[r_{13} - (r_{14} \times r_{34})] \times [r_{24} - (r_{12} \times r_{14})]\} +$$
$$\{[r_{14} - (r_{12} \times r_{24})] \times [r_{23} - (r_{24} \times r_{34})]\}\}$$

and

$$B = (1 - r_{12}^2) \times (1 - r_{34}^2)$$

Imagine that we wanted to find out whether the correlation between coursework marks and preparation at pre-test differed from that at post-test for the 10 women where the correlation at pre-test and and post-test was 0.49 (r_{12}) and 0.55 (r_{34}) respectively. In order to conduct a Z_2* test we also need to know the four other correlations between the four variables. The (test–retest) correlation between pre- and post-test for both these measures is 0.77 for the marks (r_{13}) and 0.40 for the preparation ratings (r_{24}). The (cross-lagged) correlation between pre-test marks and post-test preparation is 0.80 (r_{14}) and that between pre-test preparation and post-test marks is 0.76 (r_{23}). All six correlations for this example are shown in Figure 6.3.

Placing the appropriate values in the formula we find that Z_2* is 0.21:

$$A = 0.5 \times \{\{[0.77 - (0.49 \times 0.76)] \times [0.40 - (0.76 \times 0.55)]\} +$$
$$\{[0.80 - (0.77 \times 0.55)] \times [0.76 - (0.49 \times 0.77)]\} +$$
$$\{[0.77 - (0.80 \times 0.55)] \times [0.40 - (0.49 \times 0.80)]\} +$$
$$\{[0.80 - (0.49 \times 0.40)] \times [0.76 - (0.40 \times 0.55)]\}\}$$

$$= 0.5 \times [(0.40 \times -0.02) + (0.38 \times 0.38) + (0.33 \times 0.01) + (0.60 \times 0.54)]$$

$$= 0.5 \times (-0.01 + 0.14 + 0.00 + 0.32) = 0.5 \times 0.45$$

$$= 0.23$$

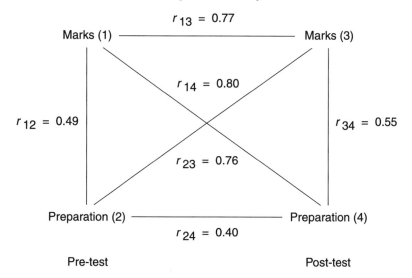

Figure 6.3 Correlations between coursework marks and preparation for women at pre- and post-test

and

$$B = (1 - 0.49^2) \times (1 - 0.55^2) = 0.76 \times 0.70 = 0.53$$
$$Z_2^* = \sqrt{(10 - 3)} \times (0.536 - 0.618) \times 1/\sqrt{2 - (2 \times 0.23/0.53)}$$
$$= 2.65 \times \text{-}0.082 \times 1/\sqrt{2 - 0.87} = -0.22 \times 0.94 = -0.207$$

We look up this value in the table in Appendix 2 where we see that to be significant a z value has to be ($\pm$) 1.96 or more at the 0.05 two-tailed level and ($\pm$) 1.65 or more at the 0.05 one-tailed level, which it is not. Consequently, we would conclude that there was no significant difference in the size of these two correlations. Note that it does not matter which way round we put the two z correlations.

The following SPSS commands could be employed to compute Z_2^*:

```
data list free/no n r12 r34 r13 r24 r14 r23.
begin data.
1 10 .49 .55 .77 .40 .80 .76
end data.
compute zr12=0.5*ln(1+r12)−0.5*ln(1−r12).
compute zr34=0.5*ln(1+r34)−0.5*ln(1−r34).
compute a=0.5*((r13−r12*r23)*(r24−r23*r34)+
            (r14−r13*r34)*(r23−r12*r13)+
            (r13−r14*r34)*(r24−r12*r14)+
            (r14−r12*r24)*(r23−r24*r34)).
compute b=(1−r12**2)*(1−r34**2).
compute z2=sqrt(n−3)*(zr12−zr34)*(1/(sqrt(2−2*a/b))).
```

format r12 r34 r13 r24 r14 r23 (f3.2) zr12 zr34 a b (f5.3) z2 (f7.3).
list.

The relevant output for these commands is:

NO	N	R12	R34	R13	R24	R14	R23	ZR12	ZR34	A	B	Z2
1.00	10.00	.49	.55	.77	.40	.80	.76	.536	.618	.23	.53	-.2057

AVERAGING PEARSON'S CORRELATIONS

To find the average of a number of Pearson's correlations, we need to (1) convert them into z correlations; (2) weight each one of them by multiplying the z correlation by the number of cases in that sample minus 3; (3) sum the results and divide by the sum of, for each sample, the number of cases minus 3; and (4) convert this average z into an average r. We would use this procedure if we wanted to report, for instance, the average correlation between coursework marks and preparation for a number of samples. An example of this procedure is shown in Table 6.7 where the average r for the three samples is 0.27. As you can see from the table in Appendix 8, r correlations are very similar in size to z_r correlations when they are small. For example, an r of 0.300 is equal to a z_r of 0.310. Consequently, when r correlations are small and when the number of cases is similar in the different samples, simply summing the r correlations and dividing by the number of samples will provide a very close approximation to the more involved procedure. For instance, this simple procedure for our example will give an average r of 0.263 compared to an average r of 0.270 using the more complicated method.

POINT-BISERIAL CORRELATION

The *point-biserial correlation* is simply a Pearson correlation between a dichotomous variable such as sex and a continuous variable such as coursework marks. For example, we could compute a point-biserial or Pearson's

Table 6.7 Computations for averaging Pearson's correlations

Sample	N	N−3	r	z_r	$z_r \times (N-3)$
1	41	38	0.25	0.255	9.690
2	53	50	0.31	0.321	16.050
3	37	34	0.23	0.234	7.956
Sum		122			33.696

Notes: Average z_r = 33.696/122 = 0.276;
   Average r = 0.270

correlation between the two tutorial conditions and pre-test coursework marks for the women as shown in Table 6.8.

Note two points about this correlation. First, it does not matter how the two conditions are coded provided they have different values. Second, and more importantly, the *t* value of 2.95 is essentially the same (within rounding error) as that for the unrelated *t* test of 2.91 calculated in Chapter 5.

$$t = -0.77 \times \sqrt{\frac{8 - 2}{1 - 0.77^2}} = 0.29 \times \sqrt{\frac{6}{0.41}} = -0.77 \times 3.83 = -2.95$$

In other words, the point-biserial correlation and the unrelated *t* test are related. This relationship can be expressed as follows:

$$r^2 = \frac{t^2}{t^2 + df}$$

In our case, r^2 is 0.59 ($\sqrt{0.59} = 0.77$)

$$\frac{2.95^2}{2.95^2 + 6} = \frac{8.70}{8.70 + 6} = \frac{8.70}{14.70} = 0.59$$

This means that *t* values can always be re-expressed as coefficients of determination which is useful for describing the amount of variance accounted for by a dichotomous variable.

Furthermore, as we have already seen, the unrelated *t* test is related to a one-way analysis of variance with two groups ($t^2 = F$). Consequently, the

Table 6.8 Computation of Pearson's correlation between the two tutorial conditions (*A*) and pre-test marks (*B*) for women

	A	*B*	D_A	$D_A{}^2$	D_B	$D_B{}^2$	D_{AB}
	2	5	−0.6	0.36	1.9	3.61	−1.14
	2	3	−0.6	0.36	−0.1	0.01	0.01
	2	7	−0.6	0.36	3.9	15.21	−2.34
	3	1	0.4	0.16	−2.1	4.41	−0.84
	3	1	0.4	0.16	−2.1	4.41	−0.84
	3	2	0.4	0.16	−1.1	1.21	−0.44
	3	3	0.4	0.16	−0.1	0.01	−0.04
	3	3	0.4	0.16	−0.1	0.01	−0.04
Sum	21	25		1.88		28.88	−5.67
N	8	8					
Mean	2.6	3.1					

Note: $r = \dfrac{-5.67}{\sqrt{1.88 \times 28.88}} = \dfrac{-5.67}{7.37} = -0.769$

relationship between the point-biserial correlation and the F ratio (with one degree of freedom in the numerator) can be expressed as follows:

$$r^2 = \frac{F}{F + \text{denominator } df}$$

Substituting the appropriate values we obtained for the one-way analysis of variance in Chapter 4 comparing the pre-test mean marks for women in the two tutorial conditions, we obtain an r^2 of 0.59

$$r^2 = \frac{8.45}{8.45 + 6} = \frac{8.45}{14.45} = 0.59$$

ETA

The eta coefficient provides a useful measure of the strength of the association between an interval/ratio variable (the dependent variable) and a categorical/ordinal variable (the independent variable) when this association is non-linear (Pearson 1905). Eta varies from zero to +1 and eta squared or the *correlation ratio* indicates the percentage of the total variance in the dependent variable that can be accounted for by the independent variable. Eta squared is the between-groups sum of squares divided by the total sum of squares. In this section we will demonstrate how eta can be calculated for the data in Table 6.3 which represent a curvilinear relationship between coursework marks and fear of failure. As eta is an asymmetric measure we could compute eta with fear of failure as the dependent variable and coursework marks as the independent variable, or vice versa. In drawing a graph it is customary to place the independent variable along the horizontal axis and the dependent variable along the vertical axis. Note that the shape of the relationship between coursework marks and fear of failure would not be curvilinear if fear of failure was the dependent variable and coursework marks the independent variable. Consequently, we will compute eta with coursework marks as the dependent variable.

The data in Table 6.3 have been arranged in Table 6.9 so that the coursework marks have been grouped in terms of the fear of failure ratings. Eta is calculated with the following steps.

Step 1   Work out the between-groups sum of squares by subtracting the grand mean from the group means, squaring the differences, multiplying the squared differences by the number of cases in each group and summing the products for all the groups.

The between-groups sum of squares for these data is 5.85:

$$[(1.5 - 2.1)^2 \times 2] + [(2.0 - 2.1)^2 \times 1] + [(3.5 - 2.1)^2 \times 2] +$$
$$[(2.0 - 2.1)^2 \times 1] + [(1.0 - 2.1)^2 \times 1] =$$
$$0.72 + 0.0 + 3.92 + 0.0 + 1.21 = 5.85$$

Table 6.9 Data and initial computations for eta

	1	2	*Fear of failure* 3	4	5		
	1 2	2	3 4	2	1		
Sum	3	2	7	2	1	Grand sum	15
N	2	1	2	1	1		
Mean	1.5	2	3.5	2	1	Grand mean	2.1

Step 2 Calculate the total sum of squares by subtracting each score from the grand mean, squaring the difference and summing the squared differences.

The total sum of squares for these data is 6.8:

$$(2.1 - 1)^2 + (2.1 - 2)^2 + (2.1 - 2)^2 + (2.1 - 3)^2 + (2.1 - 4)^2 +$$
$$(2.1 - 2)^2 + (2.1 - 1)^2 =$$
$$1.2 + 0.0 + 0.0 + 0.8 + 3.6 + 0.0 + 1.2 = 6.8$$

Step 3 Divide the between-groups sum of squares by the total sum of squares and take the square root of the result to give eta.

For this example, eta is 0.93 ($\sqrt{5.85/6.8} = \sqrt{0.860} = 0.928$).

In research papers often only the *F* ratio and its degrees of freedom are presented. In these cases, it is possible to work out eta using the following formula:

$$\text{eta} = \sqrt{\frac{\text{between-groups } df \times F}{(\text{between-groups } df \times F) + \text{within-groups } df}}$$

For our example, the between-groups mean square is 1.46 [5.85/(5 − 1) = 1.463]. The within-groups sum of squares is 0.95 (6.80 − 5.85 = 0.95) and so the within-groups mean square is 0.48 [0.95/(2 − 1) + (1 − 1) + (2 − 1) + (1− 1) + (1 − 1) = 0.95/2 = 0.475]. *F* is 3.04 (1.46/0.48 = 3.04), the between-groups *df* are 4 and the within-groups *df* are 2. Consequently, eta is 0.93:

$$\sqrt{\frac{4 \times 3.04}{(4 \times 3.04) + 2}} = \sqrt{\frac{12.16}{14.16}} = \sqrt{0.86} = 0.927$$

One SPSS procedure for deriving eta is the following one.

→**Statistics** →**Compare <u>M</u>eans** →**<u>M</u>eans . . .** [opens **Means** dialog box as in Box 4.3]
→dependent variable [e.g. **a**] →▶button beside **Dependent List:** [puts variable in this box] →independent variable [e.g. **b**] →▶button beside

Independent List: [puts variable in this box] →**Options** ... [opens **Means: Options** dialog box as in Box 4.4]
→**ANOVA table and eta** →**Continue** [closes **Means: Options** dialog box]
→**OK**

Table 6.10 presents the last section of the output showing the analysis of variance and eta.

PEARSON'S PARTIAL CORRELATION

A significant association between two measures does not necessarily mean that the two variables are causally related. For instance, if students who attend tutorials were found to have higher coursework marks, then this relationship does not necessarily imply that there is a causal link between these two variables such that attending tutorials leads to higher marks. It is possible that this association is *spurious* in the sense that it is the result of one or more other factors which are genuinely related to these two variables. For example, greater coursework preparation may be related to both tutorial attendance and higher marks. When coursework preparation is taken into account there may be no association between tutorial attendance and coursework marks.

A less extreme version of a spurious relationship is one in which part but not all of the association between two measures may be due to one or more other factors. For example, students who attend tutorials may prepare more and may also produce better work. Part of their higher marks may be due to their attendance at tutorials while another part may be due to their coursework preparation. If we removed the influence of their preparation on the association between tutorial attendance and their marks, we can assume that the remaining association between these latter two variables is not the direct result of their preparation. Similarly, we could remove the influence of tutorial attendance from the relationship between coursework preparation and coursework marks to determine how much of the association between these two variables was not due to tutorial attendance.

Table 6.10 SPSS output for eta comparing coursework marks across five fear of failure ratings

Source	Sum of Squares	d.f.	Mean Square	F	Sig.
Between Groups	5.8571	4	1.4643	2.9286	.2704
Within Groups	1.0000	2	.5000		
	Eta = .9242	Eta Squared =	.8542		

It is important to note that a significant reduction in the size of an association between two variables by partialling out the influence of a third variable does not necessarily mean that that reduction indicates the degree of spuriousness in the original relationship between the two variables. An alternative possibility that should be seriously considered is that one of the two variables is an *intervening* or *mediating* variable which is influenced by the third variable and which affects the other variable. For example, attending tutorials may cause students to prepare more which in turn may improve their marks.

tutorial attendance $\rightarrow$ more preparation $\rightarrow$ higher marks

If this is the case, then the correlation between tutorial attendance and coursework preparation and between coursework preparation and coursework marks should be more positive than that between tutorial attendance and coursework marks. Whether coursework preparation is seen as a confounding variable or an intervening variable depends on theoretical argument and not statistical considerations and appears unclear in this situation.

A partially spurious or intervening relationship may be visualised in terms of the Venn diagrams in Figure 6.4. The first diagram depicts the original relationship between the two variables A and B. The second diagram shows that part of the relationship between A and B is shared with a third variable C. When this third variable is taken into account, the proportion of variance shared by A and B is reduced.

The absence of a significant association between two measures, on the other hand, does not necessarily signify no causal connection between those two variables. It is possible that the relationship is suppressed or hidden by the influence of one or more other variables. For example, tutorial attendance may appear not to be associated with coursework marks because attending tutorials may have been compulsory for the less interesting courses which also had lower grades. If we remove the effect of course interest, we may find that attendance is related to higher marks. For the same reasons, an association may appear to be less strong than it is because part of this relationship is being suppressed by one or more variables.

A suppressed relationship may be depicted in terms of the Venn diagrams in Figure 6.5. The first diagram indicates that the two variables A and B are not related since there is no overlap in their variance. The second diagram shows that when the influence of a third variable C is removed from the relationship between A and B some overlap between A and B is revealed, indicating that these two variables do share some variance.

An index of association between two variables where no other variables have been controlled or partialled out is known as a *zero-order* association. .A *first-order* association is one where one other variable has been controlled, a *second-order* association is one in which two other variables have been controlled and so on.

Relationship between two variables

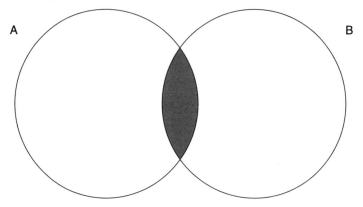

Relationship between two variables controlling for a third variable

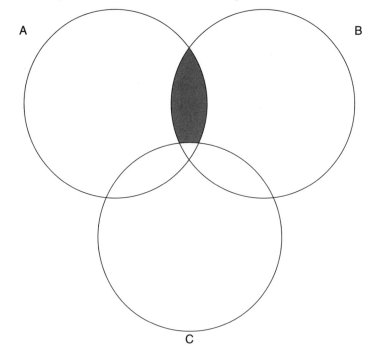

Figure 6.4 Venn diagram showing a partially spurious or intervening relationship between two variables

To remove the influence of one or more variables from a Pearson's correlation (r_{12}) between the two main variables of interest, we calculate the Pearson's partial correlation (Yule 1896). For a first-order partial correlation ($r_{12.3}$) the following formula is used:

Relationship between two variables

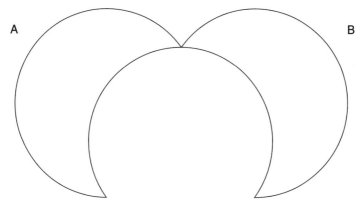

Relationship between two variables controlling for a third variable

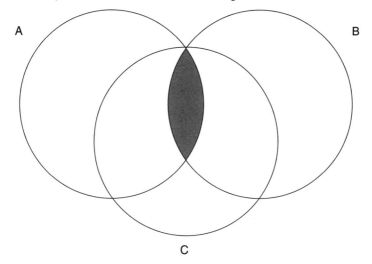

Figure 6.5 Venn diagram showing a suppressed relationship between two variables

$$r_{12.3} = \frac{r_{12} - (r_{13} \times r_{23})}{\sqrt{(1 - r_{13}{}^2) \times (1 - r_{23}{}^2)}}$$

To calculate a second-order partial correlation ($r_{12.34}$), which involves controlling two variables, the same general formula holds except that the zero-order correlations are replaced with first-order correlations:

$$r_{12.34} = \frac{r_{12.3} - (r_{14.3} \times r_{24.3})}{\sqrt{(1 - r^2{}_{14.3}) \times (1 - r^2{}_{24.3})}}$$

Similarly, third-order partial correlations are based on second-order partial correlations and so on.

Suppose we wished to calculate for our study the second-order partial correlation ($r_{12.34}$) between post-test marks (variable 1) and the sex of the student (variable 2), controlling for the two variables of coursework interest (variable 3) and coursework preparation (variable 4) at pre-test which we knew to be positively related to these two variables. The correlations between these four variables are presented in Table 6.11.

We initially have to calculate the first-order partial correlations between coursework marks and student's sex partialling out each of these control variables. We will demonstrate the calculation of the first-order partial correlation controlling for course interest ($r_{12.3}$). Inserting the appropriate correlations into the formula, we see that this partial correlation is −0.58:

$$r_{12.3} = \frac{-0.47 - (0.78 \times -0.14)}{\sqrt{(1 - 0.78^2) \times (1 - -0.14^2)}} = \frac{-0.47 - -0.11}{\sqrt{0.39 \times 0.98}}$$

$$= \frac{-0.36}{0.62} = -0.58$$

The correlation between coursework marks and student's sex is increased from −0.47 to −0.58 when we control for course interest. In other words, course interest acts as a suppressor variable.

To calculate the second-order partial correlation we also need to compute the first-order partial correlation of coursework marks and coursework preparation controlling for course interest ($r_{14.3}$) and that of student's sex and coursework preparation controlling for course interest ($r_{24.3}$). The partial correlation of coursework marks and coursework preparation controlling for course interest is 0.38:

$$r_{14.3} = \frac{0.74 - (0.78 \times 0.74)}{\sqrt{(1 - 0.78^2) \times (1 - 0.74^2)}} = \frac{0.74 - 0.58}{\sqrt{0.39 \times 0.45}}$$

$$= \frac{0.16}{0.42} = 0.38$$

In other words, controlling for course interest reduces considerably the

Table 6.11 Correlations between pre-test coursework preparation (4), pre-test course interest (3), student's sex (2) and post-test coursework marks (1)

	4 *Preparation*	*3* *Interest*	*2* *Sex*
3 Interest	0.74		
2 Sex	−0.48	−0.14	
1 Marks	0.74	0.78	−0.47

correlation between coursework marks and coursework preparation from 0.74 to 0.38.

The partial correlation of student's sex and coursework preparation controlling for course interest is -0.58:

$$r_{24.3} = \frac{-0.48 - (-0.14 \times 0.74)}{\sqrt{(1 - -0.14^2) \times (1 - 0.74^2)}} = \frac{-0.48 - -0.10}{\sqrt{0.98 \times 0.45}}$$

$$= \frac{-0.38}{0.66} = -0.58$$

Controlling for course interest increases the correlation between student's sex and coursework preparation from -0.48 to -0.58, indicating that course interest acts as a suppressor.

The second-order partial correlation between coursework marks and student's sex covarying out course interest and coursework preparation is -0.48:

$$r_{12.34} = \frac{-0.58 - (0.38 \times -0.58)}{\sqrt{(1 - 0.38^2) \times (1 - -0.58^2)}} = \frac{-0.58 - -0.22}{\sqrt{0.86 \times 0.66}}$$

$$= \frac{-0.36}{0.75} = -0.48$$

In other words, the correlation between coursework marks and student's sex increases very slightly from -0.47 to -0.48 when both coursework preparation and course interest are controlled.

The significance level of the partial correlation can be computed by converting it into t using the following formula

$$t = \text{partial } r \times \sqrt{\frac{\text{degrees of freedom}}{1 - \text{partial } r^2}}$$

The degrees of freedom are the number of cases (N) minus 2 minus the number of control variables. Substituting the values of our example into this formula we find that t is 2.19.

$$-0.48 \times \sqrt{\frac{20 - 2 - 2}{1 - -0.48^2}} = -0.48 \times \sqrt{\frac{16}{0.77}} =$$

$$-0.48 \times \sqrt{20.78} = -0.48 \times 4.56 = 2.1888$$

We look up the statistical significance of t in the table in Appendix 4 where we see that with 16 degrees of freedom t has to be 2.120 or bigger to be significant at the 0.05 two-tailed level, which it is. Alternatively we could look up the statistical significance of r in the table in Appendix 7 where we see that with 16 degrees of freedom r has to be 0.4683 or larger to be significant at the 0.05 two-tailed level.

To carry out this partial correlation with SPSS, we would use the following procedure:

→**Statistics** →**Correlate** →**Partial . . .** [opens **Partial Correlations** dialog box as in Box 6.5]
→variables to be correlated [e.g. **markpos** and **sex**] →▶button besides **Variables:** text box [puts variables in this box] →control variables [e.g. **intpre** and **prepre**] →button besides **Controlling for:** text box [puts variables in this box] →**OK**

If you want the zero-order correlations at the same time, select **Zero-order correlations** in the **Partial Correlations: Options** dialog box.

Table 6.12 displays the output for this procedure.

SUMMARY

The computation of Pearson's product moment correlation and first- and second-order partial correlations is described together with the calculation of eta and tests for determining whether correlations from the same or different samples differ. Pearson's correlation assesses the strength,

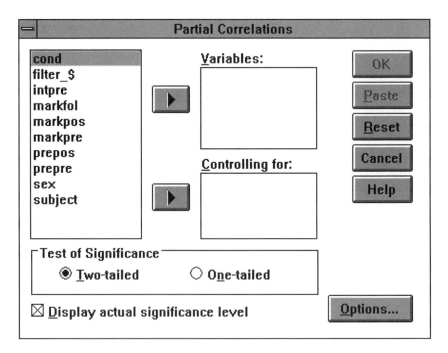

Box 6.5 **Partial Correlations** dialog box

Table 6.12 SPSS output showing a second-order partial correlation between post-test marks and student's sex controlling for pre-test course interest and coursework preparation

---

```
- - - P A R T I A L   C O R R E L A T I O N   C O E F F I C I E N T S - - -
```

Controlling for ..	INTPRE	PREPRE
	SEX	MARKPOS
SEX	1.0000	-.4783
	(0)	(16)
	P= .	P= .045
MARKPOS	-.4783	1.0000
	(16)	(0)
	P= .045	P= .

(Coefficient / (D.F.) / 2-tailed Significance)

" . " is printed if a coefficient cannot be computed

---

direction and probability of the linear association between two interval or ratio variables and varies from -1 to $+1$. It reflects the ratio of the variance shared by two variables compared to the overall variance of the two variables. This coefficient is the same as the point-biserial correlation (which measures the association between a dichotomous variable and an interval/ratio variable) and the phi coefficient (which assesses the association between two dichotomous variables). The percentage of variance shared by the two variables is the square of Pearson's correlation and is called the coefficient of determination. A correlation of close to zero may mean that the relationship between the two variables is curvilinear which can be checked with a scatterplot. The size of Pearson's correlation is affected by the variance of one or both variables as well as the presence of extreme scores which influence the variance. The z test determines whether the size of two correlations from two samples differs significantly. For correlations from the same sample, the T_2 test compares those having a variable in common while the Z_2^* test compares those having no variable in common. Eta measures the strength of a non-linear association between an interval/ratio variable and a categorical/ordinal variable and varies from zero to $+1$. Eta squared indicates the percentage of the total variance in the dependent variable explained by the independent variable.

EXERCISES

Use the data in Table 5.12 for the following exercises.

1 Calculate Pearson's correlation between educational interest at 12 and at 15.
   (a) What is the size of the correlation?
   (b) What are its degrees of freedom?
   (c) Is educational interest at 12 and 15 significantly positively correlated at the 0.05 one-tailed level?

2 Compare the size of the correlation between educational interest at 12 and 15 for single- and mixed-sex schools.
   (a) Which test would you use?
   (b) What is the correlation for single-sex schools?
   (c) What is the correlation for mixed-sex schools?
   (d) What is the value of this test?
   (e) Do the two correlations differ significantly at the 0.05 two-tailed level?

3 Compare the size of the correlation of educational interest at 12 and 15 with that at 9 and 12.
   (a) Which test would you use?
   (b) What is the correlation between educational interest at 9 and 12?
   (c) What is the correlation between educational interest at 9 and 15?
   (d) What is the value of this test?
   (e) What are its degrees of freedom?
   (f) Do the two correlations differ significantly at the 0.05 two-tailed level?

4 Compare the size of the correlation between socio-economic status and educational interest at 9 with that of educational interest at 12 and 15.
   (a) Which test would you use?
   (b) What is the correlation between socio-economic status and educational interest at 9?
   (c) What is the correlation between socio-economic status and educational interest at 12?
   (d) What is the correlation between socio-economic status and educational interest at 15?
   (e) What is the value of this test?
   (f) Do the two correlations differ significantly at the 0.05 two-tailed level?

5 What is Pearson's correlation between educational interest at 12 and at 15 controlling for educational interest at 9?

6 What is the value of eta for socio-economic status and educational interest at 15 with socio-economic status as the independent variable?

7 Bivariate and multiple regression

Regression analysis estimates or predicts the scores of one variable (called the *criterion* or the dependent variable) from one or more other variables (called *predictors* or independent variables). In order to predict the criterion, the criterion is related to or regressed on the predictor(s). *Simple* or *bivariate* regression (Galton 1886) involves one predictor whereas *multiple* regression uses two or more predictors. One of the main purposes of multiple regression in the social sciences is not so much to predict the score of one variable from others but to determine the minimum number of a set of variables which is most strongly related to the criterion and to estimate the percentage of variance in the criterion explained by those variables. For example, we may be interested in finding out which variables are most strongly related to coursework marks and how much of the variance in the marks these variables explain. Generally, the variable which is most highly related to the marks is entered first into the regression equation followed by variables which are the next most strongly related to the marks once their relationship with the other variables is taken into account. If later variables are strongly associated with the variables already entered, then it is less likely that they will independently account for much more of the variance than those previously entered and so they are unlikely to be included as predictors. Although we will demonstrate the calculation of multiple regression with a few cases, this technique should only be used when a relatively large number of cases is available. Under these circumstances, multiple regression is a very valuable statistical procedure. We will begin by describing bivariate regression which just involves one predictor.

BIVARIATE REGRESSION

If we want to predict a score on a criterion from a score on another variable and we know that there is no association between the two variables, then our best guess is the mean of the criterion since this score is the closest to all other scores. If, on the other hand, the two variables are perfectly correlated, then we could predict the criterion perfectly. Indeed, the higher the correlation the more accurate our prediction could be. However, the correlation only tells us how much of the variance is shared by both variables. It does not by itself enable us to predict the actual score of the criterion from the score of the other variable. In order to do this we also need to know the way in which those scores are scaled. What linear regression does is to find the straight line that lies closest to the joint values of the two variables. Provided that there is variation in both variables, the closer the joint values are to the straight line the more accurately we can predict the scores of the criterion.

Linear regression may be best explained in terms of the scatterplot of two variables where it is possible to draw the straight line that comes closest to the points on the graph. Take our earlier example of the pre-test and post-test marks for the women in the no and individual tutorial condition in Table 6.1 which have been re-presented in Table 7.1. Previously we worked out that the Pearson correlation between these two sets of marks was 0.62. In other words, there is a moderately strong association between the two groups of marks. Consequently, we should be able to predict to some degree the post-test marks from the pre-test marks provided we know the scales of the two sets of scores. The scatterplot of these two sets of marks is shown in Box 7.1 where, as is usual, the vertical or y axis represents the criterion (post-test marks) and the horizontal or x axis the predictor (pre-test marks).

Before we can draw a straight line in two-dimensional space (i.e. the space described by the horizontal and vertical axes) we need to know the slope of the line and its position. The position of the line can be described by the point where the line intercepts the vertical axis when the position on the horizontal axis corresponds to zero. This point is known as the *intercept*. The minimum number of points needed to draw a straight line is two. A point on a straight line can be defined by the following equation where y

Table 7.1 Data and computations for the regression coefficient between pre-test (A) and post-test (B) marks for women in the no and individual tutorial conditions

	A	B	D_A	$D_A{}^2$	D_B	D_{AB}
	3	4	−0.8	0.64	−2.8	2.24
	1	6	−2.8	7.84	−0.8	2.24
	5	7	1.2	1.44	0.2	0.24
	3	8	−0.8	0.64	1.2	−0.96
	7	9	3.2	10.24	2.2	7.04
Sum	19	34		20.80		10.80
N	5	5				
Mean	3.8	6.8				

Note: $b = \dfrac{10.80}{20.80} = 0.519$

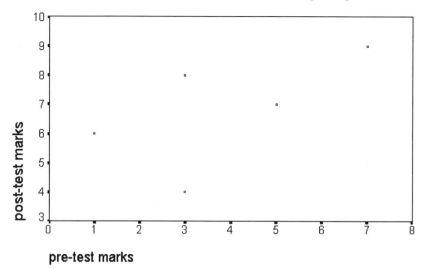

pre-test marks

Box 7.1 SPSS output of a scattergram of pre- and post-test marks for women in the no and individual tutorial groups

represents the position on the vertical or y axis, a the intercept of the line on the y axis, b the slope of the line and x the position on the horizontal or x axis:

$$y = a + bx$$

While for any line the values of y and x vary, the values of a and b remain the same and are known as *constants*.

We will illustrate the formula for a straight line with the three following pairs of scores

y	x
3	1
4	3
5	7

which represent a straight line and which is drawn as such in Figure 7.1. The slope of the line or b is the ratio of the vertical distance covered (called the *rise*) over a particular horizontal distance (called the *run*).

$$\text{slope or } b = \frac{\text{vertical distance (rise)}}{\text{horizontal distance (run)}}$$

We can see that the line rises by one unit for every two units along the horizontal axis giving a slope of 0.5 (1/2 = 0.5). If the horizontal distance is fixed at one unit, then b is a measure of the change on the vertical axis which corresponds to a change of one unit on the horizontal axis.

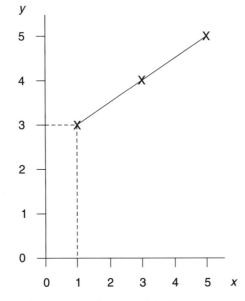

Figure 7.1 Three points representing a straight line

$$b = \frac{b}{1}$$

In this case the line rises by 0.5 for every horizontal unit of 1. If we know any three of the four values in the equation for a straight line, we can work out the fourth. So, for example, we could work out a if we subtract bx from each side of the equation to give the following expression

$$y - bx = a$$

Substituting a pair of y and x values (3 and 1) in the equation we see that a is 2.5

$$3 - (0.5 \times 1) = 2.5$$

Similarly, we can predict a particular y value from an x value if we know the other two values.

$$a + bx = y$$

For example, an x value of 1 corresponds to a y value of 3.0:

$$2.5 + (0.5 \times 1) = 3.0$$

If we know one pair of y and x values, we can define one point on the line which is simply the point where lines drawn from these two values intersect as shown in Figure 7.1. All we need now to draw the straight line is to determine the intersection of another pair of y and x values.

It is important to understand what the expression *bx* means. The value *x* indicates the distance from zero to the value *x* which is 1 unit where *x* is 1. Multiplying *x* by *b* gives the number of units on the vertical axis that *y* must change by over a horizontal distance of *x* units. So for one horizontal *x* unit *y* changes by 0.5 of a vertical unit ($0.5 \times 1 = 0.5$). To find out what value of *y* this represents we add a change of 0.5 vertical units to the vertical value of the intercept which in this example is 2.5 giving a *y* value of 3 ($0.5 + 2.5 = 3.0$).

In the social sciences, however, the relationship between two variables is rarely perfect and so determining the two points is more complicated. The formula for finding any point is the same as before except that we are interested in determining what the value of the criterion or *y* would be when a straight line is drawn that lies closest to the joint values of the criterion and the predictor. In this formula, the slope or *b* is known as the *regression* or *beta* coefficient.

criterion predicted score = intercept constant + [regression coefficient × predictor score]

To calculate the regression coefficient we use the following formula which is the sum of products of the deviation of the score of the criterion from its mean multiplied by the deviation of the corresponding score of the predictor for all pairs of scores, which is then divided by the sum of squares of the predictor:

$$b = \frac{\text{sum of products of the criterion and predictor}}{\text{predictor sum of squares}}$$

Note that the regression coefficient is similar to the correlation coefficient except that it describes the relationship between the predictor and the criterion in terms of the units of the predictor and not in terms of *standardised* units as does the correlation. Because the variables have been standardised, the intercept is zero for a correlation line. The formula for the correlation coefficient expressed in the same terms as that for the regression coefficient is as follows

$$r = \frac{\text{sum of products of the criterion and predictor}}{\sqrt{\text{criterion sum of squares} \times \text{predictor sum of squares}}}$$

Since the sum of products of the criterion and the predictor can equal but not exceed the square root of the product of the criterion and predictor sum of squares, the maximum value that the correlation coefficient can attain is ±1.0. The value of the regression coefficient can be larger than ±1.0 because the sum of products of the criterion and predictor can be bigger than the predictor sum of squares.

We compute the intercept constant with the following formula which is the predictor mean score multiplied by the regression coefficient which is then subtracted from the criterion mean score:

a = criterion mean $-$ (regression $\times$ predictor coefficient mean)

The regression line runs from the intercept constant on the vertical axis through the point where one of the predicted values of the criterion meets with the corresponding value for the predictor.

So to determine the regression line we first have to compute the regression coefficient. The steps involved in calculating this coefficient for our example are presented in Table 7.1. The means of the predictor (A) and the criterion (B) are first calculated, followed by the deviation of each score from its mean (D_A and D_B). Squaring (D_A^2) and summing the deviations of the predictor scores gives a sum of squares of 20.80, while multiplying the deviations of the criterion and predictor (D_{AB}) and summing them produces a sum of products of 10.80. Dividing the sum of products of the criterion and predictor by the sum of squares of the predictor produces a regression coefficient of 0.52 (10.8/20.8 = 0.52).

Once we have calculated the regression coefficient, we can work out from the predictor and criterion means the intercept constant which is 4.82 [6.8 $-$ (0.52 $\times$ 3.8) = 4.82]. Using the intercept and one predictor value we work out the corresponding predicted value for the criterion. For example, the predictor value of 2 would give a predicted value for the criterion of 5.86 [4.82 + (0.52 $\times$ 2) = 5.86]. We can then draw a regression line which stretches from the point on the vertical axis of 4.82 through the point where the predictor value of 2 intersects with a predicted value for the criterion of 5.86 as shown in Box 7.2.

It is useful to understand the reason for the formula for determining the

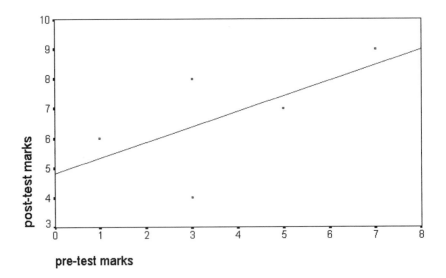

Box 7.2 SPSS output of a regression line of post-test marks on pre-test marks for women in the no and individual tutorial groups

intercept. The mean represents the centre of a distribution of values. In other words, the mean is the point in that set of values which lies closest to all the values. Multiplying the mean of the predictor (3.8) by the regression coefficient (0.52) gives the number of vertical units that the criterion must change by (1.98) over the horizontal distance that the mean value of the predictor represents (3.8). Subtracting the number of vertical units (1.98) from the mean value of the criterion (6.8) gives the value on the criterion (4.82) that corresponds to a value on the horizontal axis of zero which is the value of subtracting the number of horizontal units (3.8) from the predictor mean (3.8).

Knowing the regression coefficient and the intercept constant, we can use the regression equation to predict the value of the criterion from any value of the predictor. For example, using this information we would predict that if the pre-test mark was 1, the post-test mark would be 5.34 [4.82 + (0.52 × 1) = 5.34]. Note that where a student obtained a pre-test mark of 1 (case 2), she received a post-test mark of 6. In other words, there is a difference between the predicted score and the actual score of the criterion which in this case is 0.66 (6 − 5.34 = 0.66). This difference is called a *residual*. Although this residual is positive, others will be negative. For example, the pre-test mark of 3 for the first woman has a predicted score of 6.38 [4.82 + (0.52 × 3) = 6.38] although her actual post-test mark is 4. In other words, the difference between the actual and the predicted mark is −2.38 (4 − 6.38 = −2.38). The actual criterion value is given by the following equation:

criterion value = $a + (b ×$ predictor value) + residual

Therefore, if the re-test mark is 3, the post-test mark is 4.0:

4.82 + (0.52 × 3) + −2.38 = 4.00

The regression line is the straight line that is closest to the points on the scatterplot. To determine how close this line lies to these points we add together the squares of the residuals. If we simply added the residuals together, they would sum to zero since the sum of the negative differences equals the sum of the positive differences as shown in Table 7.2. Since the sum of squared residuals is the smallest it can be, the regression line is also called the *least-squares line* or *line of best fit*.

Since regression is sometimes used for prediction it is useful to know how accurate the prediction is. A measure of this is the *standard error of estimate* which is the square root of the sum of squared residuals divided by the number of cases minus 2:

$$\text{standard error of estimate} = \sqrt{\frac{\text{sum of squared residuals}}{N - 2}}$$

Table 7.2 Sum of residuals and residuals squared

Pre-test marks			
Actual	Predicted	Residuals	Residuals^2
3	4.82 + (0.52 × 3) = 6.38	4 − 6.38 = −2.38	5.66
1	4.82 + (0.52 × 1) = 5.34	6 − 5.34 = 0.66	0.44
5	4.82 + (0.52 × 5) = 7.42	7 − 7.42 = −0.42	0.18
3	4.82 + (0.52 × 3) = 6.38	8 − 6.38 = 1.62	2.62
7	4.82 + (0.52 × 7) = 8.46	9 − 8.46 = 0.54	0.29
Sum		0.0	9.19

It is the standard deviation of the errors of prediction. It provides an estimate of the probability of a particular criterion score occurring in that 68 per cent of scores will lie within one standard deviation of the predicted score, 95 per cent within two standard deviations and 99 per cent within three standard deviations. The standard error of estimate of the post-test marks is about 1.75 [$\sqrt{9.19/(5 - 2)} = 1.750$]. For example, when the pre-test mark is 3, the predicted post-test mark is calculated to be 6.38 using the regression equation. As the standard error of estimate of the post-test marks is about 1.75 there is a 68 per cent probability that the actual post-test mark will fall within the range of 6.38 ± 1.75 (i.e. 4.63 to 8.13), a 95 per cent probability that it will fall within 6.38 ± 3.5 (2 × 1.75 = 3.5) and a 99 per cent probability that it will fall within 6.38 ± 5.25 (3 × 1.75 = 5.25).

A measure of the accuracy of the regression coefficient is the *standard error of the regression coefficient*. This is the square root of the sum of squared residuals divided by the number of cases minus 2 and then divided by the sum of squares of the predictor variable:

$$\text{standard error of } b = \sqrt{\frac{\text{sum of squared residuals}/(N - 2)}{\text{sum of squares of predictor}}}$$

If the sample size is greater than 200, it gives an estimate of the probability of the regression coefficient occurring within one standard deviation of its value. For our example it is about 0.38:

$$\sqrt{\frac{9.19/(5 - 2)}{20.80}} = \sqrt{\frac{3.06}{20.80}} = \sqrt{0.147} = 0.383$$

Consequently, the regression coefficient would have a 95 per cent probability of falling within the range 0.52 ± (0.38 × 1.96) if the sample was greater than 200. With smaller samples, the *b* estimates follow the *t* distribution with the degrees of freedom equal to the number of cases minus 2. According to the table in Appendix 4, the *t* value for 3 degrees of freedom is 3.182 at the 0.05 two-tailed level. Therefore, the regression coefficient has a 95 per cent probability of falling within the interval 0.52 ± (0.38 × 3.182).

We use a *t* test to determine the statistical significance of the regression coefficient. This *t* test is the unstandardised regression coefficient divided by its standard error which is 1.37 (0.52/0.38 = 1.368). Its degrees of freedom are equal to those associated with the residual sum of squares which is the number of cases minus 2. Using the table in Appendix 4, we see that with 3 degrees of freedom *t* has to be 3.182 or bigger to be significant at the 0.05 level, which it is not. In other words, the regression coefficient is not statistically significant.

An index of the accuracy of the intercept is the *standard error of the intercept* which is (1) the sum of squared residuals divided by the number of cases minus 2, which is then (2) multiplied by 1 divided by the number of cases plus the square of the predictor mean divided by the predictor sum of squares, and (3) the square root is then taken of this result:

standard error of *a* =

$$\sqrt{\frac{\text{sum of squared residuals}}{n-2} \times \left(\frac{1}{n} + \frac{\text{predictor mean squared}}{\text{predictor sum of squares}}\right)}$$

For our example it is about 1.65:

$$\sqrt{\frac{9.19}{5-2} \times \left(\frac{1}{5} + \frac{3.8^2}{20.80}\right)} = \sqrt{\frac{9.19}{3} \times (0.2 + 0.69)} =$$

$$\sqrt{3.06 \times 0.89} = \sqrt{2.72} = 1.649$$

With samples greater than 200, the intercept would have a 95 per cent probability of falling within the range 4.82 ± (1.65 × 1.96). With smaller samples, the *a* estimates follow the *t* distribution with the degrees of freedom equal to the number of cases minus 2. According to the table in Appendix 4, the *t* value for 3 degrees of freedom is 3.182 at the 0.05 two-tailed level. Therefore, the intercept has a 95 per cent probability of falling within the interval 4.82 ± (1.65 × 3.182).

We can use a *t* test to determine the statistical significance of the intercept constant. This *t* test is the intercept constant divided by its standard error which is 2.92 (4.82/1.65 = 2.921). Its degrees of freedom are equal to those associated with the residual sum of squares which is the number of cases minus 2. Using the table in Appendix 4, we see that with 3 degrees of freedom *t* has to be 3.182 or bigger to be significant at the 0.05 level, which it is not. This means that the intercept constant does not differ significantly from zero.

If the variances of the two variables are the same, the regression coefficient will be the same as the correlation coefficient. The formula for the correlation coefficient is essentially the sum of products of the criterion and predictor divided by the square root of the product of the sum of squares of the criterion and the predictor:

$$r = \frac{\text{sum of products of criterion and predictor}}{\sqrt{\text{criterion sum of squares} \times \text{predictor sum of squares}}}$$

Consequently, if the sum of squares for both the criterion and the predictor is the same, the denominator of this formula is the sum of squares of the predictor.

When the variances of the two variables differ as they do here, the regression coefficient for predicting post-test marks from pre-test marks will not be the same as that for predicting pre-test marks from post-test marks since the sum of squares in the denominator will differ. However, when the criterion and the predictor are standardised so that they both have a standard deviation of 1, the regression coefficient is standardised so that the *standardised* regression coefficient or B is the same for predicting post-test marks from pre-test marks as it is for predicting pre-test marks from post-test marks. The standardised regression coefficient is the same as Pearson's correlation and can be calculated by multiplying the unstandardised regression coefficient by the standard deviation of the predictor and dividing by the standard deviation of the criterion:

$$\text{standardised regression coefficient} = \text{unstandardised regression coefficient} \times \frac{\text{predictor std dev}}{\text{criterion std dev}}$$

The standardised regression coefficient in this case is 0.62 (0.52 × 2.28/ 1.92 = 0.617). The standardised regression coefficient indicates how many standard deviation units the criterion will change for one standard deviation unit change in the predictor. In other words, post-marks will increase by 0.62 of a standard unit for every increase of one standard unit in pre-test marks.

This formula for the standardised regression coefficient is equivalent to the formula for the correlation coefficient given above. We can see this if we replace the terms in the formula for the standardised regression coefficient with their formulae as follows where SP stands for the sum of products for the criterion and predictor and SS their sum of squares:

$$B = \frac{SP}{\text{predictor SS}} \times \frac{\dfrac{\sqrt{\text{predictor SS}}}{\sqrt{N-1}}}{\dfrac{\sqrt{\text{criterion SS}}}{\sqrt{N-1}}}$$

To divide a numerator fraction by a denominator fraction, we inverse the denominator fraction and multiply it by the numerator fraction:

$$B = \frac{SP}{\text{predictor SS}} \times \frac{\sqrt{\text{predictor SS}}}{\sqrt{N-1}} \times \frac{\sqrt{N-1}}{\sqrt{\text{criterion SS}}}$$

The $\sqrt{N-1}$ terms cancel out:

$$B = \frac{SP}{\text{predictor SS}} \times \frac{\sqrt{\text{predictor SS}}}{\sqrt{\text{criterion SS}}}$$

The position of the denominators can be switched round:

$$B = \frac{SP}{\sqrt{\text{criterion SS}}} \times \frac{\sqrt{\text{predictor SS}}}{\text{predictor SS}}$$

The square root of a number ($\sqrt{\text{predictor SS}}$) divided by that number (predictor SS) gives the reciprocal square root of that number ($1/\sqrt{\text{predictor SS}}$):

$$B = \frac{SP}{\sqrt{\text{criterion SS}}} \times \frac{1}{\sqrt{\text{predictor SS}}}$$

$$= \frac{SP}{\sqrt{\text{criterion SS}} \times \sqrt{\text{predictor SS}}}$$

$$= \frac{SP}{\sqrt{\text{criterion SS} \times \text{predictor SS}}}$$

The steps in this derivation can be checked using simple whole numbers.

Regression analysis can be thought of in terms of analysis of variance where the total sum of squares for the criterion can be divided or partitioned into a sum of squares due to regression and a residual sum of squares which is left over:

criterion total sum of squares = regression sum of squares + residual sum of squares

The total sum of squares for the criterion can be calculated by subtracting the criterion mean score from each of its individual scores, squaring and summing them. If we do this for the post-test marks, the total sum of squares for the post-test marks is 14.80.

$$(4 - 6.8)^2 + (6 - 6.8)^2 + (7 - 6.8)^2 + (8 - 6.8)^2 + (9 - 6.8)^2 =$$
$$-2.8^2 + -0.8^2 + 0.2^2 + 1.2^2 + 2.2^2 =$$
$$7.84 + 0.64 + 0.04 + 1.44 + 4.84 = 14.80$$

The regression sum of squares is the sum of squared differences between the predicted criterion score and the mean criterion score:

regression sum of squares = sum of (predicted criterion score − mean criterion score)^2

Alternatively, subtracting the residual sum of squares from the criterion total sum of squares gives the regression sum of squares:

regression sum of squares = criterion total sum of squares − residual sum of squares

The predicted criterion scores and squared residual scores are shown in Table 7.2. The residual sum of squares is 9.19. Therefore, the regression sum of squares for our example is 5.61 (14.80 − 9.19 = 5.61). The analysis of variance table for this regression is presented in Table 7.3.

The *squared multiple correlation* or R^2 is the proportion of the regression sum of squares over the criterion total sum of squares:

$$R^2 = \frac{\text{regression sum of squares}}{\text{criterion total sum of squares}}$$

It represents the proportion of variance in the criterion accounted for by the linear combination of the independent variables which in this case is only one variable. The squared multiple correlation for our example is 0.38 (5.61/14.80 = 0.379). In other words, 38 per cent of the variance in the post-test marks is explained by or shared with the pre-test marks.

The adjusted squared multiple correlation is a more conservative estimate of explained variance than the squared multiple correlation since it takes into account the size of the sample and the number of predictors in the equation. Its formula is:

$$\text{adjusted } R^2 = R^2 - \frac{(1 - R^2) \times \text{no. of predictors}}{\text{no. of cases} - \text{no. of predictors} - 1}$$

Since there is only one predictor in this equation, the adjusted squared multiple correlation is about 0.17:

$$0.38 - \frac{(1 - 0.38) \times 1}{5 - 1 - 1} = 0.38 - \frac{0.62}{3} = 0.38 - 0.21 = 0.17$$

The *multiple correlation* or R is the square root of the squared multiple correlation:

$$R = \sqrt{R^2}$$

The multiple correlation for our example is 0.62 ($\sqrt{0.38} = 0.616$).

Table 7.3 Analysis of variance table for regression

Sources of variation	SS	df	MS	F	p
Regression	5.61	1	5.61	1.83	ns
Residual	9.19	3	3.06		
Total	14.80	4			

The statistical significance of the squared multiple correlation can be tested by computing the F ratio of the regression mean square to the residual mean square:

$$F = \frac{\text{regression mean square}}{\text{residual mean square}}$$

The regression mean square is the regression sum of squares divided by its degrees of freedom which is the number of predictors in the regression equation. The residual mean square is the residual sum of squares divided by its degrees of freedom which are the number of cases minus the number of predictors minus 1.

For our example the regression mean square is 5.61 (5.61/1 = 5.61) and the residual mean square is 3.06 [9.19/(5 − 1 − 1) = 3.06)]. Therefore, the F ratio is 1.83 (5.61/3.06 = 1.833). With 1 and 3 degrees of freedom in the numerator and denominator respectively, the F ratio has to be 10.128 or larger to be significant at the 0.05 level, which it is not. Consequently we would conclude that the squared multiple correlation between the pre- and post-test marks is not significant.

An alternative method of computing the F ratio for the squared multiple correlation is multiplying the squared multiple correlation by the degrees of freedom for the residual sum of squares and dividing the result by the squared multiple correlation subtracted from one and multiplied by the degrees of freedom for the regression sum of squares:

$$F = \frac{R^2 \times (\text{no. of cases} - \text{no. of predictors} - 1)}{(1 - R^2) \times \text{no. of predictors}}$$

This F ratio for our example is 1.84:

$$\frac{0.38 \times (5 - 1 - 1)}{(1 - 0.38) \times 1} = \frac{0.38 \times 3}{0.62 \times 1} = \frac{1.14}{0.62} = 1.838$$

The degrees of freedom for this F ratio are the same as the previous one.

With only one predictor, the statistical significance of the F ratio of the squared multiple correlation is the same as that of the t test of the unstandardised regression coefficient in that t^2 equals F (3.576^2 = 12.787).

To run a simple regression on these data with SPSS, first select the women in the no and individual tutorial groups (i.e. **sex = 1 & cond ~= 3**) and then carry out the following procedure:

→**Statistics** →**Regression** →**Linear** . . . [opens **Linear Regression** dialog box as in Box 7.3]
→dependent variable [e.g. **markpos**] →▶ button beside **Dependent:** box [puts variable in this box] →independent variable [e.g. **markpre**] →▶ button beside **Independent[s]:** box [puts variable in this box] →**OK**

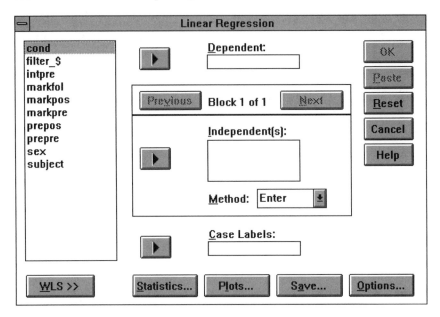

Box 7.3 **Linear Regression** dialog box

Table 7.4 displays the output for this example. **Multiple R, R Square, Adjusted R Square** and the **Standard Error** of the estimate are presented first, followed by the **Analysis of Variance** table and the values of the regression equation (**Variables in the Equation**). **B** is the unstandardised regression coefficient and **Beta** the standardised regression coefficient. The **(Constant)** is the intercept and its **SE B** is its standard error. The **T** values and the statistical significance of the *t* values (**Sig T**) are also given. These values correspond to those we have previously calculated.

To produce with SPSS a scatterplot with a regression line like that in Box 7.2, first select the women in these two tutorial groups (i.e. **sex = 1 & cond ~= 3**) and then execute the following procedure:

→**Graphs** →**Scatter** . . . [opens **Scatterplot** dialog box as in Box 6.2]
→**Define** [opens **Simple Scatterplot** dialog box as in Box 6.3]
→dependent variable [e.g. **markpos**] →▶ button beside **Y** **Axis:** box [puts variable in this box] →independent variable [e.g. **markpre**] →▶ button beside **X** **Axis:** box [puts variable in this box] →**OK** [displays scattergram in **Chart Carousel** window as in Box 7.1] →**Edit** →**Chart** →**Options** . . . →**Total** in **Fit Line** box →**OK** [draws regression line in scattergram in **Chart Carousel** window]

Correlation and regression provide a good index of the association between two variables when the assumptions of normality, linearity and *homoscedasticity* are met. Homoscedasticity refers to the variance of one

Table 7.4 SPSS output of post-test marks regressed on pre-test marks for women in the no and individual tutorial groups

* * * * M U L T I P L E   R E G R E S S I O N   * * * *

Listwise Deletion of Missing Data

Equation Number 1   Dependent Variable..   MARKPOS   post-test marks

Block Number 1.   Method: Enter   MARKPRE

Variable(s) Entered on Step Number
    1..   MARKPRE pre-test marks

Multiple R	.61555
R Square	.37890
Adjusted R Square	.17186
Standard Error	1.75046

Analysis of Variance

	DF	Sum of Squares	Mean Square
Regression	1	5.60769	5.60769
Residual	3	9.19231	3.06410

F =   1.83013   Signif F =   .2690

- - - - - - - - - - - - - - - - - Variables in the Equation - - - - - - - - - - - - - - - - - -

Variable	B	SE B	Beta	T	Sig T
MARKPRE	.519231	.383813	.615547	1.353	.2690
(Constant)	4.826923	1.655299		2.916	.0617

End Block Number 1 All requested variables entered.

variable being similar for all values of the other variable. A way of checking these three assumptions visually is to produce a scatterplot of the residuals with the predicted values. The assumption of normality is met if the residuals are normally distributed around each predicted score so that most of the residuals for that predicted score are concentrated at the centre of its distribution. The assumption of linearity holds if the overall shape of the distribution of points is rectangular. A curved shape implies that the relationship is not linear. The assumption of homoscedasticity is fulfilled if the spread of residuals does not change with an increase in the predicted values. An example of heteroscedasticity is when the distribution of residuals becomes wider at higher values.

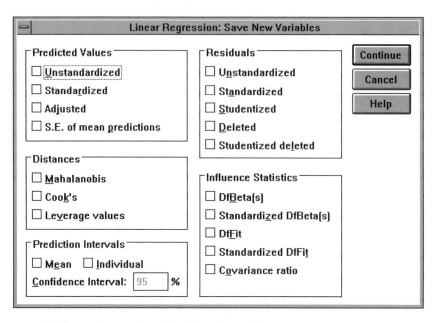

Box 7.4 **Linear Regression: Save New Variables** dialog box

To produce a scatterplot between the residuals and the predicted values for our example with SPSS we would use the following procedure:

→**Statistics** →**Regression** →**Linear** . . . [opens **Linear Regression** dialog box as in Box 7.3]
→dependent variable [e.g. **markpos**] →▶button beside **Dependent:** box [puts variable in this box] →independent variable [e.g. **markpre**] →▶button beside **Independent[s]:** box [puts variable in this box] →**Save** . . . [opens **Linear Regression: Save New Variables** dialog box as in Box 7.4]
→**Unstandardized** [**Predicted Values**] →**Unstandardized** [**Residuals**] →**Continue** →**OK**
→**Graphs** →**Scatter** . . . [opens **Scatterplot** dialog box as in Box 6.2]
→**Define** [opens **Simple Scatterplot** dialog box as in Box 6.3]
→dependent variable [e.g. **res_1**] →▶button beside **Y Axis:** box [puts variable in this box] →independent variable [e.g. **pre_1**] →▶button beside **X Axis:** box [puts variable in this box] →**OK** [displays scattergram in **Chart Carousel** window as in Box 7.5]
→**Edit** →**Chart** →**Options** . . . →**Total** in **Fit Line** box →**OK** [draws regression line in scattergram in **Chart Carousel** window]

Box 7.5 displays the output for this procedure.

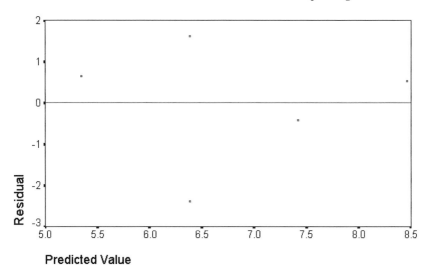

Box 7.5 SPSS output of a scattergram of residuals and predicted values with regression line

MULTIPLE REGRESSION

Multiple regression is the extension of bivariate regression to two or more predictors. We would use multiple regression if we wanted to find out, for example, how much of the variance in post-test marks was explained by the predictors of student's sex, pre-test coursework preparation, and pre-test course interest. The regression equation for multiple regression is as follows:

criterion predicted score = $a + (b_1 \times$ predictor$_1$ score) + $(b_2 \times$ predictor$_2$ score)

where b_1 is the unstandardised partial regression coefficient of the criterion with the first predictor controlling for the other predictors in the equation, b_2 is the unstandardised partial regression coefficient of the criterion with the second predictor controlling for the other predictors in the equation and so on.

As the calculation of partial regression coefficients with more than two predictors is complicated and is more appropriately carried out with matrix algebra, we will only demonstrate the calculation of a multiple regression with two predictors. The formula for computing the standardised partial regression coefficient of the criterion (c) with the first predictor (1) controlling for the second predictor (2) is:

$$B_1 = \frac{r_{c1} - (r_{c2} \times r_{12})}{1 - r^2_{12}}$$

To convert the standardised partial regression coefficient into the unstandardised coefficient, we multiply the standardised coefficient by the standard deviation of the criterion divided by the standard deviation of the predictor:

$$b_1 = \frac{\text{criterion std dev}}{\text{predictor}_1 \text{ std dev}} \times B_1$$

Similarly, the formula for computing the standardised partial regression coefficient of the criterion (c) with the second predictor (2) controlling for the first predictor (1) is:

$$B_2 = \frac{r_{c2} - (r_{c1} \times r_{12})}{1 - r^2_{12}}$$

The formula for the unstandardised partial regression coefficient is:

$$b_2 = \frac{\text{criterion std dev}}{\text{predictor}_2 \text{ std dev}} \times B_2$$

As an illustration, we will compute the multiple regression between the criterion of post-test marks (c) and the two predictors of pre-test coursework preparation (1) and student's sex (2) for the data in our sample. The correlations for these variables are shown in Table 6.11 but are re-presented in Table 7.5 together with the means and standard deviations.

Using the above formulae we find that the standardised partial regression coefficient between post-test marks and coursework preparation is about 0.66 while the unstandardised partial regression coefficient is about 1.31:

$$B_1 = \frac{0.74 - (-0.47 \times -0.48)}{1 - -0.48^2} = \frac{0.74 - 0.23}{1 - 0.23} = \frac{0.51}{0.77} = 0.662$$

$$b_1 = \frac{2.30}{1.16} \times 0.66 = 1.309$$

Similarly, the standardised partial regression coefficient between post-

Table 7.5 Correlations, means and standard deviations for pre-test coursework preparation (1), student's sex (2) and post-test coursework marks (c)

	1 *Preparation*	*2* *Sex*	*c* *Marks*
1 Preparation			
2 Sex	−0.48		
c Marks	0.74	−0.47	
Mean	2.25	1.50	4.85
Standard deviation	1.16	0.51	2.30

test marks and sex is about -0.14 while the unstandardised partial regression coefficient is about -0.63:

$$B_2 = \frac{-0.47 - (0.74 \times -0.48)}{1 - -0.48^2} = \frac{-0.47 - -0.36}{1 - 0.23} = \frac{-0.11}{0.77} = -0.143$$

$$b_2 = \frac{2.30}{0.51} \times -0.14 = -0.631$$

In this case both the standardised and the unstandardised partial regression coefficients for coursework preparation are bigger than those for sex which means that more of the variance in post-test marks is accounted for by coursework preparation than sex.

Note that the standardised partial regression coefficient may be greater than ± 1, when two predictors are highly correlated as in the following example.

$$\frac{0.48 - (0.12 \times 0.87)}{1 - 0.87^2} = \frac{0.48 - 0.10}{1 - 0.76} = \frac{0.38}{0.24} = 1.58$$

We can calculate the intercept constant from the following formula:

$$a = \text{criterion mean} - (b_1 \times \text{predictor}_1 \text{ mean}) + (b_2 \times \text{predictor}_2 \text{ mean})$$

Substituting the appropriate values in the formula gives an intercept constant of about 2.77:

$$4.85 - (1.31 \times 2.25) + (-0.63 \times 1.50) = 4.85 - 2.95 + -0.87 = 2.77$$

The formula for computing the squared multiple correlation is as follows:

$$R^2 = \frac{r^2_{c1} + r^2_{c2} - (2 \times r_{c1} \times r_{c2} \times r_{12})}{1 - r^2_{12}}$$

Placing the appropriate correlations into this formula produces a squared multiple correlation of about 0.57:

$$\frac{0.74^2 + -0.47^2 - (2 \times 0.74 \times -0.47 \times -0.48)}{1 - -0.48^2} =$$

$$\frac{0.55 + 0.22 - 0.33}{1 - 0.23} = \frac{0.44}{0.77} = 0.571$$

The formula for the adjusted squared multiple correlation is:

$$\text{adjusted } R^2 = R^2 - \frac{(1 - R^2) \times \text{no. of predictors}}{\text{no. of cases} - \text{no. of predictors} - 1}$$

Inserting the pertinent values into this formula we see that the adjusted squared multiple correlation for our example is about 0.49:

$$0.57 - \frac{(1 - 0.57^2) \times 2}{20 - 2 - 1} = 0.57 - \frac{(1 - 0.32) \times 2}{17} = 0.57 - \frac{1.36}{17} =$$

$$0.57 - 0.08 = 0.49$$

The multiple correlation is the square root of the squared multiple correlation:

$$R = \sqrt{R^2}$$

Consequently, the multiple correlation for our example is about 0.75 ($\sqrt{0.57} = 0.75$).

The formula for computing the F ratio for testing the significance of the multiple correlation is:

$$F = \frac{R^2 \times (\text{no. of cases} - \text{no. of predictors} - 1)}{(1 - R^2) \times \text{no. of predictors}}$$

The degrees of freedom are the number of predictors for the numerator and the number of cases minus the number of predictors minus 1 for the denominator.

The F ratio for our example is about 11.27:

$$\frac{0.57 \times (20 - 2 - 1)}{(1 - 0.57) \times 2} = \frac{0.57 \times 17}{0.43 \times 2} = \frac{9.69}{0.86} = 11.267$$

Looking up this value in the table in Appendix 3, we see that with 2 and 17 degrees of freedom in the numerator and denominator respectively F has to be 3.5915 or bigger to be significant at the 0.05 level, which it is. Consequently, we would conclude that the multiple correlation between posttest marks and the two predictors of coursework preparation and sex is significant.

Note that the size of the F test depends partly on the number of cases in the numerator. If the number of cases is decreased then the size of the F ratio decreases. For example, with 10 cases F is about 4.60:

$$\frac{0.57 \times (10 - 2 - 1)}{(1 - 0.57) \times 2} = \frac{0.57 \times 7}{0.43 \times 2} = \frac{3.99}{0.86} = 4.60$$

With 2 and 7 degrees of freedom respectively F has to be 4.7374 or larger to be significant at the 0.05 level, which it is not.

The SPSS procedure for running this multiple regression analysis is:

→**Statistics** →**Regression** →**Linear** . . . [opens **Linear Regression** dialog box as in Box 7.3]
→dependent variable [e.g. **markpos**] →▶button beside **Dependent:** box [puts variable in this box] →independent variable [e.g. **markpre**] →▶button beside **Independent[s]:** box [puts variable in this box]

→**Statistics** . . . [opens **Linear Regression: Statistics** dialog box as in Box 7.6]
→**Descriptives** [gives means, standard deviations and correlation matrix]
→**Continue** [closes **Linear Regression: Statistics** dialog box]
→**OK**

The output for this example is displayed in Table 7.6. As we can see, only pre-test coursework preparation significantly predicts post-test marks.

Although the standardised and unstandardised partial regression coefficients provide an index of the contributions made by the predictors, they do not offer an estimate of the amount of variance in the criterion which is accounted for by each of the predictors. One coefficient which does this is the *part* (or *semipartial*) *correlation*. A first-order part correlation can be thought of as a simple correlation between the criterion and first predictor, from the latter of which the effect of the second predictor has been taken out. This is illustrated with the Venn diagram in Figure 7.2 in which sections *b* and *f* represent the variance that is common to both the first and second predictor and which is removed from the first predictor. A first-order part correlation should be distinguished from a first-order partial correlation in which the second predictor has been removed from both the criterion and the first predictor. This is shown in Figure 7.2 where sections *e*, *b* and *f* reflect the variance of the criterion and first predictor that is also shared with the second predictor. The squared part correlation indicates the proportion of variance in the criterion that is uniquely shared with the first predictor having taken into account the variance shared by the first and second predictor. This proportion can be thought of as the ratio of the variance represented by *a* to that represented by *a*, *b*, *c* and *e*. The squared partial correlation, in contrast, is the proportion of variance in the criterion that is shared with the first predictor taking into account the proportion of variance in the criterion that is also shared with the second predictor. This proportion can be conceptualised as the ratio of the variance represented by *a* to that represented by *a* and *c*. The squared first-order part correlation is the absolute increase in the amount of variance in the

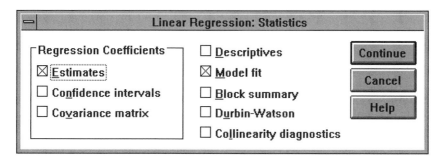

Box 7.6 **Linear Regression: Statistics** dialog box

Table 7.6 SPSS output for post-test marks (**markpos**) regressed on pre-test coursework preparation (**prepre**) and sex (**sex**)

* * * *   M U L T I P L E   R E G R E S S I O N   * * * *

Listwise Deletion of Missing Data

	Mean	Std Dev	Label
MARKPOS	4.850	2.300	post-test marks
SEX	1.500	.513	
PREPRE	2.250	1.164	

N of Cases = 20

Correlation, 1-tailed Sig:

	MARKPOS	SEX	PREPRE
MARKPOS	1.000	-.468	.742
	.	.019	.000
SEX	-.468	1.000	-.485
	.019	.	.015
PREPRE	.742	-.485	1.000
	.000	.015	.

* * * * M U L T I P L E   R E G R E S S I O N * * * *

Equation Number 1   Dependent Variable..   MARKPOS   post-test marks

  Descriptive Statistics are printed on Page   ..

Block Number 1. Method: Enter   SEX   PREPRE

Variable(s) Entered on Step Number
   1..   PREPRE
   2..   SEX

Multiple R	.75222
R Square	.56583
Adjusted R Square	.51476
Standard Error	1.60249

Analysis of Variance

	DF	Sum of Squares	Mean Square
Regression	2	56.89467	28.44734
Residual	17	43.65533	2.56796

F =   11.07779   Signif F =   .0008

Table 7.6 (continued)

- - - - - - - - - - - - - - - - - - Variables in the Equation - - - - - - - - - - - - - - - - - - -

Variable	B	SE B	Beta	T	Sig T
SEX	-.637056	.819341	-.142060	-.778	.4475
PREPRE	1.329949	.361045	.673027	3.684	.0018
(Constant)	2.813198	1.807389		1.556	.1380

End Block Number 1 All requested variables entered.

criterion which is explained by the first predictor taking the second predictor into account. Consequently, the squared part correlation is often used to determine whether adding a further variable to the regression equation provides a significant increase in the overall proportion of explained variance in the criterion.

The formula for the first-order part correlation between the criterion (c) and the first predictor (1) controlling for the second predictor (2) is:

$$r_{c1.2} = \frac{r_{c1} - (r_{c2} \times r_{12})}{\sqrt{1 - r_{12}^2}}$$

We will calculate the first-order part correlation between the criterion of post-test marks and the two predictors of coursework preparation and sex.

Using this formula, we find that the first-order part correlation between post-test marks (c) and coursework preparation (1) controlling for sex (2) is about 0.58:

$$\frac{0.74 - (-0.47 \times -0.48)}{\sqrt{1 - -0.48^2}} = \frac{0.74 - 0.23}{\sqrt{1 - 0.23}} = \frac{0.51}{0.88} = 0.58$$

This first-order part correlation squared is about 0.34 ($0.58^2=0.336$) which means that adding the predictor of coursework preparation to that of sex increases the percentage of variance explained in post-test marks by about 34.

To determine whether the increase in variance explained by the additional variable of coursework preparation is significant we carry out the following F test:

$$F = \frac{\text{squared part correlation}/1}{(1 - R^2)/(\text{no. of cases} - \text{no. of predictors} - 1)}$$

The squared part correlation involves the additional variable in question while the squared multiple correlation (R^2) includes both the additional variable and the others in the regression equation. The degrees of freedom

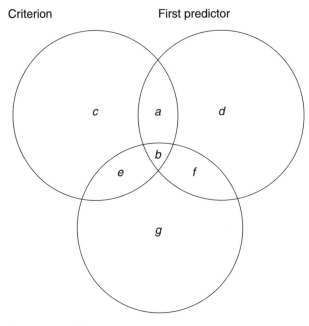

Criterion   First predictor

Second predictor

Squared semipartial correlation = $a/(a+b+c+e)$
Squared partial correlation = $a/(a+c)$

Figure 7.2 Areas representing a semipartial and a partial correlation between the criterion and the first predictor in standard multiple regression

for the numerator is 1 and for the denominator are the number of cases minus the number of predictors minus 1.

The F ratio for adding coursework preparation to the regression equation is about 13.6.

$$\frac{0.34/1}{(1-0.57)/(20-2-1)} = \frac{0.34}{0.43/17} = \frac{0.34}{0.025} = 13.60$$

Turning to the table in Appendix 3, we see that with 1 and 17 degrees of freedom respectively, F has to be 4.4513 or bigger to be significant at the 0.05 level. Consequently, adding coursework preparation to the regression equation makes a significant increase to the proportion of variance already explained. Note, however, that if the number of cases had been decreased to 9, including coursework preparation would not have made a significant contribution to the percentage of variance explained. With 9 cases, F is about 4.86 [$0.34/(0.43/6) = 0.34/0.07 = 4.857$]. With 1 and 6 degrees of freedom respectively F has to be 5.9874 or larger to be significant at the 0.05 level, which it is not.

The first-order part correlation between post-test marks (c) and sex (1) controlling for coursework preparation (2) is about -0.13:

$$\frac{-0.47 - (0.74 \times -0.48)}{\sqrt{1 - -0.48^2}} = \frac{-0.47 - -0.36}{\sqrt{1 - 0.23}} = \frac{-0.11}{0.88} = -0.125$$

This first-order part correlation squared is about 0.02 ($-0.13^2 = 0.017$). In other words, adding sex to coursework preparation increases the percentage of variance explained in post-test marks by about 2.

The F ratio for adding sex to the regression equation is about 0.80:

$$\frac{0.02/1}{(1 - 0.57)/(20 - 2 - 1)} = \frac{0.02}{0.43/17} = \frac{0.02}{0.025} = 0.80$$

With 1 and 17 degrees of freedom respectively, F has to be 4.4513 or bigger to be significant at the 0.05 level, which it is not. Therefore, we could conclude that adding sex to the regression equation does not result in a significant increase in the percentage of variance explained in post-test marks.

To find out with SPSS how much variance coursework preparation adds in addition to the variance explained by sex, we run the following procedure:

→**Statistics** →**Regression** →**Linear** . . . [opens **Linear Regression** dialog box as in Box 7.3]
→dependent variable [e.g. **markpos**] →▶button beside **Dependent:** box [puts variable in this box] →first independent variable [e.g. **sex**] →▶button beside **Independent[s]:** box [puts variable in this box] →**Next** →second independent variable [e.g. **prepre**] →▶button beside **Independent[s]:** box [puts variable in this box] →**OK**

Table 7.7 shows the **R Square** output from this procedure. To calculate the increment in variance explained by coursework preparation we subtract the **R Square** of sex only (**.21929**) from the **R Square** of sex and coursework preparation together (**.56583**) which is about 0.347 (**.56583** − **.21929** = 0.34654) or 35 per cent.

To find out with SPSS how much variance sex explains in addition to the variance accounted for by coursework preparation, we run the following procedure:

→**Statistics** →**Regression** →**Linear** . . . [opens **Linear Regression** dialog box as in Box 7.3]
→dependent variable [e.g. **markpos**] →▶button beside **Dependent:** box [puts variable in this box] →first independent variable [e.g. **prepre**] →▶button beside **Independent[s]:** box [puts variable in this box] →**Next** →second independent variable [e.g. **sex**] →▶button beside **Independent[s]:** box [puts variable in this box] →**OK**

Table 7.7 SPSS output for post-test marks regressed on first student's sex and second coursework preparation showing **R Square** for each step

---

* * * * M U L T I P L E   R E G R E S S I O N * * * *

Listwise Deletion of Missing Data

Equation Number 1   Dependent Variable. .   MARKPOS   post-test marks

Block Number 1.   Method: Enter   SEX

Variable(s) Entered on Step Number
    1. .   SEX

Multiple R	.46829
R Square	.21929
Adjusted R Square	.17592
Standard Error	2.08833

.

.

.

* * * * M U L T I P L E   R E G R E S S I O N * * * *

Equation Number 1   Dependent Variable. .   MARKPOS   post-test marks

Block Number 2.   Method: Enter   PREPRE

Variable(s) Entered on Step Number
    2. .   PREPRE

Multiple R	.75222
R Square	.56583
Adjusted R Square	.51476
Standard Error	1.60249

Table 7.8 shows the **R Square** output from this procedure. To work out the increment in variance explained by sex we subtract the **R Square** of coursework preparation on its own (**.55040**) from the **R Square** of coursework preparation and sex combined (**.56583**) which is about 0.015 (**.56583** − **.55040** = 0.01543) or 1.5 per cent.

SPSS will provide the part correlation (**zpp**) and the increase in variance explained by each variable if the appropriate command is run in the **Syntax** window. The command for running the last procedure, for example, is:

regression variables=markpos sex prepre/sta r cha zpp/dep markpos/enter prepre/enter sex.

Table 7.9 displays the last part of the output for this procedure. Note that the **Part Cor** for **SEX** controlling for **PREPRE** is **-.124256** which squared gives an **R Square Change** of **.01544**. The *F* test for this change (**F Change**) is:

$$\frac{\textbf{R Square Change}/1}{(1 - \textbf{R Square})/(\text{no. of cases} - \text{no. of predictors} - 1)}$$

which works out to be **.60454**:

Table 7.8 SPSS output for post-test marks regressed on first coursework preparation and second sex showing **R Square** for each step

---

* * * * M U L T I P L E   R E G R E S S I O N * * * *

Listwise Deletion of Missing Data

Equation Number 1   Dependent Variable . .   MARKPOS   post-test marks

Block Number 1.   Method: Enter   PREPRE

Variable(s) Entered on Step Number
   1 . .   PREPRE

Multiple R	.74189
R Square	.55040
Adjusted R Square	.52542
Standard Error	1.58478

.

.

.

* * * * M U L T I P L E   R E G R E S S I O N * * * *

Equation Number 1   Dependent Variable . .   MARKPOS   post-test marks

Block Number 2.   Method: Enter   SEX

Variable(s) Entered on Step Number
   2 . .   SEX

Multiple R	.75222
R Square	.56583
Adjusted R Square	.51476
Standard Error	1.60249

Table 7.9 SPSS output for post-test marks regressed on first student's sex and second coursework preparation showing part correlations for second step

* *

Block Number 2.   Method: Enter   SEX

Variable(s) Entered on Step Number

   2 . .   SEX

Multiple R	.75222		
R Square	.56583	R Square Change	.01544
Adjusted R Square	.51476	F Change	.60454
Standard Error	1.60249	Signif F Change	.4475

F =   11.07779   Signif F =   .0008

* * * * M U L T I P L E   R E G R E S S I O N * * * *

Equation Number 1   Dependent Variable . .   MARKPOS   post-test marks

- - - - - Variables in the Equation - - - - -

Variable	Correl	Part Cor	Partial
SEX	-.468288	-.124256	-.185311
PREPRE	.741886	.588677	.666244

End Block Number 2 All requested variables entered.

$$\frac{.01544}{(1 - .56583)/20 - 2 - 1} = \frac{.01544}{0.43417/17} = \frac{.01544}{0.02554} = 0.60454$$

The statistical significance of this F ratio (**Signif F Change**) is **.4475** which is not dissimilar to our figure of 0.80 when rounding error is taken into account.

PROCEDURES FOR SELECTING PREDICTORS

The number of potential regression equations increases with the number of predictors and is a function of 2 to the power of the number of predictors minus 1. With only two predictors the maximum number of regression equations or models that can be tested is three ($2^2 - 1 = 3$): the two predictors on their own and combined. With three predictors seven different equations can be examined ($2^3 - 1 = 7$): three with only one predictor, three with two predictors and one with all three. With four predictors there are fifteen different equations ($2^4 - 1 = 15$). As the number of predictors increases it takes more and more time to investigate and compare the different equations. In order not to have to examine every possible equation, a number of different approaches for selecting and testing predictors have been suggested, including *hierarchical* (or *blockwise*) *selection, forward selection, backward elimination* and *stepwise selection*. The first of these selects predictors on practical or theoretical grounds while the last three involve statistical criteria and are used to choose the smallest set of predictors that might explain most of the variance in the criterion. In contrast to these methods, entering all predictors into the equation is known as *standard* multiple regression while comparing all possible sets of predictors is called *setwise* regression. The method(s) used should mirror the purpose of the analysis.

In hierarchical selection predictors are entered singly or in blocks according to some rationale. For example, potentially confounding variables such as socio-demographic factors may be entered first in order to control for their effects. Or similar variables may be grouped together (such as attitudes) and entered as a block. Hierarchical regression was demonstrated previously when estimating the increase in variation explained by the two variables of pre-test coursework preparation and student's sex. To give another example, we would use the following procedure if we wanted to enter both pre-test course interest (**intpre**) and sex (**sex**) first:

→**Statistics** →**Regression** →**Linear** . . . [opens **Linear Regression** dialog box as in Box 7.3]
→dependent variable [e.g. **markpos**] →▶ button beside **Dependent:** box [puts variable in this box] →first block [e.g. **sex intpre**] →▶ button beside **Independent[s]:** box [puts block in this box] →**Next** →second block [e.g. **sex intpre prepre**] →button beside **Independent[s]:** box [puts block in this box] →**OK**

Subtracting the R Square of the first step from that of the second step shows how much variation coursework preparation explains when course interest and student's sex are controlled. Note that if the order of variables in each block is important then the order used in previous blocks must be specified in the current block by listing all the variables as has been done here.

In forward selection the predictor with the smallest probability of the *F* ratio is considered first for entry into the regression equation. This predictor is entered into the equation if the previously specified probability is larger. In SPSS this probability is set at 0.05 by default but can be changed. If the previously specified probability is not larger, this variable is not entered and the analysis ends. If this value is larger, then this predictor is entered and the analysis continues. The next predictor considered for entry is that with the next smallest *p*. If it meets the statistical criterion, it will be entered into the regression equation and the predictor with the next smallest *p* will be evaluated. The selection stops when no other predictor satisfies the entry criterion. Once a predictor has been entered into the equation it remains there even though it may no longer make a significant contribution to the amount of variance explained. The following procedure can be used to run a forward analysis

→**Statistics** →**Regression** →**Linear** . . . [opens **Linear Regression** dialog box as in Box 7.3]
→dependent variable [e.g. **markpos**] →▶ button beside **Dependent:** box [puts variable in this box] →independent variables [e.g. **sex intpre prepre**] →▶ button beside **Independent[s]:** box [puts variables in this box] →box beside **Method:** →**Forward** →**Options** . . . [opens **Linear Regression: Options** dialog box as in Box 7.7]
→box beside **Entry:** and change value if necessary →**Continue** →**OK**

In backward elimination all the predictors are initially entered into the regression equation. The predictor with the largest probability of the *F* ratio is examined first. If it is larger than the previously specified *p* value for removing predictors (which is set by default at 0.10 in SPSS), it is excluded from the regression equation and the predictor with the next largest *p* value

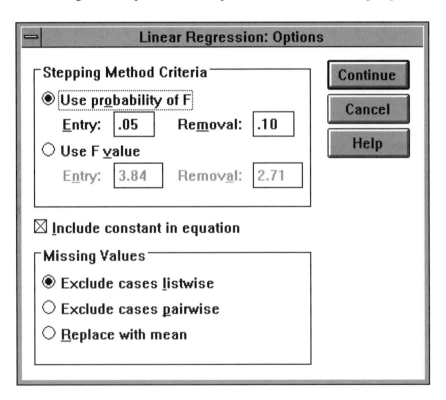

Box 7.7 **Linear Regression: Options** dialog box

is considered. No predictor can ever reenter the model. The analysis stops when no further predictors satisfy this criterion. The following procedure can be used to run a backward analysis

→**Statistics** →**Regression** →**Linear . . .** [opens **Linear Regression** dialog box as in Box 7.3]
→dependent variable [e.g. **markpos**] → ▶ button beside **Dependent:** box [puts variable in this box] →independent variables [e.g. **sex intpre prepre**] → ▶ button beside **Independent[s]:** box [puts variables in this box] →box beside **Method:** →**Backward** →**Options . . .** [opens **Linear Regression: Options** dialog box as in Box 7.7]
→box beside **Removal:** and change value if necessary →**Continue** →**OK**

Stepwise selection is a combination of forward selection and backward elimination. The predictor which has the smallest p for the F ratio is entered first if the previously specified p value for entering predictors is met. If the predictor does not meet this criterion, the analysis stops. If it meets the criterion, it is entered into the equation. The first predictor is then examined to see whether it satisfies the criterion to stay in the regression equation. If it does not, it is removed and the analysis ceases. If it does, the second predictor which has the next smallest p value is chosen and the process is repeated. If this second predictor is entered, both predictors are then considered for removal. The procedure stops when no more variables are entered into or removed from the regression equation. Note that these three different selection methods may give different results with the same data so it may be worthwhile comparing the results of the three methods. Stepwise is probably the most commonly used method of the three.

We will illustrate stepwise regression with the three predictors of student's sex, pre-test course interest and pre-test coursework preparation. The following procedure can be used to run this analysis:

→**Statistics** →**Regression** →**Linear . . .** [opens **Linear Regression** dialog box as in Box 7.3]
→dependent variable [e.g. **markpos**] → ▶ button beside **Dependent:** box [puts variable in this box] →independent variables [e.g. **sex intpre prepre**] → ▶ button beside **Independent[s]:** box [puts variables in this box] →box beside **Method:** →**Stepwise** →**OK**

Table 7.10 presents the output for this procedure. Pre-test course interest (**intpre**) is the predictor that explains the highest percentage of the variance in post-test marks (**.61266** $\times$ 100 = 61.27) followed by sex (**sex**) which accounts for a further 13.25 per cent (**.74516** − **.61266** = 0.1325). Altogether these two predictors account for 74.52 (**.61266** + 0.1325 = **.74516**) per cent of the variance in post-test marks.

As shown in Table 6.11, post-test marks are strongly correlated with both pre-test course interest (0.78) and coursework preparation (0.74). If we apply the T_2 test described in Chapter 6, we see there is no significant

Table 7.10 SPSS output showing stepwise multiple regression output of post-test marks (**markpos**) regressed on course interest (**intpre**) and sex (**sex**)

* * * *   M U L T I P L E   R E G R E S S I O N   * * * *

Listwise Deletion of Missing Data

Equation Number 1   Dependent Variable . .   MARKPOS   post-test marks

Block Number 1. Method: Stepwise   Criteria   PIN   .0500   POUT   .1000
    SEX   PREPRE   INTPRE

Variable(s) Entered on Step Number
    1 . .   INTPRE pre-test course interest

Multiple R	.78272
R Square	.61266
Adjusted R Square	.59114
Standard Error	1.47097

Analysis of Variance

	DF	Sum of Squares	Mean Square
Regression	1	61.60263	61.60263
Residual	18	38.94737	2.16374

F =   28.47041   Signif F = .0000

- - - - - - - - - - - - - - - - - Variables in the Equation - - - - - - - - - - - - - - - - - -

Variable	B	SE B	Beta	T	Sig T
INTPRE	1.610526	.301836	.782724	5.336	.0000
(Constant)	.421053	.892843		.472	.6429

- - - - - - - - - - - - - - Variables not in the Equation - - - - - - - - - - - - - - -

Variable	Beta In	Partial	Min Toler	T	Sig T
SEX	-.367510	-.584881	.981053	-2.973	.0085
PREPRE	.360689	.391090	.455391	1.752	.0978

* * * *   M U L T I P L E   R E G R E S S I O N   * * * *

Equation Number 1   Dependent Variable . .   MARKPOS   post-test marks

Variable(s) Entered on Step Number
    2 . .   SEX

Table 7.10 (continued)

Multiple R	.86323
R Square	.74516
Adjusted R Square	.71518
Standard Error	1.22772

Analysis of Variance

	DF	Sum of Squares	Mean Square
Regression	2	74.92597	37.46298
Residual	17	25.62403	1.50730

F = 24.85443   Signif F = .0000

- - - - - - - - - - - - - - - - - Variables in the Equation - - - - - - - - - - - - - - - - -

Variable	B	SE B	Beta	T	Sig T
SEX	-1.648069	.554330	-.367510	-2.973	.0085
INTPRE	1.506438	.254344	.732136	5.923	.0000
(Constant)	3.179399	1.189992		2.672	.0161

- - - - - - - - - - - - - - Variables not in the Equation - - - - - - - - - - - - - -

Variable	Beta In	Partial	Min Toler	T	Sig T
PREPRE	.076688	.084001	.305763	.337	.7404

End Block Number 1 PIN = .050 Limits reached.

difference in the size of these correlations ($T_2 = 0$). Course interest is entered first because it has the slightly higher correlation. As course interest and coursework preparation are strongly correlated (0.74), coursework preparation is not entered into the regression equation because it does not explain any more of the variance in the post-test marks than that already accounted for by course interest. Note that suppressor variables which are entered later into the equation may explain a larger proportion of the variance than earlier variables (Cramer 1997).

BIVARIATE REGRESSION AND ONE-WAY ANALYSIS OF VARIANCE WITH TWO GROUPS

Regression analysis can be used to carry out analysis of variance. As we shall see in Chapter 9 this is neccessary in analysis of variance designs which have more than one independent variable and where the cell sizes are unequal. It may be initially more instructive to show how regression analysis can be applied to simpler analysis of variance designs such as a one-way design. We will show how bivariate regression can be employed to perform a one-way analysis of variance comparing pre-test marks between the individual and the group tutorial conditions in women. This analysis of variance was previously worked out in Chapter 4 and the analysis of variance table is presented in Table 4.21.

First, we have to calculate the regression coefficient and intercept for the relationship between the two conditions and the pre-test marks. The computations for the regression coefficient are shown in Table 7.11. The regression coefficient is -3.0. The intercept is 11.0 [3.13 $-$ $(-3.0 \times 2.63) = 3.13 - -7.89 = 11.02$]. With only two groups as the predictor, the point that lies closes to all the values in a group is its mean and so the regression line simply connects the means of the two groups as shown in Box 7.8. In other words, the predicted criterion score for a condition will be its mean.

Then, we have to work out the regression and residual sum of squares as presented in Table 7.12. The regression sum of squares is simply the sum of squared deviations of the mean criterion score from the predicted criterion score. This is the same as the between-groups sum of squares which is the sum of squared deviations of the group mean from the grand mean for the two conditions. The residual sum of squares is the sum of the squared deviations of the predicted criterion score from the original criterion score. This is the same as the within-groups sum of squares which is the sum of squared deviations of the group mean from the individual scores for that group for the two groups. In other words, the regression sum of squares is the same as the between-groups sum of squares and the residual sum of squares is the same as the within-groups sum of squares. We derive the regression and residual mean square by dividing their sums of squares by their respective degrees of freedom and obtain the F ratio by dividing the regression mean square by the residual mean square. These steps are portrayed in the analysis of variance table in Table 7.13. If we compare the values in this table with those in the analysis of variance table in Table 4.21, we see that the results are the same.

MULTIPLE REGRESSION AND ONE-WAY ANALYSIS OF VARIANCE WITH THREE GROUPS

While the regression equation for performing a one-way analysis of variance with only two groups consists of only one predictor, that for performing a one-way analysis of variance with three groups contains two predictors. The first predictor defines the first and third group while the second predictor defines the second and third group. The groups are defined through *effect coding* with a 1, 0 or -1. For the first predictor, the

Table 7.11 Data and computations for the regression coefficient between two conditions (*A*) and pre-test marks (*B*) for women in the individual and group tutorial conditions

	A	B	D_A	$D_A{}^2$	D_B	D_{AB}
	2	5	−0.63	0.40	1.87	−1.18
	2	3	−0.63	0.40	−0.13	0.08
	2	7	−0.63	0.40	3.87	−2.44
	3	1	0.37	0.14	−2.13	−0.79
	3	1	0.37	0.14	−2.13	−0.79
	3	2	0.37	0.14	−1.13	−0.42
	3	3	0.37	0.14	−0.13	−0.05
	3	3	0.37	0.14	−0.13	−0.05
Sum	21	25		1.90		−5.64
N	8	8				
Mean	2.63	3.13				

Note: $b = \dfrac{-5.64}{1.90} = -2.968 = -3.0$

Table 7.12 Regression and residual sum of squares for the pre-test marks in women regressed on the two tutorial conditions

	Pre-test marks					
	Actual	Predicted	Reg	Reg^2	Resid	Resid^2
	5	11 + (−3 × 2) = 5	1.87	3.50	5 − 5 = 0	0
	3	11 + (−3 × 2) = 5	1.87	3.50	3 − 5 = −2	4
	7	11 + (−3 × 2) = 5	1.87	3.50	7 − 5 = 2	4
	1	11 + (−3 × 3) = 2	−1.13	1.28	1 − 2 = −1	1
	1	11 + (−3 × 3) = 2	−1.13	1.28	1 − 2 = −1	1
	2	11 + (−3 × 3) = 2	−1.13	1.28	2 − 2 = 0	0
	3	11 + (−3 × 3) = 2	−1.13	1.28	3 − 2 = 1	1
	3	11 + (−3 × 3) = 2	−1.13	1.28	3 − 2 = 1	1
Sum	25			16.90		12.00
N	8					
Mean	3.13					

Table 7.13 Analysis of variance table for the pre-test marks in women regressed on the two tutorial conditions

Sources of variation	SS	df	MS	F	p
Regression	16.90	1	16.90	8.45	<.05
Residual	12.00	6	2.00		
Total	28.90	7			

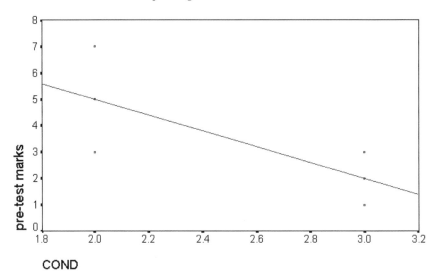

Box 7.8 SPSS output of a scattergram with a regression line between pre-test marks and the two tutorial conditions

first group is identified with 1, the second group by 0 and the third group by −1. For the second predictor the first group is identified by 0, the second group by 1 and the third group by −1. Effect coding is shown in Table 7.14 for pre-test marks in women for the three conditions. Note that a third predictor for defining the first and second group is not necessary since this predictor can be derived by subtracting the codes of the second predictor from those of the first predictor as indicated in Table 7.14. The number of predictors needed to define conditions is always one less than the total number of conditions. These predictors are known as *dummy* variables.

We will show how multiple regression can be used to compute a one-way analysis of variance with three groups, comparing pre-test marks for women across the three conditions. This analysis of variance was previously worked out in Chapter 5 and the analysis of variance table is displayed in Table 5.6.

First, we compute the correlations, means and standard deviations for the two dummy variables and pre-test marks for women which are presented in Table 7.15.

Second, we work out the two partial regression coefficients and the intercept as shown in Table 7.16.

Third, we derive the regression and residual sum of squares as depicted in Table 7.17.

And finally, we calculate the F ratio as produced in Table 7.18. The values in this table are the same as those in Table 5.6.

Table 7.14 Effect coding for pre-test marks in women regressed on three conditions

Condition	Pre-test marks	First predictor (D1)	Second predictor (D2)	Difference (D1 − D2)
1	3	1	0	1
1	1	1	0	1
2	5	0	1	−1
2	3	0	1	−1
2	7	0	1	−1
3	1	−1	−1	0
3	1	−1	−1	0
3	2	−1	−1	0
3	3	−1	−1	0
3	3	−1	−1	0

Table 7.15 Correlations, means and standard deviations for pre-test marks (c) and the two dummy variables, Dummy1 (1) and Dummy2 (2)

	1 Dummy1	*2* Dummy2	*c* Marks
1 Dummy1			
2 Dummy2	0.65		
c Marks	0.19	0.68	
Mean	−0.30	−0.20	2.90
Standard deviation	0.82	0.92	1.91

Table 7.16 Computations for the two partial regression coefficients and the intercept for pre-test marks in women and the two dummy variables

$$B_1 = \frac{0.19 - (0.68 \times 0.65)}{1 - 0.65^2} = \frac{0.19 - 0.44}{1 - 0.42} = \frac{-0.25}{0.58} = -0.431$$

$$b_1 = \frac{1.91}{0.82} \times -0.43 = -1.002 = -1.0$$

$$B_2 = \frac{0.68 - (0.19 \times 0.65)}{1 - 0.65^2} = \frac{0.68 - 0.12}{1 - 0.42} = \frac{0.56}{0.58} = 0.966$$

$$b_2 = \frac{1.91}{0.92} \times 0.966 = 2.006 = 2.0$$

$$a = 2.90 - (-1.0 \times -0.30) + (2.0 \times -0.20) = 2.90 - (0.30 + -0.40) = 3.0$$

Table 7.17 Regression and residual sum of squares for the pre-test marks in women regressed on the three tutorial conditions

	Pre-test marks		Reg	Reg²	Resid			Resid²
	Actual	Predicted						
	3	3 + (−1 × 1) + (2 × 0) = 2	−0.9	0.81	3 − 2 =	1		1
	1	3 + (−1 × 1) + (2 × 0) = 2	−0.9	0.81	1 − 2 =	−1		1
	5	3 + (−1 × 0) + (2 × 1) = 5	2.1	4.41	5 − 5 =	0		0
	3	3 + (−1 × 0) + (2 × 1) = 5	2.1	4.41	3 − 5 =	−2		4
	7	3 + (−1 × 0) + (2 × 1) = 5	2.1	4.41	7 − 5 =	2		4
	1	3 + (−1 × −1) + (2 × −1) = 2	−0.9	0.81	1 − 2 =	−1		1
	1	3 + (−1 × −1) + (2 × −1) = 2	−0.9	0.81	1 − 2 =	−1		1
	2	3 + (−1 × −1) + (2 × −1) = 2	−0.9	0.81	2 − 2 =	0		0
	3	3 + (−1 × −1) + (2 × −1) = 2	−0.9	0.81	3 − 2 =	1		1
	3	3 + (−1 × −1) + (2 × −1) = 2	−0.9	0.81	3 − 2 =	1		1
Sum	29			18.90				14.00
N	10							
Mean	2.9							

Table 7.18 Analysis of variance table for the pre-test marks in women regressed on the three tutorial conditions

Sources of variation	SS	df	MS	F	p
Regression	18.90	2	9.45	4.73	ns
Residual	14.00	7	2.00		
Total	32.90	9			

SUMMARY

The computation of bivariate regression and multiple regression with two predictors is described. One use of regression analysis is to estimate the likely score of a criterion from one or more predictors. Another use is to determine the minimum number of predictors needed to explain the maximum variance in the criterion. The regression coefficient (b) is the straight line lying closest to the points on the scatterplot. It provides a good index of the association between two variables when the assumptions of normality, linearity and homoscedasticity are met, which can be visually checked through a scatterplot of the residuals with the predicted values. The accuracy of prediction is given by the standard error of estimate. The proportion of variance in the criterion accounted for by the linear combination of predictors is assessed by the squared multiple correlation (R^2), the statistical significance of which is tested by the F ratio. A more conservative estimate of explained variance which takes account of the size of the sample and the number of predictors is the adjusted squared multiple correlation. Multiple regression uses partial regression coefficients. The squared part correlation is the absolute increase in the amount of variance in the criterion explained by the predictors and is often used to determine whether adding a further variable to the regression equation significantly increases the overall proportion of variance explained. With a large number of potential predictors, various procedures may be used to select those predictors which maximise the explained variation. Regression analysis can be used to compute analysis of variance. The F ratio is the regression mean square divided by the residual mean square.

EXERCISES

Use the data in Table 5.12 for the following exercises.

1 Conduct a bivariate regression with educational interest at 15 as the criterion and educational interest at 12 as the predictor.
(a) What is the unstandardised regression coefficient?
(b) What is the standardised regression coefficient?
(c) What is the intercept constant?
(d) What is the predicted value of educational interest at 15 if the value of educational interest at 12 is 2?
(e) What is the standard error of estimate?
(f) What is the standard error of the regression coefficient?
(g) What is the standard error of the intercept?
(h) What is the squared multiple correlation?
(i) What is the adjusted squared multiple correlation?
(j) What is the F ratio of the squared multiple correlation?
(k) What are its degrees of freedom?
(l) What is its probability value?
2 Carry out a multivariate regression with educational interest at 15 as the criterion and educational interest at 12 and at 9 as the predictors.
(a) What is the standardised partial regression coefficient between educational interest at 15 and at 12?
(b) What is the unstandardised partial regression coefficient between educational interest at 15 and at 12?
(c) What is the standardised partial regression coefficient between educational interest at 15 and at 9?
(d) What is the unstandardised partial regression coefficient between educational interest at 15 and at 9?
(e) What is the squared multiple correlation?
(f) What is the adjusted squared multiple correlation?
(g) What is the F ratio of the squared multiple correlation?
(h) What are its degrees of freedom?
(i) What is its probability value?
(j) What is the part correlation between educational interest at 15 and educational interest at 12 controlling for educational interest at 9?
(k) What is the F ratio for adding educational interest at 12 to the regression equation?
(l) What are its degrees of freedom?

(m) What is its probability value?
(n) What is the part correlation between educational interest at 15 and educational interest at 9 controlling for educational interest at 12?
(o) What is the F ratio for adding educational interest at 9 to the regression equation?
(p) What are its degrees of freedom?
(q) What is its probability value?

8 Tests of difference for interval/ratio data on related samples for one factor

The statistical tests described in this chapter ascertain whether the means of two or more related samples differ. For example, we may wish to know whether coursework marks are higher after attending tutorials compared with before attending any tutorials and whether any increase in marks is maintained later on at follow-up.

t TEST FOR TWO RELATED SAMPLES

The *t* test for related samples determines if the means of two such samples differ. The formula can be represented by the difference between the two sample means divided by the standard error of the difference in means.

$$t = \frac{\text{mean of one sample} - \text{mean of other sample}}{\text{standard error of the difference in means}}$$

The means of related samples are less likely to differ than the means of unrelated samples because the scores come from the same or similar cases. Consequently, the *t* test for related samples takes into account the extent to which the scores of the two samples are correlated by modifying the way the standard error of the difference in means is computed. This standard error can be calculated with the following formula:

$$\text{standard error of the difference in means} = \sqrt{\frac{\text{variance}_1 + \text{variance}_2 - (2 \times \text{covariance}_{1.2})}{N}}$$

where N is the total number of pairs of cases. The covariance is defined as the mean cross product of two sets of deviation scores and is calculated by: (1) subtracting each of a pair of scores from their respective means; (2) multiplying the deviations together; (3) summing the product for all pairs of scores; and (4) dividing this sum by the number of pairs of cases. If the two sets of scores were perfectly related the standard error of the difference in means is zero since twice the covariance is the same as the sum of the two variances. If, at the other extreme, the two sets of scores were totally unrelated, the covariance is zero.

To illustrate the computation of the *t* test for related samples, we will compare the pre-test with the post-test coursework marks for the women in the individual tutorial condition. The individual scores for these women are shown in Table 8.1 together with the results of the computational procedure needed to calculate the variance and covariance of pre-test and post-test coursework marks. To calculate a *t* test for related samples, carry out the following steps:

Step 1 Calculate the variance for each of the samples by subtracting each score from the mean score for that sample, squaring these differences, adding the squared differences together and dividing this total by the number of scores minus 1.

When this is done, we obtain a variance of 4.0 for pre-test marks and 1.0 for post-test marks.

Step 2 Compute the covariance for the two samples by subtracting each score from the mean score for that sample, multiplying this difference with the difference from the corresponding score, summing the products for all pairs of scores and dividing this sum by the number of cases minus 1. Ignore the sign of the covariance.

The covariance for these scores is 1.0.

Step 3 Work out the standard error of the difference in means by multiplying the covariance by 2, subtracting this product from the sum of the variances, dividing this result by the number of cases and taking the square root of this value.

The standard error of the difference in means for our example is 1.0:

$$\sqrt{\frac{4.0 + 1.0 - (2 \times 1.0)}{3}} = \sqrt{\frac{5.0 - 2.0}{3}} = \sqrt{\frac{3.0}{3}} = \sqrt{1.0} = 1.00$$

Table 8.1 Pre- and post-test coursework marks for women in the individual tutorial condition with initial computations

	Pre-test			Post-test			Pre-test × Post-test Difference
	Original	*Difference*	*Squared*	*Original*	*Difference*	*Squared*	*Difference*
	5	0	0	7	−1	1	0
	3	−2	4	8	0	0	0
	7	2	4	9	1	1	2
Sum	15		8	24		2	2
N	3			3			
Mean	5			8			
df			2			2	2
Variance			4.0			1.0	
Covariance							1.0

Step 4 Subtract one sample mean from the other and divide by the standard error of the difference in the mean to give the *t* value.

In this case, *t* is 3.0:

$$\frac{8.0 - 5.0}{1.0} = \frac{3.0}{1.0} = 3.00$$

Step 5 Look up the *t* value in the table in Appendix 4 where the degrees of freedom are the number of cases minus 1.

For *t* to be significant at the 0.05 one-tailed level with 2 degrees of freedom it has to be 2.920 or bigger, which it is. Consequently, we would conclude that coursework marks in the individual tutorial condition is significantly higher at post-test than at pre-test.

A simpler procedure for calculating *t* uses the following formula which is mathematically the same as the previous one:

$$t = \frac{\text{difference between sample means}}{\sqrt{\dfrac{\text{sum of } D^2 - \dfrac{(\text{sum of } D)^2}{N}}{N \times (N - 1)}}}$$

where *D* stands for the difference between pairs of scores and *N* refers to the number of pairs of scores. It is also more accurate since it involves less rounding error.

The pairs of scores for our example are shown in Table 8.2 together with the difference between these pairs (*D*) and the square of this difference (*D²*).

Substituting the appropriate values in the computational formula gives a *t* of 3.0:

$$\frac{8.0 - 5.0}{\sqrt{\dfrac{33 - \dfrac{(-9)^2}{3}}{3 \times (3 - 1)}}} = \frac{3.0}{\sqrt{\dfrac{33 - 27}{6}}} = \frac{3.0}{\sqrt{\dfrac{6}{6}}} = \frac{3.0}{\sqrt{1.0}} = \frac{3.0}{1.0} = 3.00$$

If the scores in the two samples are not correlated, the related *t*-test is less sensitive than the unrelated *t*-test as the degrees of freedom for the related *t*-test are half those for the unrelated *t*-test where the conditions have the same number of cases. For example, with three scores in the two conditions the degrees of freedom are 2 for the related *t*-test (3 − 1 = 2) and 4 for the unrelated *t*-test [(3 − 1) + (3 − 1) = 4]. The lower the degrees of freedom the larger the *t* value has to be for it to be significant, which in this case is 4.303 for the related *t*-test compared with 2.776 for the unrelated *t*-test at the 0.05 two-tailed level.

Table 8.2 Pre- and post-test coursework marks with their differences and squared differences

	Pre-test	Post-test	D	D^2
	5	7	−2	4
	3	8	−5	25
	7	9	−2	4
Sum	15	24	−9	33
N	3	3		
Mean	5	8		

To carry out a related *t* test with SPSS comparing pre- with post-test coursework marks in women in the individual tutorial condition, we first select the women in this condition (**sex = 1 & cond = 2**) and then we carry out the following procedure:

> →**Statistics** →**Compare Means** →**Paired-Samples T Test** ... [opens **Paired-Samples T Test** dialog box as in Box 5.1]
> →first variable [e.g. **markpre**] [puts variable beside **Variable 1:** in **Current Selections** section] →second variable [e.g. **markpos**] [puts variable beside **Variable 2:** in **Current Selections** section] →▶ button [puts these variables under **Paired Variables:**] →**OK**

Table 8.3 shows the output from this procedure. To obtain the one-tailed *p* value we divide the **2-tail Sig** *p* value of **.095** by 2 to give 0.0475 which is significant at the 0.05 one-tailed level.

t TEST FOR TWO RELATED VARIANCES

To determine whether the variances of two related samples are significantly different from one another, we use the following formula (McNemar 1969):

$$t = \frac{(\text{larger variance} - \text{smaller variance}) \times \sqrt{(\text{number of cases} - 2)}}{\sqrt{\begin{array}{c}(1 - \text{correlation of 2 sets of} \\ \text{scores squared})\end{array} \times \begin{array}{c}(4 \times \text{larger variance} \times \\ \text{smaller variance})\end{array}}}$$

To compare the variances of the pre- and post-test coursework marks of women in the individual tutorial condition, we would first have to work out Pearson's product moment correlation (*r*) which is described in Chapter 6 and which can be computed with the following formula:

$$r = \frac{\text{sum of products of pre- and post-test scores}}{\sqrt{\text{pre-test sum of squares} \times \text{post-test sum of squares}}}$$

The correlation between the pre- and post-test marks is 0.5 ($2/\sqrt{8 \times 2} = 2/4 = 0.5$).

Table 8.3 SPSS output of a related *t* test comparing the difference between pre- and post-test coursework marks in women in the individual tutorial condition

t-tests for Paired Samples

Variable		Number of pairs	Corr	2-tail Sig	Mean	SD	SE of Mean
MARKPOS	post-test marks				8.0000	1.000	.577
		3	.500	.667			
MARKPRE	pre-test marks				5.0000	2.000	1.155

Paired Differences				t-value	df	2–tail Sig
Mean	SD	SE of Mean				
3.0000	1.732	1.000		3.00	2	.095

95% CI (−1.303, 7.303)

Substituting the appropriate values in the above equation, we find that *t* is 0.87.

$$\frac{(4.0 - 1.0) \times \sqrt{3 - 2}}{\sqrt{(1 - 0.5^2) \times (4 \times 4.0 \times 1.0)}} = \frac{3 \times \sqrt{1}}{\sqrt{(1 - 0.25) \times 16}} = \frac{3 \times 1.0}{\sqrt{0.75 \times 16}} =$$

$$\frac{3}{3.46} = 0.867$$

We look up the significance of this value in the table in Appendix 4 where the degrees of freedom are the number of cases minus 1. At the 0.05 two-tailed level *t* would have to be 4.303 or bigger to be statistically significant, which it is not. Consequently, we would conclude that the variances do not differ significantly. This procedure is not available on SPSS.

SINGLE FACTOR REPEATED MEASURES

Analysis of variance also determines whether the means of two or more related samples differ. Since measures from the same or similar cases are taken more than once, this analysis is often known as a *repeated measures* analysis. In this analysis the total variation in the scores consists of three sources of variation: (1) the variation within the conditions of the factor being investigated called the *within-factor* or *between-treatments* variation; (2) the variation between cases usually called the *between-subjects* variation; and (3) the residual variation. The between-subjects and residual variation constitute the *within-treatments* or *within-subjects* variation. The sources of variation for a single factor repeated measures analysis of variance are shown in Table 8.4 together with their associated degrees of freedom. The *F* ratio for determining whether the two or more means differ is the mean square for the factor or treatments divided by the residual mean square. Note that in an independent measures analysis of variance the within-treatments mean square acts as the error term. In a repeated measures analysis of variance, however, subjects act as their own controls. Consequently, in this analysis the variance due to subjects is removed from the within-treatments variance to form the error term which will, as a result, be smaller than that in an independent measures analysis of variance when there is individual variation.

The procedure for calculating a single factor repeated measures analysis of variance will be illustrated by comparing the pre-test, post-test and follow-up coursework marks for the women in the individual tutorial condition. Their individual scores are shown in Table 8.5. The total and mean score are presented in the last two columns of the table while the total and mean score for the three occasions are displayed in the last two rows. The overall total and mean score (grand mean) are in the bottom right hand corner of the table. Means have been calculated to two decimal places.

Table 8.4 Sources of variation and degrees of freedom in a single factor repeated measures analysis

Sources of variation	Degrees of freedom
Between-treatments/within-factor	No. of conditions − 1
Within-treatments/within-subjects	No. of cases × (no. of conditions − 1)
Between-subjects	No. of cases − 1
Residual	(No. of cases − 1) × (no. of conditions − 1)
Total	(No. of cases × no. of conditions) − 1

Table 8.5 Pre-test, post-test and follow-up individual, total and mean coursework marks in women in the individual tutorial condition

	Pre-test	*Post-test*	*Follow-up*	*Sum*	*Mean*
	5	7	7	19	6.33
	3	8	5	16	5.33
	7	9	9	25	8.33
Sum	15	24	21	60	
N	3	3	3		
Mean	5	8	7		6.67

Step 1 Work out the between-treatments sum of squares by subtracting the grand mean from the mean score for each of the conditions, squaring the difference, multiplying the squared difference by the number of cases and summing the products.

between-treatments sum of squares = sum of [(condition mean − grand mean)^2 × no. of cases] for all conditions

The between-treatments sum of squares for our example is 14.01:

$$[(5.00-6.67)^2 \times 3] + [(8.00-6.67)^2 \times 3] + [(7.00-6.67)^2 \times 3] =$$
$$(-1.67^2 \times 3) + (1.33^2 \times 3) + (0.33^2 \times 3) =$$
$$(2.79 \times 3) + (1.77 \times 3) + (0.11 \times 3) = 8.37 + 5.31 + 0.33 =$$
$$14.01$$

Step 2 Calculate the between-treatments degrees of freedom which are the number of conditions minus 1. For this example they are 2 (3 − 1 = 2).

Step 3 Compute the between-treatments mean square which is the between-treatments sum of squares divided by its degrees of freedom. In this instance it is 7.01 (14.01/2 = 7.01).

Step 4 Calculate the between-subjects sum of squares by subtracting the grand mean from the mean score for each subject, squaring the difference, multiplying the squared difference by the number of conditions and adding the products.

between-subjects sum of squares = sum of [(subject mean − grand mean)^2 × no. of conditions] for all subjects

The between-subjects sum of squares for our example is 14.04:

$$[(6.33-6.67)^2 \times 3] + [(5.33-6.67)^2 \times 3] + [(8.33-6.67)^2 \times 3] =$$
$$(-0.34^2 \times 3) + (-1.34^2 \times 3) + (1.66^2 \times 3) =$$
$$(0.12 \times 3) + (1.80 \times 3) + (2.76 \times 3) =$$
$$0.36 + 5.40 + 8.28 = 14.04$$

Step 5 Derive the within-treatments sum of squares by subtracting the condition mean from the subject score for that condition for each condition, and then squaring and summing the results.

within-treatments sum of squares = sum of (subject score − condition mean)^2 for all conditions

The within-treatments sum of squares for our example is 18.

$$(5-5)^2 + (3-5)^2 + (7-5)^2 + (7-8)^2 + (8-8)^2 + (9-8)^2 + (7-7)^2 +$$
$$(5-7)^2 + (9-7)^2 =$$
$$0^2 + -2^2 + 2^2 + -1^2 + 0^2 + -1^2 + 0^2 + -2^2 + 2^2 =$$
$$0 + 4 + 4 + 1 + 0 + 1 + 0 + 4 + 4 = 18$$

Step 6   Calculate the residual sum of squares by subtracting the between-subjects sum of squares from the within-treatments sum of squares.

residual sum of squares = within-treatments sum of squares − between-subjects sum of squares

The residual sum of squares for our example is 3.96 (18 − 14.04 = 3.96).

Step 7   Work out the residual degrees of freedom which are the number of cases minus 1 multiplied by the number of conditions minus 1. For our example the residual degrees of freedom are 4 [(3 − 1) × (3 − 1) = 2 × 2 = 4].

Step 8   Compute the residual mean square which is the residual sum of squares divided by its degrees of freedom. In this case, the residual mean square is 0.99 (3.96/4 = 0.99).

Step 9   The *F* ratio is the between-treatments mean square divided by the residual mean square. For our example the *F* ratio is 7.08 (7.01/0.99 = 7.081).

We look up the significance of this *F* ratio in the table in Appendix 3. We see that with 2 degrees of freedom in the numerator and 4 degrees of freedom in the denominator, *F* has to be 6.9443 or larger to be significant at the 0.05 level, which it is. Consequently, we would conclude that there is a significant difference in coursework marks across the three tests.

Finally, to calculate the total sum of squares, we subtract the grand mean from each score, square them and add them together.

If we do this for our example, the total sum of squares is 32.01:

$$(5 - 6.67)^2 + (3 - 6.67)^2 + (7 - 6.67)^2 +$$
$$(7 - 6.67)^2 + (8 - 6.67)^2 + (9 - 6.67)^2 +$$
$$(7 - 6.67)^2 + (5 - 6.67)^2 + (9 - 6.67)^2 =$$
$$-1.67^2 + -3.67^2 + 0.33^2 + 0.33^2 + 1.33^2 + 2.33^2 + 0.33^2 +$$
$$-1.67^2 + 2.33^2 =$$
$$2.79 + 13.47 + 0.11 + 0.11 + 1.77 + 5.43 + 0.11 +$$
$$2.79 + 5.43 = 32.01$$

The results of these steps are presented in Table 8.6 which shows the sums of squares, the degrees of freedom, the mean squares and the *F* ratio. Note that the total sum of squares is the sum of the between- and the within-treatments sum of squares.

As was the case for the one-way analysis of variance test, the *F* test only tells us whether there is a significant difference between the three related scores but does not inform us where this difference lies. To determine which pair of means differ significantly, we need to carry out some supplementary analyses. If we had predicted a difference between two scores, we determine if this prediction was confirmed by conducting a

Table 8.6 Single factor repeated measures analysis of variance table comparing pre-test, post-test and follow-up coursework marks in women in the individual tutorial condition

Sources of variation	SS	df	MS	F	p
Between-treatments	14.01	2	7.01	7.01	<.05
Within-treatments	18.00	6			
Between-subjects	14.04	2			
Residual	3.96	4	0.99		
Total	32.01	8			

related *t* test as described above. If we had not predicted a difference, then Maxwell (1980) recommends the Bonferroni inequality test. The Bonferroni test is based on the related *t* test but modifies the significance level to take account of the fact that more than one comparison is being made (Fisher 1935). To calculate this, work out the total number of possible comparisons between any two groups, divide the chosen significance level (which is usually 0.05) by this number, and treat the result as the appropriate significance level for comparing more than three groups. In the case of three groups, the total number of possible comparisons is 3 which means the appropriate significance level is 0.017 (0.05/3 = 0.0167).

To determine whether the variances of three or more related groups are different, Rosenthal and Rosnow (1991) recommend an extension of Levene's test. In this test a new score is created which is the absolute difference between the original score and the mean score for the group. The absolute deviation scores for pre-test, post-test and follow-up coursework marks for women in the individual tutorial condition are shown in Table 8.7.

We then perform a single factor repeated measures analysis of variance on these absolute deviation scores. The total and mean scores for the rows

Table 8.7 Original and absolute difference score for pre-test, post-test and follow-up coursework marks in women in the individual tutorial condition

	Pre-test		Post-test		Follow-up	
	Original	Absolute difference	Original	Absolute difference	Original	Absolute difference
	5	0	7	1	7	0
	3	2	8	0	5	2
	7	2	9	1	9	2
Sum	15		24		21	
N	3		3		3	
Mean	5		8		7	

Table 8.8 Pre-test, post-test and follow-up individual, total and mean absolute deviation coursework marks in women in the individual tutorial condition

	Pre-test	Post-test	Follow-up	Sum	Mean
	0	1	0	1	0.33
	2	0	2	4	1.33
	2	1	2	5	1.67
Sum	4	2	4	10	
N	3	3	3		
Mean	1.33	0.67	1.33		1.11

and columns are displayed in Table 8.8 together with the grand total and mean.

We calculate the F ratio with following steps.

Step 1 The between-treatments sum of squares for our example is 0.87:

$[(1.33-1.11)^2 \times 3] + [(0.67-1.11)^2 \times 3] + [(1.33-1.11)^2 \times 3] =$
$(0.22^2 \times 3) + (-0.44^2 \times 3) + (0.22^2 \times 3) =$
$(0.05 \times 3) + (0.19 \times 3) + (0.05 \times 3) =$
$0.15 + 0.57 + 0.15 = 0.87$

Step 2 The between-treatments degrees of freedom are 2 (3 − 1 = 2).

Step 3 The between-treatments mean square is 0.44 (0.87/2 = 0.435).

Step 4 The between-subjects sum of squares is 2.91:

$[(0.33-1.11)^2 \times 3] + [(1.33-1.11)^2 \times 3] + [(1.67-1.11)^2 \times 3] =$
$(-0.78^2 \times 3) + (0.22^2 \times 3) + (0.56^2 \times 3) =$
$(0.61 \times 3) + (0.05 \times 3) + (0.31 \times 3) =$
$1.83 + 0.15 + 0.93 = 2.91$

Step 5 The within-treatments sum of squares is 6.01.

$(0-1.33)^2 + (2-1.33)^2 + (2-1.33)^2 + (1-0.67)^2 + (0-0.67)^2 +$
$(1-0.67)^2 + (0-1.33)^2 + (2-1.33)^2 + (2-1.33)^2 =$
$-1.33^2 + 0.67^2 + 0.67^2 + 0.33^2 + -0.67^2 + 0.33^2 + -1.33^2 + 0.67^2$
$+ 0.67^2 =$
$1.77 + 0.45 + 0.45 + 0.11 + 0.45 + 0.11 + 1.77 + 0.45 + 0.45 =$
6.01

Step 6 The residual sum of squares is 3.10 (6.01 − 2.91 = 3.10).

Step 7 The residual degrees of freedom are 4 [(3 − 1) x (3 − 1) = 2 x 2 = 4].

Step 8 The residual mean square is 0.78 (3.10/4 = 0.775).

Step 9   The F ratio is 0.56 (0.44/0.78 = 0.564).

We look up the significance of this F ratio in the table in Appendix 3. We see that with 2 degrees of freedom in the numerator and 4 degrees of freedom in the denominator, F has to be 6.9443 or larger to be significant at the 0.05 level, which it is not. Consequently, we would conclude that there is no significant difference in the variance of the coursework marks across the three tests.

The results of these steps are presented in Table 8.9 which shows the sums of squares, the degrees of freedom, the mean squares and the F ratio.

Once again, note that if there is no between-subjects effect, any between-treatment effect is less likely to be significant in a related than an unrelated one-way analysis of variance when the number of cases are the same in each condition. This is because the error term in the related analysis will then be the same as that in the unrelated analysis while the degrees of freedom will be smaller in the related than in the unrelated analysis. For instance, with three scores in each of three conditions, the degrees of freedom for a related one-way analysis of variance are 4 [(3 − 1) × (3 − 1) = 4] compared with 6 [(3 −1) + (3 −1) + (3 − 1) = 6] in an unrelated one-way analysis of variance. The lower the degrees of freedom for the error term, the higher F has to be to be significant. So in this case with 2 degrees of freedom in the numerator, F has to be 6.9443 with 4 degrees of freedom in the denominator and 5.1433 with 6 degrees of freedom in the denominator to be significant at the 0.05 level.

To conduct a single factor repeated measures analysis of variance with SPSS comparing coursework marks in women in the individual tutorial condition across the three occasions, we first select the women in this group (**sex=1 & cond=2**) and then perform the following sequence:

→**Statistics** →**ANOVA Models** →**Repeated Measures** ... [opens **Repeated Measures Define Factor(s)** dialog box as in Box 8.1]
→type repeated measures name [e.g. **time**] in **Within-Subject Factor Name** box →**Number of Levels:** box and type number of levels [e.g. **3**]
→**Add** →**Define** [opens **Repeated Measures ANOVA** dialog box as in Box 8.2]

Table 8.9 Single factor repeated measures analysis of variance table comparing pre-test, post-test and follow-up absolute deviation coursework marks in women in the individual tutorial condition

Sources of variation	SS	df	MS	F	p
Between-treatments	0.87	2	0.44	0.56	*ns*
Within-treatments	6.01				
Between-subjects	2.91				
Residual	3.10	4	0.78		
Total	6.88				

→first variable [e.g. **markpre**] → ▶ button [puts variable under **Within-Subjects Variables [time]:**] →second variable [e.g. **markpos**] → ▶ button →third variable [e.g. **markfol**] → ▶ button
→**OK**

Table 8.10 displays the relevant output from this procedure which shows the factor (**TIME**) and residual (**WITHIN+RESIDUAL**) sum of squares (**SS**), degrees of freedom (**DF**), mean squares (**MS**), *F* ratio (**F**) and probability level (**Sig of F**).

ANALYSIS OF VARIANCE AND THE *t* TEST

It is worth noting that a single factor repeated measures analysis of variance for two conditions gives the same results as a related *t* test since *F* is equal to t^2 (Fisher 1924/1950). This analysis for comparing pre- and post-test marks in women for the individual tutorial condition would give an *F* ratio of 9 which is equivalent to the *t* value of 3 ($\sqrt{9} = 3$) calculated earlier in this chapter.

REGRESSION ANALYSIS AND SINGLE FACTOR REPEATED MEASURES ANALYSIS OF VARIANCE

Regression analysis can also be used to perform a single factor repeated measures analysis of variance. We will illustrate this with the three coursework marks for women in the individual tutorial condition. As with the one-way analysis of variance in Chapter 7, the regression equation has two

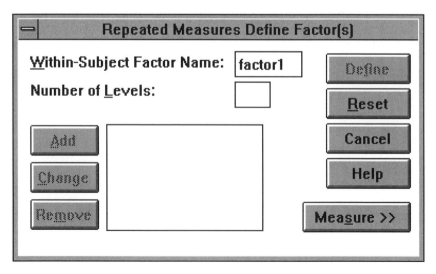

Box 8.1 **Repeated Measures Define Factor(s)** dialog box

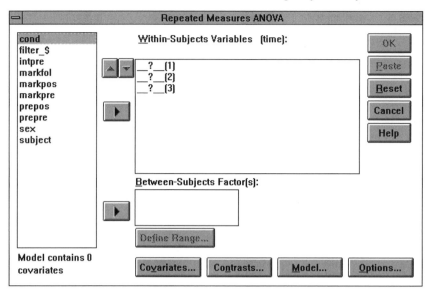

Box 8.2 **Repeated Measures ANOVA** dialog box

Table 8.10 SPSS output for the single factor repeated measures analysis of variance comparing coursework marks in women in the individual tutorial condition across the three occasions

* * * * * * A n a l y s i s   o f   V a r i a n c e   –   design 1   * * * * * *

EFFECT .. TIME

Tests involving 'TIME' Within-Subject Effect.

AVERAGED Tests of Significance for MEAS.1 using UNIQUE sums of squares

Source of Variation	SS	DF	MS	F	Sig of F
WITHIN+RESIDUAL	4.00	4	1.00		
TIME	14.00	2	7.00	7.00	.049

predictors to identify the three conditions or the between-treatments effect. In addition it has one less than the number of subjects to describe the subjects or the between-subjects effect. As there are only three cases there are only two predictors, giving four in all. Table 8.11 shows the effect coding for this example.

To obtain the between-treatments sum of squares, we regress the marks on the two condition dummy variables. Table 8.12 shows the analysis of

Table 8.11 Effect coding for marks in women regressed on three occasions and three subjects

| Marks | Occasions | | Subjects | |
	D1	D2	D3	D4
5	1	0	1	0
3	1	0	0	1
7	1	0	−1	−1
7	0	1	1	0
8	0	1	0	1
9	0	1	−1	−1
5	−1	−1	1	0
7	−1	−1	0	1
9	−1	−1	−1	−1

Table 8.12 SPSS output of the analysis of variance table for marks in women regressed on the two condition dummy variables

Analysis of Variance

	DF	Sum of Squares	Mean Square
Regression	4	14.00000	7.00000
Residual	4	18.00000	3.00000

F =   2.33333   Signif F =   .1780

variance table for this analysis. The between-treatments sum of squares is **14.00000**.

To find the residual sum of squares, regress the marks on all four dummy variables. Table 8.13 presents the output for this analysis. The residual sum of squares is **4.00000**. To calculate F we divide the between-treatment mean square (**7.00000**) by the residual mean square (**1.00000**) to give **7.00000** ($7.00000/1.00000 = 7.00000$).

SUMMARY

The computation of parametric tests for assessing whether the means of interval or ratio data from two or more related samples differ significantly across the samples is described. The related t test compares the difference between the means of two related samples taking into account the extent to which the scores of the two samples are correlated by modifying the way the standard error of the difference in means is computed. Single factor

Table 8.13 SPSS output of the analysis of variance table for marks in women regressed on all four dummy variables

Analysis of Variance

	DF	Sum of Squares	Mean Square
Regression	4	28.00000	7.00000
Residual	4	4.00000	1.00000

F = 7.00000   Signif F = .0430

repeated measures analysis of variance determines whether the means of three or more related samples differ. Differences between pairs of groups are examined with the related *t* test where differences were predicted and the Bonferroni test where differences were not predicted. Regression analysis can be used to perform a single factor repeated analysis of variance with dummy variables specifying the between-treatments and between-subjects effects.

EXERCISES

The data for these exercises are available in Table 5.12.

1 Use the related *t* test to compare educational interest at 12 and 15 for pupils from mixed-sex schools.
   (a) What is the value of the *t* test?
   (b) What are its degrees of freedom?
   (c) What is its two-tailed probability level?
   (d) Is educational interest significantly greater at 15 than at 12 for pupils from mixed-sex schools?
2 Use a single factor repeated measures analysis of variance to compare educational interest at 9, 12 and 15 for pupils from mixed-sex schools.
   (a) What is the value of the *F* test?
   (b) What are its degrees of freedom?
   (c) What is its probability level?
   (d) Does educational interest at 9, 12 and 15 differ significantly for pupils from mixed-sex schools?

9 Tests of difference for interval/ratio data on unrelated samples for two factors

This chapter will look at the analysis of variance of two factors and their interaction. Two-way analysis of variance compares the means of groups made up of two variables or *factors*. The two factors in our example are sex and treatment. With two categories or *levels* of sex and three of treatment (no tutorial, individual tutorial and group tutorial), we have what is known as a *2 × 3* analysis of variance. If we just had two levels of treatment (e.g. no tutorial and group tutorial), we would have a *2 × 2* analysis of variance. The variable being compared is often called the *dependent* variable because it is usually assumed that the values of this variable *depend* on, or are affected by, the factors being investigated. As a consequence, the factors being investigated are frequently referred to as *independent* variables since in the design they are not thought to be affected by the dependent variable. Furthermore, their statistical association with the dependent variable is called an *effect*.

There are two main advantages of analysing two factors at a time. The first is that it enables us to determine whether the two factors affect each other or *interact*. An interaction is when the effect of one variable is not the same under all conditions of the other variable. An example of an interaction would be if pre-test marks in the individual tutorial condition were higher for women than for men while in the group tutorial condition there was no difference between women and men. Interactions are often more readily grasped when they are portrayed in the form of a graph. This example is shown in Figure 9.1. The vertical axis represents the mean pre-test marks while the horizontal axis can depict either of the other two variables. In this case it is used to show the two conditions. The effects of the other variable are indicated by points on the graph and lines joining them. Women are represented by a circle and a broken line and men by a cross and a continuous line.

An interaction is likely when the lines representing the variable are not parallel. Another example of an interaction is illustrated in Figure 9.2 where pre-test marks are higher for women in both treatments but the difference between women and men is greater in the group tutorial treatment.

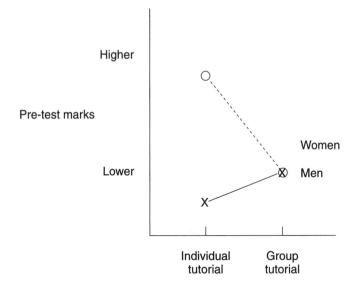

Figure 9.1 An example of an interaction

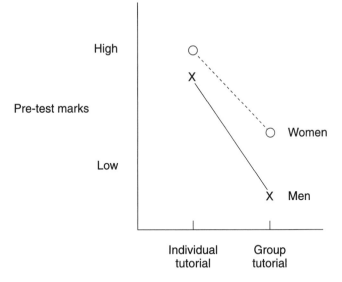

Figure 9.2 Another example of an interaction

The absence of an interaction is likely when the lines representing the second independent variable are more or less parallel as shown in Figures 9.3 and 9.4. In Figure 9.3 women have higher marks than men in both treatments but the two conditions do not differ from one another. In Figure 9.4 women also have higher marks than men but the marks for the two

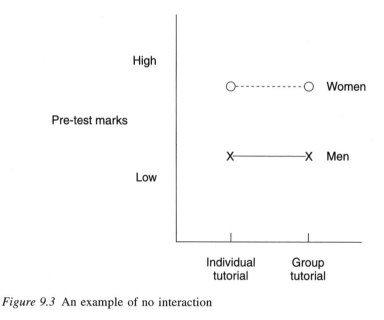

Figure 9.3 An example of no interaction

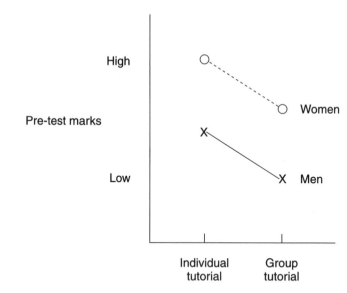

Figure 9.4 Another example of no interaction

conditions differ with the individual tutorial condition having the higher marks. Although interactions are more easily conveyed graphically, whether an interaction actually exists needs to be determined statistically and not graphically.

The second advantage of a two-way over a one-way analysis of variance is that it provides a more sensitive or powerful test of the effect of either factor than evaluating them singly, provided that the two factors do not interact substantially. The variance of the dependent variable is made up of variance attributed to the independent variable (explained variance) and variance that is unaccounted for (error or residual variance). When two variables are being analysed separately, the residual error is likely to be greater than when the two variables are being examined together since part of the residual error may be due to the other variable and to their interaction. Since the *F* ratio is derived by dividing the explained variance by the error variance, the *F* ratio is likely to be smaller and hence less likely to be significant when variables are analysed separately.

In a two-way analysis of variance there are four sources of variance as shown in Table 9.1: (1) the between-groups variance of the first factor; (2) the between-groups variance of the second factor; (3) the between-groups variance of the interaction of the two factors; and (4) the within-groups variance. Consequently, three main *F* ratios have to be calculated which respectively compare the variance of the first and second factor and their interaction with the within-groups variance.

In many factorial designs the number of cases in cells is unequal. These designs are sometimes called *unbalanced* or *non-orthogonal*. Their analysis is more problematical in that there are three different ways of analysing or partitioning the variance. These three procedures are (1) the *regression* or *unweighted means* approach, (2) the *classic experimental* or *least squares* approach and (3) the *hierarchical* approach. All three methods produce the same result when there are equal numbers of participants in cells. For a two-way design the three approaches only differ in the way they handle main effects so the results for the interaction effect are the same. The residual and the total sum of squares are also the same for all three approaches. Where the main effects are not independent the component sums of squares do not add up to the total sum of squares. The classic experimental and the hierarchical approach produce the same result if the cell frequencies are proportional with respect to their marginal distributions since the main effects are unrelated.

A design with proportional cell frequencies is shown in Table 9.2. The

Table 9.1 A two-way analysis of variance table

Source of variance	SS	df	MS	F	p
Between-groups					
First main effect					
Second main effect					
Two-way interaction					
Within-groups/Residual					
Total					

ratio of the row frequencies is 1:2:3 and that of the column frequencies is 1:2. Proportionality of cell frequencies generally holds when the frequency of a cell is equal to the product of its row and column frequencies divided by the total frequency. This is the case for all six cells in this example. For instance, the frequency of the cell in the first row of the first column is 5 which is the same as $15 \times 30/90$.

When numbers are unequal we could equalise them by randomly omitting cases from conditions. However, this procedure wastes valuable data and so is not recommended. Consequently, one of these three methods has to be selected as the preferred method since the results they give may differ. The regression approach assigns equal weight to the means in all cells regardless of their size. In other words, interaction effects have the same importance as main ones. This approach is recommended for a true experimental design where cases have been randomly assigned to treatments. The classic experimental approach places greater weight on cells with larger numbers of cases and is recommended for non-experimental designs in which the number of cases in each cell may reflect its importance. This approach gives greater weight to main effects than to interaction ones. The hierarchical approach allows the investigator to determine the order of the effects. If one factor is thought to precede another, then it can be placed first. This approach should be used in non-experimental designs where the factors can be ordered in some sequential manner. If, for example, we are interested in the effect on pre-tests marks of student's sex and course interest, then sex may be entered first since course interest cannot determine sex.

Since multiple regression is used to carry out these three procedures we can describe the differences between them in terms of multiple regression. The regression approach is like standard multiple regression with each main effect and interaction assessed after being adjusted for all other main effects, interactions and covariates. In the classic experimental approach the main effects are only adjusted for each other and for the covariates, while interactions are adjusted for the same and lower order interactions, for main effects and for covariates. In the hierarchical approach, each effect is entered sequentially taking account of the effects previously entered. These procedures are described in more detail later on in this chapter. Examples of the kinds of regression equations used in these three approaches are shown in Table 9.9.

Table 9.2 A 2 × 3 design with proportional cell frequencies

	B1	B2	B3	Row totals
A1	5	10	15	30
A2	10	20	30	60
Column totals	15	30	45	90

It may be helpful to visualise the differences between the three approaches in handling a two-way non-orthogonal design in terms of the Venn diagram in Figure 9.5 where the three circles represent the variation for the two main effects of *A* and *B* and their interaction *AB*. The overlap between the circles indicates the extent to which they are related or non-orthogonal. The variation for the interaction *AB* is the same for all three approaches and is signified by the section *g*. The variation for the main effect *A* is depicted by the section *a* in the regression approach, the sections *a* and *d* in the classic experimental approach and the sections *a*, *b*, *d* and *e* in the hierarchical approach where *A* is entered first. The variation for the main effect *B* is reflected in the section *c* for the regression approach and the sections *c* and *f* for both the classic experimental approach and the hierarchical approach where *B* is entered second.

We begin by working through the calculation of a two-way analysis of variance with equal cell frequencies. We then show how the same analysis can be conducted with multiple regression. Finally we apply multiple

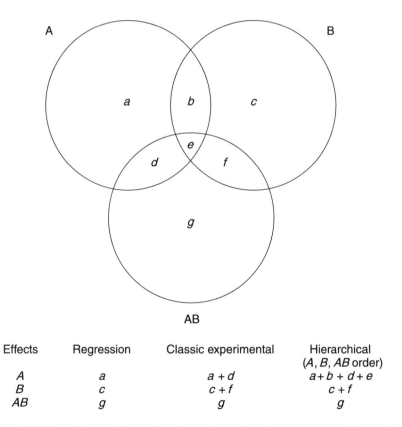

Effects	Regression	Classic experimental	Hierarchical (*A, B, AB* order)
A	*a*	*a + d*	*a + b + d + e*
B	*c*	*c + f*	*c + f*
AB	*g*	*g*	*g*

Figure 9.5 Venn diagram illustrating the variance in a two-way non-orthogonal design accounted for by the three approaches

regression to a two-way analysis of variance with unequal cell frequencies. To simplify matters a little, we illustrate the computation of a two-way analysis of variance with the post-test marks from only two of the three treatment conditions, namely the individual and group tutorial conditions. The individual scores together with the group sums and means (rounded to two decimal places) are presented in Table 9.3. The scores for the first and last case in the group tutorial condition for women have been omitted to equalise cell sizes for this analysis. In addition, the sum and mean for women and men (across treatments) is shown as the row sum and mean while the sum and mean for the two treatments (ignoring sex) is presented as the column sum and mean, together with the grand sum and mean.

Step 1   To compute the between-groups sum of squares for the first factor: (1) calculate the mean of each group of this factor (ignoring the other factor); (2) subtract the grand mean from the group mean of this factor; (3) square this difference; (4) multiply this squared difference by the number of cases within that group; and (5) sum these products for all the groups of that factor.

The sum of squares for the sex factor is 6.72:

$$[(6.5 - 5.75)^2 \times 6] + [(5 - 5.75)^2 \times 6] = (0.75^2 \times 6) + (-0.75^2 \times 6) =$$
$$(0.56 \times 6) + (0.56 \times 6) = 3.36 + 3.36 = 6.72$$

Table 9.3 Post-test marks of women and men in the individual and group tutorial conditions with initial computations

Sex	Tutorial condition			Row sum and mean
	Individual	Group		
Women	7	4		
	8	5		
	9	6		
Sum	24	15		39
N	3	3		6
Mean	8	5		6.5
Men	2	5		
	5	5		
	5	8		
Sum	12	18		30
N	3	3		6
Mean	4	6		5
Column sum	36	33	Grand sum	69
Column N	6	6	Grand N	12
Column mean	6	5.5	Grand mean	5.75

Step 2 Repeat the same procedure for the second factor except use the group means of the second factor (ignoring the first factor).

The sum of squares for the tutorial factor is 0.72:

$$[(6 - 5.75)^2 \times 6] + [(5.5 - 5.75)^2 \times 6] = (0.25^2 \times 6) + (-0.25^2 \times 6) =$$
$$(0.06 \times 6) + (0.06 \times 6) = 0.36 + 0.36 = 0.72$$

Step 3 To compute the between-groups sum of squares for the interaction we calculate the overall between-groups sum of squares and subtract from it the sum of squares for the first and second factor.

between-groups interaction sum of squares = overall between-groups sum of squares − first factor between-groups sum of squares − second factor between-groups sum of squares

The overall between-groups sum of squares is calculated using the means of the groups formed by the two factors. We subtract the grand mean from the mean of each of these groups, square this difference, multiply this squared difference by the number of cases within that group and sum these products for all the groups.

overall between-groups sum of squares = sum of [(first group mean − grand mean)^2 × no. of cases in first group)] for each group

In this example, there are four such groups so the overall between-groups sum of squares is 26.22:

$$[(8 - 5.75)^2 \times 3] + [(5 - 5.75)^2 \times 3] +$$
$$[(4 - 5.75)^2 \times 3] + [(6 - 5.75)^2 \times 3] =$$
$$(2.25^2 \times 3) + (-0.75^2 \times 3) + (-1.75^2 \times 3) + (0.25^2 \times 3) =$$
$$(5.06 \times 3) + (0.56 \times 3) + (3.06 \times 3) + (0.06 \times 3) =$$
$$15.18 + 1.68 + 9.18 + 0.18 = 26.22$$

Subtracting the sum of squares for the two factors from the overall between-groups sum of squares gives the sum of squares for the interaction which is 18.78:

$$26.22 - 6.72 - 0.72 = 18.78$$

Step 4 Calculate the within-groups or residual sum of squares by adding together the sum of squares for each group. The within-groups sum of squares is 16:

$$(7 - 8)^2 + (8 - 8)^2 + (9 - 8)^2 + (4 - 5)^2 + (5 - 5)^2 + (6 - 5)^2 +$$
$$(2 - 4)^2 + (5 - 4)^2 + (5 - 4)^2 + (5 - 6)^2 + (5 - 6)^2 + (8 - 6)^2 =$$
$$(-1)^2 + 0^2 + 1^2 + (-1)^2 + 0^2 + 1^2 + (-2)^2 + 1^2 + 1^2 + (-1)^2 + (-1)^2 + 2^2 =$$
$$1 + 0 + 1 + 1 + 0 + 1 + 4 + 1 + 1 + 1 + 1 + 4 = 16$$

Note that to complete the two-way analysis of variance table the total sum of squares can be obtained by subtracting the grand mean from each score, squaring the differences, and adding the squared differences together.

The total sum of squares for our example is 42.22:

$$(7 - 5.75)^2 + (8 - 5.75)^2 + (9 - 5.75)^2 + (4 - 5.75)^2 +$$
$$(5 - 5.75)^2 + (6 - 5.75)^2 + (2 - 5.75)^2 + (5 - 5.75)^2 +$$
$$(5 - 5.75)^2 + (5 - 5.75)^2 + (5 - 5.75)^2 + (8 - 5.75)^2 =$$
$$1.25^2 + 2.25^2 + 3.25^2 + -1.75^2 + -0.75^2 + 0.25^2 +$$
$$-3.75^2 + -0.75^2 + -0.75^2 + -0.75^2 + -0.75^2 + 2.25^2 =$$
$$1.56 + 5.06 + 10.56 + 3.06 + 0.56 + 0.06 + 14.06 +$$
$$0.56 + 0.56 + 0.56 + 0.56 + 5.06 = 42.22$$

Step 5   Calculate the residual mean square by dividing the residual sum of squares by its degrees of freedom. To compute the residual degrees of freedom subtract 1 from the number of cases in each group and sum the results across all the groups.

The residual mean square for our example is 2.0:

$$\frac{16}{(3 - 1) + (3 - 1) + (3 - 1) + (3 - 1)} = \frac{16}{2 + 2 + 2 + 2} = \frac{16}{8} = 2.0$$

Step 6   To derive the mean square for the first factor or main effect, divide the sum of squares for this factor by its degrees of freedom, which are the number of groups making up this factor minus 1.

The mean square for the sex factor is 6.72:

$$\frac{6.72}{2 - 1} = \frac{6.72}{1} = 6.72$$

Step 7   To calculate the *F* ratio for the first main effect, divide its mean square by the residual mean square.

The *F* ratio for the sex effect is 3.36:

$$\frac{6.72}{2.0} = 3.36$$

Look up the statistical significance of this *F* ratio in the table in Appendix 3. With 1 degree of freedom in the numerator and 8 degrees in the denominator, the *F* ratio has to be 5.3177 or larger to be statistically significant at the 0.05 level, which it is not. Consequently, we would conclude that post-test marks did not differ significantly between women and men.

Step 8   Repeat this procedure for working out the mean square and *F* ratio for the second main effect.

The mean square for the tutorial effect is 0.72:

$$\frac{0.72}{2-1} = \frac{0.72}{1} = 0.72$$

The F ratio for the tutorial effect is 0.36:

$$\frac{0.72}{2.0} = 0.36$$

Since this F ratio is also smaller than 5.3177, we would conclude that post-test marks did not differ significantly between the individual and the group tutorial conditions. If there were more than two conditions in this factor, we would use tests such as the unrelated t or Scheffé to determine which if any pair of conditions differed significantly.

Step 9   Repeat this procedure for calculating the mean square and F ratio for the interaction effect. The degrees of freedom for the interaction effect are calculated by subtracting 1 from the number of groups in each factor and multiplying the resulting values.

The mean square for the interaction effect is 18.78:

$$\frac{18.78}{(2-1) \times (2-1)} = \frac{18.78}{1} = 18.78$$

The F ratio for the interaction effect is 9.39:

$$\frac{18.78}{2.0} = 9.39$$

Since this F ratio is larger than 5.3177, we would conclude that there was a significant interaction between the tutorial conditions and sex on post-test marks. The results of this two-way analysis of variance are presented in Table 9.4.

If we had predicted an interaction effect, we could use the unrelated t tests to determine whether our predictions were confirmed. If, on the other hand, we had not anticipated an interaction effect, we could use a *post hoc* test such as the Scheffé test.

Table 9.4 A two-way analysis of variance table for post-test marks for women and men in the individual and group tutorial conditions (two cases dropped)

Source of variance	SS	df	MS	F	p
Between-groups					
Sex main effect	6.72	1	6.72	3.36	*ns*
Tutorial main effect	0.72	1	0.72	0.36	*ns*
Tutorial × sex interaction	18.78	1	18.78	9.39	<.05
Within-groups/Residual	16.00	8	2.0		
Total	42.22	11			

The formula for computing the Scheffé test for a two-way analysis of variance is modified by multiplying the degrees of freedom for the first factor by those for the second:

$$\sqrt{\frac{\text{within-groups}}{\text{mean square}} \times (\text{no. of groups in factor } A - 1) \times (\text{no. of groups in factor } B - 1) \times F \times \left(\frac{1}{n_1} + \frac{1}{n_2}\right)}$$

where n_1 and n_2 is the number of cases in the two groups being compared and where F refers to the desired probability level (e.g. 0.05). The appropriate degrees of freedom for F in the numerator are the product of the number of groups in the first factor (A) minus 1 times the number of groups in the second factor (B) minus 1, and in the denominator the total number of cases minus the product of the number of groups in the first and second factor.

With four groups, as in our example, we would have to make six comparisons:

1 Women in the individual tutorial group vs Women in the group tutorial group
2 Men in the individual tutorial group vs Men in the group tutorial group
3 Women in the individual tutorial group vs Men in the individual tutorial group
4 Women in the group tutorial group vs Men in the group tutorial group
5 Women in the individual tutorial group vs Men in the group tutorial group
6 Men in the individual tutorial group vs Women in the group tutorial group

We will illustrate the computation of this Scheffé test with the third comparison where the absolute difference between the two group means is 4 ($8 - 4 = 4$). The 0.05 F ratio with 1 degree of freedom in the numerator [$(2 - 1) \times (2 - 1) = 1$] and 8 in the denominator [$12 - (2 \times 2) = 8$] is 5.3177. Substituting the appropriate values in the formula for the Scheffé test, this difference would have to exceed 2.66 to be statistically significant, which it does:

$$\sqrt{2.0 \times (2 - 1) \times (2 - 1) \times 5.3177 \times (1/3 + 1/3)} =$$

$$\sqrt{2.0 \times 1 \times 1 \times 5.3177 \times 0.667} = \sqrt{7.09} = 2.66$$

Thus, women have higher post-test marks than men in the individual tutorial condition.

The proportion of variance in the dependent variable that is explained by the independent variables can be described by a statistic called *eta squared*. Eta squared is defined as the ratio of the between-groups sum of squares to the total sum of squares:

$$\text{eta squared} = \frac{\text{between-groups sum of squares}}{\text{total sum of squares}}$$

To calculate the amount of variance explained by the sex factor we divide the between-groups sum of squares for this factor by the total sum of squares which gives 0.159:

$$\frac{6.72}{42.22} = 0.1592$$

In this instance, 15.9 per cent of the variance in post-test marks is explained by the sex factor. To work out the proportion of variance explained by two factors, we would add together the two eta squared values. Since eta squared for the tutorial condition is 0.0171 (0.72/42.22 = 0.0171), the percentage of variance explained by both the sex and tutorial conditions is 17.6 (15.9 + 1.7 = 17.6).

To conduct this analysis with SPSS, delete the values for the first and last case in the group tutorial condition for women and then carry out the following procedure:

→**Statistics** →**ANOVA Models** →**Simple Factorial** . . . [opens **Simple Factorial ANOVA** dialog box as in Box 9.1]
→dependent variable [e.g. **markpos**] →▶button beside **Dependent:** [puts variable in this box] →first independent variable [e.g. **sex**] →▶button beside **Factor(s):** [puts variable in this box] →**Define Range** . . . [opens **Simple Factorial ANOVA: Define Range** dialog box as in Box 9.2]
→in box beside **Minimum:** type lower code value [e.g. **1**] →box beside **Maximum:** and type upper code value [e.g. **2**] →**Continue** [closes **Simple Factorial ANOVA: Define Range** dialog box]
→second independent variable [e.g. **cond**] →▶button beside **Factor(s):** [puts variable in this box] →**Define Range** . . . [opens **Simple Factorial ANOVA: Define Range** dialog box]
→in box beside **Minimum:** type lower code value [e.g. **2** for individual tutorial group] →box beside **Maximum:** and type upper code value [e.g. **3**] →**Continue** [closes **Simple Factorial ANOVA: Define Range** dialog box]
→**Options** . . . [opens **Simple Factorial ANOVA: Options** dialog box as in Box 9.3]
→**Hierarchical** or **Experimental** [in **Method** section] [for statistics in **Statistics** section] →**Means and counts** [in **Statistics** section] →**MCA** [in **Statistics** section] →**Continue** [closes **Simple Factorial ANOVA: Options** dialog box]
→**OK**

Table 9.5 shows the group means and numbers of cases on which they are based. Table 9.6 displays the analysis of variance table for this two-way design. The small differences between the manual calculations and the SPSS output are due to rounding differences.

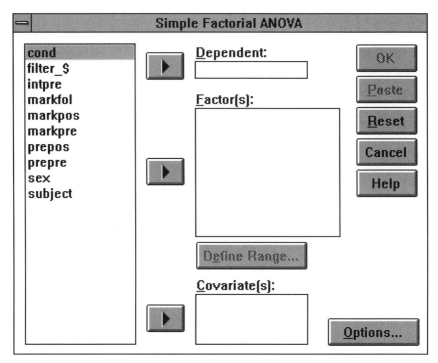

Box 9.1 **Simple Factorial ANOVA** dialog box

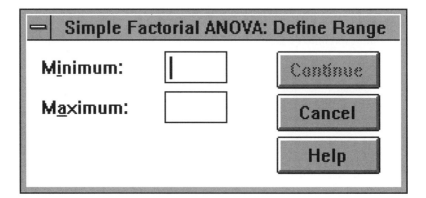

Box 9.2 **Simple Factorial ANOVA: Define Range** dialog box

Table 9.7 presents the multiple classification analysis. The grand mean, the categories of the two factors and the number of cases in those categories are presented. The column labelled **Unadjusted Dev'n** shows the amount of deviation of the mean of that group from the grand mean. For example, the mean of the women as shown in Table 9.5 is 6.5. Subtracting the grand mean (**5.75**) from this value gives **0.75** (6.5 − **5.75** = **0.75**). Since

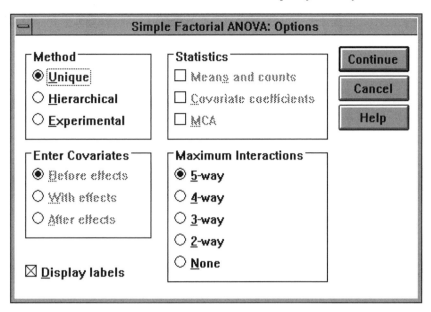

Box 9.3 **Simple Factorial ANOVA: Options** dialog box

eta squared is the between-groups sum of squares for that factor divided by the total sum of squares, eta is the square root of eta squared. As displayed in Table 9.6 the between-groups sum of squares for the sex factor is **6.750** while the total sum of squares is **42.250**. Consequently, unadjusted eta for the sex factor is **.40** ($\sqrt{6.750/42.250}$ = 0.399).

The column called **Adjusted for Independents Dev'n** presents what the deviation would be if adjusted for the effects of the other variable. Since the other variable has no effect in this case, the adjusted deviations are the same as the unadjusted ones. Beta is actually partial beta and is discussed in the chapter on regression. **Multiple R Squared** is the combined sum of squares for the two main effects divided by the total sum of squares (**7.500/42.250** = 0.1775 = **.178**) while **Multiple R** is the square root of this value ($\sqrt{0.1775}$ = **.421**). Because there were no covariates in this analysis, the final columns are empty.

MULTIPLE REGRESSION AND TWO-WAY ANALYSIS OF VARIANCE

To carry out a multiple regression we first have to effect code the two main effects and their interaction as shown in Table 9.8. Since we only have two categories per factor one category will be coded 1 and the other −1. Women are coded 1 and men −1. The individual tutorial condition is coded 1 and the group tutorial condition −1. The code for the interaction

Table 9.5 SPSS output for a two-way analysis of variance showing means and numbers of cases of post-test marks for women and men in the individual and group tutorial conditions (two cases dropped)

* * * C E L L   M E A N S * * *

MARKPOS post-test marks

by SEX

COND

Total Population

5.75

(12)

SEX

1	2
6.50	5.00
(6)	(6)

COND

2	3
6.00	5.50
(6)	(6)

COND

	2	3
SEX 1	8.00	5.00
	(3)	(3)
2	4.00	6.00
	(3)	(3)

of the two factors is simply the product of the codes for the two main effects.

The regression equations for the three approaches to analysing a two-way factorial design are shown in Table 9.9. The equations only contain the relevant effect codes for the two main effects (*A* and *B*) and their interaction (*AB*). So, for example, to work out the sum of squares for sex (*A*) in the regression approach, we subtract the sum of squares for the condition (*B*) and interaction (*AB*) dummy variables from the sum of squares for all three dummy variables (*A*, *B*, *AB*).

Table 9.6 SPSS output of a two-way analysis of variance of student's sex and tutorial condition on post-test marks (two cases dropped)

* * * A N A L Y S I S   O F   V A R I A N C E * * *

MARKPOS   post-test marks

by SEX

COND

HIERARCHICAL sums of squares

Covariates entered FIRST

Source of Variation	Sum of Squares	DF	Mean Square	F	Sig of F
Main Effects	7.500	2	3.750	1.875	.215
SEX	6.750	1	6.750	3.375	.104
COND	.750	1	.750	.375	.557
2-Way Interactions	18.750	1	18.750	9.375	.016
SEX COND	18.750	1	18.750	9.375	.016
Explained	26.250	3	8.750	4.375	.042
Residual	16.000	8	2.000		
Total	42.250	11	3.841		

19 cases were processed.

7 cases (36.8 pct) were missing.

With an orthogonal design the sums of squares for the effects are the same for all three approaches. The sums of squares and the *F* ratio for the three approaches for the present example are shown in Table 9.10.

We will illustrate a two-way analysis of variance for an unbalanced design with post-test marks for women and men in the individual and group tutorial conditions. The sums of squares and the *F* ratio for the three approaches for the present example are shown in Table 9.11. The sums of squares differ for the two main effects for the three approaches but are the same for the interaction, the residual and the total. The sum of squares for the regression and the classic experimental approach are greater than the total since the main effects are not independent.

The SPSS procedure was used to obtain these values. To run the regres-

Table 9.7 SPSS output of a multiple classification table from the same two-way analysis of variance as in Table 9.6

* * *   M U L T I P L E   C L A S S I F I C A T I O N   A N A L Y S I S   * * *

MARKPOS   post-test marks

by SEX

COND

Grand Mean =   5.75

Variable + Category	N	Unadjusted Dev'n Eta		Adjusted for Independents Dev'n Beta	
SEX					
1 women	6	.75		.75	
2 men	6	-.75		-.75	
			.40		.40
COND					
2 indivtut	6	.25		.25	
3 grouptut	6	-.25		-.25	
			.13		.13
Multiple R Squared					.178
Multiple R					.421

Table 9.8 Effect coding for two-way analysis of variance with equal cell frequencies

Marks	Sex	Condition	Interaction
7	1	1	1
8	1	1	1
9	1	1	1
4	1	−1	−1
5	1	−1	−1
6	1	−1	−1
2	−1	1	−1
5	−1	1	−1
5	−1	1	−1
5	−1	−1	1
5	−1	−1	1
8	−1	−1	1

Table 9.9 Regression equations for producing the appropriate sums of squares for the three approaches

Effects	Regression	Classic experimental	Hierarchical (A, B, AB order)
A	A, B, AB − B, AB	A, B − B	A
B	A, B, AB − A, AB	A, B − A	A, B − A
AB	A, B, AB − A, B	A, B, AB − A, B	A, B, AB − A, B

Table 9.10 Sums of squares and *F* ratio for three approaches to a two-way analysis of variance for a balanced design

Source of variation	Regression		Classic experimental		Hierarchical (A, B, AB order)	
	SS	F	SS	F	SS	F
A	6.750	3.375	6.750	3.375	6.750	3.375
B	.750	.375	.750	.375	.750	.375
AB	18.750	9.375	18.750	9.375	18.750	9.375
Residual	16.000		16.000		16.000	
Total	42.250		42.250		42.250	

Table 9.11 Sums of squares and *F* ratio for three approaches to a two-way analysis of variance for an unbalanced design

Source of variation	Regression		Classic experimental		Hierarchical (A, B, AB order)	
	SS	F	SS	F	SS	F
A	7.500	4.167	5.042	2.801	4.339	2.411
B	.833	.463	2.042	1.134	2.042	1.134
AB	20.833	11.574	20.833	11.574	20.833	11.574
Residual	18.000		18.000		18.000	
Total	45.214		45.214		45.214	

sion approach, select **Unique** in the **Method** section of the **Simple Factorial ANOVA: Options** dialog box. Table 9.12 shows the output for the regression approach. To run the classic experimental approach, select **Experimental**. Table 9.13 displays the output for the classic experimental approach. To run a hierarchical approach with the order of sex, tutorial conditions and then the interaction, select **Hierarchical**. Table 9.14 presents the output for the hierarchical approach.

We will illustrate the computation of the sum of squares for the main

Table 9.12 SPSS output of the regression approach to a two-way analysis of variance for an unbalanced design

---

*** A N A L Y S I S   O F   V A R I A N C E ***

MARKPOS   post-test marks

by SEX

COND

UNIQUE sums of squares

All effects entered simultaneously

Source of Variation	Sum of Squares	DF	Mean Square	F	Sig of F
Main Effects	7.875	2	3.938	2.188	.163
SEX	7.500	1	7.500	4.167	.069
COND	.833	1	.833	.463	.512
2-Way Interactions	20.833	1	20.833	11.574	.007
SEX COND	20.833	1	20.833	11.574	.007
Explained	27.214	3	9.071	5.040	.022
Residual	18.000	10	1.800		
Total	45.214	13	3.478		

21 cases were processed.

7 cases (33.3 pct) were missing.

---

effect of sex in the regression approach for the unbalanced design using SPSS. The post-test marks are the criterion or dependent variable while the codes for the three dummy variables are the independent variables or predictors. We need to enter the data in Table 9.8 in **Newdata** together with the two excluded rows and the effect coding for the group tutorial condition. For this analysis we enter the dummy variables in the order shown in Table 9.9 as follows:

→**Statistics** →**Regression** →**Linear** . . . [opens **Linear Regression** dialog box as in Box 7.3]
→dependent variable [e.g. **markpos**] →▶button beside **Dependent:** box [puts variable in this box] →first block [e.g. **cond interact**]

Table 9.13 SPSS output of the classical experimental approach to a two-way analysis of variance for an unbalanced design

* * * A N A L Y S I S   O F   V A R I A N C E   * * *

MARKPOS   post-test marks

by SEX

COND

EXPERIMENTAL sums of squares

Covariates entered first

Source of Variation	Sum of Squares	DF	Mean Square	F	Sig of F
Main Effects	6.381	2	3.190	1.772	.219
SEX	5.042	1	5.042	2.801	.125
COND	2.042	1	2.042	1.134	.312
2-Way Interactions	20.833	1	20.833	11.574	.007
SEX COND	20.833	1	20.833	11.574	.007
Explained	27.214	3	9.071	5.040	.022
Residual	18.000	10	1.800		
Total	45.214	13	3.478		

21 cases were processed.

7 cases (33.3 pct) were missing.

→▶button beside **Independent[s]:** box [puts block in this box] →**Next** →second block [e.g. **sex**] →button beside **Independent[s]:** box [puts block in this box] →**OK**

Table 9.15 displays the output for this procedure. We subtract the sum of squares in the first step for the tutorial condition and the interaction combined (**19.71429**) from the sum of squares in the second step for the three dummy variables together (**27.21429**) to obtain the sum of squares for sex on its own (**27.21429 − 19.71429 = 7.5**) which is the same as the figure of 7.5 in Table 9.11. We divide the mean square of sex (7.5/1 = 4.339) by the residual mean square (18/10 = 1.8) for the equation containing all three predictors to obtain an *F* of 4.167 (7.5/1.8 = 4.1666).

Table 9.14 SPSS output of the hierarchical approach to a two-way analysis of variance for an unbalanced design

*** A N A L Y S I S   O F   V A R I A N C E ***

MARKPOS   post-test marks

by SEX

COND

HIERARCHICAL sums of squares

Covariates entered first

Source of Variation	Sum of Squares	DF	Mean Square	F	Sig of F
Main Effects	6.381	2	3.190	1.772	.219
SEX	4.339	1	4.339	2.411	.152
COND	2.042	1	2.042	1.134	.312
2-Way Interactions	20.833	1	20.833	11.574	.007
SEX COND	20.833	1	20.833	11.574	.007
Explained	27.214	3	9.071	5.040	.022
Residual	18.000	10	1.800		
Total	45.214	13	3.478		

21 cases were processed.

7 cases (33.3 pct) were missing.

To give two further examples, we will compute the sum of squares for the two main effects in the hierarchical approach for the unbalanced design using SPSS. The sum of squares for the tutorial condition will be the same for both the hierarchical and the classic experimental approach. The SPSS procedure for this is:

→**Statistics** →**Regression** →**Linear** . . . [opens **Linear Regression** dialog box as in Box 7.3]
→dependent variable [e.g. **markpos**] →▶ button beside **Dependent:** box [puts variable in this box] →first block [e.g. **sex**] →▶ button beside **Independent[s]:** box [puts block in this box] →**Next** →second block [e.g. **cond**] →button beside **Independent[s]:** box [puts block in this box] →**OK**

Table 9.15 SPSS output of the tutorial conditions, the interaction and then sex regressed on post-test marks

---

* * * *   M U L T I P L E   R E G R E S S I O N   * * * *

Listwise Deletion of Missing Data

Equation Number 1   Dependent Variable. .   MARKPOS

Block Number 1. Method: Enter   COND   INTERACT

Variable(s) Entered on Step Number
  1 . .   INTERACT
  2 . .   COND

Multiple R	.66032
R Square	.43602
Adjusted R Square	.33348
Standard Error	1.52256

Analysis of Variance

	DF	Sum of Squares	Mean Square
Regression	2	19.71429	9.85714
Residual	11	25.50000	2.31818

F =   4.25210   Signif F   = .0429

- - - - - - - - - - - - - - - - - Variables in the Equation - - - - - - - - - - - - - - - - - -

Variable	B	SE B	Beta	T	Sig T
COND	.166667	.414388	.091790	.402	.6952
INTERACT	1.166667	.414388	.642533	2.815	.0618
(Constant)	5.833333	.414388		14.077	.0000

- - - - - - - - - - - - - - Variables not in the Equation - - - - - - - - - - - - - -

Variable	Beta In	Partial	Min Toler	T	Sig T
SEX	.413057	.542326	.972222	2.041	.0685

End Block Number 1   All requested variables entered.

Table 9.15 (continued)

---

* * * *   M U L T I P L E   R E G R E S S I O N   * * * *

Equation Number 1   Dependent Variable..   MARKPOS

Block Number 2. Method: Enter   SEX

Variable(s) Entered on Step Number
    3..   SEX

Multiple R	.77582
R Square	.60190
Adjusted R Square	.48246
Standard Error	1.34164

Analysis of Variance

	DF	Sum of Squares	Mean Square
Regression	3	27.21429	9.07143
Residual	10	18.00000	1.80000

F =   5.03968   Signif F =   .0221

- - - - - - - - - - - - - - - - - Variables in the Equation - - - - - - - - - - - - - - - - - -

Variable	B	SE B	Beta	T	Sig T
COND	.250000	.367423	.137686	.680	.5117
INTERACT	1.250000	.367423	.688428	3.402	.0067
SEX	.750000	.367423	.413057	2.041	.0685
(Constant)	5.750000	.367423		15.650	.0000

End Block Number 2   All requested variables entered.

Table 9.16 displays the output for this procedure. The sums of squares for the dummy variable of sex on its own is **4.33929** which is the same as the figure of 4.339 in Table 9.11. We divide the mean square of sex (4.339/1 = 4.339) by the residual mean square for the equation having all three predictors (18/10 = 1.8) to obtain an F of 2.411 (4.339/1.8 = 2.41055). We subtract from the sum of squares in the second step for sex and the tutorial condition combined (**6.38095**) the sum of squares in

Table 9.16 SPSS output of sex and then sex and tutorial condition regressed on post-test marks

* * * * M U L T I P L E   R E G R E S S I O N   * * * *

Listwise Deletion of Missing Data

Equation Number 1   Dependent Variable. .   MARKPOS

Block Number 1. Method: Enter   SEX

Variable(s) Entered on Step Number
   1. .   SEX

Multiple R	.30979
R Square	.09597
Adjusted R Square	.02064
Standard Error	1.84560

Analysis of Variance

	DF	Sum of Squares	Mean Square
Regression	1	4.33929	4.33929
Residual	12	40.87500	3.40625

F =   1.27392   Signif F   = .2811

- - - - - - - - - - - - - - - - - Variables in the Equation - - - - - - - - - - - - - - - - - - -

Variable	B	SE B	Beta	T	Sig T
SEX	.562500	.498370	.309793	1.129	.2811
(Constant)	5.562500	.498370		11.161	.0000

- - - - - - - - - - - - - - Variables not in the Equation - - - - - - - - - - - - - - -

Variable	Beta In	Partial	Min Toler	T	Sig T
COND	.214178	.223493	.984375	.760	.4360

End Block Number 1   All requested variables entered.

Table 9.16 (continued)

---

* * * *   M U L T I P L E   R E G R E S S I O N   * * * *

Equation Number 1   Dependent Variable. .   MARKPOS

Block Number 2. Method: Enter   COND

Variable(s) Entered on Step Number
  2. .   COND

Multiple R	.37567
R Square	.14113
Adjusted R Square	-.01503
Standard Error	1.87891

Analysis of Variance

	DF	Sum of Squares	Mean Square
Regression	2	6.38095	3.19048
Residual	11	38.83333	3.53030

F =   .90374   Signif F =   .4331

- - - - - - - - - - - - - - - - - - Variables in the Equation - - - - - - - - - - - - - - - - - - -

Variable	B	SE B	Beta	T	Sig T
SEX	.611111	.511375	.336565	1.195	.2572
COND	.388889	.511375	.214178	.760	.4630
(Constant)	5.611111	.511375		10.973	.0000

End Block Number 2   All requested variables entered.

---

the first step for sex on its own (**4.33929**) to obtain the sum of squares for the tutorial condition (**6.38095** − **4.33929** = 2.04166) which is the same as the value of 2.042 in Table 9.11. We divide the mean square of the tutorial condition (2.042/1 = 2.042) by the residual mean square (18/10 = 1.8) for the equation containing all three predictors to obtain an F of 1.134 (2.042/1.8 = 1.13444). Table 9.17 shows the sums of squares involved in deriving the sums of squares for the three effects in the three approaches.

Table 9.17 Derivation of sums of squares for the three effects in the three approaches

Regression			
A	27.21429 − 19.71429 =		7.50000
B	27.21429 − 26.38095 =		0.83334
AB	27.21429 − 6.38095 =		20.83334
Classic experimental			
A	6.38095 − 1.33929 =		5.04166
B	6.38095 − 4.33929 =		2.04166
AB	27.21429 − 6.38095 =		20.83334
Hierarchical (A, B, AB order)			
A			4.33929
B	6.38095 − 4.33929 =		2.04166
AB	27.21429 − 6.38095 =		20.83334

SUMMARY

Two-way analysis of variance compares the means of groups made up of two variables or factors and enables the interaction between those two factors to be examined. It is a more sensitive test of the effect of either factor than evaluating them singly provided that the two factors do not interact substantially. To test for significant differences between pairs of means, the unrelated *t* test should be employed when differences are predicted, otherwise a range test such as the Scheffé test should be used. The proportion of variance explained by one or more factors is estimated by eta squared. There are three approaches for handling analyses with unequal numbers of cases in cells, called the regression or unweighted means approach, the classic experimental or least squares approach and the hierarchical approach. They all use regression to compute sums of squares and produce the same result when there are equal numbers of participants in cells. For a two-way design the three approaches differ only in the way they handle main effects so the results for the interaction effect are the same as are those for the residual and the total sum of squares. The regression approach assigns equal weight to the means in all cells regardless of their size and is recommended for a true experimental design where cases have been randomly assigned to treatments. The classic experimental approach places greater weight on cells with larger numbers of cases and is recommended for non-experimental designs in which the number of cases in each cell may reflect its importance. The hierarchical approach allows the investigator to determine the order of the effects and should be used in non-experimental designs where the factors can be ordered in some sequential manner.

EXERCISES

The data for these exercises are provided in Table 5.12.

1 Use a two-way analysis of variance to determine the effect of socio-economic status and type of school on educational interest at 12.

   (a) What is the F ratio for the effect of socio-economic status?

   (b) What are its degrees of freedom?

   (c) What is its probability?

   (d) Does educational interest at 12 differ significantly between pupils of different socio-economic status?

   (e) What is the F ratio for the effect of type of school?

   (f) What are its degrees of freedom?

   (g) What is its probability?

   (h) Is educational interest at 12 significantly greater in single- than in mixed-sex schools?

   (i) What is the F ratio for the interaction between socio-economic status and type of school?

   (j) What are its degrees of freedom?

   (k) What is its probability?

   (l) Is there a significant interaction between socio-economic status and type of school on educational interest at 12?

10 Tests of difference for interval/ratio data on mixed samples for two factors

This chapter describes analysis of variance for examining together data from both related and unrelated samples. For example, we may be interested in determining whether any increase in post-test marks for women is greater in the individual than in the group tutorial condition. If so, we would use a two-way analysis of variance with repeated measures on one factor. Alternatively, we may want to determine whether post-test marks in women differ between the individual and the group tutorial condition when we control for differences in these two conditions at pre-test. In this case, we would use a one-way analysis of covariance.

TWO-WAY ANALYSIS OF VARIANCE WITH REPEATED MEASURES ON ONE FACTOR

Two-way analysis of variance with repeated measures on one factor compares the means of groups consisting of two factors, one of which is repeated. We could employ this analysis to determine whether post-test marks in women increased more in the individual than in the group tutorial condition. In this kind of analysis the total variation in the scores is broken down into five main sources of variation: (1) between-subjects factor (i.e. independent variable); (2) between-subjects error; (3) within-subjects factor (i.e. repeated measures); (4) within-subjects error; and (5) interaction of between- and within-subjects factor. These sources of variation are presented in Table 10.1 together with their associated degrees of freedom. The F ratio for determining whether there is a significant effect for the between-subjects factor is the between-subjects mean square divided by the between-subjects error mean square. The F ratio for finding out whether the within-subjects factor is significant is the within-subjects factor mean square divided by the within-subjects error mean square, while the F ratio for seeing whether the interaction effect is significant is the interaction mean square divided by the within-subjects error mean square.

The procedure for calculating this analysis will be illustrated by comparing pre- and post-test marks in the individual and group tutorial condition for women. Their individual scores are presented in Table 10.2. The total

Table 10.1 Sources of variation and degrees of freedom in a two-way analysis of variance with repeated measures on one factor

Sources of variation	Degrees of freedom
Between-subjects factor (A)	No. of conditions in $A - 1$
Between-subjects error	No of conditions in $A \times$ (no. of cases $- 1$)
Within-subjects factor (B)	No. of conditions in $B - 1$
Within-subjects error	No. of conditions in $A \times$ (no. of cases $- 1$) $\times$ (no. of conditions in $B - 1$)
$A \times B$ interaction	(No. of conditions in $A - 1$) $\times$ (no. of conditions in $B - 1$)
Total	No. of scores $- 1$

and mean score of the pre-test and post-test are shown in the last two columns of the table while the total and mean score for the two conditions are displayed at the bottom of each condition and in the bottom rows. The overall total and mean score (grand mean) are in the bottom right hand corner of the table. Means have been calculated to two decimal places.

Step 1 Compute the sum of squares for the between-subjects factor by subtracting the grand mean from the overall mean score for each condition (ignoring time of testing), squaring the differences, multiplying the squared

Table 10.2 Pre- and post-test marks of women in the individual and group tutorial conditions with initial computations

Condition	Pre-test	Post-test	Sum	Mean
Individual	5	7	12	6.0
tutorial	3	8	11	5.5
	7	9	16	8.0
Sum	15	24	39	
N	3	3	6	
Mean	5	8	6.5	
Group	1	4	5	2.5
tutorial	1	4	5	2.5
	2	5	7	3.5
	3	6	9	4.5
	3	6	9	4.5
Sum	10	25	35	
N	5	5	10	
Mean	2	5	3.5	
Column sum	25	49	Grand sum	74
Column N	8	8	Grand N	16
Column mean	3.13	6.13	Grand mean	4.63

differences by the number of scores in each condition and adding the products together.

The sum of squares for the between-subjects factor for our example is 33.80:

$$[(6.5 - 4.63)^2 \times 6] + [(3.5 - 4.63)^2 \times 10] =$$
$$(1.87^2 \times 6) + (-1.13^2 \times 10) = (3.50 \times 6) + (1.28 \times 10) =$$
$$21.0 + 12.8 = 33.80$$

Step 2 Compute the between-subjects sum of squares by subtracting the grand mean from the mean score for each case, squaring the differences, multiplying the squared differences by the number of scores for each case and then summing the products.

The between-subjects sum of squares for our example is 48.80:

$$[(6.0 - 4.63)^2 \times 2] + [(5.5 - 4.63)^2 \times 2] + [(8.0 - 4.63)^2 \times 2] +$$
$$[(2.5 - 4.63)^2 \times 2] + [(2.5 - 4.63)^2 \times 2] + [(3.5 - 4.63)^2 \times 2] +$$
$$[(4.5 - 4.63)^2 \times 2] + [(4.5 - 4.63)^2 \times 2] =$$
$$(1.37^2 \times 2) + (0.87^2 \times 2) + (3.37^2 \times 2) + (-2.13^2 \times 2) +$$
$$(-2.13^2 \times 2) + (-1.13^2 \times 2) + (-0.13^2 \times 2) + (-0.13^2 \times 2) =$$
$$(1.88 \times 2) + (0.76 \times 2) + (11.36 \times 2) + (4.54 \times 2) +$$
$$(4.54 \times 2) + (1.28 \times 2) + (0.02 \times 2) + (0.02 \times 2) =$$
$$3.76 + 1.52 + 22.72 + 9.08 + 9.08 + 2.56 + 0.04 + 0.04 =$$
$$48.80$$

Step 3 Compute the sum of squares for the between-subjects error by subtracting the between-subjects factor sum of squares from the between-subjects sum of squares

between-subjects error sum of squares = between-subjects sum of squares − between-subjects factor sum of squares

The between-subjects error sum of squares for our example is 15.0

$$48.80 - 33.80 = 15.0$$

Step 4 Work out the sum of squares for the within-subjects factor by subtracting the grand mean from the overall mean score for each of the tests, squaring the differences, multiplying the squared differences by the number of cases and summing the products.

The sum of squares for the within-subjects factor for our example is 36.0:

$$[(3.13 - 4.63)^2 \times 8] + [(6.13 + 4.63)^2 \times 8] =$$
$$(-1.5^2 \times 8) + (1.5^2 \times 8) = (2.25 \times 8) + (2.25 \times 8) =$$
$$18.0 + 18.0 = 36.0$$

Step 5 Calculate the sum of squares for the interaction term by subtracting the grand mean from the mean for each of the conditions formed by the two factors, squaring the differences, multiplying the squared differences by the number of cases in each condition, summing the products and subtracting from the result the sum of squares for the between-subjects and within-subjects factors.

The sum of squares for the interaction term in our example is 0:

$[(5 - 4.63)^2 \times 3] + [(8 - 4.63)^2 \times 3] +$
$[(2 - 4.63)^2 \times 5] + [(5 - 4.63)^2 \times 5] - 33.80 - 36.0 =$
$(0.37^2 \times 3) + (3.37^2 \times 3) + (-2.63^2 \times 5) +$
$(0.37^2 \times 5) - 69.80 =$
$(0.14 \times 3) + (11.36 \times 3) + (6.92 \times 5) + (0.14 \times 5) - 69.80 =$
$0.42 + 34.08 + 34.60 + 0.70 - 69.80 = 69.80 - 69.80 = 0$

Step 6   Calculate the total sum of squares by subtracting the grand mean from each score, squaring the differences and adding the squared differences together.

If we do this for our example, the total sum of squares is 87.80:

$(5 - 4.63)^2 + (3 - 4.63)^2 + (7 - 4.63)^2 + (7 - 4.63)^2 +$
$(8 - 4.63)^2 + (9 - 4.63)^2 + (1 - 4.63)^2 + (1 - 4.63)^2 +$
$(2 - 4.63)^2 + (3 - 4.63)^2 + (3 - 4.63)^2 + (4 - 4.63)^2 +$
$(4 - 4.63)^2 + (5 - 4.63)^2 + (6 - 4.63)^2 + (6 - 4.63)^2 =$
$0.37^2 + -1.63^2 + 2.37^2 + 2.37^2 + 3.37^2 + 4.37^2 +$
$-3.63^2 + -3.63^2 + -2.63^2 + -1.63^2 + -1.63^2 + -0.63^2 +$
$-0.63^2 + 0.37^2 + 1.37^2 + 1.37^2 =$
$0.14 + 2.66 + 5.62 + 5.62 + 11.36 + 19.10 +$
$13.18 + 13.18 + 6.92 + 2.66 + 2.66 + 0.40 +$
$0.40 + 0.14 + 1.88 + 1.88 = 87.80$

Step 7   Calculate the sum of squares for the within-subjects error by subtracting from the total sum of squares the sum of squares for the between-subjects factor, the between-subjects error, the within-subjects factor, and the interaction.

The sum of squares for the within-subjects error for our example is 3.0:

$87.80 - 33.80 - 15.0 - 36.0 - 0.0 = 3.0$

Table 10.3 presents the sums of squares for six of these sources of variation together with the degrees of freedom, mean squares and *F* ratios.

Step 8   Compute the between-subjects factor mean square which is the between-subjects factor sum of squares divided by its degrees of freedom. The degrees of freedom are the number of conditions minus 1 which in this case is 1 $(2 - 1 = 1)$. Consequently, the between-subjects factor mean square is 33.80 $(33.80/1 = 33.80)$.

Table 10.3 Two-way analysis of variance table with repeated measures on one factor comparing pre- and post-test marks in the individual and group tutorial condition in women

Sources of variation	SS	df	MS	F	p
Between-subjects factor	33.80	1	33.80	13.52	<0.05
Between-subjects error	15.00	6	2.50		
Within-subjects factor	36.00	1	36.00	72.00	<0.05
Within-subjects error	3.00	6	0.50		
Interaction	0.00	1	0.00	0.00	*ns*
Total	87.80	15			

Step 9 Compute the between-subjects error mean square which is the between-subjects error sum of squares divided by its degrees of freedom. The degrees of freedom are the mean number of cases in each condition minus 1 multiplied by the number of conditions. As the mean number of cases in each condition is 4 and the number of conditions is 2 the degrees of freedom for the between-subjects error are 6 [2 × (4 − 1) = 2 × 3 = 6]. Thus the between-subjects error mean square for our example is 2.50 (15.0/6 = 2.50).

Step 10 The *F* ratio for the between-subjects factor is its mean square divided by the between-subjects error mean-square.

For our example the *F* ratio for the between-subjects factor is 13.52 (33.80/2.50 = 13.52). If we look up the significance of this value in the table in Appendix 3 with 1 and 6 degrees of freedom in the numerator and denominator respectively, the *F* ratio has to be 5.9874 or bigger to be significant at the 0.05 level, which it is. Accordingly, we would conclude that the tutorial condition effect is significant. In this instance we would not be interested in this effect since it collapses the pre-test and post-test marks and so does not provide any evidence as to whether the post-test marks differ among the two conditions.

Step 11 Work out the mean square for the within-subjects factor which is its sum of squares divided by its degrees of freedom. The degrees of freedom for the within-subjects factor are the number of conditions minus 1. Since the number of conditions in our example is 2 (pre- and post-test), the degree of freedom is 1 (2 − 1 = 1) and the within-subjects factor mean square is 36.0 (36.0/1 = 36.0).

Step 12 Compute the within-subjects error mean square which is the within-subjects error sum of squares divided by its degrees of freedom. The degrees of freedom for the within-subjects error is the average number of cases in each condition minus 1 multiplied by the number of within-subjects conditions minus 1 multiplied by the number of between-subjects conditions. The degrees of freedom for our example are 6 [(4 − 1) × (2 − 1) × 2 = 3 × 1 × 2 = 6]. The within-subjects error mean square, therefore, is 0.50 (3.0/6 = 0.50).

Step 13 The *F* ratio for the within-subjects factor is its mean square divided by the within-subjects error mean square.

The *F* ratio for the within-subjects factor of time of testing is 72.0 (36.0/0.50 = 72.0). From the table in Appendix 3, we can see that with 1 and 6 degrees of freedom in the numerator and denominator respectively the *F* ratio has to be 5.9874 or larger to be statistically significant at less than the 0.05 level, which it is. Therefore, we would conclude that there was a significant time of testing effect across the two treatments. In other words, coursework marks were significantly higher at post-test than at pre-test.

Step 14 The mean square for the interaction effect, which is of main concern to us, is its sum of squares divided by its degrees of freedom. The degrees of freedom for the interaction effect are the number of between-subjects conditions minus 1 multiplied by the number of within-subjects conditions minus 1. The degree of freedom for our example is 1 [(2 − 1) × (2 − 1) = 1 × 1 = 1], giving a mean square of 0 (0/1 = 0).

Step 15 The *F* ratio for the interaction effect is its mean square divided by the mean square of the within-subjects error.

The *F* ratio for the interaction between the two conditions and time of testing is 0 (0/0.25 = 0.0). With 1 and 6 degrees of freedom in the numerator and denominator respectively, the *F* value has to be 5.9874 or greater to be statistically significant at the 0.05 level, which it is not. So, we would conclude that the interaction effect was not statistically significant. If a significant interaction was predicted, *t* tests could be used to determine where the significant differences lay. If a significant interaction was not expected, a *post hoc* test such as the Bonferroni test could be applied to related scores and the Scheffé test to unrelated scores. Since we found in Chapter 5 that the pre-test marks differed significantly between the individual and group tutorial condition, we should consider using a one-way analysis of covariance to determine if post-test marks were significantly higher for women in the individual than in the group tutorial condition.

To conduct with SPSS on these data a two-way analysis of variance with repeated measures on one factor, we first select the women (**sex=1**) and then carry out the following procedure:

→**Statistics** →**ANOVA Models** →**Repeated Measures** ... [opens **Repeated Measures Define Factor(s)** dialog box as in Box 8.1]
→type within-subjects independent variable [e.g. **time**] in **Within-Subject Factor Name:** box →type number of levels in this factor [e.g **2**] in

Number of Levels: box →**Add** →**Define** [opens **Repeated Measures ANOVA** dialog box as in Box 8.2]
→first dependent variable [e.g. **markpre**] →▶button beside **Within-Subjects Variables:** **[time]** [puts variable in this box] →second dependent variable [e.g. **markpos**] →▶button beside **Within-Subjects Variables:** **[time]** [puts variable in this box] →between-subjects independent variable [e.g. **cond**] →▶button beside **Between-Subjects Factor(s):** [puts variable in this box] →**Define Range . . .** [opens **Repeated Measures ANOVA: Define Range** dialog box as in Box 10.1]
→in box beside **Minimum:** type lower code value [e.g. **2**] →box beside **Maximum:** and type higher code value [e.g. **3**] →**Continue** [closes **Repeated Measures ANOVA: Define Range** dialog box]
→**Options . . .** [opens **Repeated Measures ANOVA: Options** dialog box as in Box 10.2]
→between-subjects independent variable [e.g. **cond**] →▶button [puts variable under **Display Means for:**] →**Continue** [closes **Repeated Measures ANOVA: Options** dialog box]
→**OK**

Table 10.4 shows the weighted and unweighted means for pre- and post-test marks in women for the two tutorial conditions. Table 10.5 presents the between-subjects effect where the between-subjects error is called the **WITHIN+RESIDUAL** source of variation. Table 10.6 displays the within-subjects factor and the interaction effect where the within-subjects error is called the **WITHIN+RESIDUAL** source of variation, the within-subjects factor **TIME** and the interaction effect **COND BY TIME**. The effect that we are interested in is the interaction between **COND** (i.e. the two conditions) and **TIME** (i.e. the two times of testing). If we divide the mean square of the interaction term (**.00**) by the mean square of the error

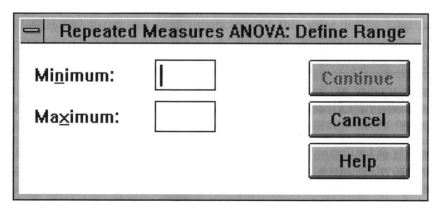

Box 10.1 **Repeated Measures ANOVA: Define Range** dialog box

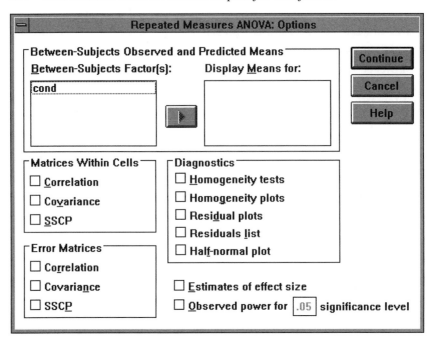

Box 10.2 **Repeated Measures ANOVA: Options** dialog box

term (**.50**), we obtain an *F* ratio of **.00** (**.00/.50** = **.00**) which, with a *p* of **1.000,** is not statistically significant.

REGRESSION ANALYSIS AND A TWO-WAY ANALYSIS OF VARIANCE WITH REPEATED MEASURES ON ONE FACTOR

To carry out a two-way analysis of variance with repeated measures on one factor using regression analysis, we create 10 dummy variables as shown in Table 10.7: one for the two occasions; one for the two conditions; one for the interaction; and seven for the between-subjects.

To work out the sum of squares for the between-subjects factor we regress the marks on the conditions dummy variable. Table 10.8 shows the analysis of variance table for this analysis. The between-subjects factor sum of squares is **33.75000**.

To obtain the between-subjects error subtract the between-subjects factor sum of squares from the between-subjects sum of squares. The between-subjects sum of squares is derived by regressing marks on the between-subjects factor and the between-subjects dummy variables. Table 10.9 displays the analysis of variance table for this analysis. As the between-subjects sum of squares is **48.75000**, the between-subjects error is 15.00 (**48.75000** − **33.75000** = 15.00).

To calculate the sums of squares for the within-subjects factor, regress

Table 10.4 SPSS output for the two-way analysis of variance with repeated measures on one factor comparing pre- and post-test marks in the individual and group tutorial condition in women

* * * * * * * A n a l y s i s   o f   V a r i a n c e -- design 1 * * * * * *

Combined Observed Means for COND

Variable . . MARKPRE

COND		
indivtut	WGT.	5.00000
	UNWGT.	5.00000
grouptut	WGT.	2.00000
	UNWGT.	2.00000

- -

Variable . . MARKPOS

COND		
indivtut	WGT.	8.00000
	UNWGT.	8.00000
grouptut	WGT.	5.00000
	UNWGT.	5.00000

- -

Table 10.5 SPSS output for the between-subjects effects of the two-way analysis of variance with repeated measures on one factor comparing pre- and post-test marks in the individual and group tutorial condition in women

* * * * * * A n a l y s i s   o f   V a r i a n c e -- design 1 * * * * * *

Tests of Between-Subjects Effects.

Tests of Significance for T1 using UNIQUE sums of squares

Source of Variation	SS	DF	MS	F	Sig of F
WITHIN+RESIDUAL	15.00	6	2.50		
COND	33.75	1	33.75	13.50	.010

Table 10.6 SPSS output for the within-subjects and interaction effects of the two-way analysis of variance with repeated measures on one factor comparing pre- and post-test marks in the individual and group tutorial condition in women

* * * * * * A n a l y s i s   o f   V a r i a n c e -- design 1 * * * * * *

Tests involving 'TIME' Within-Subject Effect.

Tests of Significance for T2 using UNIQUE sums of squares

Source of Variation	SS	DF	MS	F	Sig of F
WITHIN+RESIDUAL	3.00	6	.50		
TIME	33.75	1	33.75	67.50	.000
COND BY TIME	.00	1	.00	.00	1.000

Table 10.7 Effect coding for the two-way analysis of variance with repeated measures on one factor comparing pre- and post-test marks in the individual and group tutorial condition in women

Marks	Time	Condition	Interaction	S1	S2	S3	S4	S5	S6	S7
5	1	1	1	1	0	0	0	0	0	0
3	1	1	1	0	1	0	0	0	0	0
7	1	1	1	0	0	1	0	0	0	0
1	1	−1	−1	0	0	0	1	0	0	0
1	1	−1	−1	0	0	0	0	1	0	0
2	1	−1	−1	0	0	0	0	0	1	0
3	1	−1	−1	0	0	0	0	0	0	0
3	1	−1	−1	−1	−1	−1	−1	−1	−1	−1
7	−1	1	−1	1	0	0	0	0	0	0
8	−1	1	−1	0	1	0	0	0	0	0
9	−1	1	−1	0	0	1	0	0	0	0
4	−1	−1	1	0	0	0	1	0	0	0
4	−1	−1	1	0	0	0	0	1	0	0
5	−1	−1	1	0	0	0	0	0	1	0
6	−1	−1	1	0	0	0	0	0	0	1
6	−1	−1	1	−1	−1	−1	−1	−1	−1	−1

Table 10.8 SPSS output showing analysis of variance table for marks regressed on the between-subjects factor dummy variable only

Analysis of Variance

	DF	Sum of Squares	Mean Square
Regression	1	33.75000	33.75000
Residual	14	54.00000	3.85714

F =	8.75000	Signif F =	.0104

Table 10.9 SPSS output showing analysis of variance table for marks regressed on the between-subjects factor and between-subjects dummy variables

Analysis of Variance

	DF	Sum of Squares	Mean Square
Regression	7	48.75000	6.96429
Residual	8	39.00000	4.87500

F =	1.42857	Signif F =	.3126

the marks on the within-subjects factor dummy variable. Table 10.10 presents the analysis of variance table for this analysis. The within-subjects factor sum of squares is **36.00000**.

To find the within-subjects error, regress the marks on all the dummy variables. Table 10.11 shows the analysis of variance table for this analysis. The within-subjects error is **3.00000**.

To determine the interaction sum of squares, regress the marks on all the dummy variables except that for the interaction. Table 10.12 displays the analysis of variance table for this analysis. Subtract the sum of squares of the previous analysis (**84.75000**) from the sum of squares of this analysis (**84.75000**) to give the sum of squares for the interaction, which is 0 (**84.75000** − **84.75000** = 0).

Table 10.10 SPSS output showing analysis of variance table for marks regressed on the within-subjects factor dummy variable

Analysis of Variance

	DF	Sum of Squares	Mean Square
Regression	1	36.00000	36.00000
Residual	14	51.75000	3.69643

F =	9.73913	Signif F =	.0075

Table 10.11 SPSS output showing analysis of variance table for marks regressed on all the dummy variables

Analysis of Variance

	DF	Sum of Squares	Mean Square
Regression	9	84.75000	9.41667
Residual	6	3.00000	.50000

F =	18.83333	Signif F =	.0010

Table 10.12 SPSS output showing analysis of variance table for marks regressed on all the dummy variables except that for the interaction

Analysis of Variance

	DF	Sum of Squares	Mean Square
Regression	8	84.75000	10.59375
Residual	7	3.00000	.42857

F =	24.71875	Signif F =	.0002

ONE-WAY ANALYSIS OF COVARIANCE

One-way analysis of covariance compares the means of two or more groups controlling for the effects of a second factor which is known to be associated with the first factor. The variable which is controlled is called a *covariate*. Suppose, for example, that we found as shown in Figure 10.1 that the pre-test marks of the women in the individual tutorial condition were higher than those in the group tutorial condition and that we knew that pre-test marks were positively correlated with post-test marks so that women with higher pre-test marks also had higher post-test marks. If we observed that post-test marks were also higher in the individual than in the group tutorial condition, then this difference may be due not to the result of individual tutorials but to the fact that marks in these women were initially higher. One way of taking into account these pre-test differences is to

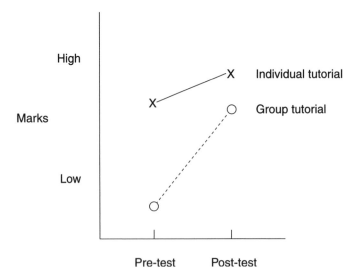

Figure 10.1 Example of pre- and post-test differences

conduct a one-way analysis of covariance on the post-test marks covarying out the pre-test marks.

In an analysis of covariance the variation in the scores of the dependent variable is adjusted to take account of the relationship between the dependent variable and the covariate. In effect, variance in the dependent variable that is shared with the covariate is removed. In an analysis of variance the between-groups variance is compared with the within-groups variance. If the between-groups variance is substantially bigger than the within-groups variance, the means of the groups or treatments differ. Similarly, in an analysis of covariance the between-groups variance is compared with the within-groups variance except that the variances have been adjusted according to their relationship with the covariate. In other words, the adjusted between-groups variance is compared with the adjusted within-groups variance.

The total variance in an analysis of covariance will generally be less than that in an analysis of variance since some of the variance will be shared with the covariate. The adjusted total variance will be the unadjusted total variance minus the total variance that is shared with the covariate.

adjusted total variance = unadjusted total variance − total variance shared with covariate

The extent to which the dependent variable is related to the covariate is expressed as the *unstandardised regression coefficient* (see Chapter 7), the square of which reflects the proportion of variance shared between the two variables. Consequently, the adjusted total variance is the unadjusted total variance minus the product of the squared unstandardised regression coefficient and the covariate total variance.

adjusted total variance = unadjusted total variance − (squared unstandardised regression coefficient × covariate total variance)

In other words, the adjusted total sum of squares of the dependent variable (TSS_{adj}) is the unadjusted total sum of squares for the dependent variable (TSS_{dep}) minus the product of the squared unstandardised regression coefficient (β^2) and the covariate total sum of squares (TSS_{cov}).

$$TSS_{adj} = TSS_{dep} - (\beta^2 \times TSS_{cov})$$

The formula for the unstandardised regression coefficient is the total sum of products divided by the covariate total sum of squares

$$\beta = \frac{TSP}{TSS_{cov}}$$

The sum of products is simply the deviation of the dependent variable multiplied by the deviation of the covariate for each pair of scores summed across all scores. The formula for calculating the adjusted total sum of squares can be re-expressed as follows

$$TSS_{adj} = TSS_{dep} - \left(\frac{TSP^2}{TSS_{cov}{}^2} \times TSS_{cov}\right)$$

which by cancelling the covariate total sum of squares in the denominator and numerator becomes

$$TSS_{adj} = TSS_{dep} - \frac{TSP^2}{TSS_{cov}}$$

We follow a similar procedure for working out the adjusted within-groups sum of squares ($WGSS_{adj}$) where the unstandardised regression coefficient represents the relationship between the dependent variable and the covariate within the groups or treatments.

$$WGSS_{adj} = WGSS_{dep} - (\beta^2 \times WGSS_{cov})$$

$$= WGSS_{dep} - \left(\frac{WGSP^2}{WGSS_{cov}{}^2} \times WGSS_{cov}\right)$$

$$= WGSS_{dep} - \frac{WGSP^2}{WGSS_{cov}}$$

We cannot obtain the adjusted between-groups sum of squares ($BGSS_{adj}$) in the same way because the regression coefficient in this case is partly determined by the dependent variable which itself is partly determined by the treatments. Since the adjusted total sum of squares is the sum of the between- and within-groups sums of squares,

$$TSS_{adj} = BGSS_{adj} + WGSS_{adj}$$

the adjusted between-groups sum of squares is most easily derived by subtracting the adjusted within-groups sum of squares from the adjusted total sum of squares

$$BGSS_{adj} = TSS_{adj} - WGSS_{adj}$$

The sources of variation in an analysis of covariance and their associated degrees of freedom are shown in Table 10.13. The between-groups mean square is simply the between-groups sum of squares divided by its degrees of freedom while the within-groups mean square is the within-groups sum of squares divided by its degrees of freedom. The F ratio is the between-groups mean square divided by the within-groups mean square.

In trying to understand and remember what an analysis of covariance is, it may be useful to think of it in terms of the Venn diagram shown in Figure 10.2 where the area enclosed by the circle represents the total variance of that variable. The total variance of the criterion or dependent variable has been divided into four sections labelled *a*, *b*, *c* and *d*. The extent of the relationship between the two variables is reflected in the overlap of the two circles. This area comprises the two sections *a*

Table 10.13 Sources of variation and degrees of freedom in a one-way analysis of covariance

Sources of variation	Degrees of freedom
Between-groups	No. of groups − 1
Within-groups	No. of cases − no. of groups − 1
Total	No. of cases − 1

and *b* whereas the two remaining sections of *c* and *d* represents the adjusted total variance of the dependent variable. Sections *a* and *c* reflect the unadjusted between-groups variance while section *c* is the between-groups variance which has been adjusted for the covariate. Sections *b* and *d* represent the unadjusted within-groups variance whereas section *d* is the within-groups variance adjusted for the covariate. The *F* ratio is the adjusted between-groups mean square (represented by section *c*) divided by the within-groups mean square (signified by section *d*).

The procedure for carrying out a one-way analysis of covariance will be illustrated by comparing post-test marks in women in the individual and group tutorial condition while covarying pre-test marks. The scores for these conditions are displayed in Table 10.14 together with the means for each condition and the grand means for the pre- and post-tests.

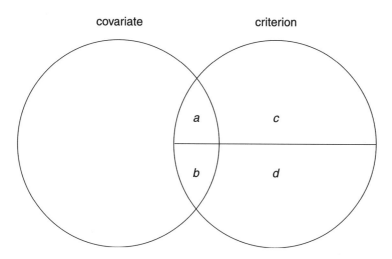

Figure 10.2 Venn diagram illustrating a one-way analysis of covariance

Table 10.14 Pre- and post-test marks of women in the individual and group tutorial conditions with initial computations

Condition	Pre-test	Post-test
Individual	5	7
tutorial	3	8
	7	9
Sum	15	24
N	3	3
Mean	5	8
Group	1	4
tutorial	1	4
	2	5
	3	6
	3	6
Sum	10	25
N	5	5
Mean	2	5
Grand sum	25	49
Grand N	8	8
Grand mean	3.13	6.13

Step 1 Calculate the within-groups sum of squares for the dependent variable by subtracting the group mean from the individual score, squaring the difference and summing the squared difference for all scores

within-groups sum of squares = sum of (individual score − group mean)^2 for all scores

The within-groups sum of squares for post-test marks is 6:

$$(7 - 8)^2 + (8 - 8)^2 + (9 - 8)^2 +$$
$$(4 - 5)^2 + (4 - 5)^2 + (5 - 5)^2 + (6 - 5)^2 + (6 - 5)^2 =$$
$$-1^2 + 0^2 + 1^2 + -1^2 + -1^2 + 0^2 + 1^2 + 1^2 =$$
$$1 + 0 + 1 + 1 + 1 + 0 + 1 + 1 = 6$$

Step 2 Calculate the within-groups sum of products for the covariate and dependent variable by (1) subtracting the covariate group mean from each of the individual scores within that group; (2) subtracting the dependent variable group mean from each of the individual scores within that group; (3) multiplying the deviation for each pair of scores of the covariate and dependent variable; and (4) summing the products for all the groups.

within-groups sum of products = sum of [(covariate individual score − covariate group mean) × (dependent variable individual score − dependent variable group mean)] for all groups

The within-groups sum of products for the covariate and the dependent variable is 6:

$[(5 - 5) \times (7 - 8)] + [(3 - 5) \times (8 - 8)] + [(7 - 5) \times (9 - 8)] +$
$[(1 - 2) \times (4 - 5)] + [(1 - 2) \times (4 - 5)] + [(2 - 2) \times (5 - 5)] +$
$[(3 - 2) \times (6 - 5)] + [(3 - 2) \times (6 - 5)] =$
$(0 \times -1) + (-2 \times 0) + (2 \times 1) + (-1 \times -1) + (-1 \times -1) + (0 \times 0)$
$+ (1 \times 1) + (1 \times 1) =$
$0 + 0 + 2 + 1 + 1 + 0 + 1 + 1 = 6$

Step 3 Calculate the within-groups sum of squares for the covariate by subtracting the group mean from the individual score, squaring the difference and summing the squared difference for all scores.

The within-groups sum of squares for pre-test marks is 12:

$(5 - 5)^2 + (3 - 5)^2 + (7 - 5)^2 +$
$(1 - 2)^2 + (1 - 2)^2 + (2 - 2)^2 + (3 - 2)^2 + (3 - 2)^2 =$
$0^2 + -2^2 + 2^2 + -1^2 + -1^2 + 0^2 + 1^2 + 1^2 =$
$0 + 4 + 4 + 1 + 1 + 0 + 1 + 1 = 12$

Step 4 Calculate the adjusted within-groups sum of squares for the dependent variable by substituting the pertinent values in the following formula:

$$\text{WGSS}_{adj} = \text{WGSS}_{dep} - \frac{\text{WGSP}^2}{\text{WGSS}_{cov}}$$

The adjusted within-groups sum of squares for post-test marks is 3:

$$6 - \frac{6^2}{12} = 6 - \frac{36}{12} = 6 - 3 = 3$$

Step 5 Calculate the total sum of squares for the dependent variable by deriving the between-groups sum of squares and adding it to the within-groups sum of squares

$$\text{TSS}_{dep} = \text{BGSS}_{dep} + \text{WGSS}_{dep}$$

Work out the between-groups sum of squares for the dependent variable by subtracting its grand mean from its mean for each group, squaring these differences, multiplying the squared differences by the number of cases in each of the groups and summing the products for all the groups.

between-groups sum of squares = sum of $[(\text{group mean} - \text{grand mean})^2$
$\times$ number of cases] for all groups

The between-groups sum of squares for post-test marks is 16.90:

$[(8.0 - 6.13)^2 \times 3] + [(5.0 - 6.13)^2 \times 5] =$
$(1.87^2 \times 3) + (-1.13^2 \times 5) = (3.50 \times 3) + (1.28 \times 5) =$
$10.50 + 6.40 = 16.90$

Consequently, the total sum of squares for post-test marks is 22.90:

$16.90 + 6.0 = 22.90$

Step 6 Calculate the total sum of products for the covariate and dependent variable by working out the between-groups sum of products and adding it to the within-groups sum of products

TSP = BGSP + WGSP

Calculate the between-groups sum of products for the covariate and dependent variable by (1) subtracting the covariate grand mean from each of its group means; (2) subtracting the dependent variable grand mean from each of its group means; (3) multiplying the deviation for each pair of group means of the covariate and dependent variable; (4) multiplying them by the number of pairs in each of the groups; and (5) summing the products for all the groups.

> between-group sum of products = sum of [(covariate group mean − covariate grand mean) × (dependent variable group mean − dependent variable grand mean) × no. of cases] for all groups

The between-groups sum of products for pre-test and post-test marks is 16.90:

$[(5 - 3.13) \times (8 - 6.13) \times 3] + [(2 - 3.13) \times (5 - 6.13) \times 5] =$
$(1.87 \times 1.87 \times 3) + (-1.13 \times -1.13 \times 5) = (3.50 \times 3) + (1.28 \times 5) =$
$10.50 + 6.40 = 16.90$

Thus, the total sum of products for pre- and post-test marks is 22.90:

$16.90 + 6.0 = 22.90$

Step 7 Calculate the total sum of squares for the covariate by obtaining the between-groups sum of squares and adding it to the within-groups sum of squares

$TSS_{cov} = BGSS_{cov} + WGSS_{cov}$

Calculate the between-groups sum of squares for the covariate by subtracting its grand mean from the mean for each group, squaring these differences, multiplying the squared differences by the number of cases in each of the groups and summing the products for all the groups.

The between-groups sum of squares for pre-test marks is 16.90:

$[(5 - 3.13)^2 \times 3] + [(2 - 3.13)^2 \times 5] =$
$(1.87^2 \times 3) + (-1.13^2 \times 5) = (3.50 \times 3) + (1.28 \times 5) =$
$10.50 + 6.40 = 16.90$

Accordingly, the total sum of squares for pre-test marks is 28.90:

$16.90 + 12.0 = 28.90$

Step 8 Calculate the adjusted total sum of squares for the dependent variable by substituting the appropriate values in the following formula:

$$TSS_{adj} = TSS_{dep} - \frac{TSP^2}{TSS_{cov}}$$

The adjusted total sum of squares for post-test marks is 4.75:

$$22.90 - \frac{22.90^2}{28.90} = 22.90 - \frac{524.41}{28.90} = 22.90 - 18.15 = 4.75$$

Step 9 Calculate the adjusted between-groups sum of squares for the dependent variable by subtracting its adjusted within-groups sum of squares from its adjusted total sum of squares

$$BGSS_{adj} = TSS_{adj} - WGSS_{adj}$$

The adjusted between-groups sum of squares for post-test marks is 1.75:

$$4.75 - 3.00 = 1.75$$

Step 10 Calculate the adjusted between-groups mean square by dividing the adjusted between-groups sum of squares by its degrees of freedom which are the number of groups minus 1.

The adjusted between-groups mean square for post-test marks is 1.75 $[1.75/(2 - 1) = 1.75/1 = 1.75]$.

Step 11 Calculate the adjusted within-groups mean square by dividing the adjusted within-groups sum of squares by its degrees of freedom which are the total number of cases minus the number of groups minus 1.

The adjusted within-groups mean square for post-test marks is 0.60 $[3.0/(8 - 2 - 1) = 3.0/5 = 0.60]$.

Step 12 Calculate the F ratio for the between-groups effect by dividing the adjusted between-groups mean square by the adjusted within-groups mean square.

The F ratio for the between-groups effect of treatment is 2.92 $[1.75/0.60 = 2.9166]$.

Step 13 Look up the F ratio in the table in Appendix 3.

With 1 and 5 degrees of freedom in the numerator and denominator respectively, F has to be 6.6079 or larger to be significant at the 0.05 level, which it is not. Consequently, we would conclude that there is no significant difference in post-test marks between the individual and group tutorial condition when pre-test marks are covaried.

The sums of squares, degrees of freedom, mean squares and F ratio for this analysis of covariance are shown in Table 10.15.

Table 10.15 One-way analysis of covariance table comparing post-test marks in the individual tutorial and group tutorial conditions in women covarying out pre-test marks

Source of variation	SS	df	MS	F	p
Between-groups	1.75	1	1.75	2.92	*ns*
Within-groups	3.00	5	0.60		
Total	4.75	7			

Since the means have been adjusted for the influence of the covariate, the adjusted means may differ from the unadjusted ones. Consequently, when interpreting the between-groups treatment effect, we should look at the adjusted means. The group means for the dependent variable can be adjusted according to the following formula:

$$\text{adjusted group mean} = \text{unadjusted group mean} - \left(\frac{\text{WGSP}}{\text{WGSS}_{\text{cov}}} \times (\text{covariate group mean} - \text{covariate grand mean}) \right)$$

Substituting the pertinent values into this formula, the adjusted group mean for the individual tutorial condition is 7.06:

$$8 - \left(\frac{6}{12} \times (5 - 3.13) \right) = 8 - (0.5 \times 1.87) = 8 - 0.94 = 7.06$$

For the group tutorial condition it is 5.57:

$$5 - \left(\frac{6}{12} \times (2 - 3.13) \right) = 5 - (0.5 \times -1.13) = 5 - -0.57 = 5.57$$

Although the difference for the adjusted means for post-test marks is smaller than that for the unadjusted means, post-test marks in the individual tutorial condition are still higher than those in the group tutorial condition.

One requirement that has to be met before a significant between-groups effect can be interpreted is that the statistical association known as the *regression coefficient* is the same within each of the treatment groups and is linear in the sense that higher levels of the dependent variable indicate higher levels of the covariate. This assumption is called *homogeneity of regression*. It is based on dividing or partitioning the adjusted within-groups sum of squares for the dependent variable into the *between-regressions* sum of squares and the remaining sum of squares (the remainder). These sums of squares and their associated degrees of freedom are shown in Table 10.16. The between-regressions mean square is its sum of squares divided by its degrees of freedom which are the number of groups minus 1. The remainder mean square is its sum of squares divided by its degrees of freedom which are the number of cases minus twice the number of groups. The F test for homogeneity of regression is the between-regressions mean square divided by the remainder mean square.

We have already described how to calculate the adjusted within-groups sum of squares for the dependent variable. The between-regressions sum of squares (BRSS) is the sum of the sum of products for each group (SP_1, SP_2 ...) squared and then divided by the covariate sum of squares for each group (SS_{1cov}, SS_{2cov} ...) from which is subtracted the within-groups sum of products (WGSP) squared and then divided by the within-groups sum of squares ($WGSS_{cov}$) for the covariate:

$$BRSS = \left(\frac{SP_1{}^2}{SS_{1cov}} + \frac{SP_2{}^2}{SS_{2cov}} + \ldots \right) - \frac{WGSP^2}{WGSS_{cov}}$$

The remainder sum of squares is simply obtained by subtracting the between-regressions sum of squares from the adjusted within-groups sum of squares:

remainder SS = $WGSS_{adj}$ − BRSS

To compute the F test for homogeneity of regression we carry out the following steps which will be illustrated with the pre- and post-test marks of the women in the individual and group tutorial conditions.

Step 1 Calculate the sum of products for each group by: (1) subtracting the covariate group mean from each of its individual scores in the group; (2) subtracting the dependent variable group mean from each of its individual scores in the group; (3) multiplying the deviation for each pair of covariate and dependent individual scores; and (4) summing the products within each group.

The sum of products for the individual tutorial condition is 2:

$[(5 - 5) \times (7 - 8)] + [(3 - 5) \times (8 - 8)] + [(7 - 5) \times (9 - 8)] =$
$(0 \times -1) + (-2 \times 0) + (2 \times 1) = 0 + 0 + 2 = 2$

Table 10.16 Between-regressions and remaining sums of squares and degrees of freedom

Source of variation	Degrees of freedom
Between-regressions	No. of groups − 1
Remainder	No. of cases − (2 × no. of groups)
Adjusted within-groups	No. of cases − no. of groups − 1

The sum of products for the group tutorial condition is 4:

$$[(1 - 2) \times (4 - 5)] + [(1 - 2) \times (4 - 5)] + [(2 - 2) \times (5 - 5)] +$$
$$[(3 - 2) \times (6 - 5)] + [(3 - 2) \times (6 - 5)] =$$
$$(-1 \times -1) + (-1 \times -1) + (0 \times 0) + (1 \times 1) + (1 \times 1) =$$
$$1 + 1 + 0 + 1 + 1 = 4$$

Step 2   Calculate the covariate sum of squares for each group by (1) subtracting the covariate group mean from each of its individual scores in the group; (2) squaring the differences; and (3) summing the results within each group.

The sum of squares for pre-test marks in the individual tutorial condition is 8:

$$(5 - 5)^2 + (3 - 5)^2 + (7 - 5)^2 = 0^2 + -2^2 + 2^2 =$$
$$0 + 4 + 4 = 8$$

The sum of squares for pre-test marks in the group tutorial condition is 4:

$$(1 - 2)^2 + (1 - 2)^2 + (2 - 2)^2 + (3 - 2)^2 + (3 - 2)^2 =$$
$$-1^2 + -1^2 + 0^2 + 1^2 + 1^2 = 1 + 1 + 0 + 1 + 1 = 4$$

Step 3   Calculate the between-regressions sum of squares by substituting the appropriate values into the following formula:

$$\text{BRSS} = \left(\frac{\text{SP}_1{}^2}{\text{SS}_{1\text{cov}}} + \frac{\text{SP}_2{}^2}{\text{SS}_{2\text{cov}}} + \ldots \right) - \frac{\text{WGSP}^2}{\text{WGSS}_{\text{cov}}}$$

The between-regressions sum of squares for post-test marks is 1.5:

$$\left(\frac{2^2}{8} + \frac{4^2}{4} \right) - \frac{6^2}{12} = \frac{4}{8} + \frac{16}{4} - \frac{36}{12} = 0.5 + 4.0 - 3.0 = 1.5$$

Step 4   Calculate the remainder sum of squares by subtracting the between-regressions sum of squares from the adjusted within-groups sum of squares.

The remainder sum of squares for post-test marks is 1.5 ($3.0 - 1.5 = 1.5$).

Step 5   Calculate the between-regressions mean square by dividing the between-regressions sum of squares by its degrees of freedom.

The between-regressions mean square for post-test marks is 1.5 [$1.5/(2 - 1) = 1.5$].

Step 6   Calculate the remainder mean square by dividing the remainder sum of squares by its degrees of freedom.

The remainder mean square for post-test marks is its sum of squares (1.5) divided by its degrees of freedom $[8 - (2 \times 2) = 4]$ which gives 0.375 (1.5/4 = 0.375).

Step 7 Calculate the F test for homogeneity of regression by dividing the between-regressions mean square by the remainder mean square.
The F test in this case is 4.0 (1.5/0.375 = 4.00).

Step 8 Look up the statistical significance of the F ratio in the table in Appendix 3.
With 1 and 4 degrees of freedom in the numerator and denominator respectively, F has to be 7.7086 or bigger to be significant at the 0.05 level, which it is not. Therefore, the regression coefficient is the same in each of the groups.

The sum of squares, degrees of freedom, mean square and F ratio for these two sources of variation are presented in Table 10.17.

If we had more than two conditions, we would need to determine which of the adjusted means in the conditions differed significantly from one another. For planned or *a priori* comparisons we could run separate analyses of covariance on the pairs of groups being compared.

For unplanned or *post hoc* comparisons, we would use the Bryant–Paulson procedure (Stevens 1992). The following formula is used for a non-randomised study with one covariate where the subscripts 1 and 2 denote the two groups being compared and n is the sample size of the group.

$$\frac{\text{adjusted mean}_1 - \text{adjusted mean}_2}{\sqrt{\dfrac{\text{adjusted error mean square} \times \left(\dfrac{2}{n} + \dfrac{(\text{covariate mean}_1 - \text{covariate mean}_2)^2}{\text{covariate error sum of squares}}\right)}{2}}}$$

The error term must be computed separately for each comparison.

Table 10.17 Analysis of covariance table for between-regressions and remaining sources of variation

Source of variation	SS	df	MS	F	p
Between-regressions	1.50	1	1.500	4.00	*ns*
Remainder	1.50	4	0.375		
Adjusted within-groups	3.00	5			

For a randomised study with one covariate we need to use the following formula

$$\frac{\text{adjusted mean}_1 - \text{adjusted mean}_2}{\sqrt{\dfrac{\text{adjusted error mean square} \times \left(1 + \dfrac{\text{covariate between-groups mean square}}{\text{covariate error sum of squares}}\right)}{\text{number of cases in each group}}}}$$

Where the group sizes are unequal, the *harmonic* mean of the sample size is used. For two groups the harmonic mean is defined as follows:

$$\text{harmonic mean} = \frac{2 \times n_1 \times n_2}{n_1 + n_2}$$

The harmonic mean for the individual and group tutorial conditions is 3.75 [$(2 \times 3 \times 5)/(3 + 5) = 30/8 = 3.75$].

We will show the calculation of the second procedure by comparing the adjusted mean post-test mark of the individual and group tutorial condition for women. Inserting the pertinent values in this formula we find that the value for this procedure is 2.37:

$$\frac{7.06 - 5.57}{\sqrt{\dfrac{0.60 \times \left(1 + \dfrac{16.90}{12}\right)}{3.75}}} = \frac{1.49}{\sqrt{\dfrac{0.60 \times (1 + 1.408)}{3.75}}} =$$

$$\frac{1.49}{\sqrt{\dfrac{0.60 \times 2.408}{3.75}}} = \frac{1.49}{\sqrt{\dfrac{1.45}{3.75}}} = \frac{1.49}{\sqrt{0.39}} = \frac{1.49}{0.63} = 2.37$$

We look up the two-tailed 0.05 critical value of this procedure in the table in Appendix 9 where we see that with 5 degrees of freedom for the error term, one covariate and two groups the value has to be 4.06 or bigger to be significant, which it is not.

One-way analysis of covariance may be computed in SPSS with either the **Simple Factorial ANOVA** or the **General Factorial ANOVA** procedure. The advantage of using the latter procedure is that the output includes the F test for homogeneity of regression. To carry out this analysis with either procedure, first select the women (**sex=1**).

The **Simple Factorial ANOVA** procedure is:

→**Statistics** →**ANOVA Models** →**Simple Factorial** . . . [opens **Simple Factorial ANOVA** dialog box as in Box 9.1]

→dependent variable [e.g. **markpos**] → ▶button beside **Dependent:** [puts variable in this box] →independent variable [e.g. **cond**] → ▶button beside **Factor(s):** [puts variable in this box] →**Define Range . . .** [opens **Simple Factorial ANOVA: Define Range** dialog box as in Box 9.2] →in box beside **Minimum:** type lower code value [e.g. **2** for individual tutorial group] →box beside **Maximum:** and type upper code value [e.g. **3**] →**Continue** [closes **Simple Factorial ANOVA: Define Range** dialog box] →covariate [e.g. **markpre**] → ▶button beside **Covariate(s):** [puts covariate in this box] →**Options . . .** [opens **Simple Factorial ANOVA: Options** dialog box as in Box 9.3] →**Hierarchical** or **Experimental** [in **Method** section] [for statistics in **Statistics** section] →**Means and counts** [in **Statistics** section] →**MCA** [in **Statistics** section] →**Continue** [closes **Simple Factorial ANOVA: Options** dialog box] →**OK**

Table 10.18 shows the analysis of covariance table for this analysis. The sum of squares for the covariate (**18.122**) is that for the post-test marks regressed on the pre-test marks and represents the variation in the post-test marks that is accounted for by the pre-test marks. Table 10.19 displays the multiple classification table. The adjusted mean for post-test marks in the individual tutorial condition can be calculated by adding the deviation adjusted for the covariate (**.94**) to the grand mean (**6.13**) giving a value of 7.07. Similarly, the adjusted mean for post-test marks in the group tutorial condition is worked out by subtracting the deviation adjusted for the covariate (**−.56**) from the grand mean (**6.13**) giving a value of 5.57.

Eta is the square root of eta squared which in turn is the between-groups variance divided by the total variance, both of which are unadjusted. From our manual calculations, the between-groups sum of squares was 16.90 and the total sum of squares was 22.90. Dividing 16.90 by 22.90 and taking the square root of the result ($\sqrt{0.738}$) yields an eta of **.86**. **Multiple R Squared** is based on the sums of squares shown in Table 10.18. It is the covariate and main effect sums of squares added together (**18.122 + 1.753 = 19.875**) and divided by the total sum of squares (**22.875**) which gives a squared multiple correlation of **.869 (19.875/22.875** = 0.8689). **Multiple R** is the square root of this value ($\sqrt{.869}$ = **.932**).

For the **General Factorial ANOVA** procedure, we first carry out the following procedure to test whether the regression lines are the same in each of the cells:

→**Statistics** →**ANOVA Models** →**General Factorial . . .** [opens **General Factorial ANOVA** dialog box as in Box 10.3] →dependent variable [e.g. **markpos**] → ▶button beside **Dependent Variable:** [puts variable in this box]

Table 10.18 SPSS output for a one-way analysis of covariance table using the **Simple Factorial ANOVA** procedure

A N A L Y S I S   O F   V A R I A N C E

MARKPOS post-test marks

by   COND

with MARKPRE pre-test mark

HIERARCHICAL sums of squares

Covariates entered FIRST

Source of Variation	Sum of Squares	DF	Mean Square	F	Sig of F
Covariates	18.122	1	18.122	30.203	.003
MARKPRE	18.122	1	18.122	30.203	.003
Main Effects	1.753	1	1.753	2.922	.148
COND	1.753	1	1.753	2.922	.148
Explained	19.875	2	9.938	16.563	.006
Residual	3.000	5	.600		
Total	22.875	7	3.268		

10 cases were processed.
2 cases (20.0 pct) were missing.

→independent variable [e.g. **cond**] →▶button beside **Factor(s):** [puts variable in this box] →**Define Range . . .** [opens **General Factorial ANOVA: Define Range** dialog box as in Box 10.4]
→in box beside **Minimum:** type lower code value [e.g. **2**] →box beside **Maximum:** and type upper code value [e.g. **3**] →**Continue** [closes **General Factorial ANOVA: Define Range** dialog box]
→covariate [e.g. **markpre**] →▶button beside **Covariate(s):** [puts covariate in this box]
→**Model . . .** [opens **General Factorial ANOVA: Model** dialog box as in Box 10.5]
→**Custom** →independent variable [e.g. **cond**] →▶button [puts variable under **Model:**] →covariate [e.g. **markpre**] →▶button [puts covariate under **Model:**] →**Interaction** →independent variable [e.g. **cond**] →covariate [e.g. **markpre**] →▶button [puts **cond*markpre** under **Model:**]
→**Continue** [closes **General Factorial ANOVA: Model** dialog box]
→**OK**

Table 10.19 SPSS output of the multiple classification table for a one-way analysis of covariance

---

* * * M U L T I P L E   C L A S S I F I C A T I O N   A N A L Y S I S * * *

MARKPOS post-test marks

by   COND

with MARKPRE pre-test marks

				Adjusted for
Grand Mean =	6.13			Independents
			Unadjusted	+ Covariates
Variable + Category	N	Dev'n	Eta	Dev'n	Beta
COND					
2 indivtut	3	1.88		.94	
3 grouptut	5	-1.13		-.56	
			.86		.43
Multiple R Squared				.869	
Multiple R				.932	

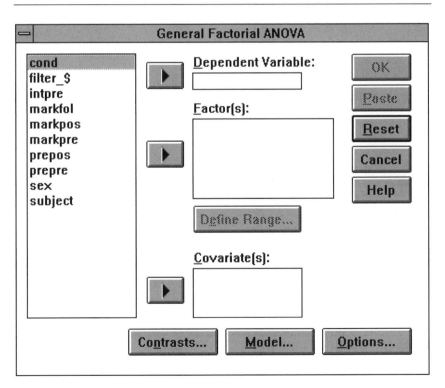

Box 10.3 **General Factorial ANOVA** dialog box

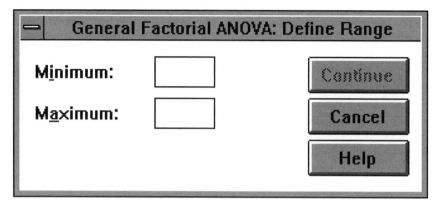

Box 10.4 **General Factorial ANOVA: Define Range** dialog box

Box 10.5 **General Factorial ANOVA: Model** dialog box

Table 10.20 presents the *F* ratio of the interaction between the independent variable of treatment and the covariate (**COND * MARKPRE**) which is not significant since *p* is **.116**. This means that the slope of the regression line in each of the cells is similar and therefore the homogeneity of regression assumption is met.

Table 10.20 SPSS output of the *F* test of homogeneity of regression for a one-way analysis of covariance using the **General Factorial ANOVA** procedure

* * * * * * A n a l y s i s   o f   V a r i a n c e -- design 1 * * * * * *

Tests of Significance for MARKPOS using UNIQUE sums of squares

Source of Variation	SS	DF	MS	F	Sig of F
WITHIN+RESIDUAL	1.50	4	.37		
COND	3.02	1	3.02	8.05	.047
MARKPRE	4.17	1	4.17	11.11	.029
COND * MARKPRE	1.50	1	1.50	4.00	.116
(Model)	21.38	3	7.13	19.00	.008
(Total)	22.88	7	3.27		

R-Squared = .934
Adjusted R-Squared = .885

Consequently we can proceed with the main analysis of covariance using the following procedure:

→**Statistics** →**ANOVA Models** →**General Factorial . . .** [opens **General Factorial ANOVA** dialog box as in Box 10.3]
→dependent variable [e.g. **markpos**] →▶button beside **Dependent Variable:** [puts variable in this box] →independent variable [e.g. **cond**] →▶button beside **Factor(s):** [puts variable in this box] →**Define Range . . .** [opens **General Factorial ANOVA: Define Range** dialog box as in Box 10.4]
→in box beside **Minimum:** type lower code value [e.g. **2**] →box beside **Maximum:** and type upper code value [e.g. **3**] →**Continue** [closes **General Factorial ANOVA: Define Range** dialog box]
→covariate [e.g. **markpre**] →▶button beside **Covariate(s):** [puts variable in this box]
→**Model . . .** [opens **General Factorial ANOVA: Model** dialog box as in Box 10.5]
→**Full factorial** →**Continue** [closes **General Factorial ANOVA: Model** dialog box]
→**Options . . .** [opens **General Factorial ANOVA: Options** dialog box as in Box 10.6]
→independent variable [e.g. **cond**] →▶button [puts variable under **Display Means for:**] →**Continue** [closes **General Factorial ANOVA: Options** dialog box]
→**OK**

```
┌─────────────────────────────────────────────────────────────────────────────┐
│ ▭              General Factorial ANOVA: Options                               │
│ ┌─Observed and Predicted Means──────────────────────────────┐  ┌──────────┐  │
│ │  Factor(s):                    Display Means for:          │  │ Continue │  │
│ │  ┌────────────────────┐        ┌────────────────────┐     │  └──────────┘  │
│ │  │cond                │        │                    │     │  ┌──────────┐  │
│ │  │                    │  ┌───┐ │                    │     │  │ Cancel   │  │
│ │  │                    │  │ ▶ │ │                    │     │  └──────────┘  │
│ │  │                    │  └───┘ │                    │     │  ┌──────────┐  │
│ │  │                    │        │                    │     │  │ Help     │  │
│ │  └────────────────────┘        └────────────────────┘     │  └──────────┘  │
│ └───────────────────────────────────────────────────────────┘                │
│ ┌─Matrices Within Cells──────┐  ┌─Diagnostics───────────────┐                 │
│ │  ☐ Correlation             │  │  ☐ Homogeneity tests      │                 │
│ │  ☐ Covariance              │  │  ☐ Homogeneity plots      │                 │
│ │  ☐ SSCP                    │  │  ☐ Residual plots         │                 │
│ └────────────────────────────┘  │  ☐ Residuals list         │                 │
│    ☐ Estimates of effect size   └───────────────────────────┘                 │
│    ☐ Observed power for │.05│ significance level                              │
└─────────────────────────────────────────────────────────────────────────────┘
```

Box 10.6 **General Factorial ANOVA: Options** dialog box

Table 10.21 SPSS output of the means of the pre- and post-test marks for women in the two tutorial conditions

* * * * * * A n a l y s i s   o f   V a r i a n c e -- design 1 * * * * * *

Combined Observed Means for COND

Variable . . MARKPOS

	COND		
	indivtut	WGT.	8.00000
		UNWGT.	8.00000
	grouptut	WGT.	5.00000
		UNWGT.	5.00000

- -

Variable . . MARKPRE

	COND		
	indivtut	WGT.	5.00000
		UNWGT.	5.00000
	grouptut	WGT.	2.00000
		UNWGT.	2.00000

- -

Table 10.22 SPSS output of a one-way analysis of covariance using the **General Factorial ANOVA** procedure

---

* * * * * * A n a l y s i s o f V a r i a n c e -- design 1 * * * * * *

Tests of Significance for MARKPOS using UNIQUE sums of squares

Source of Variation	SS	DF	MS	F	Sig of F
WITHIN+RESIDUAL	3.00	5	.60		
REGRESSION	3.00	1	3.00	5.00	.076
COND	1.75	1	1.75	2.92	.148
(Model)	19.88	2	9.94	16.56	.006
(Total)	22.88	7	3.27		

R-Squared =   .869
Adjusted R-Squared = .816

- -

Regression analysis for WITHIN+RESIDUAL error term

--- Individual Univariate .9500 confidence intervals

Dependent variable . . MARKPOS   post-test marks

COVARIATE	B	Beta	Std. Err.	t-Value	Sig. of t
MARKPRE	.50000	.56176	.224	2.236	.076

COVARIATE	Lower -95%	CL- Upper
MARKPRE	−.075	1.075

- -

Adjusted and Estimated Means

Variable . . MARKPOS   post-test marks

CELL	Obs. Mean	Adj. Mean	Est. Mean	Raw Resid.	Std. Resid.
1	8.000	7.250	8.000	.000	.000
2	5.000	5.750	5.000	.000	.000

- -

Table 10.21 shows the pre- and post-test means for women in the individual and group tutorial conditions. Table 10.22 presents much of the rest of the output. The F ratio for the tutorial groups (**COND**) is **2.92** and is not significant with a p of **.148**. The unstandardised partial regression coefficient (**B**) between **MARKPOS** and **MARKPRE** is **.50000**. The adjusted mean (**Adj. Mean**) for the individual tutorial condition (**CELL 1**) is **7.250** and for the group tutorial condition (**CELL 2**) is **5.750**. The adjusted means for the present procedure differ somewhat from those in the previous one in that the unweighted rather than the weighted covariate grand mean is used. The unweighted covariate grand mean is 3.5 while the weighted covariate grand mean is 3.15. If we substitute the unweighted for the weighted covariate grand mean, the adjusted post-test mark is 7.25 for the individual tutorial condition and 5.75 for the group tutorial condition.

$$8 - \left(\frac{6}{12} \times (5 - 3.5) \right) = 8 - (0.5 \times 1.5) = 8 - 0.75 = 7.25$$

$$5 - \left(\frac{6}{12} \times (2 - 3.5) \right) = 5 - (0.5 \times -1.5) = 5 - -0.75 = 5.75$$

REGRESSION ANALYSIS AND ONE-WAY ANALYSIS OF COVARIANCE

To carry out a one-way analysis of covariance with regression analysis, we create an effect dummy variable for the two tutorial conditions with 1 representing the individual tutorial condition and -1 the group tutorial condition. To work out the sum of squares for the tutorial conditions, we first regress post-test marks on pre-test marks and the conditions dummy variable. From the sum of squares for this regression (**19.87500**) we subtract the sum of squares for post-test marks regressed on pre-test marks (**18.12175**), which gives 1.75 (**19.87500 – 18.12175 = 1.75325**). The residual sum of squares is that for post-test marks regressed on pre-test marks and the conditions dummy variable (**3.00000**). Table 10.23 shows the analysis of variance table and the partial regression coefficents for the first regression and Table 10.24 that for the second regression.

SUMMARY

Two-way analysis of variance with repeated measures on one factor compares the means of groups consisting of two factors, one of which is repeated. Where differences were predicted a related t test is used for related pairs of groups and an unrelated t test for unrelated pairs. Where differences were not predicted, the Bonferroni test could be applied to related scores and the Scheffé test to unrelated scores. One-way analysis of covariance compares the means of two or more groups controlling for

Table 10.23 SPSS output showing the analysis of variance table and partial regression coefficients for post-test marks regressed on the pre-test marks and the conditions dummy variable

Analysis of Variance

	DF	Sum of Squares	Mean Square
Regression	2	19.87500	9.93750
Residual	5	3.00000	.60000

F = 16.56250   Signif F = .0062

---------------- Variables in the Equation ----------------

Variable	B	SE B	Beta	T	Sig T
DCOND	.750000	.438748	.429449	1.709	.1481
MARKPRE	.500000	.223607	.561760	2.236	.0756
(Constant)	4.750000	.832166		5.708	.0023

Table 10.24 SPSS output showing the analysis of variance table for post-test marks regressed on the pre-test marks

Analysis of Variance

	DF	Sum of Squares	Mean Square
Regression	1	18.12175	18.12175
Residual	6	4.75325	.79221

F = 22.87500   Signif F = .0031

the effects of a second factor known to be associated with the first factor and called a covariate. Interpretation of the analysis depends on the regression coefficient being the same within each of the groups. A two-group analysis of covariance tests for differences between pairs of groups which were predicted and the Bryant–Paulson procedure for differences which were not predicted.

EXERCISES

Use the data in Table 5.12 for these exercises.

1 Use a two-way analysis of variance with repeated measures on one factor to determine whether any change in educational interest between 12 and 15 differs for pupils from single- and mixed-sex schools.
   (a) What is the value of the F test?

   (b) What are its degrees of freedom?

   (c) What is its probability level?

   (d) Does any change in educational interest between 12 and 15 differ for pupils from single- and mixed-sex schools?

2 Use a one-way analysis of covariance to determine whether there is a significant difference in educational interest at 12 between single- and mixed-sex schools when socio-economic status is covaried.

   (a) What is the value of the F test for the adjusted between-groups effect?

   (b) What are its degrees of freedom?

   (c) What is its probability level?

   (d) What is the value of the F test for homogeneity of regression?

   (e) What are its degrees of freedom?

   (f) What is its probability level?

   (g) Is the regression coefficient the same in the two groups of single- and mixed-sex schools?

   (h) What is the adjusted mean of educational interest at 12 for pupils from single-sex schools?

   (i) What is the adjusted mean of educational interest at 12 for pupils from mixed-sex schools?

   (j) Is educational interest at 12 significantly greater in single- than in mixed-sex schools when socio-economic status is covaried?

11 Tests of difference for categorical data

The statistical tests covered in this chapter only apply to data in which the number of cases falling into various categories is simply counted. The tests determine whether the frequency of cases in the different categories varies across one or more groups or from some expected distribution. We would use these tests to answer the following kinds of questions. Is the number of students in a sample obtaining above a particular mark similar to the number achieving that level in the population from which the sample was drawn? Is the number of students attaining that level similar for coursework carried out at pre-test, post-test and follow-up? Are the numbers of management, sociology, education and psychology students in the sample similar to the numbers studying those subjects in the student population? New sets of data will be introduced to illustrate many of the points covered in this chapter since the number of cases in the example used up to now is generally not ideal for this purpose. The same variables, however, will be used.

BINOMIAL TEST FOR ONE SAMPLE

The binomial test determines whether the number of cases that fall into one of only two categories differs significantly from some expected proportion. Suppose, for instance, we know that half the students in the population achieve a mark of 3 or less on their first piece of coursework and that of a small sample of five students all five obtained a mark of more than 3. On the basis of these figures, can we assume that in terms of their marks our sample represents the population? The binomial test can be used to answer this question, the only two categories being a mark of 3 or less and a mark of more than 3.

The following formula can be used for calculating the probability of obtaining a particular number of cases in categories A and B

$$\frac{\text{total number of cases } (N)!}{\text{number of } A\ (n)! \times \text{number of } B\ (N-n)!} \times \text{probability of } A^n \times \text{probability of } B^{N-n}$$

where the exclamation mark (!) signifies a *factorial* expression. For example, $N!$ means $N \times (N - 1) \times (N - 2) \ldots N \times [N - (N - 1)]$.

We can illustrate the use of this formula to find out what the probability is of obtaining five marks bigger than 3 ($n = 5$) in a sample of five ($N = 5$) when the probability of obtaining a mark of more than 3 is 0.5 and the probability of obtaining a mark of 3 or less is therefore also 0.5. Inserting the relevant values into the above formula, we see that the probability of obtaining a sample of five marks greater than 3 and no marks of 3 or less is 0.031.

$$\frac{5!}{5! \times (5 - 5)!} \times 0.5^5 \times 0.5^{5-5} =$$

$$\frac{5!}{5! \times 1} \times 0.03125 \ (\times 1) = \frac{5 \times 4 \times 3 \times 2 \times 1}{5 \times 4 \times 3 \times 2 \times 1} \times 0.03125 =$$

$$1 \times 0.03125 = 0.03125$$

The probability of obtaining a sample of four marks greater than 3 and one mark of 3 or less is 0.156.

$$\frac{5!}{4! \times (5 - 4)!} \times 0.5^4 \times 0.5^{5-4} =$$

$$\frac{5!}{4! \times 1!} \times 0.0625 \times 0.5 = \frac{5 \times 4 \times 3 \times 2 \times 1}{4 \times 3 \times 2 \times 1 \times 1} \times 0.03125 =$$

$$5 \times 0.03125 = 0.15625$$

Consequently, the probability of obtaining five marks of more than 3 and no marks of 3 or less as well as four marks of more than 3 and one mark of 3 or less is the sum of their separate probabilities which is the cumulative probability of 0.188 ($0.03125 + 0.15625 = 0.1875$).

If the size of the sample is less than 26 and the probability of obtaining either outcome is 0.5, we can look up the cumulative probability of finding a particular outcome in the table in Appendix 10. To use the table we need to know the size of the sample (which is represented by N and which in this case is 5) and the smaller of the two frequencies (which is indicated by n and which is 0 for men). The size of the sample being investigated is given in the left hand column of the table and varies from 1 to 25, while the smaller frequency is presented along the top row of the table and ranges from 0 to 15.

Reading from the table, the relevant part of which has been reproduced in Table 11.1, we can see that the probability of obtaining five marks of more than 3 and no marks of 3 or less is 0.031. Incidentally, this figure is identical to that worked out in Chapter 4 for the probability of finding all five people in a sample to be women when there are equal numbers of women and men in the population. The probability values in this table are

Table 11.1 Part of the binomial test one-tailed probabilities table

N\n	0	1	2	. . . 15
4	0.062	0.312	0.687	
5	0.031	0.188	0.500	
6	0.016	0.109	0.344	
.				
.				
.				
25				

one-tailed. Since we have not specified the direction of the results we expected to find, a two-tailed probability level is more appropriate. To obtain this, we simply double the one-tailed level which gives a two-tailed probability of 0.062 ($0.031 \times 2 = 0.062$). Since the figure of 0.062 is larger than 0.05, we would conclude that our sample of marks does not differ significantly from the expected proportion of marks in the population which is 0.5. Note also that the probability of a sample of five marks of more than 3 and one or no marks of 3 or less is 0.188, which is the same as the figure previously calculated.

If the size of our sample is larger than 25 and the probability of obtaining either outcome is near to 0.5, then the binomial distribution tends to be similar to the normal distribution which may be used instead. So, to determine the probability of a particular outcome under these circumstances, we calculate the z value of finding this result by using the following formula:

$$z = \frac{\text{smaller frequency} - (\text{number of cases} \times \text{expected probability of one category})}{\sqrt{(\text{number of cases} \times \text{expected probability of one category} \times \text{expected probability of other category})}}$$

Suppose that 30 of the 40 people in our sample attained a mark of more than 3. On the basis of these figures, could we argue that with respect to their marks our sample was representative of the population? To work out whether this is the case, we need to substitute the following numbers into the formula:

$$\frac{10 - (40 \times 0.5)}{\sqrt{40 \times 0.5 \times 0.5}} = \frac{-10}{3.162} = -3.16$$

The category with the smaller frequency is marks of 3 or less, of which there are 10. The expected probability of sampling a mark of either more than 3 or 3 or less is 0.5 and the total number of people in the sample is 40. To determine the statistical significance of this z value, we ignore its sign and look it up in the table in Appendix 2 where we see that the probability of this value occurring by chance is 0.0009.

The normal distribution is based on a continuous variable (consisting of non-whole numbers) whereas the binomial distribution assumes a discrete variable (comprising whole numbers). The binomial distribution can be made more similar to the normal distribution when a correction for continuity is included. This is done by presupposing that the frequency of cases in the smaller category (e.g. 10) occupies an interval, the lower limit of which is half a unit (0.5) below its observed value (10 − 0.5 = 9.5) while its upper limit is half a unit (0.5) above it (10 + 0.5 = 10.5). The correction for continuity consists of reducing by 0.5 the difference between the observed value of the smaller category (10) and its expected value (40 × 0.5 = 20). So, in this case, where the observed frequency (10) is less than the expected frequency (20), we would add 0.5 to 10. If we substitute this new value in the formula for calculating z, we would obtain a z value of -3.00:

$$\frac{10.5 - 20}{3.162} = \frac{-9.5}{3.162} = -3.00$$

Looking up this figure in the table in Appendix 2, we see that the probability of obtaining this result at the one-tailed level is slightly higher at 0.0013 which when doubled gives a two-tailed level of 0.0026. Consequently, we would conclude that the proportion of marks of more than 3 in our sample was significantly greater than that in the population.

To carry out the first analysis with SPSS, we code marks of more than 3 and 3 or less as, say, **1** and **0** respectively and enter this code into **Newdata** in, say, the first five rows of the first column. We then execute the following procedure:

→**Statistics** →**Nonparametric Tests** →**Binomial** . . . [opens **Binomial Test** dialog box as in Box 11.1]
→variable [e.g. **marks**] →▶ button [puts variable under **Test Variable List:**] →box called **Test Proportion:** and type expected proportion [**.5** is the default value]→**OK**

Table 11.2 presents the output for this analysis which gives an **Exact Binomial 2–Tailed P** of .0625.

To enter the data for the second analysis we can enter **1** in the first row of the first column and **0** in the second row of that column. Next we enter **30** in the first row of the second column and **10** in the second row of that column. We then perform the following sequence to weight the values in the first column by those in the second:

→**Data** →**Weight Cases** . . . [opens **Weight Cases** dialog box as in Box 11.2]
→**Weight cases by** →weighting factor [e.g. **var00002**] →▶ button [puts weighting factor in **Frequency Variable:** text box →**OK**

Table 11.3 shows the output for this second analysis which gives a **Z Approximation 2-Tailed P** of **.0027**.

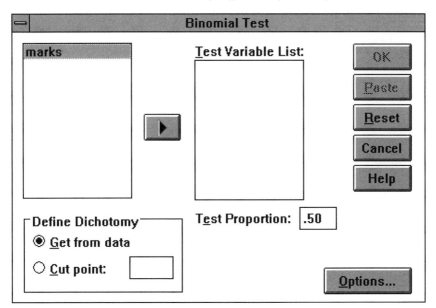

Box 11.1 **Binomial Test** dialog box

Table 11.2 SPSS output for the binomial test with all five cases having the same value

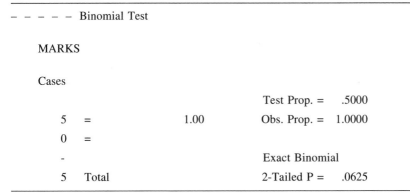

CHI-SQUARE TEST FOR ONE OR MORE UNRELATED SAMPLES

The Pearson chi-square (pronounced 'ky-square' and symbolized as χ^2) test compares the observed frequency of cases against the expected frequency for one or more unrelated samples on a variable which may have two or more categories (Pearson 1900). It does this for each category of the sample. The closer the expected number is to the observed number across

```
┌─────────────────────────────────────────────────────────────────────┐
│ ▭                        Weight Cases                                 │
├─────────────────────────────────────────────────────────────────────┤
│ ┌──────────────┐   ┌──────────────────────────────────┐  ┌─────────┐ │
│ │ marks        │   │ ◉ Do not weight cases            │  │   OK    │ │
│ │ var00002     │   │                                  │  └─────────┘ │
│ │              │   │ ○ Weight cases by                │  ┌─────────┐ │
│ │              │   │        Frequency Variable:       │  │  Paste  │ │
│ │              │   │   ┌───┐ ┌──────────────────────┐ │  └─────────┘ │
│ │              │   │   │ ▶ │ │                      │ │  ┌─────────┐ │
│ │              │   │   └───┘ └──────────────────────┘ │  │  Reset  │ │
│ │              │   │                                  │  └─────────┘ │
│ │              │   └──────────────────────────────────┘  ┌─────────┐ │
│ │              │                                         │ Cancel  │ │
│ │              │    Current Status: Do not weight cases  └─────────┘ │
│ └──────────────┘                                         ┌─────────┐ │
│                                                          │  Help   │ │
│                                                          └─────────┘ │
└─────────────────────────────────────────────────────────────────────┘
```

Box 11.2 **Weight Cases** dialog box

Table 11.3 SPSS output for the binomial test with 30 of the 40 cases having the same value

---

– – – – – Binomial Test

MARKS

Cases

			Test Prop. =	.5000
30	=	1.00	Obs. Prop. =	.7500
10	=	.00		
--			Z Approximation	
40	Total		2-Tailed P =	.0027

---

all categories, the less likely it is that any difference between the observed and expected frequency is statistically significant. The general formula for calculating chi-square is:

$$\text{chi-square} = \text{sum of } \frac{(\text{observed frequency} - \text{expected frequency})^2}{\text{expected frequency}} \text{ for each category}$$

Note, however, that many textbooks on statistics suggest that chi-square should only be used when the expected frequency is not too small. The reason for this restriction is that the distribution of the chi-square statistic, like the normal distribution, is a smooth, continuous curve. Observed frequencies, however, change in discrete steps, such as from 1 to 2 and 2 to 3. Discrepancies between the smooth distribution of chi-square and the steplike distribution of frequencies are likely to be bigger when the frequencies are small.

Based on the recommendations of Cochran (1954), Siegel in his influential text on non-parametric statistics (Siegel 1956; Siegel and Castellan

1988) suggested that, with two categories from one sample, the minimum expected frequency in either category should be 5. If one or both of the expected frequencies is less than 5, the binomial test should be used. In the case of one sample with three or more categories, chi-square should not be used when any expected frequency is less than 1 or when more than 20 per cent of the expected frequencies are smaller than 5. This restriction also applies to the following two situations: (1) two samples with a variable of three or more categories; and (2) three or more samples with a variable of only two categories. In all three of these cases, it may be possible to increase the expected frequencies in a category by combining it with those of another. Siegel's suggestions for the special case of two samples with a variable of two categories will be discussed when we present this case later on.

CHI-SQUARE TEST FOR ONE SAMPLE

Because it is the simplest, we will begin by describing the calculation of chi-square for two categories for one sample. We will use the previous example to illustrate its calculation in that we wish to determine whether a sample containing 30 out of 40 marks greater than 3 differs significantly from a population where the expected proportion of such marks is 0.5. Computing chi-square involves carrying out the following six steps:

Step 1   Calculate the expected frequency for each cell. Since the expected proportion of marks greater than 3 is 0.5 and the total number of cases in the sample is 40, then the expected frequency of such marks should be 20 ($0.5 \times 40 = 20$). Similarly, the expected frequency of marks of 3 or less is also 20 ($0.5 \times 40 = 20$). The observed and expected frequencies for this example are shown in Table 11.4.

Step 2   Subtract the expected frequency from the observed frequency for each cell and square the difference. The differences are squared to remove the minus values. If this was not done the sum of differences equals zero since the sum of negative differences is equal to the sum of positive differences.

Step 3   Divide the squared difference by the expected frequency of that cell (to take account of the expected size of that cell). Note that in this case the expected frequencies are the same although this is often not the case.

Table 11.4 Observed and expected frequency for one sample with two categories

Frequencies	4+	3−
Observed	30	10
Expected	20	20

Step 4   Add together the results for all the cells.

Applying Steps 2 to 4, we see that chi-square is 10.

$$\frac{(30-20)^2}{20} + \frac{(10-20)^2}{20} = \frac{10^2}{20} + \frac{-10^2}{20} = \frac{100}{20} + \frac{100}{20} = 5 + 5 = 10$$

Note that if we had not squared the difference between the observed and expected difference, chi-square equals 0 since the sum of the negative differences equals the sum of the positive differences.

$$\frac{(30-20)}{20} + \frac{(10-20)}{20} = \frac{10}{20} + \frac{-10}{20} = 0.5 + -0.5 = 0$$

Note also that it does not matter whether we subtract the expected frequency from the observed frequency (observed frequency – expected frequency), as shown in the above formula, or the observed frequency from the expected frequency (expected frequency – observed frequency) provided that we adopt one or other order for the test.

$$\frac{(20-30)^2}{20} + \frac{(20-10)^2}{20} = \frac{-10^2}{20} + \frac{10^2}{20} = \frac{100}{20} + \frac{100}{20} = 5 + 5 = 10$$

Step 5   Calculate the degrees of freedom for a one sample chi-square which are the number of categories minus 1. In this case the degree of freedom is 1 ($2 - 1 = 1$).

Step 6   Look up the value of chi-square against the appropriate degrees of freedom in the table in Appendix 11, part of which has been reproduced in Table 11.5. We see that for chi-square with 1 degree of freedom to be statistically significant at the two-tailed 0.05 level, it has to be 3.84 or bigger. Since our chi-square value of 10 is larger than 3.84, we would conclude that the number of marks more than 3 in this sample is significantly greater than the expected proportion of 0.5.

Table 11.5 Part of the chi-square two-tailed critical values table

| df | Level of significance | | |
	0.10	0.05	0.01
1	2.71	3.84	6.64
2	4.60	5.99	9.21
3	6.25	7.82	11.34
.			
.			
.			
30	40.26	43.77	50.89

A number of other points should be noted about chi-square at this stage. Chi-square is 0 when the observed frequency is exactly the same as the expected frequency.

$$\frac{(20-20)^2}{20} + \frac{(20-20)^2}{20} = \frac{0^2}{20} + \frac{0^2}{20} = \frac{0}{20} + \frac{0}{20} = 0 + 0 = 0$$

The larger chi-square is for the same number of categories, the more likely it is to be statistically significant since this means that the difference between the observed and expected frequencies is bigger.

Other things being equal, the larger the sample, the bigger chi-square is and so the more likely it is to be statistically significant. This can be illustrated with the three samples of data shown in Table 11.6. If there is a real difference in the observed frequency between two categories, then this difference as a proportion of the total frequency should remain the same for different sized samples. In Table 11.6 the proportional difference has been set at 0.2 for Sample 1 (4/20 = 0.2), Sample 2 (8/40 = 0.2) and Sample 3 (16/80 = 0.2). If we calculate chi-square for the three samples of data, we see that as the sample size doubles from 20 to 40 to 80, so chi-square doubles from 0.8 to 1.6 to 3.2. As the size of the sample increases, so the exact probability of finding such a difference by chance decreases from 0.37 to 0.20 to 0.07. In other words, this proportional difference would be statistically significant at the one-tailed level in Sample 3 (0.07/2 = 0.035) whereas it is not significant at either the one- or two-tailed level for Samples 1 (0.37/2 = 0.185) and 2 (0.20/2 = 0.10).

Because chi-square sums the squared difference between the observed and the expected frequencies, it is likely to be bigger with more categories. Consequently, the critical values of chi-square are adjusted for the number of categories which is done through the degrees of freedom.

The distribution of chi-square, like the distribution of most of the other test statistics described in this text, is determined by the degrees of freedom and is unique for each such number. In chi-square the degrees of freedom refer to the number of categories and not the number of cases. With only two categories, chi-square has one degree of freedom because if the total frequency is known and the frequency of one of the categories (which is

Table 11.6 Chi-square and sample size

	Sample 1		Sample 2		Sample 3	
Observed frequencies	12	8	24	16	48	32
Expected frequencies	10	10	20	20	40	40
Sample size		20		40		80
Proportional difference		4/20 = 0.2		8/40 = 0.2		16/80 = 0.2
Chi-square		0.80		1.60		3.20
Exact *p*		0.37		0.20		0.07

free to vary) is also known, then the frequency of the other category is fixed. For example, if the total frequency is 20 and the frequency of one of the categories is 15, then the frequency of the other category must be 5 (20 − 15 = 5). With three categories, chi-square has two degrees of freedom because if the total frequency and the frequency of two of the categories is known, the frequency of the third category is fixed. For instance, if the total frequency is 60, and the frequencies of the two categories free to vary are 10 and 20, then the frequency of the third category is fixed at 30 (60 − 10 − 20 = 30).

Chi-square with one degree of freedom is related to the standard normal curve in that it is equal to z^2. For example, looking at the table in Appendix 2, we see that a z value of 1.96 cuts off a proportion of 0.025 (0.5 − 0.4750 = 0.025) at either end of the distribution which means that this z value represents a two-tailed probability of 0.05. The square of 1.96 is 3.84 which is the same value as a two-tailed chi-square with one degree of freedom.

Up to 30 degrees of freedom, the chi-square distribution is skewed to the right. As the degrees of freedom increase, it becomes more symmetrical and begins to look like the normal curve with more than 30 degrees of freedom.

The chi-square test is, in effect, non-directional because all differences between observed and expected frequencies are squared making them all positive. In other words, any negative differences (e.g. fewer marks than expected of 3 or less) are made positive by squaring. Consequently, observed frequencies which lie in one direction (e.g. fewer marks than expected of 3 or less) are combined with observed frequencies which lie in the other direction (e.g. more marks than expected of more than 3) so that it is not possible to distinguish the direction of any difference. The critical values for chi-square are two-tailed in the sense that the test is non-directional. However, in the case of one sample with only two categories it is possible to determine whether the difference obtained is in the predicted direction because there are only two cells. So, for example, we can tell whether there are more marks of greater than 3 than marks of 3 or less. Consequently, in this case it is possible to use a one-tailed level by dividing the two-tailed critical value by 2. If we do this for our example above, we can conclude that the statistical significance of our finding at the one-tailed level has a probability of less than 0.025 (0.5/2 = 0.025). The chi-square test may also be directional (and hence one-tailed) in two samples with only two categories in each, as we shall explain when we discuss this case.

When a sample has three or more categories, the chi-square test is non-directional. Suppose, for example, that we were interested in whether the distribution of the major subject studied of our sample of 100 students differed from that of the student population. As shown in Table 11.7, the proportion of those studying sociology, management, education and psychology in the student population was 0.20, 0.70, 0.06 and 0.04 respectively while our sample consisted of 30 reading sociology, 50 management, 10 education and 10 psychology. If the distribution of the discipline studied in the sample is the same as that in the population, then we can work out that the expected number of people in our sample studying sociology, management, education and psychology is 20 (0.20 × 100 = 20), 70 (0.70 × 100 = 70), 6 (0.06 × 100 = 6) and 4 (0.04 × 100 = 4) respectively.

Since the expected frequency of those studying psychology in our sample is less than 5, it would be inappropriate to apply chi-square. To carry out chi-square we could either omit them from the analysis or, if we can justify this, group them with another category so that no category would have an expected frequency of less than 5. To demonstrate this procedure, we have grouped those studying education and psychology together into one category. The expected frequency of this combined category is 10 (0.10 × 100 = 10) and its observed frequency 20 (10 + 10 = 20). Chi-square for these three groups is 20.71.

$$\frac{(30-20)^2}{20} + \frac{(50-70)^2}{70} + \frac{(20-10)^2}{10} = \frac{10^2}{20} + \frac{-20^2}{70} + \frac{10^2}{10} =$$

$$\frac{100}{20} + \frac{400}{70} + \frac{100}{10} = 5 + 5.71 + 10 = 20.71$$

We can use this example, where the expected frequencies for categories differ, to illustrate the reason for and the effect of dividing the squared difference between the observed and expected frequencies by the expected frequency. What this does is to weight the squared difference by the expected frequency so that the same squared difference has a smaller effect on chi-square when the expected frequency is greater. For instance, the squared difference between the observed and expected frequency for the sociology students is 100 [$(30-20)^2 = 10^2 = 100$] which is the same size as the squared difference between the observed and expected frequency for the combined group [$(20-10)^2 = 10^2 = 100$]. However, since the expected frequency of the sociology students (20) is greater than that of the

Table 11.7 Expected frequency of subject studied in a sample based on observed proportion in the population

Subject	Frequency		
	Population Proportion	Sample	
		Observed n	Expected n
Sociology	0.20	30	0.20 × 100 = 20
Management	0.70	50	0.70 × 100 = 70
Education	0.06	10	0.06 × 100 = 6
Psychology	0.04	10	0.04 × 100 = 4
Total	1.00	100	100

combined group (10), the contribution to chi-square of the difference for the sociology students (100/20 = 5) is less than that for the combined group (100/10 = 10). If we had not weighted the differences according to expected frequency, both differences would have made the same contribution.

Looking at the table in Appendix 11, we can see that the 0.01 two-tailed critical value of chi-square with 2 (3 − 1 = 2) degrees of freedom is 9.21. Since the chi-square value of 20.71 for our sample is greater than this critical value, we can conclude that the distribution of subject studied in our sample differs significantly from that in the population. Note that we cannot use a one-tailed test in this case where there are more than two categories because, even if we had predicted that there would be proportionately more sociology students in our sample than in the population, the test compares the distribution of the observed and expected frequency across all three categories and so does not tell us which differences are significant.

To carry out the first analysis with SPSS we use the following procedure:

→**Statistics** →**Nonparametric Tests** →**Chi-Square** . . . [opens **Chi-Square Test** dialog box as in Box 11.3]
→variable [e.g. **marks**] →▶button [puts variable under **Test Variable List:**] →**OK**

Table 11.8 displays the output for this analysis. The value of **Chi-Square** is **10.0000** and its **Significance** is **.0016**.

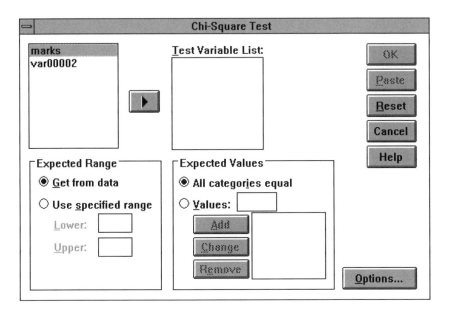

Box 11.3 **Chi-Square Test** dialog box

Table 11.8 SPSS output for the one-sample chi-square with two categories

─ ─ ─ ─ ─ ─ Chi-Square Test

MARKS

	Cases		
Category	Observed	Expected	Residual
.00	10	20.00	-10.00
1.00	30	20.00	10.00
	--		
Total	40		

| Chi-Square | D.F. | Significance |
| 10.0000 | 1 | .0016 |

Table 11.9 SPSS output for the one-sample chi-square with three categories

─ ─ ─ ─ ─ ─ Chi-Square Test

SUBJECT

		Cases		
	Category	Observed	Expected	Residual
Sociology	1.00	30	20.00	10.00
Management	2.00	50	70.00	-20.00
Combined	3.00	20	10.00	10.00

	Total	100		

| Chi-Square | D.F. | Significance |
| 20.7143 | 1 | .0000 |

To conduct the second analysis, we first need to enter the data appropriately, coding the three subjects (sociology, management and combined) and weighting them accordingly. Then in the **Chi-Square Test** dialog box, we select **Values:** , type the expected value for the first category which is **20** and select **Add** which puts this value in the box beside it. Repeat this sequence for the other two expected values of **70** and **10**. Table 11.9

presents the output for this analysis. The value of **Chi-Square** is **20.7143** and its **Significance** is **.0000** which means that it is less than 0.00005.

MULTIPLE COMPARISON TESTS FOR THREE OR MORE GROUPS

With three categories or groups, we can compare three pairs of groups (i.e. 1 vs 2, 1 vs 3 and 2 vs 3). The major problem with this approach is that the more pairwise comparisons we make on the same set of data, the more likely it is that one of these comparisons will be statistically significant. In other words, the probability of making a Type I error (finding a difference when there is none) increases with the number of comparisons. For example, if we make one comparison, the probability of finding a statistically significant difference at the 0.05 critical level by chance is 5 out of 100 or 1 out of 20. The rate of making this type of error is known as the *per comparison error rate*. If we make two comparisons on the same set of data and the comparisons are independent of one another, the probability of obtaining a statistically significant difference at the same critical level by chance is 10 out of 100 or 1 out of 10. This error rate is known as the *familywise* or *experimentwise* error rate. The relationship between these two error rates is given by the following formula

familywise error rate $= 1 - (1 - $ per comparison error rate$)^c$

where c represents the number of independent or orthogonal comparisons.

Note that with three groups, only two of the possible three pairwise comparisons are orthogonal while the third is not orthogonal. We can illustrate this by comparing the differences in the observed percentage of cases in our example shown in Table 11.10. The observed frequencies in the three categories of sociology, management and the combined group are also observed percentages since the total number of cases is 100 (e.g. 30/ 100 × 100 = 30). If we know the difference in percentage frequencies of any two comparisons, we can work out the absolute difference for the third comparison by subtracting one of the differences from the other. For instance, if we know that the difference between sociology and management is −20 and the difference between the sociology and the combined group is 10, then if we subtract one from the other we obtain the absolute difference between management and the combined group, which is 30

Table 11.10 Differences in percentage frequencies of three pairwise comparisons

Pairwise comparisons	Differences in percentage frequencies
Sociology *vs* Management	30 − 50 = −20
Sociology *vs* Combined	30 − 20 = 10
Management *vs* Combined	50 − 20 = 30

[(−20) − 10 or 10 − (−20) = 30]. Similarly, if we know that the difference between sociology and the combined group is 10 and the difference between management and the combined group is 30, then the absolute difference between sociology and management is 20 (10 − 30 = − 20 or 30 − 10 = 20).

BONFERRONI'S TEST

Some authors suggest that we do not need to correct the per comparison error rate when we carry out planned or *a priori* orthogonal comparisons to test for predicted differences between particular groups because this was the reason for conducting the study in the first place (e.g. Keppel 1991). Others recommend that *Bonferroni's* test or procedure, also known as *Dunn's* test or the *Dunn–Bonferroni* test, should be used to adjust the per comparison error rate (Marascuilo and McSweeney 1977).

Suppose, for example, that prior to conducting our study we had predicted that there would be proportionately more sociology and combined students than management ones. To carry out Bonferroni's test on these two orthogonal comparisons, we would first conduct a chi-square test for each of them. The observed frequencies and expected percentages for these two comparisons are presented in Table 11.11. Note that the expected percentages for each of the categories have had to be slightly adjusted so that, for example, what was 20 per cent for sociology is now 22.22 per cent (i.e. 20/90 × 100 = 22.22) in the first comparison. Chi-square for comparing the proportion of sociology students with management students is about 10.80.

$$\frac{(30 - 17.78)^2}{17.78} + \frac{(50 - 62.22)^2}{62.22} = \frac{12.22^2}{17.78} + \frac{-12.22^2}{62.22} =$$

$$\frac{149.33}{17.78} + \frac{149.33}{62.22} = 8.40 + 2.40 = 10.80$$

Chi-square for comparing the proportion of the combined group with the management students is 16.53

$$\frac{(50 - 61.25)^2}{61.25} + \frac{(20 - 8.75)^2}{8.75} = \frac{-11.25^2}{61.25} + \frac{11.25^2}{8.75} =$$

Table 11.11 Observed frequencies and expected percentages and frequencies for the two comparisons

| | Comparisons | | | |
	First		Second	
Observed frequencies	30	50	50	20
Expected percentages	22.22	77.78	87.50	12.50
Expected frequencies	17.78	62.22	61.25	8.75

$$\frac{126.56}{61.5} + \frac{126.56}{8.75} = 2.07 + 14.46 = 16.53$$

Inspecting the table in Appendix 11, we can see that for 1 degree of freedom chi-squares of 6.64 or more are statistically significant at the 0.01 two-tailed or the 0.005 one-tailed level. Looking at the observed and expected frequencies for the first comparison in Table 11.11 and as predicted, the observed frequency of the sociology students (30) is greater than their expected frequency (17.78) while the observed frequency of the management students (50) is less than their expected frequency (62.22). The prediction for the second comparison was also confirmed, with the observed frequency of the combined group (20) being bigger than their expected frequency (8.75) and the observed frequency of the management students (50) being smaller than their expected frequency (61.25).

The last column in the table of Appendix 12 presents the 0.05 critical values of the Bonferroni test for different numbers of comparisons when used with the z distribution. The 0.05 critical value of z for two comparisons is 2.24. Since z^2 equals chi-square with one degree of freedom, values of chi-square of 5.08 ($2.24^2 = 5.08$) or more are statistically significant at the 0.05 level with Bonferroni's test. Since both our chi-square values exceed this figure, both comparisons are statistically significant when adjusted for the number of orthogonal comparisons made.

MODIFIED SCHEFFÉ'S TEST

If we had not predicted any differences before carrying out the study, Marascuilo and McSweeney (1977) recommend that we apply the Scheffé test to the chi-square distribution. This will enable us to compare the observed proportions across all three categories. This test may be thought of as calculating the particular confidence limit of finding a certain difference in the observed proportions between two categories. When the confidence interval fails to include 0, the comparison is said to be significant (Hays 1994). To execute this test, perform the following 11 steps which are illustrated with the example of the three categories of subject studied. The statistics for Steps 1 to 3 are shown in Table 11.12. The statistics for Steps 4, 5, 8, 9 and 10 are displayed in Table 11.13.

Step 1 Calculate the proportion of cases in each category by dividing the number of cases in that category with the total number of cases. The observed proportion of the sociology students, management students and the combined group are 0.30 (30/100 = 0.30), 0.50 (50/100 = 0.50) and 0.20 (20/100 = 0.20) respectively.

Step 2 Work out the remaining proportion of cases in each category by subtracting the observed proportion of cases from 1. The remaining pro-

Table 11.12 Observed proportion of cases in three categories of subject studied and their squared standard error

	Sociology	Management	Combined
Observed frequency	30	50	20
Observed proportion	0.30	0.50	0.20
Remaining proportion	0.70	0.50	0.80
Squared standard error of proportion	0.0021	0.0025	0.0016

Table 11.13 Confidence limits for differences in proportions for three categories

Comparisons	Difference	Estimated variance	Confidence interval	Lower limit	Upper limit
Sociology *vs* Management	−0.20*	0.0046	0.166	−0.366	−0.034
Sociology *vs* Combined	0.10	0.0037	0.149	−0.049	0.249
Management *vs* Combined	0.30*	0.0041	0.157	0.143	0.457

*$p < .0.05$

portion for the three categories are 0.70 (1 − 0.30 = 0.70), 0.50 (1 − 0.50 = 0.50) and 0.80 (1 − 0.20 = 0.80) respectively.

Step 3 Calculate the squared standard error of the observed proportion by multiplying the observed proportion in a category by its remaining proportion and dividing by the number of cases. The squared standard error of the observed proportion for the three categories are 0.0021 (0.30 × 0.70/100 = 0.0021), 0.0025 (0.50 × 0.50/100 = 0.0025) and 0.0016 (0.20 × 0.80/100 = 0.0016).

For each comparison, perform the following eight steps.

Step 4 Work out the difference in the observed proportion of cases in the two categories by subtracting one from the other. The difference in the observed proportion of cases is −0.20 (0.30 − 0.50 = −0.20) for the sociology students vs the management students, 0.10 (0.30 − 0.20 = 0.10) for the sociology students vs the combined group and 0.30 (0.50 − 0.20 = 0.30) for the management students vs the combined group.

Step 5 Calculate the estimated variance by adding together the squared standard error for each category. The estimated variance for the three comparisons is 0.0046, 0.0037 and 0.0041 respectively.

Step 6 Work out the required degrees of freedom for chi-square which is the number of comparisons minus 1. This is 2 (3 − 1 = 2) for this example.

Step 7   Find the value of chi-square for these degrees of freedom. In the table in Appendix 11, we see that at the 0.05 two-tailed critical level, this value is 5.99.

Step 8   Calculate the confidence interval for the comparison by multiplying chi-square by the estimated variance and taking the square root of the product.

$$\text{confidence interval} = \sqrt{\text{chi-square} \times \text{estimated variance}}$$

The confidence interval for the three comparisons is 0.166 ($\sqrt{5.99 \times 0.0046}$ = $\sqrt{0.0276}$ = 0.166), 0.149 ($\sqrt{5.99 \times 0.0037}$ = $\sqrt{0.0222}$ = 0.149) and 0.157 ($\sqrt{5.99 \times 0.0041}$ = $\sqrt{0.0246}$ = 0.157) respectively.

Step 9   Work out the lower limit of the confidence interval by subtracting it from the difference for that comparison. The lower limit for the three comparisons is −0.366 (−0.20 − 0.166 = −0.366), −0.049 (0.10 − 0.149 = −0.049) and 0.143 (0.30 − 0.157 = 0.143) respectively.

Step 10   Work out the upper limit of the confidence interval by adding it to the difference for that comparison. The upper limit for the three comparisons is −0.034 (−0.20 + 0.166 = −0.034), 0.249 (0.10 + 0.149 = 0.249) and 0.457 (0.30 + 0.157 = 0.457) respectively.

Step 11   If the confidence interval fails to include 0, the comparison is statistically significant. We can see that the confidence interval for the second comparison includes a 0 (−0.049 to 0.249) so this difference is not statistically significant at the 0.05 two-tailed critical level. The confidence interval does not include a 0 for both the first (−0.366 to −0.034) and the third (0.143 to 0.457) comparison, so both these comparisons are statistically significant at the 0.05 two-tailed critical level.

CHI-SQUARE TEST FOR TWO UNRELATED SAMPLES

We can extend chi-square to more than one sample. The simplest case is one with two samples and where the variable is *dichotomous* (i.e. has only two categories). Imagine, for example, that we wanted to find out whether the number of students studying management as opposed to the other social sciences are significantly more likely to have tutorials. Illustrative data for this question are displayed in Table 11.14 in what is called a *contingency* table. A contingency table consists of a number of rows and columns which show the contingency or relationship between two variables, where the variables have been classified into mutually exclusive categories and where the data consist of frequencies. The two samples in our example may be

Table 11.14 Contingency table of number of students having tutorials in management vs other social sciences

	Management	Other	Row total
Tutorials	30	5	35
None	10	15	25
Column total	40	20	60

thought of as a second variable which consists of two categories (management and other social sciences). A contingency table is also called a *cross-tabulation* table since the frequencies in the categories of one variable are tabulated across the frequencies in the categories of the other variable.

The table shown in Table 11.14 is known as a 2 × 2 contingency table since it has 2 rows to represent the 2 categories of the first variable and 2 columns to reflect the 2 categories of the second variable. It has four *cells*. If the second variable comprised three categories, then it would be a 2 × 3 contingency table as it would consist of 2 rows and 3 columns comprising six cells. The number of students having tutorials is shown in the upper left cell for management (30) and in the upper right cell for the other social sciences (5). The number of students not having tutorials is displayed in the lower left cell for management (10) and in the lower right cell for the other social sciences (15). The total number of cases in each row, called the *row total* or the *row marginal total*, is presented in the right column of the table. The row total is 35 for those having tutorials and 25 for those not having them. The total number of cases in each column, called the *column total* or *column marginal total*, is given in the bottom row. The column total is 40 for management and 20 for the other social sciences. Finally, the total number of cases in the sample, called the *grand total*, is shown in the bottom right corner of the table and is 60.

As before, to calculate chi-square for these data we begin by working out the expected frequency of cases in each cell assuming that the two variables are unrelated. We can do this using probability theory. The probability that a person has tutorials regardless of whether they study management or some other social science is 0.58 (35/60 = 0.583). The probability that a person studies management is 0.67 (40/60 = 0.667). Therefore, the probability that a person has tutorials and studies management is the product of their separate probabilities and is 0.39 (0.583 × 0.667 = 0.389). The expected frequency that a person has tutorials and studies management is the product of that joint probability and the total number of cases and is 23.4 (0.39 × 60 = 23.4). We can translate this procedure for obtaining the expected frequency for any cell into the following general formula:

$$\text{expected frequency} = \frac{\text{row total}}{\text{grand total}} \times \frac{\text{column total}}{\text{grand total}} \times \text{grand total}$$

Since the grand total appears in one of the numerators and both the denominators, we can simplify this formula by cancelling out the grand total in the numerator and one of the denominators as follows:

$$\text{expected frequency} = \frac{\text{row total} \times \text{column total}}{\text{grand total}}$$

If we use this formula, the expected frequency for having tutorials and studying management is 23.3. The expected frequency for each of the four cells is presented in Table 11.15.

Applying the chi-square formula to these data, we see that chi-square is 13.87.

$$\frac{(30 - 23.3)^2}{23.3} + \frac{(5 - 11.7)^2}{11.7} + \frac{(10 - 16.7)^2}{16.7} + \frac{(15 - 8.3)^2}{8.3} =$$

$$\frac{6.7^2}{23.3} + \frac{-6.7^2}{11.7} + \frac{-6.7^2}{16.7} + \frac{6.7^2}{8.3} =$$

$$\frac{44.89}{23.3} + \frac{44.89}{11.7} + \frac{44.89}{16.7} + \frac{44.89}{8.3} =$$

$$1.93 + 3.84 + 2.69 + 5.41 = 13.87$$

The formula for calculating the degrees of freedom (*df*) for chi-square is:

chi-square *df* = (number of rows − 1) × (number of columns − 1)

Since we have two rows and two columns, the appropriate degree of freedom is 1 [(2 − 1) × (2 − 1) = 1]. Note that if we know the total row and column frequencies and the frequency of one of the cells, then the frequencies in the other three cells are fixed. For example, if as in Table 11.16 we know that the frequency of cell *a* is 30, then we can work out that the frequency of cell *b* is 5 (35 − 30 = 5), of cell *c* is 10 (40 − 30 = 10) and of cell *d* is 15 (20 − 5 = 15 or 25 − 10 = 15).

Looking at the table in Appendix 11, we see that chi-square to be

Table 11.15 Expected frequencies of students having tutorials in management vs other social sciences

	Management	Other	Row total
Tutorials	23.3	11.7	35
None	16.7	8.3	25
Column total	40	20	60

Table 11.16 Cell frequencies in a 2 × 2 contingency table

	Management	*Other*	*Row total*
Tutorials	a 30	b	35
None	c	d	25
Column total	40	20	60

statistically significant with one degree of freedom has to be 3.84 or larger at the 0.05 two-tailed level. As the chi-square value of 13.87 is larger than 3.84, we can conclude that there is a statistically significant difference between management and the other social sciences in the number of students having tutorials. Inspecting the relationship between the observed frequencies in Table 11.14 and the expected frequencies in Table 11.15, we can see that in management more students (30) than expected (23.3) have tutorials while in the other social sciences fewer students (5) than expected (11.7) have them, which was what we predicted. Since it is possible to specify the direction of the results in a 2 × 2 table and since we did so, we could use a one-tailed probability level.

Siegel (1956), on the basis of Cochran (1954), recommended that in the case of a 2 × 2 contingency table the general formula for chi-square should be corrected for continuity either when the number of cases is greater than 40 or when the number of cases is between 20 and 40 and all four expected frequencies are 5 or more. On the other hand, *Fisher's exact test* should be used either when the number of cases is between 20 and 40 and the smallest expected frequency is less than 5 or when the number of cases is less than 20.

The correction for continuity is known as *Yates's correction* (Yates 1934) and consists of subtracting 0.5 from each of the absolute differences (i.e. ignoring the sign of the differences) between the observed and expected frequencies before squaring them. This has the effect of reducing the size of chi-square which was thought to decrease the probability of making a Type I error (i.e. assuming there is a difference when none exists).

Since the number of cases in our example is greater than 40, we could follow Siegel's recommendation and apply Yates's correction. If we do this, chi-square corrected for continuity is 11.87 which is slightly smaller than an uncorrected chi-square of 13.87.

$$\frac{(|30 - 23.3| - 0.5)^2}{23.3} + \frac{(|5 - 11.7| - 0.5)^2}{11.7} + \frac{(|10 - 16.7| - 0.5)^2}{16.7} +$$

$$\frac{(|15 - 8.3| - 0.5)^2}{8.3} =$$

$$\frac{6.2^2}{23.3} + \frac{6.2^2}{11.7} + \frac{6.2^2}{16.7} + \frac{6.2^2}{8.3} = \frac{38.44}{23.3} + \frac{38.44}{11.7} + \frac{38.44}{16.7} + \frac{38.44}{8.3} =$$

$$1.65 + 3.29 + 2.30 + 4.63 = 11.87$$

Based on this reasoning, earlier texts on statistics used to suggest that Yates's correction should be made when the frequency of one or more of the cells in a 2 × 2 contingency is less than 5. Since none of the expected frequencies in Table 11.15 is less than 5, we will use the data in Table 11.17 for computing chi-square uncorrected and corrected for continuity. The expected frequencies are given in brackets. We can see that the expected frequency for students in the other social sciences not having tutorials is 2.1. Chi-square uncorrected for continuity is 5.07.

$$\frac{(6 - 4.1)^2}{4.1} + \frac{(1 - 2.9)^2}{2.9} + \frac{(1 - 2.9)^2}{2.9} + \frac{(4 - 2.1)^2}{2.1} =$$

$$\frac{1.9^2}{4.1} + \frac{-1.9^2}{2.9} + \frac{-1.9^2}{2.9} + \frac{1.9^2}{2.1} = \frac{3.6}{4.1} + \frac{3.6}{2.9} + \frac{3.6}{2.9} + \frac{3.6}{2.1} =$$

$$0.88 + 1.24 + 1.24 + 1.71 = 5.07$$

Looking at the table in Appendix 11, we see that for chi-square to be statistically significant it has to be 3.84 or larger at the two-tailed 0.05 level, which it is. Chi-square corrected for continuity, however, is 2.82.

$$\frac{(|6 - 4.1| - 0.5)^2}{4.1} + \frac{(|1 - 2.9| - 0.5)^2}{2.9} +$$

$$\frac{(|1 - 2.9| - 0.5)^2}{2.9} + \frac{(|4 - 2.1| - 0.5)^2}{2.1} =$$

$$\frac{1.4^2}{4.1} + \frac{-1.4^2}{2.9} + \frac{-1.4^2}{2.9} + \frac{1.4^2}{2.1} = \frac{2.0}{4.1} + \frac{2.0}{2.9} + \frac{2.0}{2.9} + \frac{2.0}{2.1} =$$

$$0.49 + 0.69 + 0.69 + 0.95 = 2.82$$

Table 11.17 Observed frequencies (and expected frequencies in brackets) for a smaller sample

	Management	Other	Row total
Tutorials	6 (4.1)	1 (2.9)	7
None	1 (2.9)	4 (2.1)	5
Column total	7	5	12

This figure is not statistically significant at the 0.05 two-tailed level.

Subsequent research, however, has suggested that Yates's correction may be too conservative in that it increases the probability of making a Type II error (i.e. assuming there is no difference when one exists) when the expected frequencies are small (e.g. Bradley, Bradley, McGrath and Cutcomb 1979; Camilli and Hopkins 1978, 1979; Overall 1980). Consequently, making this adjustment may no longer be necessary.

FISHER'S EXACT TEST

Siegel (1956) suggested that Fisher's (1925b) exact probability test should be used either when the number of cases is between 20 and 40 and the smallest expected frequency is less than 5 or when the number of cases is less than 20. Since the data in Table 11.17 correspond to the former condition, we will use it to illustrate the computation of this test.

The frequency data in a 2 × 2 contingency table can be represented more generally by the table shown in Table 11.18 where the letters a, b, c and d signify the frequencies in the four cells. The probability of obtaining a particular set of frequencies in such a table is given by the *hypergeometric distribution* which is determined by the following formula

$$p = \frac{(a + b)!(c + d)!(a + c)!(b + d)!}{(a + b + c + d)!a!b!c!d!}$$

The hypergeometric distribution reflects the probability of finding a particular outcome (i.e. the frequency of cases in Category 1) in a sample when an outcome, once chosen, is not replaced and when the marginal totals remain fixed (Berenson and Levine 1992).

Determining the probability of an outcome with or without replacement is like estimating the probability of obtaining, say, two aces on two draws of a well shuffled standard deck of 52 cards. The probability of drawing the first ace is the same in both situations and is 4/52 or 0.077. If the first card drawn is replaced and the deck of cards is reshuffled, then the probability of obtaining a second ace is 4/52 × 4/52 or 0.006. If the first card is an ace and if this ace is not replaced, then the probability of drawing a second ace is 4/52 × 3/51 or 0.0045.

Table 11.18 2 × 2 contingency table for calculating Fisher's exact test

		Sample		Row total
		1	*2*	
Category	1	a	b	$a + b$
	2	c	d	$c + d$
Column total		$a + c$	$b + d$	$a + b + c + d$

To calculate the probability of obtaining the particular outcome shown in Table 11.17, we substitute the appropriate values in the formula for the hypergeometric distribution which gives us a probability of 0.04419.

$$\frac{(6 + 1)!(1 + 4)!(6 + 1)!(1 + 4)!}{(6 + 1 + 1 + 4)!6!1!1!4} = \frac{7!5!7!5!}{12!6!1!1!4!} =$$

$$\frac{7 \times 5 \times 5 \times 4 \times 3 \times 2 \times 1}{12 \times 11 \times 10 \times 9 \times 8} = \frac{7 \times 5}{11 \times 9 \times 8} = \frac{35}{792} = 0.04419$$

However, to this probability we need to add the probability of obtaining distributions which deviate more extremely from the expected distribution. With the marginal totals remaining fixed, there is only one distribution which is more extreme than that shown in Table 11.17 and that is presented in Table 11.19. Two points should be noted about the data in this table. First, the expected frequencies are the same as those in Table 11.17 because the marginal totals are fixed. And second, in order to ensure the marginal totals are the same, we need to change the frequency in both the upper right cell and the lower left cell. The probability of obtaining this more extreme distribution is 0.00126.

$$\frac{(7 + 0)!(0 + 5)!(7 + 0)!(0 + 5)!}{(7 + 0 + 0 + 5)!7!0!0!5!} = \frac{7!5!7!5!}{12!7!0!0!5!} =$$

$$\frac{5 \times 4 \times 3 \times 2 \times 1}{12 \times 11 \times 10 \times 9 \times 8} = \frac{1}{11 \times 9 \times 8} = \frac{1}{792} = 0.00126$$

Consequently, the probability of finding a distribution as and more extreme than that depicted in Table 11.17 is 0.04545 (0.04419 + 0.00126 = 0.04545). Since both these distributions deviate in the same direction of there being more students in management having tutorials, this probability represents the one-tailed level.

To determine the two-tailed probability level, we need to add the one-tailed probability level to the probability level of distributions which have a lower probability than that shown in Table 11.17 and which deviate in the other direction (Siegel and Castellan 1988). Such a distribution is displayed in Table 11.20 which has a probability of 0.02652.

Table 11.19 Observed frequencies (and expected frequencies in brackets) for a more extreme distribution

	Management	Other	Row total
Tutorials	7 (4.1)	0 (2.9)	7
None	0 (2.9)	5 (2.1)	5
Column total	7	5	12

Table 11.20 Observed frequencies for a more extreme distribution in the opposite direction

	Management	Other	Row total
Tutorials	2	5	7
None	5	0	5
Column total	7	5	12

$$\frac{(2 + 5)!(5 + 0)!(2 + 5)!(5 + 0)!}{(2 + 5 + 5 + 0)!2!5!5!0!} = \frac{7!5!7!5!}{12!2!5!5!0!} =$$

$$\frac{7 \times 6 \times 5 \times 4 \times 3}{12 \times 11 \times 10 \times 9 \times 8} = \frac{7}{11 \times 3 \times 8} = \frac{7}{264} = 0.02652$$

So, the two-tailed probability of obtaining the distribution presented in Table 11.17 is 0.07197 (0.04419 + 0.00126 + 0.02652 = 0.07197).

As the calculations become more cumbersome with larger frequencies and less extreme distributions, the table in Appendix 13 can be employed to determine whether an observed distribution differs significantly from its expected one. Part of this table has been reproduced in Table 11.21 to illustrate its use. To look up the one-tailed 0.05 critical value of the frequencies in cell d for the data in Table 11.17, we first select the line which has an $a+b$ row total of 7, a $c+d$ row total of 5 and a cell b frequency of 1. Since there is not a cell b frequency of 1 in the table, we have to choose the corresponding cell a frequency of 6. If there is a

Table 11.21 Part of the table of one-tailed 0.05 critical values of d (or c) in Fisher's Test

Row totals		Cells					
$a + b$	$c + d$	b (or a)	d (or c)	b (or a)	d (or c)	b (or a)	d (or c)
.							
.							
$\underline{7}$	7	7	3	5	0	4	0
		6	2				
	6	7	2	5	0	4	0
		6	1				
	5	7	2	6	1	5	0
	4	7	1	6	0	5	0
	3	7	0	6	0		
	2	7	0				
.							
.							
.							

frequency of 1 or less in cell *c*, we would conclude that our observed distribution differs significantly from the expected one at or less than the 0.05 one-tailed level. Since the cell *c* frequency is 1, we would draw this conclusion.

For another example, we could see whether the distribution in Table 11.19 differs significantly from the expected one. Once again, we would select the line which has an *a+b* row total of 7 and a *c+d* row total of 5 but this time we would choose a cell *b* frequency of 5, which is listed in the table. In order for this distribution to differ significantly from the expected one at the 0.05 one-tailed level, the cell *d* frequency has to be 0, which it is. Consequently, we would presume that the distribution differs significantly from the expected one at this level.

CHI-SQUARE TEST FOR THREE OR MORE UNRELATED SAMPLES

Analysing frequency data from three or more unrelated samples with chi-square follows the same procedure as a one-sample chi-square for three or more categories. We will use the 3 × 4 contingency table presented in Table 11.22 to demonstrate this. Students were classified into the three categories of having individual tutorials, group tutorials or no tutorials. The four samples were students studying management, sociology, education and psychology. Assuming that we wanted to carry out a chi-square on this table, the first step would be to see if any expected frequency is less than 1 or more than 20 per cent of the expected frequencies are smaller than 5. The expected frequencies for this table are displayed in Table 11.23. There are no expected frequencies of less than 1, but 4 of the 12 cells (or 33.3 per cent) have expected frequencies of less than 5.

Table 11.22 A 3 × 4 contingency table

	Management	Sociology	Education	Psychology	Row total
Individual tutorials	14	3	5	1	23
Group tutorials	6	5	15	3	29
No tutorials	20	12	10	6	48
Column total	40	20	30	10	100

Table 11.23 Expected frequencies in a 3 × 4 table

	Management	Sociology	Education	Psychology	Row total
Individual tutorials	9.2	4.6	6.9	2.3	23
Group tutorials	11.6	5.8	8.7	2.9	29
No tutorials	19.2	9.6	14.4	4.8	48
Column total	40	20	30	10	100

Table 11.24 Expected frequencies in a 3 × 3 table

	Management	Sociology	Education	Row total
Individual tutorials	9.8	4.9	7.3	22
Group tutorials	11.6	5.8	8.7	26
No tutorials	18.7	9.3	14.0	42
Column total	40	20	30	90

One way of reducing the percentage of cells with an expected frequency of less than 5 would be to omit the psychology sample. If we do this, only 1 of the 9 cells (or 11.1 per cent) has an expected frequency of less than 5, as shown in Table 11.24. Chi-square for this 3 × 3 contingency table is 12.64.

$$\frac{(14-9.8)^2}{9.8} + \frac{(3-4.9)^2}{4.9} + \frac{(5-7.3)^2}{7.3} + \frac{(6-11.6)^2}{11.6} + \frac{(5-5.8)^2}{5.8} +$$

$$\frac{(15-8.7)^2}{8.7} + \frac{(20-18.7)^2}{18.7} + \frac{(12-9.3)^2}{9.3} + \frac{(10-14.0)^2}{14.0} =$$

$$\frac{4.2^2}{9.8} + \frac{-1.9^2}{4.9} + \frac{-2.3^2}{7.3} + \frac{-5.6^2}{11.6} + \frac{-0.8^2}{5.8} + \frac{6.3^2}{8.7} + \frac{1.3^2}{18.7} + \frac{2.7^2}{9.3} +$$

$$\frac{-4.0^2}{14.0} =$$

$$\frac{17.64}{9.8} + \frac{3.61}{4.9} + \frac{5.29}{7.3} + \frac{31.36}{11.6} + \frac{0.64}{5.8} + \frac{39.69}{8.7} + \frac{1.69}{18.7} +$$

$$\frac{7.29}{9.3} + \frac{16.00}{14.00} =$$

$$1.80 + 0.74 + 0.72 + 2.70 + 0.11 + 4.56 + 0.09 +$$

$$0.78 + 1.14 = 12.64$$

Next, we determine the degrees of freedom which are the product of the number of rows minus 1 and the number of columns minus 1. Since we have 3 rows and 3 columns, the degrees of freedom for this 3 × 3 table are 4 [(3 − 1) × (3 − 1) = 2 × 2 = 4]. In other words, if we know the total row and column frequencies and the frequencies of four of the nine cells (provided that three of these are not in the same row or column), then the frequencies of the other five cells are fixed. Suppose, for example, that we know the frequencies of the four cells (*a*, *b*, *d* and *e*) in the 3 × 3 contingency table shown in Table 11.25 are 14, 3, 6 and 5 respectively. Then the frequency must be 5 for cell *c* (22 − 14 − 3 = 5), 15 for cell *f* (26

Table 11.25 Cell frequencies in a 3 × 3 contingency table

	Management	Sociology	Education	Row total
Individual tutorials	a	b	c	
	14	3		22
Group tutorials	d	e	f	
	6	5		26
No tutorials	g	h	i	
				42
Column total	40	20	30	90

$- 6 - 5 = 15$), 20 for cell g ($40 - 14 - 6 = 20$), 12 for cell h ($20 - 3 - 5 = 12$) and 10 for cell i ($42 - 20 - 12 = 10$ or $30 - 5 - 15 = 10$).

Turning to the table in Appendix 11, we see that with 4 degrees of freedom, chi-square has to be 9.49 or larger to be significant at the 0.05 two-tailed level which, with a value of 12.64, it is. Consequently, we would conclude that the frequencies in the nine cells differ significantly from those that would be expected by chance. To determine which of the cells differ significantly, we need to carry out the appropriate multiple comparison tests as described earlier.

We will use this example to illustrate how to carry out with SPSS a chi-square for two or more samples. First we enter the data in Table 11.22 (apart from those for the psychology students) into **Newdata** using the weighting procedure as shown in Box 11.4. The values in the first column (called **tutorial**) indicate the rows of the table and those in the second column (called **subject**) represent its columns. The third column contains the frequencies of the nine cells. Then execute the following procedure:

→**Statistics** →**Summarize** →**Crosstabs** . . . [opens **Crosstabs** dialog box as in Box 11.5]
→row variable [e.g. **tutorial**] →▶ button [puts variable under **Row[s]:**]
→column variable [e.g. **subject**] →▶ button [puts variable under **Column[s]:**] →**Cells** . . . [opens **Crosstabs: Cell Display** dialog box as in Box 11.6]
→**Expected** [in **Counts** section] →**Continue** [closes **Crosstabs: Cell Display** dialog box]
→**Statistics** . . . [opens **Crosstabs: Statistics** dialog box as in Box 11.7]
→**Chi-square** →**Continue** [closes **Crosstabs: Statistics** dialog box]
→**OK**

Since chi-square is based on comparing the expected with the observed frequency in each cell, it is useful to have a display of the expected frequencies.

Table 11.26 presents the output from this procedure. The first line in each cell gives the observed number of cases for that cell (which are whole numbers) and the second line the expected number (which are given to one

	tutorial	subject	var00003	var
1	1.00	1.00	14.00	
2	1.00	2.00	6.00	
3	1.00	3.00	20.00	
4	2.00	1.00	3.00	
5	2.00	2.00	5.00	
6	2.00	3.00	12.00	
7	3.00	1.00	5.00	
8	3.00	2.00	15.00	
9	3.00	3.00	10.00	
10				

Box 11.4 **Newdata** containing frequencies for a 3 × 3 contingency table

decimal place). In addition, the number and percentage of cases in each row and column are presented together with the grand total. SPSS produces three different measures of chi-square. The value of chi-square is shown together with the appropriate degrees of freedom and the statistical significance of this value. As we can see, the value of the Pearson chi-square is **12.69930**, which when rounded to two decimal places is 12.70 and is similar to that previously calculated which was 12.64. This value is statistically significant with a *p* value of **.01284** (i.e. *p*<0.02).

The likelihood ratio chi-square is twice the sum of the observed frequency of each cell multiplied by the natural logarithm of its observed frequency divided by its expected frequency:

$$L^2 = 2 \times \text{sum of} \left[\text{observed frequency} \times \text{natural logarithm} \times \left(\frac{\text{observed frequency}}{\text{expected frequency}} \right) \right] \text{for each cell}$$

Because of the small values of the numbers involved in these calculations, it is necessary to work to 5 decimal places. Substituting the appropriate

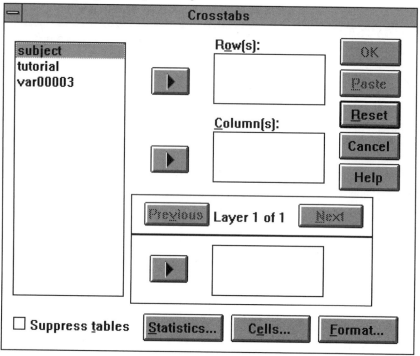

Box 11.5 **Crosstabs** dialog box

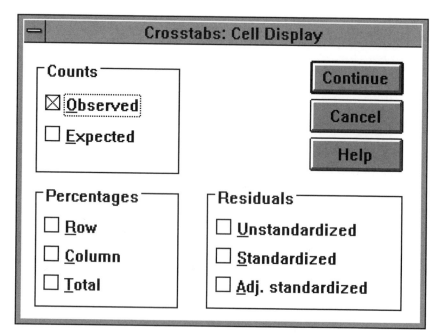

Box 11.6 **Crosstabs: Cell Display** dialog box

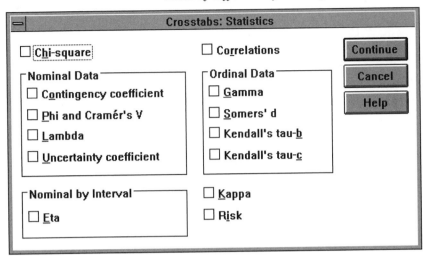

Box 11.7 **Crosstabs: Statistics** dialog box

values in the formula, we see that the likelihood ratio chi-square is 12.49648 which is almost identical to the figure of 12.49852 reported in Table 11.26:

$2 \times [(14 \times \ln(14/9.778)) + (3 \times \ln(3/4.889)) +$
   $(5 \times \ln(5/7.333)) + (6 \times \ln(6/11.556) +$
   $(5 \times \ln(5/5.778)) + (15 \times \ln(15/8.667)) +$
   $(20 \times \ln(20/18.667) + (12 \times \ln(12/9.333)) +$
   $(10 \times \ln(10/14.000)] =$

$2 \times [(14 \times \ln 1.43179) + (3 \times \ln 0.61362) +$
   $(5 \times \ln 0.68185) + (6 \times \ln 0.51921) +$
   $(5 \times \ln 0.86535) + (15 \times \ln 1.73070) +$
   $(20 \times \ln 1.07141) + (12 \times \ln 1.28576) +$
   $(10 \times \ln 0.71429)] =$

$2 \times [(14 \times 0.35893) + (3 \times -0.48838) +$
   $(5 \times -0.38295) + (6 \times -0.65545) +$
   $(5 \times -0.14462) + (15 \times 0.54853) +$
   $(20 \times 0.06898) + (12 \times 0.25135) +$
   $(10 \times -0.33647)] =$

$2 \times [5.02496 + -1.46514 + -1.91473 + -3.93268 +$
   $-0.72311 + 8.22789 + 1.37951 + 3.01620 + -3.36466] =$

$2 \times 6.24824 = 12.49648$

Table 11.26 SPSS output for chi-square on a 3 × 3 contingency table

TUTORIAL by SUBJECT

		SUBJECT			Page 1 of 1
	Count				
	Exp Val				
					Row
		1.00	2.00	3.00	Total
TUTORIAL					
1.00		14	3	5	22
		9.8	4.9	7.3	24.4%
2.00		6	5	15	26
		11.6	5.8	8.7	28.9%
3.00		20	12	10	42
		18.7	9.3	14.0	46.7%
Column		40	20	30	90
Total		44.4%	22.2%	33.3%	100.0%

Chi-Square	Value	DF	Significance
Pearson	12.69930	4	.01284
Likelihood Ratio	12.49852	4	.01400
Mantel-Haenszel test for linear association	.03241	1	.85714

Minimum Expected Frequency -   4.889

Cells with Expected Frequency < 5 -   1 OF   9 (11.1%)

Number of Missing Observations: 0

The Mantel–Haenszel chi-square of linear association will be discussed in Chapter 13.

The output also gives the smallest or minimum expected frequency for any cell which is **4.889** for the sociology students having individual tutorials. This information is useful for drawing to our attention whether

Table 11.27 SPSS output for chi-square with more than 20 per cent of cells having expected frequencies of less than five

TUTORIAL by SUBJECT

		SUBJECT			Page 1 of 1	
Count						
Exp Val						
						Row
		1.00	2.00	3.00	4.00	Total
TUTORIAL	1.00	14	6	20	1	41
		9.0	10.7	17.2	4.1	41.0%
	2.00	3	5	12	3	23
		5.1	6.0	9.7	2.3	23.0%
	3.00	5	15	10	6	36
		7.9	9.4	15.1	3.6	36.0%
Column		22	26	42	10	100
Total		22.0%	26.0%	42.0%	10.0%	100.0%

Chi-Square	Value	DF	Significance
Pearson	17.16722	6	.00869
Likelihood Ratio	17.86039	6	.00659
Mantel-Haenszel test for linear association	1.77362	1	.18294

Minimum Expected Frequency -   2.300

Cells with Expected Frequency < 5 -   3 OF   12 (25.0%)

Number of Missing Observations: 0

the expected frequencies fall above the minimum required for applying chi-square. In this case, this condition is met since only **1 OF 9 (11.1%)** cells have an expected frequency of less than 5. However, if we carried out an analysis on all the data in Table 11.22 where the conditions for a chi-square test were not met, the relevant output shown in Table 11.27 would state that

Table 11.28 SPSS output for chi-square with Yates's continuity correction

TUTORIAL by SUBJECT

		SUBJECT		Page 1 of 1
Count				
Exp Val				
				Row
		1.00	2.00	Total
TUTORIAL				
1.00	30	5		35
	23.3	11.7		58.3%
2.00	10	15		25
	16.7	8.3		41.7%
Column	40	20		60
Total	66.7%	33.3%		100.0%

Chi-Square	Value	DF	Significance
Pearson	13.71429	1	.00021
Continuity Correction	11.73429	1	.00061
Likelihood Ratio	14.02297	1	.00018
Mantel-Haenszel test for linear association	13.48571	1	.00024

Minimum Expected Frequency -   8.333

Number of Missing Observations: 0

(in addition to the minimum expected frequency) **3 OF 12 (25.0%)** had expected frequencies of less than 5.

SPSS gives Yates's correction for continuity for all 2 × 2 contingency tables where all cells have an expected frequency of 5 or more. This is shown in Table 11.28 which presents the relevant output for a chi-square of the data in Table 11.14. The value of **11.73429** for Yates's corrected chi-square is slightly smaller than the previously calculated value of 11.87. This discrepancy is due to differences in rounding decimal places, parti-

Table 11.29 SPSS output for chi-square with Fisher's exact test

TUTORIAL by SUBJECT

		SUBJECT		Page 1 of 1
Count				
Exp Val				
				Row
		1.00	2.00	Total
TUTORIAL				
1.00	6	1		7
	4.1	2.9		58.3%
2.00	1	4		5
	2.9	2.1		41.7%
Column	7	5		12
Total	58.3%	41.7%		100.0%

Chi-Square	Value	DF	Significance
Pearson	5.18204	1	.02282
Continuity Correction	2.83102	1	.09246
Likelihood Ratio	5.55499	1	.01843
Mantel-Haenszel test for linear association	4.75020	1	.02929
Fisher's Exact Test:			
One-Tail			.04545
Two-Tail			.07197

Minimum Expected Frequency -   2.083

Cells with Expected Frequency < 5 -   4 OF   4 (100.0%)

Number of Missing Observations: 0

cularly those of the expected frequencies. SPSS, for example, does not use the figures displayed in its table whereas the manual calculation did.

The values for Fisher's exact test are given for 2 × 2 contingency tables when one or more of the four cells have an expected frequency of less than

5. For example, it would be produced if we analysed the data in Table 11.17. The relevant output for these data are shown in Table 11.29. The values are the same as those previously calculated by hand.

McNEMAR TEST FOR TWO RELATED SAMPLES

The McNemar (1947) test compares the frequencies of a dichotomous variable for two related samples of cases. These two samples may consist of the same or *matched* cases tested on two occasions or receiving two treatments. Matching involves selecting samples of cases to be the same in certain respects such as age, gender and socio-economic status and is used to make the samples as similar as possible. We could employ the McNemar test, for example, to determine whether students achieving 4 or more marks on the pre-test coursework were also significantly more likely to attain 4 or more marks on the post-test coursework. The dichotomous variable in this instance would be whether the mark was 4 or more, or 3 or less and the two related samples would be the two pieces of coursework.

The data for the whole sample are displayed in Table 11.30. Of the 21 students, 4 obtained 3 marks or less on both occasions, 4 attained 4 marks or more on both occasions, 1 achieved a mark of 3 or less on the second occasion but not on the first and 12 received a mark of 3 or less on the first occasion but not on the second. Do these results suggest that students achieving a mark of 4 or more on the first piece of coursework are also more likely to attain this level for their second piece of coursework? With the McNemar test, we are only interested in whether the number of cases who have changed in one direction on the two occasions (say, those obtaining 4 or more on the first but not on the second occasion) are different from the number who have changed in the other direction (say, those receiving 4 or more on the second but not on the first occasion). In other words, we are only concerned with the number of cases who have changed from one occasion to the next (i.e. those in the top left and bottom right cell). If there was no difference between these two cells, then the expected frequency of cases in each of these two cells should be 6.5 [i.e. (1 + 12)/2 = 6.5]. If the expected frequency is less than 5, the binomial test should be used.

The McNemar test is like the chi-square test in that it compares the

Table 11.30 Pre- and post-test marks categorised into 4+ and below

		Pre-test marks	
		4+	*3−*
Post-test marks	3−	1	4
	4+	4	12

observed with the expected frequency of cases and the statistic computed is chi-square but, unlike the chi-square test, it is only based on cases who have changed from one occasion (or condition) to the next. The formula for the McNemar test is:

$$\text{chi-square} = \frac{(|\text{cell}_1 \text{ frequencies} - \text{cell}_2 \text{ frequencies}| - 1)^2}{\text{cell}_1 + \text{cell}_2}$$

where the two cells (cell_1 and cell_2) refer to the two cells which indicate change. This test has one degree of freedom.

The steps involved in calculating chi-square for the McNemar test are as follows.

Step 1   Find the absolute difference between the observed frequency of cases for the two cells representing a change from one occasion or condition to the next. Since the two cells in our example which reflect this change are the top left and the bottom right cells, the absolute difference is 11 ($|1 - 12| = 11$).

Step 2   Subtract 1 from this absolute difference to correct for continuity, which gives 10 ($11 - 1 = 10$).

Step 3   Square this difference, making 100 ($10^2 = 10$).

Step 4   Divide this squared difference by the sum of the observed frequencies in the two cells reflecting change. As the sum of the frequencies in these two cells is 13 ($1 + 12 = 13$), this result is 7.69 ($100/13 = 7.692$) which can be obtained by substituting the appropriate figures in the above formula:

$$\frac{(|1 - 12| - 1)^2}{1 + 12} = \frac{100}{13} = 7.692$$

We look up the statistical significance of this value in the table in Appendix 11. Because we specified the direction of the results we expected to find, we can use the one-tailed level of significance which simply involves halving the significance value. With one degree of freedom, the critical value at the 0.05 one-tailed level is 2.71. Since our value is more than this, we would conclude that students obtaining 4 or more on the pre-test coursework were significantly more likely to obtain this mark on the post-test coursework.

To compute with SPSS a McNemar test for this example, we first recode marks of 3 or less for **markpre** and **markpos** as, say, **0** and marks of 4 or more as **1** and save the recoded data as two new variables, say, **markprer** and **markposr**. We then carry out the following procedure on the two new variables:

```
┌─────────────────────────────────────────────────────────────────────┐
│ ▬                    Two-Related-Samples Tests                        │
├─────────────────────────────────────────────────────────────────────┤
│ ┌──────────────┬─┐   Test Pair(s) List:         ┌──────────────┐      │
│ │cond          │▲│                               │     OK       │      │
│ │filter_$      │ │                               └──────────────┘      │
│ │intpre        │ │                               ┌──────────────┐      │
│ │markfol       │ │                               │    Paste     │      │
│ │markpos       │ │      ┌───┐                    └──────────────┘      │
│ │markposr      │ │      │ ▶ │                    ┌──────────────┐      │
│ │markpre       │ │      └───┘                    │    Reset     │      │
│ │markprer      │ │                               └──────────────┘      │
│ │prepos        │ │                               ┌──────────────┐      │
│ │prepre        │▼│                               │   Cancel     │      │
│ └──────────────┴─┘                               └──────────────┘      │
│                                                  ┌──────────────┐      │
│ ┌─Current Selections─┐ ┌─Test Type──────────────┐│    Help      │      │
│ │ Variable 1:        │ │ ☒ Wilcoxon  ☐ Sign  ☐ McNemar │               │
│ │ Variable 2:        │ └────────────────────────┘                      │
│ └────────────────────┘               ┌──────────────┐                  │
│                                       │   Options... │                  │
│                                       └──────────────┘                  │
└─────────────────────────────────────────────────────────────────────┘
```

Box 11.8 **Two Related Samples Tests** dialog box

→**Statistics** →**Nonparametric Tests** →**2 Related Samples . . .** [opens **Two Related Samples Tests** dialog box as in Box 11.8] →first variable [e.g. **markprer**] [puts variable beside **Variable 1:** in **Current Selections** section] →second variable [e.g. **markposr**] [puts variable beside **Variable 2:** in **Current Selections** section] →▶button [puts both variables under **Test Pair[s] List:**] →**McNemar** →**Wilcoxon** [deselects it] →**OK**

Table 11.31 SPSS output for a McNemar test comparing pre- and post-test marks categorised into 4+ and below

– – – – – McNemar Test

    MARKPOSR

with MARKPRER

```
                           MARKPRER
                         1.00      .00              Cases        21
                    + - - - - - + - - - - - +
             .00 |      1 |       4 |
MARKPOSR            + - - - - - + - - - - - +      (Binominal)
            1.00 |      4 |      12 |            2-Tailed P     .0034
                    + - - - - - + - - - - - +
```

Table 11.31 shows the output for this procedure. McNemar's test has a two-tailed probability of **.0034**, which when halved gives a one-tailed probability of 0.0017. SPSS automatically gives the binomial value when the number of cases changing values from the first to the second occasion (or variable) is less than 10.

COCHRAN Q FOR THREE OR MORE RELATED SAMPLES

If we wanted to compare the frequencies of a dichotomous variable for three or more related samples of cases, we would use the Cochran (1950) Q test. We would apply this test if we wished to determine, for example, whether students attaining 4 marks or more on the pre-test coursework also obtained this level on the post-test and follow-up coursework. The recoded data for the 8 women having tutorials are presented in Table 11.32 where 0 represents a mark of 3 or less and 1 a mark of 4 or more.

The values of the Q test approximate those of chi-square when the number of rows is not too small, although Cochran does not specify what the minimum number is. To calculate Q, we first need to sum each of the rows (RT) and columns (CT) and then square them (RT^2 and CT^2) as

Table 11.32 Coursework marks categorised as 4+ or below for women having tutorials

Pre-test	Post-test	Follow-up
1	1	1
0	1	1
1	1	1
0	1	1
0	1	1
0	1	1
0	1	1
0	1	1

Table 11.33 Cochran Q test: Initial computations

	Pre-test	Post-test	Follow-up	RT	RT^2
	1	1	1	3	9
	0	1	1	2	4
	1	1	1	3	9
	0	1	1	2	4
	0	1	1	2	4
	0	1	1	2	4
	0	1	1	2	4
	0	1	1	2	4
CT	2	8	8	18	42
CT^2	4	64	64	132	

shown in Table 11.33. So, from this table we can see that 2 students obtained more than 4 marks on the pre-test and all 8 achieved this level on post-test and follow-up, giving a total number of 18 over all pieces of coursework. The number of marks above 4 for any one individual is 3 for the first person, 2 for the next one and so on, giving a total of 18 for all 8 students.

The formula for computing Q is:

$$Q = \frac{[(\text{number of groups} \times \text{sum of CT}^2) - \text{squared sum of RT}] \times (\text{number of groups} - 1)}{(\text{number of groups} \times \text{sum of RT}) - \text{sum of RT}^2}$$

To compute the Q value, we carry out the following steps.

Step 1   Take the sum of the row totals (which is 18 and which is the total number of 1's in this example) and square this to give the squared sum of row totals (i.e. 324).

Step 2   Multiply the sum of the squared column totals (i.e. 132) by the number of groups (i.e. 3).

Step 3   Subtract from this figure (i.e. 132 × 3 = 396) the squared sum of row totals (i.e. 324).

Step 4   Multiply this difference (i.e. 396 − 324 = 72) by the number of groups minus 1 (i.e. 3 − 1 = 2). This figure (i.e. 72 × 2 = 144) which we will call the numerator is divided by another figure which we shall call the denominator and which is calculated in the following way.

Step 5   Multiply the sum of row totals (i.e. 18) by the number of groups (i.e. 3) and subtract from this the sum of the squared row totals (i.e. 42) to give the denominator (i.e. (18 × 3) − 42 = 54 − 42 = 12).

Step 6   Divide the numerator (i.e. 144) by the denominator (i.e. 12) to produce the Q value (i.e. 12.0).

Substituting the appropriate values in the formula, we see that Q is 12.0:

$$\frac{[(3 \times 132) - 324)] \times 2}{(3 \times 18) - 42} = \frac{(396 - 324) \times 2}{54 - 42} = \frac{144}{12} = 12.0$$

To check the statistical significance of this value, we look it up in the table in Appendix 11. Since, with 2 degrees of freedom, the value of 12.0 is larger than the critical value of 5.99 at the two-tailed 0.05 level, we would conclude that the number of marks of 4 or more differed significantly across the three pieces of coursework.

In terms of analysis of variance, Cochran's Q test is the between-treatments sum of squares divided by the within-subjects mean square (Winer 1962).

$$Q = \frac{\text{between-treatments sum of squares}}{\text{within-subjects mean square}}$$

This test does not, of course, tell us where this difference arises. To find this out, Marascuilo and McSweeney (1977) recommend using either the Bonferroni or the modified Scheffé test which involve the following preliminary steps.

Step 1 Determine the number of comparisons between pairs of samples or groups. With three samples, we can compare three pairs of groups (i.e. 1 vs 2, 1 vs 3 and 2 vs 3).

Step 2 Calculate the difference in proportions for these comparisons as shown in Table 11.34.

Step 3 Work out the estimated variance of the comparisons according to the following formula:

$$\frac{(\text{number of groups} \times \text{sum of CT}) - \text{sum of RT}^2}{\text{squared number of cases} \times \text{number of groups} \times (\text{number of groups} - 1)} \times 2$$

Substituting the figures from our example into the formula, we see that the estimated variance is 0.0625.

$$\frac{(3 \times 18) - 42}{8^2 \times 3 \times 2} \times 2 = \frac{54 - 42}{64 \times 6} \times 2 = \frac{12}{384} \times 2 = 0.0625$$

To perform the Bonferroni test, carry out the following additional steps.

Step 1 With three groups there are three comparisons. Look up in the last column of the table in Appendix 12 the critical value for the 0.05 probability level for three comparisons, which is 2.39.

Step 2 Multiply this figure by the square root of the estimated variance, which gives 0.598.

$$2.39 \times \sqrt{0.0626} = 2.39 \times 0.25 = 0.598$$

The difference between any two groups must be bigger than 0.598 to be statistically significant. The difference in the proportion of students

Table 11.34 Differences in proportions for the three pairwise comparisons

Pairwise comparisons	Differences proportions
Pre-test vs Post-test	2/8 − 8/8 = −0.75
Pre-test vs Follow-up	2/8 − 8/8 = 0.75
Post-test vs Follow-up	8/8 − 8/8 = 0.00

achieving a mark of 4 or more is greater than this figure for the comparison between pre-test and both post-test and follow-up but not for that between post-test and follow-up.

To conduct a modified Scheffé test, carry out the following steps.

Step 1 The degrees of freedom for chi-square with three groups are 1 minus the total number of groups which is 2. Look up in the table in Appendix 11 the critical value for the 0.05 probability level with 2 degrees of freedom, which is 5.99.

Step 2 Multiply the square root of this value by the square root of the estimated variance, which is 0.612.

$$\sqrt{5.99} \times \sqrt{0.0626} = 2.447 \times 0.25 = 0.612.$$

The difference between any two groups must be larger than 0.612 to be statistically significant. Once again, the difference in the proportion of students achieving a mark of 4 or more is bigger than this value for the comparison between pre-test and both post-test and follow-up but not for that between post-test and follow-up.

To compute with SPSS a Cochran's Q test for this example, we first recode marks for **markfol** as we did for **markpre** and **markpos** for the McNemar test and select the women in the tutorial groups (**sex = 1 & cond ~= 1**). We then carry out the following procedure on the three new variables:

→**Statistics** →**Nonparametric Tests** →**K Related Samples . . .** [opens **Tests for Several Related Samples** dialog box as in Box 11.9]

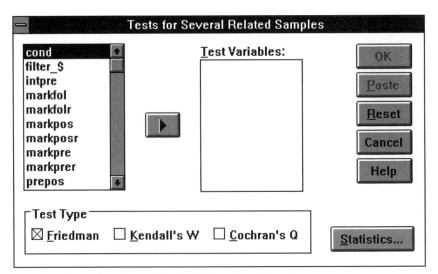

Box 11.9 **Tests for Several Related Samples** dialog box

Table 11.35 SPSS output of Cochran's *Q* test

─ ─ ─ ─ ─ Cochran Q Test

Cases

= 1.00	= .00	Variable
2	6	MARKPRER
8	0	MARKPOSR
8	0	MARKFOLR

Cases	Cochran Q	D.F.	Significance
8	12.0000	2	.0025

→first variable [e.g. **markprer**] →▶button [puts variable under **Test Variables:**] →second variable [e.g. **markposr**] →▶button [puts variable under **Test Variables:**] →third variable [e.g. **markfolr**] →▶button [puts variable under **Test Variables:**] →**Cochran's Q** →**Friedman** [deselects it] →**OK**

Table 11.35 shows the resulting output which gives a **Cochran Q** value of **12.0000**.

SUMMARY

The computation of non-parametric tests for assessing whether the number of cases in different categories varies across one or more groups or from some expected distribution is described. The binomial test determines whether the number of cases falling into one of only two categories differs significantly from some expected number or proportion. The Pearson chi-square test compares the observed frequency of cases against the expected frequency for one or more unrelated samples for variables with two or more categories. When there are only two categories the binomial test should be used when the minimum expected frequency for one of the two categories is less than 5. With three or more categories chi-square should not be used when the expected frequency is less than 1 or when more than 20 per cent of the expected frequencies are less than 5. Expected frequencies may be increased by dropping or combining appropriate categories. Applying Yates's correction may no longer be necessary when each variable has only two categories and when the number of cases is greater than 40 or when the number of cases is between 20 and 40 and all four expected frequencies are 5 or more. Fisher's exact test is used when each variable has only two categories and either the number of cases is between 20 and 40 and the smallest expected frequency is less than 5 or the number of cases is less than 20. The McNemar test compares the frequencies of a dichotomous variable which have changed values in two related samples of cases whereas the Cochran Q test compares them in three or more related samples. The *a priori* or planned test for determining which pair of three or more unrelated or related groups differ is the Bonferroni test whereas the *post hoc* test is the modified Scheffé test.

EXERCISES

1. Of a sample of 80 women, 20 are single, 40 are married, 10 are separated or divorced and 10 are widowed. The percentage of women in the population falling into these four categories are known to be 10, 70, 10 and 10.
   (a) What test would you use to determine if the distribution of marital status in the sample is similar to that of the population?
   (b) What is the value of this test?
   (c) What are the degrees of freedom?
   (d) Would you use a one- or two-tailed probability level to evaluate the significance of this value?
   (e) What is the probability value of the test?
   (f) Is the distribution of marital status in the sample significantly different from that in the population?
2. Of 90 married couples, 10 of the women compared to 25 of the men said that they fell in love with their partner at first sight.
   (a) What test would you use to determine whether this difference was significant?
   (b) What is the value of this test?
   (c) What are the degrees of freedom?
   (d) Would you use a one- or two-tailed probability level to evaluate the significance of this value?
   (e) What is the probability value of the test?
   (f) Do significantly more men than women fall in love with their future spouse at first sight?
3. Of 30 members who are supposed to meet twice, 5 attend both meetings, 5 attend neither meeting, 15 attend the first but not the second meeting and 5 attend the second but not the first meeting.
   (a) What test would you use to determine whether of the people attending the first meeting significantly fewer were present at the second meeting?
   (b) What is the value of this test?
   (c) What are the degrees of freedom?
   (d) Would you use a one- or two-tailed probability level to evaluate the significance of this value?
   (e) What is the probability value of the test?
   (f) Of the people attending the first meeting did significantly fewer attend the second?

12 Tests of difference for ordinal data

The statistical tests described in this chapter are used to analyse ordinal data for one or more groups of cases, or data which do not meet the assumptions for using parametric tests. These tests determine whether the distribution of cases differs significantly from chance across the groups or from some theoretical distribution. For example, instead of treating coursework marks as a ratio or interval scale, we could treat these scores as ordinal in the sense that a mark of 6, for example, is simply higher than the marks below it and that the difference between, say, marks of 2 and 3 is not necessarily the same as the difference between 3 and 4. We could then use some of the tests discussed in this chapter to find out whether having individual tutorials results in higher coursework marks than having group tutorials or no tutorials. We could use other tests contained in this chapter to see whether there is a significant increase in coursework marks after attending tutorials (i.e. at post-test) compared to before having them (i.e. at pre-test) and whether any increase which occurs is maintained later on (i.e. at follow-up). These tests are less powerful than parametric tests in the sense that differences are less likely to be statistically significant. We can check this by comparing the significance levels of the tests in this chapter with the significance level of parametric tests carried out on the same data in previous chapters.

KOLMOGOROV–SMIRNOV TEST FOR ONE SAMPLE

The Kolmogorov–Smirnov test for one sample determines whether the distribution of an ordinal variable differs significantly from some theoretical distribution (Kolmogorov 1933; Smirnov 1939). We could use this test to find out whether the distribution of, for example, pre-test course interest for the ten women in our study differed from the distribution of the population or some expected distribution such as that shown in Table 12.1 in which 20 percent obtained a rating of 1 or 4 and 30 per cent had one of 2 or 3. To perform this test, we carry out the following steps.

Step 1 Draw up a cumulative frequency table of the pre-test ratings for the sample in which the frequency of the previous category is added to the

Table 12.1 Proportions of expected or theoretical distribution of pre-test course interest ratings in women

Ratings	1	2	3	4
Proportions	0.20	0.30	0.30	0.20

Table 12.2 Cumulative frequency table of pre-test course interest ratings in women

Ratings	1	2	3	4
Sample	1	3	7	10

Table 12.3 Cumulative frequency proportions of pre-test course interest ratings in women

Ratings	1	2	3	4
Sample	1/10 0.10	3/10 0.30	7/10 0.70	10/10 1.00

Table 12.4 Absolute differences between the cumulative frequency proportions of the sample and the population

Ratings	1	2	3	4
Sample	0.10	0.30	0.70	1.00
Expected	0.20	0.50	0.80	1.00
Difference	0.10	0.20	0.10	0.00

frequency of the subsequent category as shown in Table 12.2. For instance, one women has a rating of 1 and two women have a rating of 2 so that the cumulative frequency of women having a rating of either 1 or 2 is 3 (1 + 2 = 3).

Step 2   Calculate the cumulative frequency proportion for each rating by dividing each cumulative frequency by the total number of cases in the sample as shown in Table 12.3.

Step 3   Work out the cumulative frequency proportion for the population (or expected) distribution and for each rating calculate the difference between the population (or expected) and the sample value as depicted in Table 12.4.

Step 4   Select the largest absolute difference between these two distributions and look up the probability of obtaining this difference in the table in

Appendix 14. As we can see from Table 12.4 the largest absolute difference is 0.20. From the table in Appendix 14, for a sample of 10 cases this difference to be significant must be equal to or bigger than 0.368 at the 0.05 one-tailed level and 0.410 at the 0.05 two-tailed level, which it is not. Consequently, we would conclude that the sample distribution does not differ significantly from the population (or expected) distribution.

With SPSS, a Kolmogorov–Smirnov test for one sample is tested against a normal, uniform, or Poisson theoretical distribution. To test this sample against a normal distribution, first select the women (**sex = 1**) and then use the following procedure:

→**S**tatistics →**N**onparametric Tests →**1**-Sample K-S . . . [opens **One-Sample Kolmogorov-Smirnov Test** dialog box as in Box 12.1]
→variable [e.g. **intpre**] →▶ button or double click [puts variable under **T**est Variable List:] →**N**ormal [under **Test Distribution**] →**OK**

Table 12.5 shows the output for this procedure. The largest or **Most extreme Absolute** difference is **.24005** which is not significant at a **2–Tailed P** of **.6119** or a one-tailed *p* of 0.3036.

KOLMOGOROV–SMIRNOV TEST FOR TWO UNRELATED SAMPLES

The Kolmogorov–Smirnov test determines whether the distribution of an ordinal variable differs significantly between two unrelated samples. We could apply this test if we wanted to compare the distribution, for example,

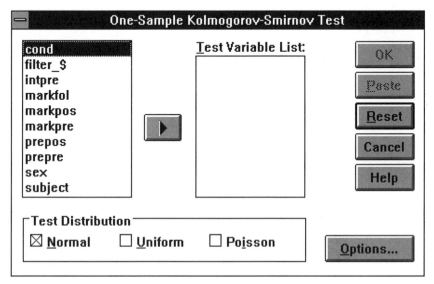

Box 12.1 **One-Sample Kolmogorov–Smirnov Test** dialog box

Table 12.5 SPSS output of the Kolmogorov–Smirnov test comparing pre-test course interest ratings in women against a normal distribution

- - - - - - - Kolmogorov - Smirnov Goodness of Fit Test

INTPRE   pre-test course interest

Test distribution - Normal   Mean: 2.90

                                Standard Deviation: .99

              Cases: 10

              Most extreme differences

Absolute	Positive	Negative	K-S Z	2-Tailed P
.24005	.15995	-.24005	.7591	.6119

of pre-test course interest ratings for women and men. To do this, we would carry out the following steps.

Step 1   Draw up a cumulative frequency table for the two groups in which the frequency of the previous category is added to the frequency of the subsequent category as shown in Table 12.6.

Step 2   Calculate the cumulative frequency proportion for each rating by dividing each cumulative frequency by the total number of cases in each sample as illustrated in Table 12.7.

Table 12.6 Cumulative frequency table of pre-test course interest ratings for women and men

Ratings	*1*	*2*	*3*	*4*
Women	1	3	7	10
Men	3	4	7	10

Table 12.7 Cumulative frequency proportions of pre-test course interest ratings for women and men

Ratings	*1*	*2*	*3*	*4*
Women	1/10	3/10	7/10	10/10
	0.10	0.30	0.70	1.00
Men	3/10	4/10	7/10	10/10
	0.30	0.40	0.70	1.00
Difference	0.20	0.10	0.00	0.00

Step 3 Compute the difference between the cumulative proportions within each rating as displayed in Table 12.7.

Step 4 for small samples When the number of cases in both samples is 25 or less as it is in this example, take the largest absolute difference which is 0.20. Multiply this difference by the number of cases in each sample which gives a value of 20.0 ($0.20 \times 10 \times 10 = 20.0$). Turn to the table in Appendix 15 for the one-tailed level and the table in Appendix 16 for the two-tailed level. As we did not predict the direction of any difference, we would use the two-tailed level in Appendix 16. When the size of both samples is 10 this absolute difference must be 70 or bigger to be statistically significant at the 0.05 level, which it is not. Consequently, we would conclude that there is no significant difference in the distribution of pre-test course interest ratings between the women and men.

Step 4: Two-tailed level for large samples When either sample is larger than 25, we would have to carry out the computation shown in the table in Appendix 17 to determine the two-tailed significance level. If we multiplied the numbers within each rating by 10, we would have 100 cases in each sample. To determine the value which an absolute difference of 0.20 from 100 cases would have to be larger than to be significant, we proceed as follows. We have to add the two sample sizes together ($100 + 100 = 200$), divide by the product of the two sample sizes [$200/(100 \times 100) = 200/10000 = 2/100 = 0.02$], take the square root of the resulting figure ($\sqrt{0.02} = 0.14$) and multiply by 1.36 which gives a value of 0.19 ($0.14 \times 1.36 = 0.19$).

Since the absolute difference of 0.20 is just larger than 0.19, we would conclude in this instance that the two distributions differed significantly at less than the 0.05 two-tailed level and that women had significantly higher pre-test course interest ratings than men. We could go on to calculate that the absolute difference of 0.20 was just smaller than the 0.025 two-tailed value (i.e. $0.14 \times 1.48 = 0.207$) and so was not significant at this level.

Step 4: One-tailed level for large samples To calculate the one-tailed probability level when either sample is larger than 25, we compute a chi-square according to the following formula where n_1 is the number of cases in one sample and n_2 is the number of cases in the other sample:

$$\text{chi-square} = \frac{n_1 \times n_2}{n_1 + n_2} \times 4 \times \text{largest absolute difference squared}$$

If we substitute the appropriate figures into this formula we see that chi-square is 8.0:

$$\frac{100 \times 100}{100 + 100} \times 4 \times 0.20^2 = \frac{10000}{200} \times 4 \times 0.04 = 50 \times 0.16 = 8.0$$

We look up this figure in the table in Appendix 11. Since this test has two degrees of freedom and since a chi-square of 8.0 is larger than 5.99 at the 0.05 two-tailed level, we can conclude that women had significantly higher pre-test course interest than men at the 0.05 two-tailed level.

To carry out this analysis with SPSS, first select the whole sample and then execute the following procedure:

→**Statistics** →**Nonparametric Tests** →**2 Independent Samples** . . . [opens **Two-Independent Samples Test** dialog box as in Box 12.2] →dependent variable [e.g. **intpre**] →▶button [puts variable under **Test Variable List:**] →independent variable [e.g. **sex**] [puts variable under **Grouping Variable:**] →**Define Groups** . . . [opens **Two Independent Samples: Define Groups** dialog box as in Box 12.3] →in box beside **Group 1:** type lower code value [e.g. **1**] →box beside **Group 2:** and type upper code value [e.g. **2**] →**Continue** [closes **Two Independent Samples: Define Groups** dialog box] →**Kolmogorov-Smirnov Z** →**Mann-Whitney U** [deselects it] →**OK**

Table 12.8 presents the output for this analysis. The **Most extreme Absolute** difference is **.20000** which is not significant at a **2–Tailed P** of **.988**.

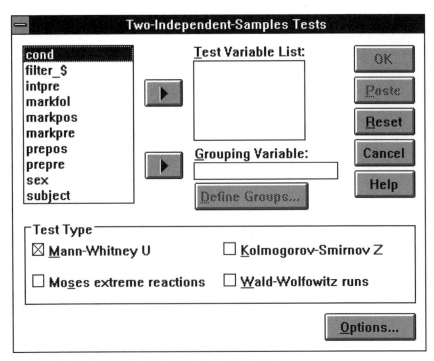

Box 12.2 **Two Independent Samples Test** dialog box

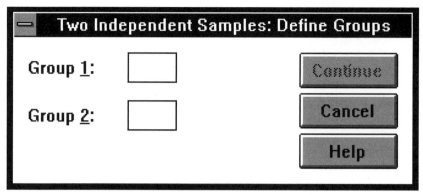

Box 12.3 **Two Independent Samples: Define Groups** dialog box

Table 12.8 SPSS output of the Kolmogorov–Smirnov test comparing pre-test course interest ratings in women and men

- - - - - - - - Kolmogorov - Smirnov 2-Sample Test

     INTPRE   pre-test course interest
     by SEX

     Cases

       10 SEX = 1 women
       10 SEX = 2 men
       –
       20 Total

Warning – Due to small sample size, probability tables should be consulted.

     Most extreme differences

Absolute	Positive	Negative	K-S Z	2-Tailed P
.20000	.00000	-.20000	.447	.988

MOOD'S MEDIAN TEST FOR TWO OR MORE UNRELATED SAMPLES

Mood's (1950) median test is used to determine if the distribution of values either side of a common median differs for two or more unrelated samples. To calculate Mood's median test to discover if the pre-test marks in women are higher for the individual than for the group tutorial condition, we would carry out the following steps.

Step 1 Combine the scores for the two groups and find the median for this combined group. The median for this example is 3.0.

1 1 2 3 3 3 5 7

Step 2 Form a contingency table where the columns represent the conditions, the first row the frequencies of values above the median and the second row the frequencies of values at or below the median as shown in Table 12.9.

Step 3 Work out the expected frequencies as displayed in Table 12.10.

Step 4 Carry out a chi-square test on the observed frequencies in this contingency table. Doing this gives a chi-square of 4.44.

$$\frac{(2 - 0.75)^2}{0.75} + \frac{(0 - 1.25)^2}{1.25} + \frac{(1 - 2.25)^2}{2.25} + \frac{(5 - 3.75)^2}{3.75} =$$

$$\frac{1.25^2}{0.75} + \frac{-1.25^2}{1.25} + \frac{-1.25^2}{2.25} + \frac{1.25^2}{3.75} = \frac{1.56}{0.75} + \frac{1.56}{1.25} + \frac{1.56}{2.25} + \frac{1.56}{3.75} =$$

$$2.08 + 1.25 + 0.69 + 0.42 = 4.44$$

Step 5 We look up this value which has 1 degree of freedom in the table in Appendix 11 where we see that chi-square has to be 2.71 or bigger to be significant at the one-tailed 0.05 level, which it is. Note, however, that because of the small expected frequencies, it would not be suitable to use a chi-square test in this instance and a Fisher's exact test is more appropriate.

To conduct with SPSS Mood's median test on this example, we first select the women (**sex=1**) and then execute the following procedure:

Table 12.9 2 × 2 contingency table of observed frequencies of pre-test marks in women in the individual and group tutorial condition above the median and at or below the median

	Individual	*Group*	*Row totals*
Above the median	2	0	2
At or below the median	1	5	6
Column totals	3	5	8

Table 12.10 2 × 2 contingency table of expected frequencies of pre-test marks in women in the individual and group tutorial condition above or at and below the median

	Individual	*Group*
Above the median	0.75	1.25
At or below the median	2.25	3.75

→**Statistics** →**Nonparametric Tests** →**K Independent Samples ...** [opens **Tests for Several Independent Samples** dialog box as in Box 12.4]
→dependent variable [e.g. **markpre**] →▶ button [puts variable under **Test Variable List:**] →independent variable [e.g. **cond**] [puts variable under **Grouping Variable:**] →**Define Range ...** [opens **Define Range** dialog box as in Box 12.5]
→in box beside **Minimum:** type lower code value [e.g. **2**] →box beside **Maximum:** and type higher code value [e.g. **3**] →**Continue** [closes **Several Independent Samples: Define Range** dialog box]
→**Median** →**Kruskal-Wallis H** [deselects it] →**OK**

Table 12.11 shows the output for this procedure. The **Exact probability** of **.1071** is the one-tailed level for Fisher's test which SPSS uses for 30 or fewer cases.

When three or more groups are being compared we can conduct *post hoc* comparisons between any two groups using the same procedure (Marascuilo and McSweeney 1977). However, we need to adjust the 0.05 significance level by dividing it by the number of comparisons being made. For example, for three comparisons the appropriate significance level is 0.0167 (0.05/3 = 0.0167).

MANN–WHITNEY *U* TEST FOR TWO UNRELATED SAMPLES

The Mann–Whitney *U* test determines the number of times a score from one of the samples is ranked higher than a score from the other sample

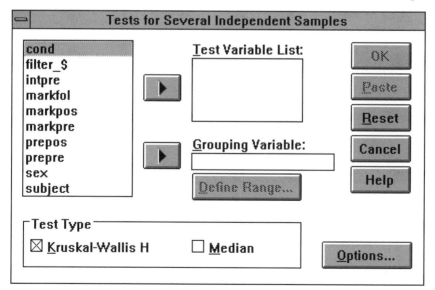

Box 12.4 **Tests for Several Independent Samples** dialog box

Box 12.5 **Define Range** dialog box

Table 12.11 SPSS output for Mood's median test comparing pre-test marks in women for the individual and group tutorial conditions

– – – – – Median Test

    MARKPRE pre-test marks

by COND

                              COND
                              2   3
                         + ----------- + ----------- +
          GT median | 2 | 0 |
MARKPRE   + ----------- + ----------- +
          LE median | 1 | 5 |
                         + ----------- + ----------- +

              Cases   Median   Exact probability
                8   3.0   .1071

(Mann and Whitney 1947). If the two sets of scores are similar, then the number of times this happens should be similar for the two samples. To calculate the Mann–Whitney test to find out if the sum of ranked pre-test marks in women is greater for the individual than for the group tutorial condition, we would carry out the following steps.

Step 1 Rank the scores of both the samples together, using rank 1 for the lowest score, rank 2 for the next lowest score and so on. If two or more scores have the same value, each of the tied scores has the same rank which

Table 12.12 Ranking of pre-test marks in women for the individual and group tutorial conditions

	Scores				
	Original	Reordered	Position	Ranked	Ranks of originals
Individual	5	1	1	1.5	7.0
tutorial	3	1	2	1.5	5.0
	7	2	3	3.0	8.0
Group	1	3	4	5.0	1.5
tutorial	1	3	5	5.0	1.5
	2	3	6	5.0	3.0
	3	5	7	7.0	5.0
	3	7	8	8.0	5.0

is equal to the average rank of those scores for the combined samples. For example, if two scores are equal and would have occupied first and second place, the two positions are added together $(1 + 2 = 3)$ and divided by the number of scores (2) to give a ranking of 1.5 $(3/2 = 1.5)$, which is then assigned to the two scores. The ranking of the pre-test marks for the two conditions is shown in Table 12.12.

Step 2 Sum the ranks for the smaller sample. The individual tutorial condition is the smaller sample and its sum of ranks is 20.0 (7.0 + 5.0 + 8.0 = 20.0).

Step 3 The Mann–Whitney U is calculated by the following formula where n_1 represents the smaller sample and n_2 the larger sample:

$$U = (n_1 \times n_2) + \frac{n_1 \times (n_1 + 1)}{2} - \text{summed ranks of } n_1$$

Substituting the appropriate values into this formula, we find that U is 1:

$$(3 \times 5) + \frac{3 \times (3 + 1)}{2} - 20 = 15 + \frac{12}{2} - 20 = 15 + 6 - 20 = 1$$

Step 4 Calculate the U value for the second sample using the following formula:

U of second sample $= n_1 \times n_2 - U$ of first sample

Putting the relevant figures into this formula, we see that the U of the second sample is 14:

$(3 \times 5) - 1 = 15 - 1 = 14$

Note that if we know the U value of one sample (e.g. 1) and the two sample sizes (i.e. 3 and 5), we can work out the U value for the other sample (15 − 1 = 14) since the two U values combined equal the product of the number of cases in the two samples ($3 \times 5 = 15$).

Step 5 for samples up to 20   If the samples are 20 or less, as they are in this case, we look up the significance of the smaller of the two U values (i.e. 1) in the appropriate table in Appendix 18 or 19. If the value of the smaller U is greater than the critical value of U in the table, we conclude that there is no significant difference between the summed ranks of the two samples. Since we specified the direction of the difference we expected to find, we would use the 0.05 one-tailed level shown in the table in Appendix 18. As the U value of 1 equals the critical value of 1 when the size of one sample is 3 and the other 5, we would argue that there is a significant difference in pre-test marks between the two conditions.

Step 5 for samples larger than 20   If the samples are greater than 20, we convert our U value into an approximate z value by using the following formula:

$$z = \frac{U - [(n_1 \times n_2)/2]}{\sqrt{[(n_1 \times n_2)(n_1 + n_2 + 1)]/12}}$$

We can change our U value into a z value by substituting the appropriate numbers into the formula which gives a z of 1.94:

$$\frac{1 - [(3 \times 5)/2]}{\sqrt{[(3 \times 5)(3 + 5 + 1)]/12}} = \frac{1 - 7.5}{\sqrt{(15 \times 9)/12}} = \frac{-6.5}{\sqrt{11.25}} = \frac{-6.5}{3.35} = -1.94$$

Since we ignore the sign of the U value, it does not matter which U value is put into the formula. If we subtracted 7.5 from 14 instead of 1 the absolute difference is still 6.5.

We look up the significance of this z value in the table in Appendix 2. The area between the middle of the curve and a z value of 1.94 is 0.4738, indicating that the area beyond the z value on one side of the curve is 0.0622 ($0.5000 - 0.4378 = 0.0622$). Since 0.0622 is larger than 0.05, we would conclude that there is no significant difference in pre-test marks in women between the individual and group tutorial condition. If we had wanted the two-tailed probability level we would double 0.0622 to give 0.1244 ($0.0622 \times 2 = 0.1244$).

When ties occur between the scores of the two samples, the U value is affected although this effect is usually slight. To correct for tied ranks in calculating z, we carry out the following steps.

Step 1   Count the number of ties for each score. So, in our example, we have two scores or ties of 1 and three ties of 3.

Step 2 For each tied score, subtract the number of ties from the number of ties cubed and divide by 12. So, two ties becomes 0.5 [$(2^3 - 2)/12 = 0.5$].

Step 3 Sum these values for each tied score, which in our example would give a figure of 2.5:

$$\frac{2^3 - 2}{12} + \frac{3^3 - 3}{12} = \frac{8 - 2}{12} + \frac{27 - 3}{12} = \frac{6}{12} + \frac{24}{12} = \frac{30}{12} = 2.5$$

Step 4 This value (which we shall call ST for sum of ties) is used in the following formula to calculate z, where N stands for the total number of cases in both samples:

$$z = \frac{U - \dfrac{(n_1 \times n_2)}{2}}{\sqrt{\dfrac{n_1 \times n_2}{N \times (N - 1)} \times \left(\dfrac{N^3 - N}{12} - ST\right)}}$$

Inserting the values of our example, we find that z is 1.9975:

$$\frac{1 - \dfrac{(3 \times 5)}{2}}{\sqrt{\dfrac{(3 \times 5)}{8 \times (8 - 1)} \times \left(\dfrac{8^3 - 8}{12} - 2.5\right)}} =$$

$$\frac{1 - 7.5}{\sqrt{\dfrac{15}{56} \times \left(\dfrac{504}{12} - 2.5\right)}} = \frac{-6.5}{\sqrt{0.268\ 3\ (42 - 2.5)}} = \frac{-6.5}{\sqrt{0.268 \times 39.5}} =$$

$$\frac{-6.5}{\sqrt{10.586}} = \frac{-6.5}{3.254} = -1.9975$$

Looking up the significance of this value of 2.00 in the table in Appendix 2, we find that we obtain a one-tailed probability value of 0.0228 (0.5000 − 0.4772 = 0.0228). Since this value is smaller than 0.05, we would conclude that there was a significant difference in pre-test marks in women between the individual and group tutorial condition.

To carry out this analysis with SPSS, after selecting the women (**sex = 1**) we conduct the following procedure:

→**Statistics** →**N**onparametric **Tests** →**2** **Independent Samples** . . .
[opens **Two-Independent Samples Test** dialog box as in Box 12.2]
→dependent variable [e.g. **markpre**] →▶ button [puts variable under **Test Variable List:**] →independent variable [e.g. **cond**] [puts variable under **Grouping Variable:**] →**D**efine **Groups** . . . [opens **Two Independent Samples: Define Groups** dialog box as in Box 12.3]
→in box beside **Group 1:** type lower code value [e.g. **2**] →box beside **Group 2:** and type upper code value [e.g. **3**] →**Continue** [closes **Two Independent Samples: Define Groups** dialog box]
[→**M**ann-Whitney U already selected] →**OK**

Table 12.13 displays the output for this procedure. The mean rank for the two conditions is given as well as the U and W value. The U and W value of the smaller group is presented, unless the two groups are of equal size when the U and W value of the group with the lower code (i.e. 2) is shown. The W value is the rank sum of the smaller group (i.e. **6.67** $\times$ **3 = 20.0**). For samples with less than 30 cases, the exact two-tailed significance level is calculated using the algorithm of Dinneen and Blakesley (1973) together with the z statistic corrected for ties. For larger samples, only the z statistic is displayed.

Table 12.13 SPSS output for the Mann–Whitney test comparing pre-test marks in women for the individual and group tutorial conditions

- - - - - - - Mann-Whitney U - Wilcoxon Rank Sum W Test

MARKPRE

by COND

Mean Rank	Cases
6.67	3 COND = 2 indivtut
3.20	5 COND = 3 grouptut
—	
	8 Total

		Exact	Corrected for ties	
U	W	2-Tailed P	Z	2-Tailed P
1.0	20.0	.0714	-1.9983	.0457

KRUSKAL–WALLIS ONE-WAY ANALYSIS OF VARIANCE OR H TEST FOR THREE OR MORE UNRELATED SAMPLES

The Kruskal–Wallis H test is similar to the Mann–Whitney U test in that the cases in the different samples are ranked together in one series except that this test can be used with more than two unrelated samples (Kruskal and Wallis 1952). If there is little difference between the sets of scores, their mean ranks should be similar. We would use the Kruskal–Wallis H test to determine if pre-test marks in women differed between the three conditions of the no, individual and group tutorials. To apply this test to these data, we would carry out the following steps:

Step 1 Rank the scores of the conditions taken together, giving rank 1 to the lowest score. Where two or more scores are tied, allocate the average rank to those scores. The pre-test marks for the three conditions are presented in Table 12.14 where they have been rearranged in three parallel columns. The ranking of these data

1	1	1	2	3	3	3	3	5	7
2.0	2.0	2.0	4.0	6.5	6.5	6.5	6.5	9.0	10.0

arranged according to condition is shown in Table 12.15.

Step 2 Sum the ranks for each group which, in this example, gives 8.5, 25.5 and 21.0 respectively.

Table 12.14 Pre-test marks for women in the three tutorial conditions

No	Individual	Group
3	5	1
1	3	1
	7	2
		3
		3

Table 12.15 Ranking of pre-test marks for women in the three tutorial conditions

	No	Individual	Group
	6.5	9.0	2.0
	2.0	6.5	2.0
		10.0	4.0
			6.5
			6.5
Total	8.5	25.5	21.0

Step 3 For each group, square the sum of ranks and divide by the number of cases. This in turn yields 36.125 (72.25/2 = 36.125), 216.75 (650.25/3 = 216.75) and 88.20 (441/5 = 88.20).

Step 4 Sum these values which, in this case, is 341.075.

Step 5 Place this figure (which we shall call SR for sum of ranks) in the following formula which gives *H*:

$$H = \frac{12 \times SR}{N \times (N + 1)} - [3 \times (N + 1)]$$

Substituting the appropriate values, *H* is 4.21:

$$\frac{12 \times 341.075}{10 \times (10 + 1)} - [3 \times (10 + 1)] = \frac{4092.9}{110} - 33 = 37.2082 - 33 = 4.2082$$

When there are more than 5 cases in each of the conditions, the significance of *H* may be determined from the chi-square table in Appendix 11. The degrees of freedom is one less than the number of samples which in this case is 2 (3 − 1 = 2). Since with 2 degrees of freedom an *H* value of 4.21 is not greater than 5.99 at the two-tailed 0.05 level, we would conclude that there was no significant difference in pre-test marks between the three conditions.

To correct for tied scores, we carry out the following steps.

Step 1 Count the number of ties for each score. In this example, we have three ties of 1 and four ties of 3.

Step 2 For each tied score, subtract the number of ties from the number of ties cubed. So, three ties becomes 24 (3^3 − 3 = 24).

Step 3 Sum these values for each tied score, which in this case gives 84:

$$(3^3 - 3) + (4^3 - 4) = 24 + 60 = 84$$

Step 4 Divide this value by the total number of cases subtracted from the total number of cases cubed, which in this instance produces a figure of 0.085:

$$\frac{84}{10^3 - 10} = \frac{84}{1000 - 10} = \frac{84}{990} = 0.0849$$

Step 5 Subtract this number from one, which gives 0.915 (1 − 0.085 = 0.915).

Step 6 Divide the uncorrected value of *H* by this figure to give the value corrected for ties, which in this example is 4.60 (4.21/0.915 = 4.60). We look up this value in the chi-square table in Appendix 11. Since with 2 degrees of freedom this figure is not greater than 5.99 at the two-tailed 0.05 level, we would conclude that there was no significant difference in pre-test marks between the three conditions.

In terms of analysis of variance, the Kruskal–Wallis *H* test may be thought of as the between-treatments sum of squares divided by the total mean square for the ranked scores (Winer 1962). This can be quickly checked by running a one-way analysis of variance on these scores with SPSS.

To conduct a Kruskal–Wallis *H* test with SPSS, we first select the women (**sex=1**) and then perform the following procedure:

→**Statistics** →**Nonparametric Tests** →**K Independent Samples . . .** [opens **Tests for Several Independent Samples** dialog box as in Box 12.4]
→dependent variable [e.g. **markpre**] →▶button [puts variable under **Test Variable List:**] →independent variable [e.g. **cond**] [puts variable under **Grouping Variable:**] →**Define Range . . .** [opens **Define Range** dialog box as in Box 12.5]
→in box beside **Minimum:** type lower code value [e.g. **1**] →box beside **Maximum:** and type upper code value [e.g. **3**] →**Continue** [closes **Several Independent Samples: Define Range** dialog box]
[→**Kruskal-Wallis H** already selected] →**OK**

Table 12.16 SPSS output for the Kruskal–Wallis *H* test comparing pre-test marks for women in the three tutorial conditions

- - - - - - - Kruskal-Wallis 1-Way Anova

MARKPRE   pre-test marks
by COND

Mean Rank   Cases

    4.25   2 COND = 1 notut
    8.50   3 COND = 2 indivtut
    4.20   5 COND = 3 grouptut
                 –
             10 Total

				Corrected for ties		
Chi-Square	D.F.		Significance	Chi-Square	D.F.	Significance
4.2082	2		.1220	4.5983	2	.1003

Table 12.16 presents the output for this procedure. The mean rank for the three conditions is given which is simply the sum of ranks for each group divided by the number of cases in that group. For example, the sum of ranks for the no tutorial condition is 8.5 which divided by 2 gives **4.25**. The chi-square test, uncorrected and corrected for ties, with its associated significance level is also depicted.

This test only tells us whether three or more groups differ but not which of any two groups differ. Marascuilo and McSweeney (1977) suggest that the Mann–Whitney U test can be used to make *post hoc* comparisons between all pairs of groups adjusting the significance level of 0.05 by dividing it by the number of comparisons. For example, with three comparisons the appropriate significance level is 0.0167 (0.05/3 = 0.0167).

SIGN TEST FOR TWO RELATED SAMPLES

The sign test compares the number of positive and negative differences between scores for the same or matched samples (Dixon and Mood 1946). If the two samples do not differ, the number of positive and negative differences should be similar. We could use the sign test to determine if there had been any change in marks between any two occasions such as at pre-test and post-test.

To apply the sign test to determine whether marks had increased from pre- to post-test for women in the individual tutorial condition, we would carry out the following steps.

Step 1   Record the direction of change between the two occasions, giving a minus $(-)$ if the second score is larger than the first, a plus $(+)$ if it is smaller and a zero (0) if there is no difference. These differences have been noted in Table 12.17 for the pre- and post-test marks scores for women in the individual condition.

Step 2   Count the number of pluses and minuses. Let n represent the less frequent sign and N the total number of pluses and minuses. In this example, n is 0 since there are no pluses and N is 3.

Step 3 for less than 26 differences   For samples containing less than 26 differences (number of pluses and minuses), look up the significance of the

Table 12.17 Pre-test and post-test marks for women in the individual condition

Pre-test	Post-test	Sign of Difference
5	7	−
3	8	−
7	9	−

results in the binomial table in Appendix 10. The one-tailed probability of obtaining this value is 0.125 which is greater than the 0.05 criterion. In other words, marks did not increase significantly from pre- to post-test for the individual tutorial condition.

Step 3 for greater than 25 differences   For samples having more than 25 differences, the less frequent difference can be converted into a z value using the following formula:

$$z = \frac{(n + 0.5) - N/2}{0.5 \times \sqrt{N}}$$

where n and N have the same meaning as before. Substituting the appropriate values in this formula, z is -1.16:

$$\frac{(0 + 0.5) - 3/2}{0.5 \times \sqrt{3}} = \frac{-1.0}{0.5 \times 1.73} = \frac{-1.0}{0.865} = -1.156$$

We look up the significance of this z value of 1.16 in the normal distribution table in Appendix 2, where we see that it has a one-tailed probability value of less than 0.1230 ($0.5000 - 0.3770 = 0.1230$).

To perform a sign test with SPSS on this example, we first select the women in the individual tutorial condition (**sex=1 & cond=2**) and then conduct the following procedure:

→**Statistics** →**Nonparametric Tests** →**2 Related Samples . . .** [opens **Two Related Samples Tests** dialog box as in Box 11.8]
→first variable [e.g. **markpre**] [puts variable beside **Variable 1:** in **Current Selections** section] →second variable [e.g. **markpos**] [puts variable beside **Variable 2:** in **Current Selections** section] →▶ button [puts the two variables under **Test Pair[s] List:**] →**Sign** →**Wilcoxon** [deselects it] →**OK**

Table 12.18 presents the output for this procedure. The number of negative, positive and zero differences are shown. The two-tailed binomial level is used with fewer than 26 differences (as in this instance) and the two-tailed z level with more than 25 differences.

WILCOXON MATCHED-PAIRS SIGNED-RANKS TEST FOR TWO RELATED SAMPLES

Whereas the sign test only makes use of the sign of the difference between the two samples, the Wilcoxon (1945) matched-pairs signed-ranks test (or Wilcoxon test for short), takes some account of the size of the difference by ranking the size of the differences and summing ranks of the same sign.

To conduct a Wilcoxon test to determine whether marks had increased

Table 12.18 SPSS output for the sign test comparing pre- and post-test marks for women in the individual tutorial condition

- - - - - - - Sign Test

     MARKPOS   post-test marks

with MARKPRE   pre-test marks

        Cases

            3 - Diffs (MARKPRE LT MARKPOS)

            0 + Diffs (MARKPRE GT MARKPOS)   (Binomial)

            0   Ties   2-Tailed P =   .2500

            –

            3   Total

Note: Although SPSS puts the two variables in their alphabetical and not their selected order, the variable higher in alphabetical order (MARKPOS) is subtracted from the variable lower in alphabetical order (MARKPRE).

from pre- to post-test for women in the individual tutorial condition, we would carry out the following steps.

Step 1 Calculate the difference between each pair of scores and rank these in size, ignoring the sign of the difference. Give a rank of 1 to the smallest difference (regardless of its sign) and omit pairs where there is no difference. For example, 2 would receive a higher rank than either 1 or −1, which would be given the same rank. The size and rank of the differences between pre- and post-test marks for the women in the individual tutorial condition are presented in Table 12.19. Where two or more differences are the same size, they are given the average of the ranks they would have received if they had differed. The smallest difference in our data is 2 and there are two such values, so its rank is 1.5.

Step 2 Sum the ranks of the difference with the less frequent sign. In this case, the less frequent sign is plus. Since there are no positive differences, the sum of ranks is zero.

Table 12.19 Ranked differences between pre- and post-test marks for women in the individual tutorial condition

Pre-test	Post-test	Difference	Rank
5	7	−2	1.5
3	8	−5	3.0
7	9	−2	1.5

Step 3 for less than 26 differences For data having fewer than 26 differences, look up the significance of the smaller sum of ranks with the same sign in the table in Appendix 20. We can use the one-tailed significance level as we are testing for an increase rather than a change in marks. The smaller sum of ranks has to be the same as or smaller than the values shown in the table to be significant at the stated level. The significance level for samples with fewer than 5 differences is not given. However, if the number of differences had been 6, we can see that a sum of ranks of 0 is smaller than 2 at the two-tailed 0.10 level (and therefore at the one-tailed 0.05 level), and so we would have concluded that marks had decreased significantly from pre- to post-test for women in the individual tutorial condition.

Step 3 for more than 25 differences For data with more than 25 differences, the following formula is used to transform the smaller sum of ranks (denoted as SR) into a z score where N stands for the number of differences:

$$z = \frac{SR - \dfrac{N \times (N + 1)}{4}}{\sqrt{\dfrac{N \times (N + 1) \times [(2 \times N) + 1]}{24}}}$$

To illustrate the use of this formula, we will substitute the values of our example which give a z of -1.60:

$$\frac{0 - \dfrac{3 \times (3 + 1)}{4}}{\sqrt{\dfrac{3 \times (3 + 1) \times [(2 \times 3) + 1]}{24}}} = \frac{0 - \dfrac{12}{4}}{\sqrt{\dfrac{12 \times 7}{24}}} = \frac{-3.0}{\sqrt{3.5}} = \frac{-3.0}{1.87} = -1.60$$

We look up the significance of this z value of 1.60 in the normal distribution table in Appendix 2, where we see that it has a one-tailed probability of less than 0.0548 ($0.5000 - 0.4452 = 0.0548$).

To run a Wilcoxon test with SPSS on this example, we first select the women in the individual tutorial condition (**sex=1 & cond=2**) and then use the following procedure:

→**Statistics** →**Nonparametric Tests** →**2 Related Samples . . .** [opens **Two Related Samples Tests** dialog box as in Box 11.8]
→first variable [e.g. **markpre**] [puts variable beside **Variable 1:** in **Current Selections** section] →second variable [e.g. **markpos**] [puts variable beside **Variable 2:** in **Current Selections** section] →▶ button [puts these variables under →**Test Pair[s] List:**] [→**Wilcoxon** already selected] →**OK**

Table 12.20 SPSS output for the Wilcoxon test comparing pre- and post-test marks for women in the individual tutorial condition

- - - - - - - Wilcoxon Matched-Pairs Signed-Ranks Test

MARKPOS	post-test marks
with MARKPRE	pre-test marks

Mean Rank	Cases
2.00	3 - Ranks (MARKPRE LT MARKPOS)
.00	0 + Ranks (MARKPRE GT MARKPOS)
	0 Ties (MARKPRE EQ MARKPOS)
	$-$
	3 Total
Z = -1.6036	2-Tailed P = .1088

Table 12.20 displays the output for this procedure. The mean negative and positive rank is shown together with the number of negative, positive and tied ranks, the **Z** statistic and its two-tailed probability. SPSS also uses the z statistic for samples with fewer than 25 differences which in this case has a one-tailed probability of 0.0544 (**.1088**/2 = 0.0544).

FRIEDMAN TWO-WAY ANALYSIS OF VARIANCE TEST FOR THREE OR MORE RELATED SAMPLES

The Friedman (1937) two-way analysis of variance test (or Friedman test for short) compares the mean ranks of three or more related samples. If the samples do not differ, the mean ranks should be similar. The Friedman test approximates a chi-square distribution where the degrees of freedom are the number of columns minus 1.

To calculate the Friedman test to determine whether pre-test, post-test and follow-up marks differ for women in the individual tutorial condition, we would carry out the following steps.

Step 1 Arrange the scores in a table where the columns represent the conditions and the rows the cases. This has been done for the pre-test, post-test and follow-up marks scores for women in the individual condition in Table 12.21.

Step 2 Rank the scores in each row across all the conditions, ranking the lowest score as 1. Where two or more scores are tied, allocate the average rank to those scores. The scores in Table 12.21 have been ranked in this

Table 12.21 Pre-test, post-test and follow-up marks for women in the individual tutorial condition

Pre-test	Post-test	Follow-up
5	7	7
3	8	5
7	9	9

Table 12.22 Ranked pre-test, post-test and follow-up marks for women in the individual tutorial condition and initial computations

	Pre-test	Post-test	Follow-up	
	1.0	2.5	2.5	
	1.0	3.0	2.0	
	1.0	2.5	2.5	
Sum	3.0	8.0	7.0	
Sum^2	9.0	64.0	49.0	122.0

way in Table 12.22. For example, in the first row 1 would be ranked 1 and the two 2s would receive the average rank of 2.5 [(2 + 3)/2 = 2.5].

Step 3   Sum the ranks for each condition, as shown in Table 12.22, which gives 3.0, 8.0 and 7.0 respectively.

Step 4   Square the sum of ranks for each condition, as indicated in Table 12.22, producing 9.0, 64.0 and 49.0 respectively.

Step 5   Add together the squared sum of ranks to form the total squared sum of ranks which we shall abbreviate as TSSR and which is 122.0.

Step 6   To obtain chi-square unadjusted for ties (referred to by Hollander and Wolfe 1973 as *S*), insert this value into the following formula where *C* represents the number of columns and *N* the number of rows or cases:

$$S = \frac{12 \times \text{TSSR}}{N \times C \times (C + 1)} - 3 \times N \times (C + 1)$$

Substituting the appropriate figures in our example, we find that *S* is 4.67:

$$\frac{12 \times 122}{3 \times 3 \times (3 + 1)} - 3 \times 3 \times (3 + 1) = \frac{1464}{36} - 36 = 40.667 - 36 = 4.67$$

We look up the significance of this value, which has 2 degrees of freedom, in the table in Appendix 11. The two-tailed probability level is used because with three conditions, we cannot specify the direction of any differences. Chi-square has to be 5.99 or larger to be significant, which it is not. Consequently, we could conclude that there is no significant difference between pre-test, post-test and follow-up marks for the individual condition when no adjustment is made for tied ranks.

To obtain chi-square adjusted for ties (called by Hollander and Wolfe 1973 S'), we would insert the TSSR into the following formula

$$S' = \frac{(12 \times \text{TSSR}) - [3 \times N^2 \times C \times (C + 1)^2]}{[N \times C \times (C + 1)] - [\text{sum of adjustments for each row}]/(C - 1)]}$$

where the adjustment for each row is the number of ties cubed for any rank added to 1 cubed (i.e. 1) for every untied rank minus the number of columns.

Rows 1 and 3 have two ties of the same rank and 1 untied rank, so the adjustment for rows with tied ranks is 12

$$[(2^3 + 1^3) - 3] + [(2^3 + 1^3) - 3] = (9 - 3) + (9 - 3) = 6 + 6 = 12$$

Consequently, chi-square adjusted for ties is 5.60

$$\frac{(12 \times 122) - [3 \times 3^2 \times 3 \times (3 + 1)^2]}{[3 \times 3 \times (3 + 1) - [12/(3 - 1)]} =$$

$$\frac{1464 - (3 \times 9 \times 3 \times 16)}{36 - 6} = \frac{1464 - 1296}{30} = \frac{168}{30} = 5.60$$

From the table in Appendix 11, we can see that this value with 2 degrees of freedom is smaller than the two-tailed 0.05 critical value of 5.99 and so we would conclude that there is no significant difference in marks between the three occasions when an adjustment is made for tied ranks.

In terms of analysis of variance, the Friedman test may be thought of as the between-treatments sum of squares divided by the within-subjects mean square (Winer 1962). The formula for the within-subjects mean square unadjusted for ties is

$$\text{within-subjects mean square} = \frac{k \times (k + 1)}{12}$$

where k is the number of treatments.

To conduct a Friedman test with SPSS on this example, we first select women in the individual tutorial condition (**sex=1 & cond=2**) and then perform the following sequence:

→**Statistics** →**Nonparametric Tests** →**K Related Samples . . .** [opens **Tests for Several Related Samples** dialog box as in Box 11.9]
→first variable [e.g. **markpre**] →▶ button [puts variable under **Test Variables:**] →second variable [e.g. **markpos**] →▶ button [puts variable

Table 12.23 SPSS output for the Friedman test comparing pre-test, post-test and follow-up marks for women in the individual tutorial condition

- - - - - - - Friedman Two-Way Anova

Mean Rank	Variable	
1.00	MARKPRE	pre-test marks
2.67	MARKPOS	post-test marks
2.33	MARKFOL	

Cases	Chi-Square	D.F.	Significance
3	4.6667	2	9.70E-02

under **Test Variables:**] →third variable [e.g. **markpre**] → ▶ button [puts variable under **Test Variables:**] [→**Friedman** already selected] →**OK**

Table 12.23 shows the output for this procedure which displays the mean rank for each variable, the chi-square statistic, its degrees of freedom and probability. The degrees of freedom are the number of conditions minus one while the probability is based on the χ^2 rather than the χ^2_r distribution. The exact probability level is 0.0970.

The Friedman test only tells us whether three or more groups differ but not which of any two groups differ. Marascuilo and McSweeney (1977) suggest that the Wilcoxon matched-pairs signed-ranks test can be used to make planned comparisons between pairs of groups adjusting the significance level of 0.05 by dividing it by the number of comparisons. For example, with three comparisons the appropriate significance level is 0.0167 (0.05/3 = 0.0167).

SUMMARY

The computation of non-parametric tests for assessing whether the distribution of ordinal data for two or more samples differs significantly across the samples is described. The Kolmogorov–Smirnov test determines whether the largest absolute difference between either one sample and a theoretical distribution or two unrelated samples is significant. The Mood median test compares the distribution of scores of two or more unrelated groups around a common median. The Mann–Whitney U test ascertains the number of times a score from one of the samples is ranked higher than a score from the other sample whereas the Kruskal–Wallis H test does this for three or more unrelated samples. If the different sets of scores are similar, then the number of times this happens should be similar for the samples being compared. A *post hoc* test for determining which pairs of samples differ is the Mann–Whitney U test. The sign test compares the number of positive and negative differences between scores for two related samples. If the two samples do not differ, then the number of positive and negative differences should be similar. The Wilcoxon test takes account of the size of the difference between the two unrelated samples by ranking the size of the differences and summing ranks of the same sign. The Friedman test compares the mean ranks of three or more related samples. If the samples do not differ, the mean ranks should be similar. The planned test for finding out which pairs of samples differ is the Wilcoxon test.

EXERCISES

The data for these exercises are available in Table 5.12.

1 Use the Mood median test to compare educational interest at 12 between single- and mixed-sex schools.
   (a) What is the value of this test?
   (b) What are the degrees of freedom?
   (c) What is the two-tailed probability level?
   (d) Is educational interest at 12 significantly greater at single- than at mixed-sex schools?
2 Use the Mann–Whitney U test to compare educational interest at 12 between single- and mixed-sex schools.
   (a) What is the U value of this test?
   (b) What is its two-tailed probability level?
   (c) Is educational interest at 12 significantly greater at single- than at mixed-sex schools?
3 Use the Kruskal–Wallis H test to compare educational interest at 12 for pupils of different socio-economic status.
   (a) What is the value of this test adjusted for ties?
   (b) What are the degrees of freedom?
   (c) What is the two-tailed probability level?
   (d) Does educational interest at 12 differ significantly between pupils of different socio-economic status?
4 Use the sign test to compare educational interest at 12 and 15 for pupils from mixed-sex schools.
   (a) What is the two-tailed probability level?
   (b) Is educational interest significantly greater at 12 than at 15 for pupils from mixed-sex schools?
5 Use the Wilcoxon test to compare educational interest at 12 and 15 for pupils from mixed-sex schools.
   (a) What is the two-tailed probability level?
   (b) Is educational interest significantly greater at 12 than at 15 for pupils from mixed-sex schools?
6 Use the Friedman test to compare educational interest at 9, 12 and 15 for pupils from single-sex schools.

(a) What is the value of this test?
(b) What are the degrees of freedom?
(c) What is the two-tailed probability level?
(d) Does educational interest differ significantly between 9, 12 and 15 for pupils from single-sex schools?

13 Tests of association for categorical and ordinal data

So far we have looked at statistical tests which determine whether the distribution of two or more variables differs significantly. However, we are often interested in the extent to which two or more variables are associated, the direction of that association and the likelihood of that association occurring by chance. For example, we may wish to know whether management students are more likely to have tutorials than other social science students and what the strength and statistical probability of any such association is. Or, we may want to find out whether higher pre-test marks are related to higher post-test marks and how strong and statistically significant such a relationship is. In addition, we may wish to discover whether an association between two variables, or the lack of one, is the result of their relationship with one or more other variables. For instance, if it was found that students with higher marks had tutorials, then this association may result from the fact that students who were more interested in their course were more likely both to obtain higher marks and to attend tutorials. To discover the answers to such questions, we would need to carry out the appropriate test of association, the selection of which partly depends on whether the data are categorical, ordinal or interval/ratio. In this chapter we will deal with tests which are suitable for categorical and ordinal data.

CATEGORICAL DATA

Tests of association for categorical data described in this chapter are divided into those that are derived from chi-square (*phi coefficient, contingency coefficient* and *Cramér's V*) and those that are based on the *proportional reduction in error* (*Goodman and Kruskal's lambda* and *tau*). We will illustrate the computation of the first and last two of these tests with the data in Table 13.1 which shows the number of management and other social science students having tutorials and which is the same as Table 11.14.

Table 13.1 Number of students having tutorials in management vs other social sciences

	Management	Other	Row total
Tutorials	30	5	35
None	10	15	25
Column total	40	20	60

Phi coefficient

The phi coefficient is suitable as a measure of association where both variables are dichotomous (Pearson 1904). One way of computing it is by dividing Pearson's chi-square by the total number of cases and taking the square root of the result:

$$\text{phi} = \sqrt{\frac{\text{chi-square}}{\text{no. of cases}}}$$

With this formula phi can vary from zero to +1.0. Since the minimum value of chi-square is 0, the minimum value of phi is also 0. If, however, the formula involves subtracting the product of two of the cells from the product of the other two cells as in the following formula

$$\text{phi} = \frac{(\text{top left cell} \times \text{bottom right cell}) - (\text{top right cell} \times \text{bottom left cell})}{\sqrt{\text{first row} \times \text{second row} \times \text{first column} \times \text{second column subtotals}}}$$

then the minimum value of phi can be −1. This form of phi is the same as Pearson's product moment correlation described in Chapter 6.

To calculate phi using the first formula, we first have to compute chi-square. As described in Chapter 11, chi-square is the sum of the squared difference between the observed and expected frequency for each cell divided by the expected frequency for that cell. As worked out in that chapter for this example, chi-square is 13.87. Consequently, phi is 0.48 ($\sqrt{13.87/60} = 0.481$). Since chi-square equals phi squared times the number of cases, the significance of phi can be tested by looking up the statistical significance of the chi-square value (13.87), which has 1 degree of freedom, in the table in Appendix 11. With 1 degree of freedom, chi-square has to be larger than 3.84 to be significant at the two-tailed 0.05 level, which it is. Therefore, we would conclude that there was a statistically significant association between studying management and having tutorials such that management students were more likely to have tutorials than other social science students.

Using the second formula, phi is also 0.48:

$$\frac{(30 \times 15) - (5 \times 1)}{\sqrt{35 \times 25 \times 40 \times 20}} = \frac{450 - 50}{\sqrt{700000}} = \frac{400}{836.66} = 0.478$$

For an example of a negative phi see Chapter 14.

To carry out phi with SPSS on this example, we enter the data into **Newdata** using the weighting procedure and then perform the following procedure:

→**Statistics** →**Summarize** →**Crosstabs** . . . [opens **Crosstabs** dialog box as in Box 11.5]
→row variable [e.g. **tutorial**] →▶button [puts variable under **Row[s]:**]
→column variable [e.g. **subject**] →▶button [puts variable under **Column[s]:**]
→**Statistics** . . . [opens **Crosstabs: Statistics** dialog box as in Box 11.7]
→**Phi and Cramér's V** →**Continue** [closes **Crosstabs: Statistics** dialog box]
→**OK**

Table 13.2 presents the output for this procedure which gives a **Phi** value of **.47809**. As shown in Table 11.28 **Pearson**'s chi-square is **13.71429**. The square root of this figure divided by 60 is **.47809** ($\sqrt{13.71429}/60 = .47809$).

Contingency coefficient

When one or both variables have more than two categories, phi is not restricted to varying between zero and $+1$ because the chi-square value can be greater than the total number of cases in the sample. To obtain a measure that must lie between zero and $+1$, Pearson (1904) devised the contingency coefficient in which chi-square has been added to the denominator of the formula for phi:

$$\text{contingency coefficient } (C) = \sqrt{\frac{\text{chi-square}}{\text{chi-square + no. of cases}}}$$

The contingency coefficient does not have $+1$ as its upper limit as this limit depends on the number of categories. For a table made up of an equal number of rows and columns, $n \times n$, the upper limit is calculated by subtracting 1 from the number of n, dividing the result by n and then taking the square root of this division. So, for a 3×3 table the upper limit is 0.82 [$\sqrt{(3 - 1)/3} = 0.82$], while for a 4×4 table it would be 0.87 [$\sqrt{(4 - 1)/4} = 0.87$]. When the number of rows and columns differ, as in a 3×4 table, the upper limit is based on the smaller number. In this case the upper limit is 0.82.

We will demonstrate the calculation of the contingency coefficient with the example from Chapter 11 of the number of management, sociology and education students having individual, group and no tutorials. These data are reproduced in Table 13.3. As calculated in Chapter 11, chi-square for these data is 12.64. Consequently, the contingency coefficent is 0.35 [$\sqrt{12.64/(12.64 + 90)} = 0.35$]. To check the statistical significance of this coefficient, we look up the statistical significance of the chi-square value used to

Table 13.2 SPSS output for phi and Cramér's *V* comparing number of students having tutorials in management and other social sciences

---

TUTORIAL by SUBJECT

	SUBJECT		Page 1 of 1
Count			
			Row
	1.00	2.00	Total

TUTORIAL	1.00	2.00	Row Total
1.00	30	5	35
			58.3
2.00	10	15	25
			41.7
Column Total	40	20	60
	66.7	33.3	100.0

Statistic	Value	AES1	VAL/ASEO	Approximate Significance
Phi	.47809			.00021 *1
Cramer's V	.47809			.00021 *1

*1 Pearson chi-square probability

Number of Missing Observations: 0

---

calculate it in the table in Appendix 11 with the appropriate degrees of freedom which are the number of rows minus 1 multiplied by the number of columns minus 1. With 4 degrees of freedom [(3 − 1) × (3 − 1)] the contingency coefficient has to be 9.49 or larger to be significant at the two-tailed 0.05 level, which it is. Consequently, we would conclude that there was a statistically significant association between the subject studied and the presence and nature of tutorials.

To perform a contingency coefficient with SPSS on this example, we enter the data into **Newdata** using the weighting procedure and then conduct the following steps:

→**Statistics** →**S**ummarize →**C**rosstabs . . .   [opens **Crosstabs** dialog box as in Box 11.5]

Table 13.3 Number of management, sociology and education students having individual, group or no tutorials

	Management	Sociology	Education	Row total
Individual tutorials	14	3	5	22
Group tutorials	6	5	15	26
No tutorials	20	12	10	42
Column total	40	20	30	90

Table 13.4 SPSS output of the contingency coefficient for management, sociology and education students having individual, group and no tutorials

TUTORIAL by SUBJECT

```
                   SUBJECT              Page 1 of 1
         Count  |
                |
                |                    Row
                |    1.00 |   2.00 |   3.00 |  Total

TUTORIAL -------+--------+--------+--------+
       1.00  |    14  |    3  |    5  |    22
             |        |       |       |    24.4
             +--------+--------+--------+
       2.00  |     6  |    5  |   15  |    26
             |        |       |       |    28.9
             +--------+--------+--------+
       3.00  |    20  |   12  |   10  |    42
             |        |       |       |    46.7
             +--------+--------+--------+
       Column      40      20      30      90
       Total      44.4    22.2    33.3   100.0
```

				Approximate
Statistic	Value	ASE1	Val/ASE1	Significance
------------------	------	-----	--------	------------
Contingency Coefficient	.35165			.01284 *1

*1 Pearson chi-square probability

Number of Missing Observations: 0

→row variable [e.g. **tutorial**] →▶button [puts variable under **Ro̲w[s]:**]
→column variable [e.g. **subject**] →▶button [puts variable under **Co̲l-umn[s]:**]
→**S̲tatistics . . .** [opens **Crosstabs: Statistics** dialog box as in Box 11.7]
→**C̲ontingency coefficient** →**Continue** [closes **Crosstabs: Statistics** dialog box]
→**OK**

Table 13.4 presents the output for this procedure which gives a **Contingency Coefficient** of **.35165**.

Cramér's V

To make the upper limit of the association +1 for tables greater than 2×2, Cramér (1946) produced V which is computed by dividing chi-square by the total number of cases multiplied by the smaller number of rows or columns and then taking the square root of the result:

$$\text{Cramér's } V = \sqrt{\frac{\text{chi-square}}{\substack{\text{no. of} \times \text{(smaller no. of} \\ \text{cases} \quad \text{rows/columns} - 1)}}}$$

Where the smaller number of rows or columns is 2, the denominator effectively becomes the number of cases [$N \times (2 - 1) = N$] and therefore Cramér's V is the same as phi as shown in Table 13.2.

For the data in Table 13.3, Cramér's V is 0.26 ($\sqrt{12.64/[(90 \times (3 - 1)]}$ = 0.26). As before, to check the statistical significance of this value, we look up the statistical significance of the chi-square value on which it is based in the table in Appendix 11 with the appropriate degrees of freedom which are the number of rows minus 1 multiplied by the number of columns minus 1. We would conclude that there was a statistically significant association between the subject studied and the presence and nature of tutorials.

To conduct Cramér's V with SPSS on this example, we enter the data into **Newdata** using the weighting procedure and then carry out the following procedure:

→**S̲tatistics** →**S̲ummarize** →**C̲rosstabs . . .** [opens **Crosstabs** dialog box as in Box 11.5]
→row variable [e.g. **tutorial**] →▶button [puts variable under **Ro̲w[s]:**]
→column variable [e.g. **subject**] →▶button [puts variable under **Co̲l-umn[s]:**]
→**S̲tatistics . . .** [opens **Crosstabs: Statistics** dialog box as in Box 11.7]
→**P̲hi and Cramér's V** →**Continue** [closes **Crosstabs: Statistics** dialog box]
→**OK**

The format of the output is similar to that in Table 13.2 except that **Cramér's V** is **.26562** with an **Approximate Significance** of **.01284 *1**.

Goodman and Kruskal's lambda

Lambda is the proportional increase in predicting the outcome of one categorical variable when knowing its combined outcome with a second categorical variable (Goodman and Kruskal 1954, 1972). The value of lambda can vary from zero to $+1$. Zero means that there is no increase in predictiveness whereas 1 indicates that prediction can be made without error. Suppose, for example, we wanted to predict from the data in Table 13.1 the larger number of cases of students having tutorials regardless of the subject they studied. The larger category is students who have tutorials (35). Consequently, if we had to predict whether a particular student had tutorials or not, our best guess would be to say they did. If we did this for all 60 students we would be wrong on 25 occasions $(60 - 35 = 25)$.

How would our ability to predict whether a particular student had tutorials be enhanced by our knowledge as to whether they studied management or not? Taking the students studying management first, if we knew that 30 of these 40 students had tutorials, our best guess for predicting which category a particular student in this group was in is to say they studied management. If we did this for all 40 students we would be wrong 10 times $(40 - 30 = 10)$. Turning next to the students studying other social sciences, if we knew that 15 of these 20 students did not have tutorials, our best guess for predicting which category a particular student in this group was in is to say they did not have tutorials. If we did this for all 20 students we would be wrong 5 times $(20 - 15 = 5)$. Therefore, if we knew whether students studied management or not, we would make 15 errors $(10 + 5 = 15)$. Knowing this information reduces our errors by 10 $(25 - 15 = 10)$ which as a proportion of the errors we made initially is 0.40 $(10/25 = 0.40)$. In other words, knowledge of the second variable reduces the proportion of errors by 0.40. Predicting students who have tutorials from the subject they study results in a lambda of 0.40.

$$\frac{25 - (10 + 5)}{60 - 35} = \frac{10}{25} = 0.40$$

We could also work out lambda for predicting whether students are studying management based on knowing whether they have tutorials. Lambda for this prediction is 0.25:

$$\frac{20 - (5 + 10)}{60 - 40} = \frac{5}{20} = 0.25$$

These two lambdas are called *asymmetric* since they are likely to vary depending on which variable is being predicted. The following formula is used for calculating asymmetric lambda:

$$\text{asymmetric lambda} = \frac{\text{sum of the largest cell frequencies in the columns} - \text{largest row total}}{\text{total number of cases} - \text{largest row total}}$$

Applying this formula to our data, we see that lambda for predicting students having tutorials is 0.40:

$$\frac{(30 + 15) - 35}{60 - 35} = \frac{10}{25} = 0.40$$

Lambda for predicting students studying managment is 0.25:

$$\frac{(30 + 15) - 40}{60 - 40} = \frac{5}{20} = 0.25$$

Note that unless we turn the table round, columns in the above formula become rows and the row becomes a column.

The formula for computing symmetric lambda is:

$$\frac{\begin{array}{l}\text{sum of the largest cell} \\ \text{frequencies in the colums}\end{array} + \begin{array}{l}\text{sum of the largest cell} \\ \text{frequencies in the rows}\end{array} - \begin{array}{l}\text{largest row} \\ \text{total}\end{array} - \begin{array}{l}\text{largest column} \\ \text{total}\end{array}}{(2 \times \text{total number of cases}) - \text{largest row total} - \text{largest column total}}$$

Applying this formula to our data we find that symmetric lambda is 0.33:

$$\frac{(30 + 15) + (30 + 15) - 35 - 40}{(2 \times 60) - 35 - 40} = \frac{90 - 75}{120 - 75} = \frac{15}{45} = 0.33$$

To compute Goodman and Kruskal's lambda with SPSS on this example, we enter the data into **Newdata** using the weighting procedure and then perform the following procedure:

→**Statistics** →**S̲ummarize** →**C̲rosstabs** . . . [opens **Crosstabs** dialog box as in Box 11.5]
→row variable [e.g. **tutorial**] →▶button [puts variable under **R̲ow[s]:**]
→column variable [e.g. **subject**] →▶button [puts variable under **C̲ol-umn[s]:**]
→**S̲tatistics** . . . [opens **Crosstabs: Statistics** dialog box as in Box 11.7]
→**L̲ambda** →**Continue** [closes **Crosstabs: Statistics** dialog box]
→**O̲K**

Table 13.5 displays the output for this procedure which also gives Goodman and Kruskal's tau. Discussion of **ASE1** (the **a**symptotic **s**tandard **e**rror when lamba is **1**) and **Val/ASE0** (a *t* value based on the **a**symptotic **s**tandard **e**rror when lamba is **0**) is beyond the scope of this book.

Goodman and Kruskal's tau

Lambda assumes that the same prediction is made for all cases in a particular row or column. Goodman and Kruskal's tau, on the other hand, presumes that the predictions are randomly made on the basis of their proportions in row and column totals (Goodman and Kruskal 1954).

Table 13.5 SPSS output for lambda comparing number of students having tutorials in management and other social sciences

---

TUTORIAL by SUBJECT

		SUBJECT		Page 1 of 1
	Count			
				Row
		1.00	2.00	Total
TUTORIAL				
1.00		30	5	35
				58.3
2.00		10	15	25
				41.7
Column		40	20	60
Total		66.7	33.3	100.0

Statistic	Value	AES1	VAL/ASEO	Approximate Significance
Lambda:				
symmetric	.33333	.16229	1.77705	
with TUTORIAL dependent	.40000	.13856	2.33550	
with SUBJECT dependent	.25000	.21651	1.00844	
Goodman & Kruskal Tau :				
with TUTORIAL dependent	.22857	.10877		.00024 *2
with SUBJECT dependent	.22857	.10996		.00024 *2

*2 Based on chi-square approximation
Number of Missing Observations: 0

For instance, if we predicted whether students had tutorials ignoring whether they studied management, we would guess this correctly for 0.58 (35/60 = 0.583) of the 35 students who had tutorials (i.e. 0.58 × 35 = about 20.3 students) and for 0.42 (25/60 = 0.416) of the 25 students who did not have tutorials (i.e. 0.42 × 25 = about 10.5 students). In other words, we would guess correctly that about 29.2 of the students had tutorials (60 − 20.3 − 10.5 = about 29.2 students) and the probability of error would be 0.49 (29.2/60 = 0.486).

If we now took into account whether these students had studied management or not, we would predict correctly whether students had tutorials for 0.86 (30/35 = 0.857) of the 30 management students with tutorials (i.e. 0.86 × 30 = about 25.8 students), 0.14 (5/35 = 0.143) of the 5 non-management students with tutorials (i.e. 0.14 × 5 = about 0.7 students), 0.40 (10/25 = 0.40) of the 10 management students without tutorials (i.e. 0.40 × 10 = 4 students) and 0.60 (15/25 = 0.60) of the 15 non-management students without tutorials (i.e. 0.60 × 15 = 9 students). In other words, the probability of error for guessing whether students had tutorials knowing whether they studied management is 0.34 [(60 − 25.8 − 0.7 − 4 − 9)/ 60 = 20.5/60 = 0.34]. Consequently, the proportional reduction of error in predicting students who had tutorials knowing whether they studied management is 0.31 [(0.49 − 0.34)/0.49 = 0.306]. In the same way, we could also work out Goodman and Kruskal's tau for predicting whether students studied management knowing whether they had tutorials which is the same for a 2 × 2 table.

To compute Goodman and Kruskal's tau with SPSS for this example, we use the above procedure. Table 13.5 displays its output. The value of **.22857** differs from that previously calculated of 0.31 because SPSS uses the following algorithm or procedure to compute this statistic:

$$\frac{\left(\begin{array}{cc} \text{Total no.} & \times \text{ Sum of squared cell frequency/} \\ \text{of cases} & \text{row total for all cells} \end{array}\right) - \begin{array}{c} \text{Sum of squared} \\ \text{column totals} \end{array}}{\text{Total no. of cases} - \text{Sum of squared column totals}}$$

Substituting the appropriate values into this formula gives a value of 0.23:

$$\frac{[60 \times (30^2/35 + 5^2/35 + 10^2/25 + 15^2/25)] - (40^2 + 20^2)}{60^2 - (40^2 + 20^2)} =$$

$$\frac{[60 \times (900/35 + 25/35 + 100/25 + 225/25)] - (1600 + 400)}{3600 - (1600 + 400)} =$$

$$\frac{[60 \times (25.714 + 0.714 + 4 + 9)] - 2000}{3600 - 2000} =$$

$$\frac{(60 \times 39.428) - 2000}{1600} = \frac{2365.68 - 2000}{1600} = \frac{365.68}{1600} = 0.2285$$

ORDINAL DATA

There are several tests of association for two ordinal variables. Apart from *Spearman's rank order correlation* and *Mantel–Haenszel's chi-square* measure of linear association, the tests discussed in this section

(*Kendall's tau a, tau b* and *tau c*; *Goodman and Kruskal's gamma*; and *Somers' d*) are based on comparing all possible pairs of cases. We will illustrate the computation of these tests by assessing the association between pre- and post-test marks in women in the no and the individual tutorial condition. To do this, we have re-ordered the pre-test marks from low to high as shown in Table 13.6. We can now compare the extent to which the rankings of the post-test marks are similar to those of the pre-test marks by counting the number of pairs of cases for post-test marks in which the first case is ranked higher than the second (called a *concordant* pair), lower (a *discordant* pair) or the same (a *tied* pair). For example, both Mary and Jo receive the same pre-test mark so this pair of ranks is tied. The post-test mark for Ann is higher than that for Mary, so this pair is discordant. Taking into account the tied pre-test ranks for Mary and Jo, the post-test marks of only Sue and Jane are ranked higher than Ann, so these two pairs are concordant.

If all pairs of cases for post-test marks were concordant, then the rankings of post-test marks would be the same as those of pre-test marks and there would be a perfect direct or *positive* association between the rankings of pre- and post-test marks so that a higher ranking of a pre-test mark always corresponds to a higher ranking of a post-test mark. Conversely, if all pairs of cases for post-test marks were discordant, then there is a perfect inverse or *negative* association between the rankings of pre- and post-test marks so that a higher ranking of a pre-test mark always corresponds to a lower ranking of a post-test mark. If there were an equal number of concordant and discordant pairs for post-test marks, then there is no association between the rankings of the two sets of marks. If there are more concordant pairs than discordant pairs, the association is positive while if there are more discordant pairs than concordant pairs, the association is negative.

The simplest method of counting the number of concordant, discordant and tied pairs is to use a matrix as shown in Table 13.7, where the pre-test marks are arranged along the side and the post-test marks along the bottom with the number of ranks specified in each cell. Concordant pairs for a joint ranking are represented by the sum of values which lie below and to the

Table 13.6 Ranking of pre- and post-test marks for women in the no and individual tutorial conditions

| Women | Pre-test | | Post-test | |
	Marks	Ranks	Marks	Ranks
Ann	1	1	6	2
Mary	3	2.5	4	1
Jo	3	2.5	8	4
Sue	5	4	7	3
Jane	7	5	9	5

Table 13.7 Matrix of ranks for pre- and post-test marks for women in the no and individual tutorial conditions

	1		1			
Pre-test marks	2.5	1			1	
	4			1		
	5					1
		1	2	3	4	5
			Post-test marks			

right of that position while discordant pairs are the sum of values which lie below and to the left of that point. So, for the joint ranking located at rank 1 for pre-test marks and rank 2 for post-test marks there are three values below and to the right of it and one value below and to the left of it. Proceeding in this way through the matrix, we can count seven concordant pairs and two discordant pairs. Ties are represented by values that lie along either the same rows (for pre-test marks) or the same columns (for post-test marks). So, there is one tie for pre-test marks.

Kendall's rank correlation coefficient or tau a

Kendall's (1948) tau a is used when there are no tied pairs and can vary from -1 to $+1$. It is the number of concordant pairs minus the number of discordant pairs over the total number of pairs:

$$\text{tau } a = \frac{\text{no. of concordant pairs} - \text{no. of discordant pairs}}{\text{total no. of pairs}}$$

As there is one tied pair for pre-test marks (Mary and Jo) for the data in Table 13.7, we will change the mark of Jo from 3 to 4. Using the matrix in Table 13.8, we can work out that there are eight concordant pairs and two discordant pairs. The total number of pairs can be calculated by subtracting 1 from the number of pairs, multiplying the result by the number of pairs and then dividing by 2. Thus, the total number of pairs is 10 [(5 − 1) × 5/2 = 10] and tau a is 0.60 [(8 − 2)/10 = 0.60].

Note there is an alternative formula which can be used to compute tau a and tau b regardless of tied pairs, which is described in the next section and which simply uses the number of concordant and discordant pairs. SPSS uses this formula and calls this option **Kendall's tau-b.**

To compute Kendall's tau a with SPSS on this example, enter the data into **Newdata** and then execute the following procedure:

→**Statistics** →**Summarize** →**Crosstabs** . . . [opens **Crosstabs** dialog box as in Box 11.5]
→row variable [e.g. **markpre**] →▶ button [puts variable under **Row[s]:**]
→column variable [e.g. **markpos**] →▶ button [puts variable under **Column[s]:**]

Table 13.8 Matrix of pre- and post-test marks with no tied pairs

		1	1		
Pre-test marks	1				
	2	1			
	3			1	
	4		1		
	5				1
		1 2	3	4	5

Post-test marks

→**Statistics** . . . [opens **Crosstabs: Statistics** dialog box as in Box 11.7]
→**Kendall's tau-b** →**Continue** [closes **Crosstabs: Statistics** dialog box]
→**OK**

Table 13.9 displays the output for this procedure which shows a contingency table and a **Kendall's Tau-b** value of **.60000**.

Kendall's tau b

Kendall's (1948) tau b is used as a test of association for ordinal data when there are tied pairs. It is the number of concordant pairs (C) minus the number of discordant pairs (D) divided by the square root of the product of the total number of pairs (T) minus the number of tied pairs for one variable (T_1) and the total number of pairs (T) minus the tied pairs for the other variable (T_2):

$$\text{tau } b = \frac{C - D}{\sqrt{(T - T_1) \times (T - T_2)}}$$

Tau b can vary from -1 to $+1$ if the table is square and if none of the row and column totals is zero.

For the data in Table 13.7 the number of concordant pairs is 7 and the number of discordant pairs is 2. There is one tied pair of ranks for pre-test marks. Consequently, tau b is 0.53:

$$\frac{7 - 2}{\sqrt{(10 - 1) \times (10 - 0)}} = \frac{5}{\sqrt{90}} = \frac{5}{9.487} = 0.527$$

We can see that the matrix in Table 13.7 is not square since it consists of four rows and five columns.

An alternative formula for computing tau b is the difference between the number of concordant (C) and discordant (D) pairs multiplied by 2 and divided by the square root of the squared number of cases (N^2) minus the sum of squared row totals (RT^2) multiplied by the squared number of cases (N^2) minus the sum of squared column totals (CT^2):

$$\text{tau } b = \frac{2 \times (C - D)}{\sqrt{(N^2 - \text{sum of } RT^2) \times (N^2 - \text{sum of } CT^2)}}$$

Table 13.9 SPSS output for tau *a*

MARKPRE by MARKPOS

		SUBJECT					Page 1 of 1
Count							Row
		4.00	6.00	7.00	8.00	9.00	Total
MARKPRE							
1.00			1				1
							20.0
3.00		1					1
							20.0
4.00					1		1
							20.0
5.00				1			1
							20.0
7.00						1	1
							20.0
Column		1	1	1	1	1	5
Total		20.0	20.0	20.0	20.0	20.0	100.0

Statistic	Value	ASE1	Val/ASE0	Approximate Significance
Kendall's Tau-b	.60000	.17889	3.35410	

Number of Missing Observations: 0

If we substitute the appropriate values into this formula, we see that tau b is 0.53:

$$\frac{2 \times (7 - 2)}{\sqrt{[5^2 - (1^2 + 2^2 + 1^2 + 1^2)] \times [5^2 - (1^2 + 1^2 + 1^2 + 1^2 + 1^2)}} =$$

$$\frac{10}{\sqrt{(25 - 7) \times (25 - 5)}} = \frac{10}{\sqrt{360}} = \frac{10}{18.97} = 0.527$$

We can also use this formula to calculate tau a. Inserting the appropriate values in the formula gives a value of 0.60:

$$\frac{2 \times (8 - 2)}{\sqrt{[5^2 - (1^2 + 1^2 + 1^2 + 1^2 + 1^2)] \times [5^2 - (1^2 + 1^2 + 1^2 + 1^2 + 1^2)}} =$$

$$\frac{12}{\sqrt{(25 - 5) \times (25 - 5)}} = \frac{12}{\sqrt{400}} = \frac{12}{20.0} = 0.60$$

To compute Kendall's tau b with SPSS we use the procedure described in the previous section. The output for this procedure for the data in Table 13.7 is presented in Table 13.10 which shows a contingency table and a **Kendall's Tau-b** value of **.52705**.

Kendall's tau c

For a rectangular table Kendall's (1948) tau c can come closer to -1 to $+1$. It is the number of concordant pairs (C) minus the number of discordant pairs (D) multiplied by twice the number of columns or rows whichever is the smaller (S), divided by the total number of cases (N) squared times 1 from the smaller number of columns or rows:

$$\text{tau } c = \frac{(C - D) \times 2 \times S}{N^2 \times (S - 1)}$$

Consequently, for the data in Table 13.7 where the number of rows (4) is smaller than the number of columns (5) tau c is 0.53:

$$\frac{(7 - 2) \times 2 \times 4}{5^2 \times (4 - 1)} = \frac{5 \times 8}{25 \times 3} = \frac{40}{75} = 0.533$$

Since tau is approximately normally distributed when the size of the sample (N) is larger than 10, we can calculate the significance level of tau by converting it into z according to the following formula

$$z = \frac{\text{tau}}{\sqrt{\dfrac{2(2N + 5)}{9N(N - 1)}}}$$

Table 13.10 SPSS output for Kendall's tau *b* for pre- and post-test marks in women in the no and individual tutorial condition

---

MARKPRE by MARKPOS

	SUBJECT					Page 1 of 1
Count						Row
	4.00	6.00	7.00	8.00	9.00	Total
MARKPRE 1.00		1				1
						20.0
3.00	1			1		2
						20.0
5.00			1			1
						20.0
7.00					1	1
						20.0
Column	1	1	1	1	1	5
Total	20.0	20.0	20.0	20.0	20.0	100.0

Statistic	Value	ASE1	Val/ASE0	Approximate Significance
Kendall's Tau-b	.52705	.23527	2.04124	

Number of Missing Observations: 0

Substituting the values in this formula for our example we find that z is 1.29.

$$\frac{0.53}{\sqrt{\dfrac{2 \times [(2 \times 5) + 5]}{9 \times 5 \times (5 - 1)}}} = \frac{0.53}{\sqrt{\dfrac{30}{180}}} = \frac{0.53}{0.41} = 1.293$$

We look up the significance of this z value in the table in Appendix 2. The area between the middle of the curve and a z value of 1.29 is 0.4015, indicating that the area beyond the z value on one side of the curve is 0.0985 (0.5000 − 0.4015 = 0.0985), which is the one-tailed probability. For the two-tailed probability we would double 0.0985 to give 0.1970 (0.0985 × 2 = 0.1970).

To compute Kendall's tau c with SPSS for this example, we carry out the procedure described in the previous section except that we select **Kendall's tau-c** instead of **Kendall's tau-b**.

Table 13.11 presents the output for the **Kendall's Tau-c** value, which is **.53333**, but omits the contingency table which is the same as that in Table 13.10. To exclude the table select **Suppress tables** in the **Crosstabs** dialog box.

Goodman and Kruskal's gamma

Goodman and Kruskal's (1954) gamma can range from −1 to +1 and takes no account of ties or the size of the table. It is simply the number of concordant pairs (C) minus the number of discordant pairs (D) divided by the number of concordant and discordant pairs:

$$\text{gamma} = \frac{C - D}{C + D}$$

So, for the data in Table 13.7 gamma is 0.56:

$$\frac{7 - 2}{7 + 2} = \frac{5}{9} = 0.556$$

To compute Goodman and Kruskal's gamma with SPSS we use the procedure described in the previous section except that we select **Gamma** instead of **Kendall's tau-c**. Table 13.12 presents the output for

Table 13.11 SPSS output for Kendall's tau c (omitting the contingency table)

MARKPRE by MARKPOS

Number of valid observations = 5

Statistic	Value	ASE1	Val/ASE0	Approximate Significance
Kendall's Tau-c	.53333	.26128	2.04124	

Number of Missing Observations: 0

Table 13.12 SPSS output for Goodman and Kruskal's gamma (but excluding the contingency table)

MARKPRE by MARKPOS

Number of valid observations = 5

Statistic	Value	ASE1	Val/ASE0	Approximate Significance
Gamma	.55556	.22630	2.04124	

Number of Missing Observations: 0

this **Gamma** value, which is **.55556**, but excludes the contingency table which is the same as that in Table 13.10.

Somers' *d*

Somers' (1962) *d* provides an asymmetric as well as a symmetric measure of association and takes account of tied pairs. The formula for computing asymmetric *d* for the first variable as the dependent variable is the difference between the number of concordant (C) and discordant (D) pairs divided by the number of concordant (C), discordant (D) and tied pairs for the first variable (T_1):

$$\text{asymmetric } d = \frac{C - D}{C + D + T_1}$$

For the data in Table 13.7, asymmetric *d* for pre-test marks as the dependent variable is 0.50:

$$\frac{7 - 2}{8 + 1 + 1} = \frac{5}{10} = 0.50$$

The formula for computing asymmetric *d* for the second variable as the dependent variable is the difference between the number of concordant (C) and discordant (D) pairs divided by the number of concordant (C), discordant (D) and tied pairs for the second variable (T_2):

$$\text{asymmetric } d = \frac{C - D}{C + D + T_2}$$

Asymmetric *d* for post-test marks as the dependent variable is 0.56:

$$\frac{7 - 2}{7 + 2 + 0} = \frac{5}{9} = 0.556$$

The formula for computing symmetric d is the difference between the number of concordant (C) and discordant (D) pairs divided by the number of concordant (C), discordant (D) and tied pairs for the first variable (T_1) added to the number of concordant (C), discordant (D) and tied pairs for the second variable (T_2) divided by 2:

$$\text{symmetric } d = \frac{C - D}{(C + D + T_1 + C + D + T_2)/2}$$

Symmetric d for this example is 0.53:

$$\frac{7 - 2}{(7 + 2 + 1 + 7 + 2 + 0)/2} = \frac{5}{9.5} = 0.526$$

An alternative formula for computing asymmetric d, where the dependent variable is represented by the row totals of the matrix of ranks, is the difference between the number of concordant (C) and discordant (D) pairs multiplied by 2 and divided by the squared number of cases (N^2) minus the sum of squared column totals (CT^2):

$$\text{asymmetric } d = \frac{2 \times (C - D)}{N^2 - \text{sum of } CT^2}$$

For the data in Table 13.7, asymmetric d for pre-test marks as the dependent variable is 0.50:

$$\frac{2 \times (7 - 2)}{5^2 - (1^2 + 1^2 + 1^2 + 1^2 + 1^2)} = \frac{10}{25 - 5} = \frac{10}{20} = 0.50$$

The corresponding formula for computing asymmetric d, where the dependent variable is represented by the column totals of the matrix of ranks, is the difference between the number of concordant (C) and discordant (D) pairs multiplied by 2 and divided by the squared number of cases (N^2) minus the sum of squared row totals (RT^2):

$$\text{asymmetric } d = \frac{2 \times (C - D)}{N^2 - \text{sum of } RT^2}$$

Asymmetric d for post-test marks as the dependent variable is 0.56:

$$\frac{2 \times (7 - 2)}{5^2 - (1^2 + 2^2 + 1^2 + 1^2)} = \frac{10}{25 - 7} = \frac{10}{18} = 0.556$$

The formula for computing symmetric d is the difference between the number of concordant (C) and discordant (D) pairs multiplied by 4 and divided by the squared number of cases (N^2) minus the sum of squared row totals (RT^2) added to the squared number of cases (N^2) minus the sum of squared column totals (CT^2):

$$\text{symmetric } d = \frac{4 \times (C - D)}{(N^2 - \text{sum of } RT^2) + (N^2 - \text{sum of } CT^2)}$$

Table 13.13 SPSS output for Somers' d (excluding the contingency table)

MARKPRE by MARKPOS

Number of valid observations = 5

Statistic	Value	ASE1	Val/ASE0	Approximate Significance
Somers' D :				
symmetric	.52632	.23494	2.04124	
with MARKPRE dependent	.50000	.24495	2.04124	
with MARKPOS dependent	.55556	.22630	2.04124	

Number of Missing Observations: 0

Symmetric d is 0.53:

$$\frac{4 \times (7 - 2)}{[5^2 - (1^2 + 2^2 + 1^2 + 1^2)] + [5^2 - (1^2 + 1^2 + 1^2 + 1^2 + 1^2)]} =$$

$$\frac{4 \times 5}{(25 - 7) + (25 - 5)} = \frac{20}{38} = 0.526$$

To compute Somers' d with SPSS we use the procedure described in the previous section except that we select **Somers' d** instead of **Gamma**. Table 13.13 displays the output for the **Somers' D** values but excludes the contingency table which is the same as that in Table 13.10.

Spearman's rank order correlation or rho

Spearman's (1904) rho ranges from -1 to $+1$ and is essentially a Pearson's correlation on data that have been ranked. The computations for the Pearson's correlation between the pre- and post-test marks for women in the no and individual tutorial conditions have been presented in Table 6.1. Pearson's correlation is 0.615. To compute Spearman's rho for these data, we first rank them as shown in Table 13.6 and then carry out a Pearson's correlation on the ranked data. The computations for this analysis are displayed in Table 13.14. Spearman's rho is 0.67.

Like Pearson's correlation. the significance level of rho can be computed by converting it into t using the following formula:

Table 13.14 Computations for rho on ranked data

Women	Pre-A	Post-B	D_A	$D_A{}^2$	D_B	$D_B{}^2$	D_{AB}
Ann	1	2	−2.0	4.00	−1.0	1.00	2.0
Mary	2.5	1	−0.5	0.25	−2.0	4.00	1.0
Jo	2.5	4	−0.5	0.25	1.0	1.00	−0.5
Sue	4	3	1.0	1.00	0.0	0.00	0.0
Jane	5	5	2.0	4.00	2.0	4.00	4.0
Sum	15	15		9.50		10.00	6.5
N	5	5					
Mean	3.0	3.0					

Note: $r = \dfrac{6.5}{\sqrt{9.5 \times 10.0}} = \dfrac{6.5}{9.75} = 0.667$

$$t = \text{rho} \times \sqrt{\dfrac{N-2}{1-\text{rho}^2}}$$

Substituting the values of our example into this formula we find that *t* is 1.57

$$0.67 \times \sqrt{\dfrac{5-2}{1-0.67^2}} = 0.67 \times \sqrt{\dfrac{3}{0.55}} = 0.67 \times \sqrt{5.46} = 0.67 \times 2.34 = 1.568$$

We look up the statistical significance of *t* in the table in Appendix 4 against the appropriate degrees of freedom which are the number of cases (*N*) minus 2. We see that with three degrees of freedom *t* has to be 2.353 or bigger to be significant at the 0.05 one-tailed level. So if we had anticipated that the two sets of rankings would be positively correlated, we could conclude that the correlation was not significantly positive. Alternatively we could look up the statistical significance of rho in the table in Appendix 21 where we see that with three degrees of freedom (*N* = 5) rho has to be 0.9000 or bigger to be significant at the 0.05 one-tailed level.

We can compute Spearman's rho either with the procedure described in the previous section except that we select **Correlations** instead of **Somers' d**. Table 13.15 displays the output for this procedure for the example with tied ranks but excludes the contingency table which is the same as that in Table 13.10. **Spearman Correlation** is **.66689**.

Or we can use the following procedure:

→**Statistics** →**Correlate** →**Bivariate** . . . [opens **Bivariate Correlations** dialog box as in Box 6.1]
→variables [e.g. **markpre** and **markpos**] →▶ button [puts variables in **Variables:** text box] →**Spearman** →**OK**

Table 13.15 SPSS output for Spearman's correlation using the **Crosstabs** procedure (excluding the contingency table)

MARKPRE by MARKPOS

Number of valid observations = 5

Statistic	Value	ASE1	Val/ASE0	Approximate Significance
Pearson's R	.61555	.18212	1.35282	.26904 *4
Spearman Correlation	.66689	.25076	1.55011	.21889 *4

*4 VAL/ASEO is a t-value based on a normal approximation, as is the significance

Number of Missing Observations: 0

Table 13.16 SPSS output for Spearman's correlation using the **Bivariate Correlations** procedure

---

- - - S P E A R M A N   C O R R E L A T I O N   C O E F F I C I E N T S - - -

MARKPRE   .6669

                 N(5)

                 Sig .219

                 MARKPOS

(Coefficient / (Cases) / 2–tailed Significance)

" . " is printed if a coefficient cannot be computed

Table 13.16 presents the output for this procedure for the same example which gives a Spearman's correlation of **.6669**.

Mantel–Haenszel's chi-square

Mantel–Haenszel's chi-square is another linear measure of association for ordinal data (Mantel and Haenszel 1959). It is calculated by multiplying the squared Pearson's correlation coefficient by the number of cases minus 1 and it has one degree of freedom. The procedure for computing Pearson's correlation is described in Chapter 6. The critical values of Mantel–Haenszel's chi-square are those of chi-square with 1 degree of freedom.

However, we can demonstrate the calculation of Mantel–Haenszel's chi-square with the output shown in Table 13.15 which gives Pearson's correlation (**Pearson's R**) as well as Spearman's correlation. When we square this correlation ($.61555^2 = 0.379$) and multiply it by 4 ($5 - 1 = 4$), we have a Mantel–Haenszel's chi-square of 1.52 ($0.379 \times 4 = 1.516$). If we look up this value in the table in Appendix 11, we see that with 1 degree of freedom chi-square has to exceed 3.84 to be significant at the 0.05 two-tailed level, which it is not. Therefore, we would conclude that the association between these two sets of rankings is not significant.

To compute Mantel–Haenszel's chi-square with SPSS for this example, we use the following **Crosstabs** procedure:

→<u>S</u>tatistics →S<u>u</u>mmarize →<u>C</u>rosstabs . . . [opens **Crosstabs** dialog box as in Box 11.5]
→row variable [e.g. **markpre**] →▶button [puts variable under **R<u>o</u>w[s]:**]
→column variable [e.g. **markpos**] →▶button [puts variable under **C<u>o</u>lumn[s]:**]
→<u>S</u>tatistics . . . [opens **Crosstabs: Statistics** dialog box as in Box 11.7]
→**C<u>h</u>i-square** →**Continue** [closes **Crosstabs: Statistics** dialog box]
→**OK**

Table 13.17 presents the output for this procedure which gives a **Mantel–Haenszel test for linear association** of **1.51559**.

Table 13.17 SPSS output showing Mantel–Haenszel's chi-square (excluding the contingency table)

MARKPRE by MARKPOS

Number of valid observations = 5

Chi-Square	Value	DF	Significance
Pearson	15.00000	12	.24144
Likelihood Ratio	13.32179	12	.34609
Mantel-Haenszel test for linear association	1.51559	1	.21829

Minimum Expected Frequency -   .200
Cells with Expected Frequency < 5 -   20 OF   20 (100.0%)

Number of Missing Observations: 0

A MEASURE OF PARTIAL ASSOCIATION

An index of association between two variables where no other variables have been controlled or partialled out is known as a *zero-order* association. A *first-order* association is one where one other variable has been controlled, a *second-order* association is one in which two other variables have been controlled and so on. The two tests of partial association we shall discuss are *Kendall's partial rank correlation coefficient* and *partial gamma* (Kendall 1948).

Kendall's partial rank correlation coefficient

The formula for computing the partial rank correlation ($tau_{12.3}$) between two variables (1 and 2) partialling out a third (3) variable is the rank correlation between the first two variables (tau_{12}) minus the product of the rank correlation between one of the two variables (1) and the third variable (tau_{13}) and the rank correlation between the other variable (2) and the third variable (tau_{23}), divided by the square root of the product of 1 minus the squared rank correlation between one of the two variables (1) and the third variable (tau_{13}^2) times 1 minus the squared rank correlation between the other variable (2) and the third variable (tau_{23}^2):

$$tau_{12.3} = \frac{tau_{12} - (tau_{13} \times tau_{23})}{\sqrt{(1 - tau_{13}^2) \times (1 - tau_{23}^2)}}$$

The rank correlation is tau *b*.

We will illustrate the partial rank correlation by computing that between post-test marks (1) and student's sex (2) controlling for pre-test course interest (3). We first calculate Kendall's rank correlation for the three variables. The rank correlation between post-test marks and student's sex (12) is -0.37, between post-test marks and pre-test course interest (13) is 0.67 and between student's sex and pre-test course interest (23) is -0.10. Substituting these values into the formula above, we see that the partial rank correlation is -0.42:

$$\frac{-0.37 - (0.67 \times -0.10)}{\sqrt{(1 - 0.67^2) \times (1 - 0.23^2)}} = \frac{-0.37 - -0.07}{\sqrt{0.55 \times 0.95}} = \frac{-0.30}{0.72} = -0.417$$

In other words, the rank correlation of -0.37 between post-test marks and student's sex is slightly increased (-0.42) when pre-test course interest is controlled.

To determine the statistical significance of the partial rank correlation for samples of up to 90 we look at the appropriate value in the table in Appendix 22, which gives the 0.05 and 0.025 one-tailed values. The 0.05 two-tailed values correspond to the 0.025 one-tailed values. To be significant at the 0.05 one-tailed level with 20 cases the partial rank correlation needs to be 0.268 or bigger, which it is.

Since partial tau is approximately normally distributed when the size of the sample (N) is large, we can calculate the significance level of partial tau by converting it into z according to the following formula

$$z = \frac{3 \times \text{tau} \times \sqrt{N(N-1)}}{\sqrt{2(2N+5)}}$$

Substituting the values in this formula for our example we find that, ignoring the minus sign, z is 2.59

$$\frac{3 \times -0.42 \times \sqrt{20(20-1)}}{\sqrt{2[(2 \times 20)+5]}} = \frac{-1.26 \times \sqrt{380}}{\sqrt{2 \times 45}} = \frac{-1.26 \times 19.49}{\sqrt{90}} = \frac{-24.56}{9.49} = -2.588$$

We look up the significance of this z value in the table in Appendix 2. The area between the middle of the curve and a z value of 2.79 is 0.4974, indicating that the area beyond the z value on one side of the curve is 0.0026 (0.5000 − 0.4974 = 0.0026), which is the one-tailed probability.

SPSS does not compute the partial rank correlation but as we have just seen this is fairly easy to do.

Partial gamma

The formula for partial gamma is the number of concordant pairs (C) minus the number of discordant pairs (D) for the two variables summed across the different levels of the third variable divided by the number of concordant and discordant pairs summed across the different levels of the third variable (Goodman and Kruskal 1954):

$$\text{partial gamma} = \frac{\text{sum of } C - D}{\text{sum of } C + D}$$

We will demonstrate the calculation of partial gamma by working out that between post-test marks and student's sex controlling for pre-test course interest. First we draw up a contingency table as we have done in Table 13.18 which contains four subtables, one for each of the four ratings for pre-test course interest. Using the matrix method of counting, the number of concordant pairs is the sum of cases which lie below and to the right of that cell multiplied by the number in that cell, whereas the number of discordant pairs is the sum of cases which lie below and to the left of that cell multiplied by the number of cases in that cell. Thus, the number of discordant and concordant pairs for each subtable are as follows: first subtable 3 discordant pairs only; second subtable 2 discordant pairs; third subtable 9 discordant and 3 concordant pairs; and fourth subtable 7 discordant and 2 concordant pairs. The total number is 21 discordant pairs

Table 13.18 Contingency subtables of post-test marks and student's sex for levels of pre-test course interest

| | | | Post-test marks | | | | | | | | |
			1	*2*	*3*	*4*	*5*	*6*	*7*	*8*	*9*
Pre-test	1	Women				1					
course		Men	2	1							
interest											
	2	Women				1	1				
		Men	1								
	3	Women				1		2		1	
		Men					3				
	4	Women						1	1		1
		Men					2			1	

and 5 concordant pairs. Substituting these values into the formula for computing partial gamma, we see that partial gamma is −0.62:

$$\frac{5 - 21}{5 + 2} = \frac{-16}{26} = -0.615$$

With SPSS we can only compute partial gamma with a syntax command which takes the following general form:

crosstabs variables = first variable (minimum value, maximum value) second variable (minimum value, maximum value) third variable (minimum value, maximum value)
/tables = first variable **by** second variable **by** third variable
/statistics gamma.

We would use the following command for our example:

crosstabs variables = markpos (1, 9) sex (1, 2) intpre (1, 4)
/tables = sex by markpos by intpre
/statistics gamma.

Table 13.19 shows the output for this command which consists of the subtables, their zero-order gammas, the zero-order gamma for the overall contingency table and the first-order partial gamma.

SUMMARY

The computation of tests of association for categorical and ordinal data is described in this chapter. Tests of association for categorical data can be divided into those derived from chi-square (phi coefficient, contingency coefficient and Cramér's *V*) and those based on the proportional reduction in error (Goodman and Kruskal's lambda and tau). The phi coefficient is

Table 13.19 SPSS output for partial gamma between post-test marks and student's sex controlling for pre-test course interest

SEX by MARKPOS post-test marks

Controlling for . .

INTPRE pre-test course interest Value = 1 slight

		MARKPOS			Page 1 of 1
	Count				
					Row
		1	2	4	Total
SEX					
1 women				1	1 25.0
2 men		2	1		3 75.0
	Column Total	2 50.0	1 25.0	1 25.0	4 100.0

Statistic	Value	ASE1	Val/ASE0	Approximate Significance
Gamma	-1.00000	.00000	-1.73205	

SEX by MARKPOS post-test marks

Controlling for . .

INTPRE pre-test course interest Value = 2 some

	Count		MARKPOS			Page 1 of 1
						Row
			1	4	5	Total
SEX						
women	1			1	1	2
						66.7
men	2		1			1
						33.3
	Column		1	1	1	3
	Total		33.3	33.3	33.3	100.0

Statistic	Value	ASE1	Val/ASE0	Approximate Significance
Gamma	-1.00000	.00000	-2.44949	

SEX by MARKPOS post-test marks

Controlling for . .

INTPRE pre-test course interest Value = 3 moderate

```
                     MARKPOS                        Page 1 of 1
             Count  |
                    |
                    |                                Row
                    |    4 |    5 |    6 |    8 |  Total
SEX          -------+------ +------ +------- +------- +
              1     |    1 |      |    2 |    1 |    4
          women     |      |      |      |      |   57.1
                    +------ +------ +------- +------- +
              2     |      |    3 |      |      |    3
          men       |      |      |      |      |   42.9
                    +------ +------ +------- +------- +
            Column       1      3      2      1      7
             Total    14.3   42.9   28.6   14.3  100.0
```

Statistic	Value	ASE1	Val/ASE0	Approximate Significance
Gamma	-5.0000	.43301	-1.14564	

SEX by MARKPOS post-test marks

Controlling for ..

INTPRE pre-test course interest Value = 4 much

	MARKPOS					Page 1 of 1

	Count	5	6	7	8	9	Row Total
SEX							
women	1		1	1		1	3 / 50.0
men	2	2			1		3 / 50.0
Column Total		2 / 33.3	1 / 16.7	1 / 16.7	1 / 16.7	1 / 16.7	6 / 100.0

Statistic	Value	ASE1	Val/ASE0	Approximate Significance
Gamma	-.55556	.40572	-1.36931	

Zero-Order Gamma	-.51064
First-Order Partial Gamma	-.61538

Number of Missing Observations: 1

---

appropriate for two dichotomous variables where it can vary from zero, or -1, to $+1$ depending on the formula used. When one or both variables have more than two categories, the contingency coefficient may be preferable since it varies between zero and less than $+1$ whereas phi may be greater than $+1$. To make the upper limit $+1$ for tables greater than 2×2, Cramér's V should be used. Goodman and Kruskal's lambda, which varies from zero to $+1$, is the proportional increase in predicting one outcome of a categorical variable when knowing its combined outcome with a second categorical variable. Whereas lambda assumes the same prediction is made for all cases in a particular row or column, Goodman and Kruskal's tau presumes the predictions are randomly made based on their proportions in row and column totals.

Tests of association for two ordinal variables, which count the number of cases higher (concordant) and lower (discordant) than the others, include Somers' d, Goodman and Kruskal's gamma, Kendall's tau a, tau b and tau c. Kendall's tau a, which is the number of concordant pairs minus the number of discordant pairs over the total number of pairs, is used when there are no tied pairs and can vary from -1 to $+1$. Tau b is employed when there are tied pairs and can vary from -1 to $+1$ if the table is square and if none of the row and column totals is zero. For a rectangular table tau c can come closer to ± 1. Goodman and Kruskal's gamma, which is the number of concordant pairs minus the number of discordant pairs divided by the number of concordant and discordant pairs, can range from -1 to $+1$ and takes no account of ties or the size of the table. Somers' d provides an asymmetric as well as a symmetric measure of association and includes tied pairs. Spearman's rho ranges from -1 to $+1$ and is a Pearson's correlation on ranked data. Mantel–Haenszel's chi-square is the squared Pearson's correlation coefficient multiplied by the number of cases minus 1. Partial gamma and Kendall's partial rank correlation coefficient are tests of partial association for ordinal data which partial out a third variable.

EXERCISES

1 Students reading an arts, social science or natural science subject were asked whether they supported an increase in direct taxation. The numbers in favour, against and undecided are shown in Table 13.20.
Calculate the association between the students' area of study and their opinion on this issue using the following tests:
(a) Phi coefficient
(b) Contingency coefficient
(c) Cramér's V
(d) Goodman and Kruskal's asymmetric lambda with opinion as the dependent variable
(e) Goodman and Kruskal's asymmetric tau with opinion as the dependent variable

Table 13.20 Opinion on increase in direct taxation of arts, social science and natural science students

	Yes	*No*	*Undecided*
Arts	45	15	9
Social science	77	13	11
Natural science	69	27	3

2 Calculate the association between educational interest at 12 and at 15 for the data in Table 5.12 using the following tests:

(a) Kendall's tau b

(b) Kendall's tau c

(c) Goodman and Kruskal's gamma

(d) Somers' asymmetric d with educational interest at 15 as the dependent variable

(e) Spearman's rho

(f) Kendall's partial rank correlation coefficent controlling for educational interest at 9

14 Measurement reliability and agreement

This chapter describes statistical tests which provide an index of how reliable a particular measure is or how much agreement exists between two or more judges. For instance, we may wish to find out to what extent two or more judges categorise or rate subjects in the same way, or to what extent the answers to questions devised to measure the same quality are consistent. The type of test to use depends on whether the data are categorical or not. The most widely recommended index of agreement between two or more judges is Cohen's (1960) *kappa coefficient* for categorical data. The most common measure of the reliability of non-categorical data for three or more judges is Ebel's (1951) *intraclass correlation* while the most frequently used index of the internal reliability for a set of questions is Cronbach's (1951) *alpha*.

CATEGORICAL DATA

Kappa coefficient

Kappa indicates the extent of agreement for categorical data between two judges or raters and can be extended to apply to more than two judges (Fleiss 1971). It measures the proportion of agreements between two judges taking into account the proportion of agreements that may occur simply by chance. It has the following formula:

$$k = \frac{\text{observed proportion of agreement} - \text{chance-expected proportion of agreement}}{1 - \text{chance-expected proportion of agreement}}$$

which can be expressed in frequencies:

$$k = \frac{\text{observed frequency of agreement} - \text{chance-expected frequency of agreement}}{\text{no. of subjects} - \text{chance-expected frequency of agreement}}$$

Kappas can range from -1 to $+1$. A kappa of 0 means that the observed agreement is exactly equal to the agreement that would be expected by chance, a negative kappa a less than chance agreement, a positive kappa a greater than chance agreement and a kappa of 1 perfect agreement. A kappa of 0.7 or more is usually considered to be an acceptable level of agreement. As will be demonstrated below, kappa is an index of agreement whereas tests such as the contingency coefficient and phi are measures of association. The contingency coefficient only varies between 0 and 1 and phi does when the first formula described in Chapter 13 is used. If there is substantial disagreement between two judges on a dichotomous judgement task, then both the contingency coefficient and phi (when the first formula is used) will be positive whereas kappa will be negative.

To illustrate the computation of kappa we will take the case where two judges are asked to indicate whether they consider each of 100 pieces of coursework to have passed or failed. The results of these two judges are shown in Table 14.1. Judge A thinks that 90 out of 100 or 90 per cent of the assignments have passed while Judge B believes that only 40 per cent of them have. The decisions of the two judges agree on only 30 per cent of the work.

To calculate kappa we first find the chance-expected frequency of agreement for the two cells. This is done for each cell by multiplying its row total by its column total and dividing by the overall total. So the chance-expected frequency for the fail category is 6 ($10 \times 60/100 = 6$) and for the pass category 36 ($90 \times 40/100 = 36$) giving a total of 42.

Applying the above formula we find that kappa is about -0.21:

$$\frac{30 - 42}{100 - 42} = \frac{-12}{58} = -0.2069$$

This indicates that the agreement between the two judges is less than would be expected by chance which implies that they are using different criteria to make their judgements.

Let us now compare this kappa with the contingency coefficient and phi. To calculate these two coefficients we first have to find chi-square which is about 16.67:

$$\frac{(0 - 6)^2}{6} + \frac{(10 - 4)^2}{4} + \frac{(60 - 54)^2}{54} + \frac{(30 - 36)^2}{36} =$$

$$6 + 9 + 0.67 + 1 = 16.67$$

Table 14.1 Categorisation of coursework by two judges

		Judge B		Row total
		Failed	Passed	
Judge A	Failed	0	10	10
	Passed	60	30	90
Column total		60	40	100

Consequently, the contingency coefficient is about $0.38[\sqrt{16.67/(16.67 + 100)}$ $= 0.378]$ and phi is $0.41(\sqrt{16.67/100} = 0.408)$. Note that both the contingency oefficient and phi are positive and larger than kappa even though the amount of disagreement is greater than the amount of agreement. What these two coefficients indicate is that there is a tendency for certain decisions of Judge A to be associated with certain decisions of Judge B but they provide no information as to whether the actual decisions are the same.

To compute kappa with SPSS for this example, first enter the data in **Newdata** using the weighting procedure and then carry out the following sequence:

→**Statistics** →**Summarize** →**Crosstabs** . . . [opens **Crosstabs** dialog box as in Box 11.5]
→row variable [e.g. **judgea**] →▶button [puts variable under **Row[s]:**]
→column variable [e.g. **judgeb**] →▶button [puts variable under **Column[s]:**]
→**Statistics** . . . [opens **Crosstabs: Statistics** dialog box as in Box 11.7]
→**Kappa** →**Continue** [closes **Crosstabs: Statistics** dialog box]
→**OK**

Table 14.2 presents the output for this procedure together with the values for phi, Cramér's *V*, the contingency coefficient and kappa. Note that phi is negative indicating that it has been computed with the second formula described in Chapter 13.

NON-CATEGORICAL DATA

When measuring a hypothetical construct such as course or educational interest, it is useful to obtain a number of separate indices of that variable in order to determine how reliably that construct is being assessed. These indices might consist of either the independent ratings of a number of judges asked to assess that variable or the answers to a number of items designed to measure that variable. These ratings or answers represent the score on that variable for the person being assessed. These scores can be thought of as reflecting two components consisting of a true score plus some error:

actual score = true score + error

For example, a person may understand the question correctly and may answer appropriately, in which case the actual score will mainly reflect the true score with very little error. Alternatively, the person may misunderstand the question and therefore respond inappropriately, in which situation the actual score will largely consist of error.

Table 14.2 SPSS output for kappa

JUDGEA by JUDGEB

```
                    JUDGEB              Page 1 of 1
            Count  |
                   |
                   |                        Row
                   |    1.00 |    2.00 |   Total
JUDGEA      - - - - + - - - - + - - - - +
        1.00 |             |    10 |     10
             |             |       |     10.0
             + - - - - + - - - - +
        2.00 |      60 |    30 |     90
             |         |       |     90.0
             + - - - - + - - - - +
            Column      60       40       100
            Total      60.0     40.0     100.0
```

Statistic	Value	ASE1	Val/ASE0	Approximate Significance
Phi	-.40825			.00004 *1
Cramer's V	.40825			.00004 *1
Contingency Coefficient	.37796			.00004 *1
Kappa	-.20690	.06308	-4.08248	

*1 Pearson chi-square probability

Number of Missing Observations: 0

The reliability of that score can be thought of as the proportion of the true score over the true score plus the error:

$$\text{reliability of a score} = \frac{\text{true score}}{\text{true score} + \text{error}}$$

Alternative ways of expressing this measure of reliability are as follows:

$$\text{reliability of a score} = \frac{\text{actual score} - \text{error}}{\text{actual score}} = \frac{\text{true score}}{\text{actual score}}$$

With only one measure of a variable it is not possible to estimate the error in that measure. In order to do this, it is necessary to have a number of indices (i.e. judges or items), where the error of those indices can be estimated with analysis of variance. Reliability is the proportion of the true variance in the scores of subjects as a function of the true variance together with the error variance:

$$\text{reliability} = \frac{\text{true variance}}{\text{true variance} + \text{error variance}}$$

Two measures of reliability are Ebel's intraclass correlation and Cronbach's alpha coefficient. The intraclass correlation is used to estimate the individual or average reliability of the ratings of judges whereas alpha is employed to assess the internal consistency of a set of items making up a scale. The difference between these two measures of reliability lies in the kind of analysis of variance conducted. Intraclass correlation is calculated with a one- or two-way analysis of variance where the ratings of the judges are treated as an unrelated factor in which the ratings are made by different people. Alpha, on the other hand, is computed with a single factor repeated measures analysis of variance in which the different items are treated as a repeated measure in that the answers to the different items are given by the same individual.

Intraclass correlation

The reliability of the non-categorical ratings of two judges is estimated with Pearson's correlation coefficient and of three or more judges with the intraclass correlation. There are four different forms of the intraclass correlation. The intraclass correlation can be generally thought of as the proportion of the true variance in the ratings of the subjects (i.e. the between-subjects variance minus the error variance) in relation to the between-subjects variance:

$$\text{intraclass correlation} = \frac{\text{between-subjects variance} - \text{error variance}}{\text{between-subjects variance}}$$

This formula gives the reliability of the average rating for all the judges and is used as the appropriate measure of reliability if the ratings of the judges were averaged to form a score for each case. For example, if three judges rated the course interest of 80 students and these three ratings were averaged for each individual to give them a course interest rating, then this index should be used as the measure of reliability.

If, on the other hand, only one of every four of these 80 students was rated by all three judges while the other three were rated by only one of the three judges, then it is more suitable to provide the reliability of the average rating for an individual judge. The reliability of the average rating for an individual judge is lower than that for all three judges since in this formula the error variance, which is multiplied by the number of judges minus 1, is added to the denominator:

$$\frac{\text{between-subjects variance} - \text{error variance}}{\text{between-subjects variance} + [\text{error variance} \times (\text{no. of judges} - 1)]}$$

Using the error variance on its own provides an index of the extent to which the judges rank the subjects in a similar order, ignoring the extent to which a similar rating (rather than ranking) is given to each case. Take, for example, the ratings shown in Table 14.3 of four subjects made by three judges. Note that while there is perfect agreement between the three judges in the rank order of the four subjects, there is total disagreement over the particular ratings given. For example, all three judges agree in giving the first case the highest rating (low numbers reflecting higher ratings) but give that case a different rating of 1, 2 and 3. An intraclass correlation which uses error variance on its own is sometimes referred to as interjudge reliability.

To determine the extent to which the mean ratings are also similar, the error variance is combined with the between-judges variance:

$$\frac{\text{between-subjects variance} - \text{error variance} - \text{between-judges variance}}{\text{between-subjects variance}}$$

and to allow for individual judge agreement we have

$$\frac{\text{between-subjects variance} - \text{error variance} - \text{between-judges variance}}{\text{between-subjects variance} + [(\text{error variance} + \text{between-judges variance}) \times (\text{no. of judges} - 1)]}$$

An intraclass correlation which includes the between-judges variance is sometimes known as a measure of interjudge agreement since it assesses the extent to which the judges also give a similar rating.

Table 14.3 Ratings of four subjects by three judges

Subjects	Judges		
	A	*B*	*C*
1	1	2	3
2	2	3	4
3	3	4	5
4	4	5	6

So the following four forms of intraclass correlation may be distinguished:

$$\text{interjudge reliability of all judges} = \frac{\text{between-subjects variance} - \text{error variance}}{\text{between-subjects variance}}$$

$$\text{interjudge reliability of individual judge} = \frac{\text{between- subjects variance} - \text{error variance}}{\text{between-subjects variance} + [\text{error variance} \times (\text{no of judges} - 1)]}$$

$$\text{interjudge agreement of all judges} = \frac{\text{between-subjects variance} - \text{error variance} - \text{between-judges variance}}{\text{between-subjects variance}}$$

$$\text{interjudge agreement of individual judge} = \frac{\text{between-subjects variance} - \text{error variance} - \text{between-judges variance}}{\text{between-subjects variance} + [(\text{error variance} + \text{between-judges variance}) \times (\text{no. of judges} - 1)]}$$

When the between-judges variance is to be included in the error variance, a one-way analysis only need be worked out as the error term will incorporate the between-judges variance:

one-way anova = between-subjects variance + error variance

When the between-judges variance is to be excluded from the error variance, then a two-way analysis of variance is necessary as the between-judges variance will be given separately from the error variance:

two-way anova = between-subjects variance + between-judges variance + error variance

Note that if a two-way analysis of variance is performed, the between-judges variance can be combined with the error variance to give the appropriate error variance for interrater reliability.

So, to demonstrate the calculation of these four kinds of intraclass correlation for the data in Table 14.3, we will carry out a two-way analysis of variance. The means for the three judges and four subjects are shown in Table 14.4 together with the grand mean.

The between-subjects sum of squares is calculated by subtracting the

Table 14.4 Sums and means of ratings of subjects and judges

Subjects	Judges			Sum	Mean
	A	B	C		
1	1	2	3	6	2
2	2	3	4	9	3
3	3	4	5	12	4
4	4	5	6	15	5
Sum	10	14	18	42	
N	4	4	4		
Mean	2.5	3.5	4.5		3.5

grand mean from each of the subject means, squaring this difference, multiplying this squared difference by the number of judges and summing the products for all the subjects. This makes it 15:

$$[(2 - 3.5)^2 \times 3] + [(3 - 3.5)^2 \times 3] + [(4 - 3.5)^2 \times 3] +$$
$$[(5 - 3.5)^2 \times 3] =$$
$$[2.25 \times 3] + [0.25 \times 3] + [0.25 \times 3] + [2.25 \times 3] =$$
$$6.75 + 0.75 + 0.75 + 6.75 = 15$$

The between-subjects mean square is its sum of squares divided by its degrees of freedom (the number of subjects minus 1) which gives 5.0 (15/3 = 5).

The between-judges sum of squares is calculated by subtracting the grand mean from the mean of each judge, squaring this difference, multiplying this squared difference by the number of subjects and summing the products for all the judges. This makes it 8:

$$[(2.5 - 3.5)^2 \times 4] + [(3.5 - 3.5)^2 \times 4] +$$
$$[(4.5 - 3.5)^2 \times 4] = 4 + 0 + 4 = 8$$

The between-judges mean square is its sum of squares divided by its degrees of freedom (the number of judges minus 1) which gives 4.0 (8/2 = 4).

The residual or error sum of squares can be calculated by subtracting the between-subjects and between-judges sum of squares from the total sum of squares. The total sum of squares is the grand mean subtracted from each rating, squared and added together which makes it 23.0:

$$(1 - 3.5)^2 + (2 - 3.5)^2 + (3 - 3.5)^2 + (4 - 3.5)^2 +$$
$$(2 - 3.5)^2 + (3 - 3.5)^2 + (4 - 3.5)^2 + (5 - 3.5)^2 +$$
$$(3 - 3.5)^2 + (4 - 3.5)^2 + (5 - 3.5)^2 + (6 - 3.5)^2 =$$
$$6.25 + 2.25 + 0.25 + 0.25 + 2.25 + 0.25 + 0.25 +$$
$$2.25 + 0.25 + 0.25 + 2.25 + 6.25 = 23.0$$

The error sum of squares is 0 (23.0 − 15.0 − 8.0 = 0.0). The degrees of freedom for the error sum of squares are the number of subjects minus 1 multiplied by the number of judges minus 1, which in this case are 6 [(4 − 1) × (3 − 1) = 3 × 2 = 6]. Since the error sum of squares is 0 its mean square is also 0 (0/6 = 0). The sums of squares, degrees of freedom and mean squares for these data are presented in Table 14.5.

Using the between-subjects and error mean square we find that the interjudge reliability of all three judges is 1.0:

$$\frac{5 - 0}{5} = \frac{5}{5} = 1.0$$

Table 14.5 Analysis of variance table for the intraclass correlation

Sources of variation	SS	df	MS
Between-subjects	15.0	3	5.0
Within-subjects	8.0	8	1.0
Between-judges	8.0	2	4.0
Error	0.0	6	0.0
Total	23.0		

as is the interjudge reliability of an individual judge:

$$\frac{5 - 0}{5 + [0 \times (3 - 1)]} = \frac{5}{5} = 1.0$$

If no account is taken of the differences in the average ratings of the judges, then the intraclass correlation indicates that there is perfect agreement between the judges even though no judge gave the same case the same rating. In other words, when the average ratings of the judges are ignored the intraclass correlation is similar to an average intercorrelation.

However, if the between-judges variance is included in the error term, the intraclass correlation is substantially smaller. To calculate the error sum of squares which includes the between-judges variance either subtract the between-subjects sum of squares from the total sum of squares which gives 8.0 (23.0 − 15.0 = 8.0) or add the between-judges sum of squares to the residual sum of squares (8.0 + 0.0 = 8.0). The degrees of freedom for this residual sum of squares are 1 subtracted from the number of judges for each case summed together. Therefore the residual mean square is 1.0 [8/(3 − 1 + 3 − 1 + 3 − 1 + 3 − 1) = 1]. Using this value, we find that the interjudge agreement for all three judges is 0.80:

$$\frac{5 - 1}{5} = \frac{4}{5} = 0.80$$

and the interjudge agreement for an individual judge is 0.57:

$$\frac{5 - 1}{5 + [1 \times (3 - 1)]} = \frac{4}{7} = 0.57$$

To produce the necessary statistics with SPSS to derive the intraclass correlation, we first enter the data into **Newdata** (as shown in Box 14.1) and we then carry out a two-way analysis of variance with the following procedure:

→**Statistics** →**ANOVA Models** →**Simple Factorial . . .** [opens **Simple Factorial ANOVA** dialog box as in Box 9.1]
→dependent variable [e.g. **ratings**] →▶button beside **Dependent:** [puts variable in this box] →first independent variable [e.g. **subjects**]

→▶button beside **Factor(s):** [puts variable in this box] →**Define Range . . .** [opens **Simple Factorial ANOVA: Define Range** dialog box as in Box 9.2]

→in box beside **Minimum:** type lower code value [e.g. **1**] →box beside **Maximum:** and type upper code value [e.g. **4**] →**Continue** [closes **Simple Factorial ANOVA: Define Range** dialog box]

→second independent variable [e.g. **judges**] →▶button beside **Factor(s):** [puts variable in this box] →**Define Range . . .** [opens **Simple Factorial ANOVA: Define Range** dialog box]

→in box beside **Minimum:** type lower code value [e.g. **1**] →box beside **Maximum:** and type upper code value [e.g. **3**] →**Continue** [closes **Simple Factorial ANOVA: Define Range** dialog box]

→**Options . . .** [opens **Simple Factorial ANOVA: Options** dialog box as in Box 9.3]

→**None** [in **Maximum Interactions** section] [suppresses interaction] →**Continue** [closes **Simple Factorial ANOVA: Options** dialog box] →**OK**

Table 14.6 shows the output for this procedure.

Alpha

The alpha coefficient determines the internal reliability or consistency of a set of items designed to measure a particular characteristic. It can be thought of as the proportion of variation in the subjects which is explained by the items:

$$\text{alpha} = \frac{\text{between-subjects variance} - \text{error variance}}{\text{between-subjects variance}}$$

or

$$1 - \frac{\text{error variance}}{\text{between-subjects variance}}$$

The difference between this formula and that for the intraclass correlation lies in the different way in which the error variance is derived. We can calculate alpha as a single factor repeated measures analysis of variance in which the error mean square is divided by the between-subjects mean square and the result subtracted from 1.

We will illustrate the computation of alpha with the data shown in Table 14.7 which represent the dichotomous answers of four subjects to three items measuring, say, course interest. A '1' might indicate a 'No' or 'Disagree' response and a '2' a 'Yes' or 'Agree' answer. Each of the three items is worded so that a 'Yes' reply indicates greater interest than a 'No' response. Apart from the fourth case the scores for each person are the same for all three items so that if a person answers 'Yes' to one

	subjects	judges	ratings	var
1	1.00	1.00	1.00	
2	2.00	1.00	2.00	
3	3.00	1.00	3.00	
4	4.00	1.00	4.00	
5	1.00	2.00	2.00	
6	2.00	2.00	3.00	
7	3.00	2.00	4.00	
8	4.00	2.00	5.00	
9	1.00	3.00	3.00	
10	2.00	3.00	4.00	
11	3.00	3.00	5.00	
12	4.00	3.00	6.00	
13				

Box 14.1 **Newdata** window with ratings of four cases by three judges

question they answer 'Yes' to the other two. This pattern of responding implies that the items are measuring the same characteristic. If some of the items had been worded so that a 'Yes' signified lower interest than a 'No', then the scorings of these items have to be reversed (i.e. a 'Yes' coded as a '1' and a 'No' as '2') so that the direction of the scoring was consistent.

The total and mean scores for the subjects and items are presented in Table 14.8 together with the grand mean. To calculate the between-subjects and error mean squares carry out the following steps.

Table 14.6 SPSS output of a two-way analysis of variance for calculating the intraclass correlation

* * * A N A L Y S I S   O F   V A R I A N C E * * *

RATINGS
by JUDGES
SUBJECTS

UNIQUE sums of squares
All effects entered simultaneously

Source of Variation	Sum of Squares	DF	Mean Square	F	Sig of F
Main Effects	23.000	5	4.600		
JUDGES	8.000	2	4.000		
SUBJECTS	15.000	3	5.000		
Explained	23.000	5	4.600		
Residual	.000	6	.000		
Total	23.000	11	2.091		

12 cases were processed.
0 cases (.0 pct) were missing.

Table 14.7 Dichotomous answers to three items

Subjects	Items		
	1	*2*	*3*
1	1	1	1
2	2	2	2
3	1	1	1
4	1	2	2

Table 14.8 Sum and means of items and subjects

Subjects	Items			Sum	Mean
	1	*2*	*3*		
1	1	1	1	3	1
2	2	2	2	6	2
3	1	1	1	3	1
4	1	2	2	5	1.67
Sum	5	6	6	17	
N	4	4	4		
Mean	1.25	1.5	1.5		1.42

Step 1   Calculate the total sum of squares by subtracting the grand mean from each score, squaring the differences and adding the squared differences together.

The total sum of squares for our example is 2.92:

$$(1 - 1.42)^2 + (2 - 1.42)^2 + (1 - 1.42)^2 + (1 - 1.42)^2 +$$
$$(1 - 1.42)^2 + (2 - 1.42)^2 + (1 - 1.42)^2 + (2 - 1.42)^2 +$$
$$(1 - 1.42)^2 + (2 - 1.42)^2 + (1 - 1.42)^2 + (2 - 1.42)^2 = 2.917$$

Step 2   Compute the between-subjects sum of squares by subtracting the grand mean from the mean score for each case, squaring the differences, multiplying the squared differences by the number of items and adding the products together.

The between-subjects sum of squares for our example is 2.25:

$$[(1.00 - 1.42)^2 \times 3] + [(2.00 - 1.42)^2 \times 3] +$$
$$[(1.00 - 1.42)^2 \times 3] + [(1.67 - 1.42)^2 \times 3] =$$
$$0.529 + 1.009 + 0.529 + 0.188 = 2.25$$

Step 3   Work out the within-factor (i.e. items) sum of squares by subtracting the grand mean from the mean score for each of the items, squaring the differences, multiplying the squared differences by the number of subjects and summing the products.

The within-factor sum of squares for our example is 0.17:

$$[(1.25 - 1.42)^2 \times 4] + [(1.5 - 1.42)^2 \times 4] +$$
$$[(1.5 - 1.42)^2 \times 4] = 0.116 + 0.026 + 0.026 = 0.168$$

Step 4   Calculate the residual sum of squares by adding together the between-subjects and within-subjects sum of squares and subtracting them from the total sum of squares.

For our example the residual sum of squares is 0.50 [2.92 − (2.25 + 0.17) = 0.50].

Step 5 Calculate the error mean square by dividing its sum of squares by its degrees of freedom which are the number of subjects minus 1 multiplied by the number of items minus 1.

For our example the degrees of freedom are 6 [(4 − 1) × (3 − 1) = 6] so the error mean square is 0.08 (0.50/6 = 0.08).

Step 6 Calculate the between-subjects mean square by dividing its sum of squares by its degrees of freedom which are the number of subjects minus 1.

The between-subjects mean square for our example is 0.75 (2.25/3 = 0.75).

Table 14.9 summarises the results of these steps.

To calculate alpha divide the error mean square by the between-subjects mean square and subtract the result from 1.

For our example alpha for the three items is 0.89:

$$1 - \frac{0.08}{0.75} = 1 - 0.1067 = 0.8933$$

Since an alpha of 0.80 or higher is generally thought to indicate an acceptable level of internal reliability, this set of three items is considered as constituting a reliable scale.

To calculate alpha with SPSS, we first enter the data and then run the following procedure:

→**Statistics** →**Sc**a**le** →**R**e**liability Analysis . . .** [opens **Reliability Analysis** dialog box as in Box 14.2]
→first variable [e.g. **item1**] →▶button beside **Items:** [puts variable in this box] →second variable [e.g. **item2**] →▶button beside **Items:** [puts variable in this box] and so on →**Statistics . . .** [opens **Reliability Analysis: Statistics** dialog box as in Box 14.3]
→**Sc**a**le if item deleted** [in **Descriptives for** section] →**Continue** [closes **Reliability Analysis: Statistics** dialog box]
→**OK**

Table 14.10 displays the output for this procedure. Note that if the first item is omitted, alpha for the remaining two items increases to **1.0000** while if either of the other two items is dropped alpha decreases to **.7273**.

Table 14.9 Analysis of variance table for alpha

Sources of variation	SS	df	MS
Between-subjects	2.25	3	0.75
Within-subjects			
Within-factor	0.17		
Residual	0.50	6	0.08
Total	2.92		

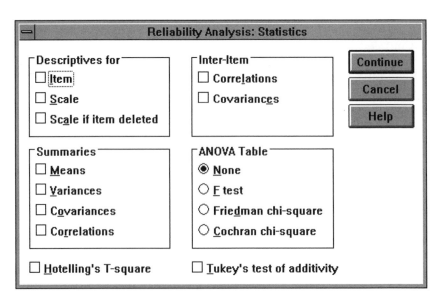

Box 14.2 **Reliability Analysis** dialog box

Box 14.3 **Reliability Analysis: Statistics** dialog box

Table 14.10 SPSS output for alpha

R E L I A B I L I T Y   A N A L Y S I S – S C A L E   (A L P H A)

Item-total Statistics

	Scale Mean if Item Deleted	Scale Variance if Item Deleted	Corrected Item-Total Correlation	Alpha if Item Deleted
ITEM1	3.0000	1.3333	.5774	1.0000
ITEM2	2.7500	.9167	.9045	.7273
ITEM3	2.7500	.9167	.9045	.7273

Reliability Coefficients

N of Cases =   4.0   N of Items = 3

Alpha =   .8889

If the wording of one or more of a series of items was reversed, then the **Recode** procedure could be used to reverse the scores of these items. Imagine, for example, that of a scale of 10 dichotomously-scored items the wording of the odd-numbered ones was reversed. We could reconvert the scores for these items so that a 1 becomes a 2 and a 2 a 1 using the **Recode** procedure described in Chapter 3.

Spearman–Brown prophecy formula

One way of estimating the number of judges or items necessary for providing a measure of acceptable reliability is to use the following Spearman–Brown prophecy formula (Brown 1910, Spearman 1910):

$$\text{estimated reliability} = \frac{n \times \text{known reliability}}{1 + [(n-1) \times \text{known reliability}]}$$

where n is the ratio by which the number of judges or items is to be increased or decreased. For example, we could use this formula to estimate the reliability of having six rather than three items to assess course interest where the alpha reliability of the three items was 0.89. The estimated reliability of the six item scale is 0.94:

$$\frac{2 \times 0.89}{1 + [(2 - 1) \times 0.89]} = \frac{1.78}{1.89} = 0.94$$

We can check the accuracy of this estimate by adding to our data an identical set of three scores as shown in Table 14.11.

The following formula is used for estimating the ratio by which the number of judges or items has to be changed in order to achieve a measure of a specified reliability:

$$\text{ratio} = \frac{\text{specified reliability} \times (1 - \text{known reliability})}{\text{known reliability} \times (1 - \text{specified reliability})}$$

Suppose, for instance, we had a scale of three items with an alpha of 0.5 and we wished to increase it to about 0.9. According to this formula, the number of items we would need to do this is 9 times 3 (i.e. 27):

$$\frac{0.9 \times (1 - 0.5)}{0.5 \times (1 - 0.9)} = \frac{0.45}{0.05} = 9$$

Correction for attenuation

Many variables are measured with a certain degree of unreliability. Consequently, the correlation between unreliably measured variables is always less strong than that between reliably measured variables. This reduced correlation is known as *attenuation*. If we wanted to find out the 'true' or theoretical correlation between two measures which had been assessed without error then we need to make a correction for their unreliability.

The following formula has been proposed for calculating the correlation between two variables where the unreliability of both measures has been taken into account:

$$r_c = \frac{\text{correlation between measure}_1 \text{ and measure}_2}{\sqrt{\text{measure}_1 \text{ reliability} \times \text{measure}_2 \text{ reliability}}}$$

Table 14.11 Dichotomous answers to six items

Subjects	Items					
	1	*2*	*3*	*4*	*5*	*6*
1	1	1	1	1	1	1
2	2	2	2	2	2	2
3	1	1	1	1	1	1
4	1	2	2	1	2	2

When the reliability of only one of the measures is being adjusted, then the formula is:

$$r_c = \frac{\text{correlation between measure}_1 \text{ and measure}_2}{\sqrt{\text{measure}_1 \text{ or measure}_2 \text{ reliability}}}$$

For instance, if the observed correlation between course interest and course preparation was 0.30 and the reliability of the course interest and course preparation measure was 0.80 and 0.70 respectively, then the theoretical correlation between course interest and course preparation is 0.40:

$$\frac{0.30}{\sqrt{0.80 \times 0.70}} = \frac{0.30}{0.75} = 0.40$$

If the attenuated correlation between two measures is close to 1.0, then the two measures would be interpreted as two forms of the same measure.

SUMMARY

The computation of various tests for assessing the agreement and reliability between judges and the internal reliability of a scale of items is described. Kappa indicates the amount of agreement for categorical data between two judges taking into account the agreement expected by chance. While it can range from -1 to $+1$, a kappa of 0.7 or higher indicates an acceptable level of agreement. For non-categorical data Pearson's correlation assesses the reliability of the ratings made by two judges and the intraclass correlation the reliability of three or more judges. Alpha assesses the internal reliability of a set of items for measuring a particular characteristic. Spearman–Brown's prophecy formula estimates the number of judges or items needed to provide a specified level of reliability. The correlation between two variables can be corrected for the known unreliability of both or either measure.

EXERCISES

1 Two clinicians categorise the problems of 100 patients into the three classes of anxiety, depression and other as shown in Table 14.12. What is the kappa coefficient of agreement for the diagnoses of the two clinicians?
2 Three judges rate the physical attractiveness of four people on a 4–point scale as presented in Table 14.13.
  (a) What is the reliability of the average rating for an individual judge not taking into account the mean levels of the judges's ratings?
  (b) What is the reliability of the average rating for an individual judge taking into account the mean levels of the judges's ratings?
  (c) What is the reliability of the average rating for all three judges not taking into account the mean levels of the judges's ratings?

Table 14.12 Categorisation of patients' problems by two clinicians

Clinician A	Clinician B		
	Anxiety	Depression	Other
Anxiety	7	2	1
Depression	6	35	4
Other	2	13	30

Table 14.13 Physical attractiveness ratings by three judges

Subjects	Judges		
	A	B	C
1	1	2	2
2	2	2	1
3	3	1	2
4	4	3	2

    (d) What is the reliability of the average rating for all three judges taking into account the mean levels of the judges's ratings?

3 Assume that the data in Table 14.13 represent answers to items rather than ratings by judges.

    (a) What is the alpha reliability of the three items?

    (b) By what factor would we have to increase the number of items to achieve an alpha of 0.80?

    (c) How many items would be needed to attain this alpha?

Appendices

APPENDIX 1: SPSS FOR WINDOWS SYNTAX COMMANDS

This appendix provides a convenient summary of SPSS for Windows syntax commands for the procedures described in this book, listed in alphabetical order. Only SPSS terms are printed in bold. Statistics given by default (i.e. without a keyword) are in square brackets and are listed first. If the keyword is underlined they are given even if the subcommand, denoted by a forward slash (/), is missing. 'Variable(s)' refer to SPSS names given to variable(s). Each command must end with a full stop. Most keywords can be shortened to the first three letters.

anova dependent variables **by** first-grouping-variable (value of first group, value of last group) second-grouping-variable (value of first group, value of last group) **with** covariate
   /method=[experimental] unique hierarchical
   /statistics=[mean] mca.

begin data.
lines of data
end data.

compute new variable=transformed old-variables.
   +   addition
   —   subtraction
   *   multiplication
   **   exponentiation
   /   division
   sqrt(variable)   square root
   lg10 (variable)   base 10 logarithm
   ln (variable)   natural logarithm
   mean. minimum number of valid scores (variables).

correlation variables
   /missing=[variable] pairwise
   /print=[twotail nosig] onetail sig
   /statistics=descriptives.

crosstabs table=row-variable **by** column-variable
 /cells=[<u>count</u>] **expected**
 /statistics=[**chisq**] **phi cc lambda btau ctau gamma d corr eta kappa.**

crosstabs variables=first-variable (minimum value, maximum value) second-variable (minimum value, maximum value) control-variable (minimum value, maximum value)
 /tables=first variable **by** second-variable **by** control-variable
 /statistics gamma.

data list [**file**='filename' if data in separate file] [**free** if format is not fixed] [**matrix** if data are in a matrix]
 /variable columns variable columns (first line of data for same case)
 /...... (second line of data for same case).

descriptives variables
 /missing=[<u>variable</u>] **listwise**
 /statistics=[<u>mean</u> <u>stddev</u> <u>min</u> <u>max</u>] **range sum variance semean skewness kurtosis all.**

frequencies variables
 /ntiles number of groups
 /statistics=[**mean stddev min max**] **mode median range variance semean sum skewness seskew kurtosis sekurt all**
 /histogram normal [**percent**].

if (logical expression) new-variable=transformed old-variables.

and	or	**&**	and
or			or
not	or	~	not
eq	or	=	equal to
ne	or	~=	**or** < >	not equal to
le	or	< =	less than or equal to
lt	or	<	less than
ge	or	> =	greater than or equal to
gt	or	>	greater than

list variables.

manova dependent-variables **by** grouping-variables (value of first group, value of last group) **with** covariates
 /wsfactor=name (number of conditions)
 /print=cellinfo (means) signif (brief)
 /pmeans
 /design
 /analysis=dependent-variables
 /design=grouping-variable, grouping-variable **by** covariates.

missing value variables (same missing value)
/variables (different missing value).

npar tests binomial [**.5**] (proportion of value 1)=variable (lowest value, highest value)
npar tests cochran=variables
npar tests friedman=variables
npar tests k-s=ordinal variable **by** grouping-variable (value of one group, value of other group)
npar tests k-w=ordinal variable **by** grouping variable (value of first group, value of last group)
npar tests m-w=ordinal variable **by** grouping-variable (value of one group, value of other group)
npar tests mcnemar=first-variable second-variable
npar tests sign=first-variable second-variable
npar tests wilcoxon=first-variable second-variable
/missing=[analysis] listwise.

oneway dependent variables **by** grouping-variable (value of first group, value of last group)
/statistics=descriptives homogeneity
/range=scheffe lsdmod
/missing=[analysis] listwise.

partial correlation variables **by** control variables (order of correlations as a value)
/significance=[onetail] twotail
/statistics=corr descriptives
/missing=[listwise] analysis.

plot /plot vertical-axis-variable **with** horizontal-axis-variable.

recode variables (old-value/s=new-value) **into** new variables.

regression criterion predictors
/descriptives=mean stddev corr
/statistics=[r anova coeff] ci cha zpp
/dependent=criterion
/method=enter or **forward** or **backward** or **stepwise** predictors.

regression criterion predictors
/scatterplot (*resid, *pred).

reliability variables=items
/scale (name)=items
/summary=total.

select if (logical expression).
and or **&**   and

or	or	|		or
not	or	~	or **a**	not
eq	or	=		equal to
ne	or	< >	or **a**	not equal to
le	or	< =		less than or equal to
lt	or	<		less than
ge	or	> =		greater than or equal to
gt	or	>		greater than

temporary.

t-test groups=grouping-variable [**1,2**] (value of one group, value of other group)
 /variables=dependent variables
 /missing=[analysis] **listwise.**

t-test pair=first-variable second-variable
 /missing=[analysis] **listwise.**

value labels variable value label/variable value label . . . .

variable label variable 'label' variable 'label' . . . .

weight by variable.

APPENDIX 2: STANDARD NORMAL DISTRIBUTION

z	0.00	0.01	0.02	0.03	0.04	0.05	0.06	0.07	0.08	0.09
0.0	0.0000	0.0040	0.0080	0.0120	0.0160	0.0199	0.0239	0.0279	0.0319	0.0359
0.1	0.0398	0.0438	0.0478	0.0517	0.0557	0.0596	0.0636	0.0675	0.0714	0.0754
0.2	0.0793	0.0832	0.0871	0.0910	0.0948	0.0987	0.1026	0.1064	0.1103	0.1141
0.3	0.1179	0.1217	0.1255	0.1293	0.1331	0.1368	0.1406	0.1443	0.1480	0.1517
0.4	0.1554	0.1591	0.1628	0.1664	0.1736	0.1700	0.1772	0.1808	0.1844	0.1879
0.5	0.1915	0.1950	0.1985	0.2019	0.2054	0.2088	0.2123	0.2157	0.2190	0.2224
0.6	0.2258	0.2291	0.2324	0.2357	0.2389	0.2422	0.2454	0.2486	0.2518	0.2549
0.7	0.2580	0.2612	0.2642	0.2673	0.2704	0.2734	0.2764	0.2794	0.2823	0.2852
0.8	0.2881	0.2910	0.2939	0.2967	0.2996	0.3023	0.3051	0.3078	0.3106	0.3133
0.9	0.3159	0.3186	0.3212	0.3238	0.3264	0.3289	0.3315	0.3340	0.3365	0.3389
1.0	0.3413	0.3438	0.3461	0.3485	0.3508	0.3531	0.3554	0.3577	0.3599	0.3621
1.1	0.3643	0.3665	0.3686	0.3708	0.3729	0.3749	0.3770	0.3790	0.3810	0.3830
1.2	0.3849	0.3869	0.3888	0.3907	0.3925	0.3944	0.3962	0.3980	0.3997	0.4015
1.3	0.4032	0.4049	0.4066	0.4082	0.4099	0.4115	0.4131	0.4147	0.4162	0.4177
1.4	0.4192	0.4207	0.4222	0.4236	0.4251	0.4265	0.4279	0.4292	0.4306	0.4319
1.5	0.4332	0.4345	0.4357	0.4370	0.4382	0.4394	0.4406	0.4418	0.4429	0.4441
1.6	0.4452	0.4463	0.4474	0.4484	0.4495	0.4505	0.4515	0.4525	0.4535	0.4545
1.7	0.4554	0.4564	0.4573	0.4582	0.4591	0.4599	0.4608	0.4616	0.4625	0.4633
1.8	0.4641	0.4649	0.4656	0.4664	0.4671	0.4678	0.4686	0.4693	0.4699	0.4706
1.9	0.4713	0.4719	0.4726	0.4732	0.4738	0.4744	0.4750	0.4756	0.4761	0.4767
2.0	0.4772	0.4778	0.4783	0.4788	0.4793	0.4798	0.4803	0.4808	0.4812	0.4817
2.1	0.4821	0.4826	0.4830	0.4834	0.4838	0.4842	0.4846	0.4850	0.4854	0.4857
2.2	0.4861	0.4864	0.4868	0.4871	0.4875	0.4878	0.4881	0.4884	0.4887	0.4890
2.3	0.4893	0.4896	0.4898	0.4901	0.4904	0.4906	0.4909	0.4911	0.4913	0.4916
2.4	0.4918	0.4920	0.4922	0.4925	0.4927	0.4929	0.4931	0.4932	0.4934	0.4936
2.5	0.4938	0.4940	0.4941	0.4943	0.4945	0.4946	0.4948	0.4949	0.4951	0.4952
2.6	0.4953	0.4955	0.4956	0.4957	0.4959	0.4960	0.4961	0.4962	0.4963	0.4964
2.7	0.4965	0.4966	0.4967	0.4968	0.4969	0.4970	0.4971	0.4972	0.4973	0.4974
2.8	0.4974	0.4975	0.4976	0.4977	0.4977	0.4978	0.4979	0.4979	0.4980	0.4981
2.9	0.4981	0.4982	0.4982	0.4983	0.4984	0.4984	0.4985	0.4985	0.4986	0.4986
3.0	0.4987	0.4987	0.4987	0.4988	0.4988	0.4989	0.4989	0.4989	0.4990	0.4990
3.1	0.4990	0.4991	0.4991	0.4991	0.4992	0.4992	0.4992	0.4992	0.4992	0.4993
3.2	0.4993	0.4993	0.4994	0.4994	0.4994	0.4994	0.4994	0.4995	0.4995	0.4995
3.3	0.4995	0.4995	0.4995	0.4996	0.4996	0.4996	0.4996	0.4996	0.4996	0.4997
3.4	0.4997	0.4997	0.4997	0.4997	0.4997	0.4997	0.4997	0.4997	0.4997	0.4998
3.5	0.4998	0.4998	0.4998	0.4998	0.4998	0.4998	0.4998	0.4998	0.4998	0.4998
3.6	0.4998	0.4998	0.4999	0.4999	0.4999	0.4999	0.4999	0.4999	0.4999	0.4999
3.7	0.4999	0.4999	0.4999	0.4999	0.4999	0.4999	0.4999	0.4999	0.4999	0.4999
3.8	0.4999	0.4999	0.4999	0.4999	0.4999	0.4999	0.4999	0.4999	0.4999	0.4999
3.9	0.5000	0.5000	0.5000	0.5000	0.5000	0.5000	0.5000	0.5000	0.5000	0.5000

Note: Proportion of area from the mean (0) to z

APPENDIX 3: TWO-TAILED 0.05 VALUES OF *F*

					df_1				
df_2	1	2	3	4	5	6	7	8	9
1	161.45	199.50	215.71	224.58	230.16	233.99	236.77	238.88	240.54
2	18.513	19.000	19.164	19.247	19.296	19.330	19.353	19.371	19.385
3	10.128	9.5521	9.2766	9.1172	9.0135	8.9406	8.8867	8.8452	8.8323
4	7.7086	6.9443	6.5914	6.3882	6.2561	6.1631	6.0942	6.0410	5.9938
5	6.6079	5.7861	5.4095	5.1922	5.0503	4.9503	4.8759	4.8183	4.7725
6	5.9874	5.1433	4.7571	4.5337	4.3874	4.2839	4.2067	4.1468	4.0990
7	5.5914	4.7374	4.3468	4.1203	3.9715	3.8660	3.7870	3.7257	3.6767
8	5.3177	4.4590	4.0662	3.8379	3.6875	3.5806	3.5005	3.4381	3.3881
9	5.1174	4.2565	3.8625	3.6331	3.4817	3.3738	3.2927	3.2296	3.1789
10	4.9646	4.1028	3.7083	3.4780	3.3258	3.2172	3.1355	3.0717	3.0204
11	4.8443	3.9823	3.5874	3.3567	3.2039	3.0946	3.0123	2.9480	2.8962
12	4.7472	3.8853	3.4903	3.2592	3.1059	2.9961	2.9134	2.8486	2.7964
13	4.6672	3.8056	3.4105	3.1791	3.0254	2.9153	2.8321	2.7669	2.7444
14	4.6001	3.7389	3.3439	3.1122	2.9582	2.8477	2.7642	2.6987	2.6458
15	4.5431	3.6823	3.2874	3.0556	2.9013	2.7905	2.7066	2.6408	2.5876
16	4.4940	3.6337	3.2389	3.0069	2.8524	2.7413	2.6572	2.5911	2.5377
17	4.4513	3.5915	3.1968	2.9647	2.8100	2.6987	2.6143	2.5480	2.4443
18	4.4139	3.5546	3.1599	2.9277	2.7729	2.6613	2.5767	2.5102	2.4563
19	4.3807	3.5219	3.1274	2.8951	2.7401	2.6283	2.5435	2.4768	2.4227
20	4.3512	3.4928	3.0984	2.8661	2.7109	2.5990	2.5140	2.4471	2.3928
21	4.3248	3.4668	3.0725	2.8401	2.6848	2.5727	2.4876	2.4205	2.3660
22	4.3009	3.4434	3.0491	2.8167	2.6613	2.5491	2.4638	2.3965	2.3219
23	4.2793	3.4221	3.0280	2.7955	2.6400	2.5277	2.4422	2.3748	2.3201
24	4.2597	3.4028	3.0088	2.7763	2.6207	2.5082	2.4226	2.3551	2.3002
25	4.2417	3.3852	2.9912	2.7587	2.6030	2.4904	2.4047	2.3371	2.2821
26	4.2252	3.3690	2.9752	2.7426	2.5868	2.4741	2.3883	2.3205	2.2655
27	4.2100	3.3541	2.9604	2.7278	2.5719	2.4591	2.3732	2.3053	2.2501
28	4.1960	3.3404	2.9467	2.7141	2.5581	2.4453	2.3593	2.2913	2.2360
29	4.1830	3.3277	2.9340	2.7014	2.5454	2.4324	2.3463	2.2783	2.2329
30	4.1709	3.3158	2.9223	2.6896	2.5336	2.4205	2.3343	2.2662	2.2507
40	4.0847	3.2317	2.8387	2.6060	2.4495	2.3359	2.2490	2.1802	2.1240
60	4.0012	3.1504	2.7581	2.5252	2.3683	2.2541	2.1665	2.0970	2.0401
120	3.9201	3.0718	2.6802	2.4472	2.2899	2.1750	2.0868	2.0164	1.9688
∞	3.8415	2.9957	2.6049	2.3719	2.2141	2.0986	2.0096	1.9384	1.8799

APPENDIX 3: *continued*

df_1									
10	12	15	20	24	30	40	60	120	∞
241.88	243.91	245.95	248.01	249.05	250.10	251.14	252.20	253.25	254.31
19.396	19.413	19.429	19.446	19.454	19.462	19.471	19.479	19.487	19.496
8.7855	8.7446	8.7029	8.6602	8.6385	8.6166	8.5944	8.5720	8.5594	8.5264
5.9644	5.9117	5.8578	5.8025	5.7744	5.7459	5.7170	5.6877	5.6381	5.6281
4.7351	4.6777	4.6188	4.5581	4.5272	4.4957	4.4638	4.4314	4.3085	4.3650
4.0600	3.9999	3.9381	3.8742	3.8415	3.8082	3.7743	3.7398	3.7047	3.6689
3.6365	3.5747	3.5107	3.4445	3.4105	3.3758	3.3404	3.3043	3.2674	3.2298
3.3472	3.2839	3.2184	3.1503	3.1152	3.0794	3.0428	3.0053	2.9669	2.9276
3.1373	3.0729	3.0061	2.9365	2.9005	2.8637	2.8259	2.7872	2.7475	2.7067
2.9782	2.9130	2.8450	2.7740	2.7372	2.6996	2.6609	2.6211	2.5801	2.5379
2.8536	2.7876	2.7186	2.6464	2.6090	2.5705	2.5309	2.4901	2.4480	2.4045
2.7534	2.6866	2.6169	2.5436	2.5055	2.4663	2.4259	2.3842	2.3410	2.2962
2.6710	2.6037	2.5331	2.4589	2.4202	2.3803	2.3392	2.2966	2.2524	2.2064
2.6022	2.5342	2.4630	2.3879	2.3487	2.3082	2.2664	2.2229	2.1778	2.1307
2.5437	2.4753	2.4034	2.3275	2.2878	2.2468	2.2043	2.1601	2.1141	2.0658
2.4935	2.4247	2.3522	2.2756	2.2354	2.1938	2.1507	2.1058	2.0589	2.0096
2.4499	2.3807	2.3077	2.2304	2.1898	2.1477	2.1040	2.0584	2.0107	1.9604
2.4117	2.3421	2.2686	2.1906	2.1497	2.1071	2.0629	2.0166	1.9681	1.9168
2.3779	2.3080	2.2341	2.1555	2.1141	2.0712	2.0264	1.9795	1.9302	1.8780
2.3479	2.2776	2.2033	2.1242	2.0825	2.0391	1.9938	1.9464	1.8963	1.8432
2.3210	2.2504	2.1757	2.0960	2.0540	2.0102	1.9645	1.9165	1.8657	1.8117
2.2967	2.2258	2.1508	2.0707	2.0283	1.9842	1.9380	1.8894	1.8380	1.7831
2.2747	2.2036	2.1282	2.0476	2.0050	1.9605	1.9139	1.8648	1.8128	1.7570
2.2547	2.1834	2.1077	2.0267	1.9838	1.9390	1.8920	1.8424	1.7896	1.7330
2.2365	2.1649	2.0889	2.0075	1.9643	1.9192	1.8718	1.8217	1.7684	1.7110
2.2197	2.1479	2.0716	1.9898	1.9464	1.9010	1.8533	1.8027	1.7488	1.6906
2.2043	2.1323	2.0558	1.9736	1.9299	1.8842	1.8361	1.7851	1.7306	1.6717
2.1900	2.1179	2.0411	1.9586	1.9147	1.8687	1.8203	1.7689	1.7138	1.6541
2.1768	2.1045	2.0275	1.9446	1.9005	1.8543	1.8055	1.7537	1.6981	1.6376
2.1646	2.0921	2.0148	1.9317	1.8874	1.8409	1.7918	1.7396	1.6835	1.6223
2.0772	2.0035	1.9245	1.8389	1.7929	1.7444	1.6928	1.6373	1.5766	1.5089
1.9926	1.9174	1.8364	1.7480	1.7001	1.6491	1.5943	1.5343	1.4673	1.3893
1.9105	1.8337	1.7505	1.6587	1.6084	1.5543	1.4952	1.4290	1.3519	1.2539
1.8307	1.7522	1.6664	1.5705	1.5173	1.4591	1.3940	1.3180	1.0214	1.0000

Notes: df_1 are the degrees of freedom for the numerator; df_2 are the degrees of freedom for the denominator

APPENDIX 4: TWO-TAILED CRITICAL VALUES OF *t*

df	Significance level		
	0.10	*0.05*	*0.02*
1	6.314	12.706	31.821
2	2.920	4.303	6.965
3	2.353	3.182	4.541
4	2.132	2.776	3.747
5	2.015	2.571	3.365
6	1.943	2.447	3.143
7	1.895	2.365	2.998
8	1.860	2.306	2.896
9	1.833	2.262	2.821
10	1.812	2.228	2.764
11	1.796	2.201	2.718
12	1.782	2.179	2.681
13	1.771	2.160	2.650
14	1.761	2.145	2.624
15	1.753	2.131	2.602
16	1.746	2.120	2.583
17	1.740	2.110	2.567
18	1.734	2.101	2.552
19	1.729	2.093	2.539
20	1.725	2.086	2.528
21	1.721	2.080	2.518
22	1.717	2.074	2.508
23	1.714	2.069	2.500
24	1.711	2.064	2.492
25	1.708	2.060	2.485
26	1.706	2.056	2.479
27	1.703	2.052	2.473
28	1.701	2.048	2.467
29	1.699	2.045	2.462
30	1.697	2.042	2.457
40	1.684	2.021	2.423
60	1.671	2.000	2.390
120	1.658	1.980	2.358
∞	1.645	1.960	2.326

Source: Adapted from Table III of Fisher, R. A. and Yates, F. (1974) *Statistical Tables for Biological, Agricultural and Medical Research* (6th edn), Longman, London, by permission of the publishers

APPENDIX 5: TWO-TAILED 0.5 CRITICAL VALUES OF F_{max}

$n-1$	Number of groups										
	2	3	4	5	6	7	8	9	10	11	12
2	39.0	87.5	142	202	266	333	403	475	550	626	704
3	15.4	27.8	39.2	50.7	62.0	72.9	83.5	93.9	104	114	124
4	9.60	15.5	20.6	25.2	29.5	33.6	37.5	41.4	44.6	48.0	51.4
5	7.15	10.8	13.7	16.3	18.7	20.8	22.9	24.7	26.5	28.2	29.9
6	5.82	8.38	10.4	12.1	13.7	15.0	16.3	17.5	18.6	19.7	20.7
7	4.99	6.94	8.44	9.70	10.8	11.8	12.7	13.5	14.3	15.1	15.8
8	4.43	6.00	7.18	8.12	9.03	9.78	10.5	11.1	11.7	12.2	12.7
9	4.03	5.34	6.31	7.11	7.80	8.41	8.95	9.45	9.91	10.3	10.7
10	3.72	4.85	5.67	6.34	6.92	7.42	7.87	8.28	8.66	9.01	9.34
12	3.28	4.16	4.79	5.30	5.72	6.09	6.42	6.72	7.00	7.25	7.48
15	2.86	3.54	4.01	4.37	4.68	4.95	5.19	5.40	5.59	5.77	5.93
20	2.46	2.95	3.29	3.54	3.76	3.94	4.10	4.24	4.37	4.49	4.59
30	2.07	2.40	2.61	2.78	2.91	3.02	3.12	3.21	3.29	3.36	3.39
60	1.67	1.85	1.96	2.04	2.11	2.17	2.22	2.26	2.30	2.33	2.36
∞	1.00	1.00	1.00	1.00	1.00	1.00	1.00	1.00	1.00	1.00	1.00

Source: Adapted from Table 31 of Pearson, E.S. and Hartley, H.O. (1976) Biometrika Tables for Statisticians, vol. 1, 3rd edn, London: Cambridge University Press, by permission of the Biometrika Trustees

APPENDIX 6: TWO-TAILED 0.05 CRITICAL VALUES OF COCHRAN'S C

n−1	Number of groups										
	2	3	4	5	6	7	8	9	10	15	20
1	0.9985	0.9669	0.9065	0.8412	0.7808	0.7271	0.6798	0.6385	0.6020	0.4709	0.3894
2	0.9750	0.8709	0.7679	0.6838	0.6161	0.5612	0.5157	0.4775	0.4450	0.3346	0.2705
3	0.9392	0.7977	0.6841	0.5981	0.5321	0.4800	0.4377	0.4027	0.3733	0.2758	0.2205
4	0.9057	0.7457	0.6287	0.5441	0.4803	0.4307	0.3910	0.3584	0.3311	0.2419	0.1921
5	0.8772	0.7071	0.5895	0.5065	0.4447	0.3974	0.3595	0.3286	0.3029	0.2195	0.1735
6	0.8534	0.6771	0.5598	0.4783	0.4184	0.3726	0.3362	0.3067	0.2823	0.2034	0.1602
7	0.8332	0.6530	0.5365	0.4564	0.3980	0.3535	0.3185	0.2901	0.2666	0.1911	0.1501
8	0.8159	0.6333	0.5175	0.4387	0.3817	0.3384	0.3043	0.2768	0.2541	0.1815	0.1422
9	0.8010	0.6167	0.5017	0.4241	0.3682	0.3259	0.2926	0.2659	0.2439	0.1736	0.1357
16	0.7341	0.5466	0.4366	0.3645	0.3135	0.2756	0.2462	0.2226	0.2032	0.1429	0.1108
36	0.6602	0.4748	0.3720	0.3066	0.2612	0.2278	0.2022	0.1820	0.1655	0.1144	0.0879
144	0.5813	0.4031	0.3093	0.2513	0.2119	0.1833	0.1616	0.1446	0.1308	0.0889	0.0675

Source: Adapted from Eisenhart, C., Hastay, M. W. and Wallis, A. (1947) Techniques of Statistical Analysis, McGraw-Hill, New York, by permission of the publishers

APPENDIX 7: TWO-TAILED CRITICAL VALUES OF PEARSON'S *r*

N−2	Significance level	
	0.10	0.05
1	0.9877	0.9969
2	0.9000	0.9500
3	0.8054	0.8783
4	0.7293	0.8114
5	0.6694	0.7545
6	0.6215	0.7067
7	0.5822	0.6664
8	0.5494	0.6319
9	0.5214	0.6021
10	0.4973	0.5760
11	0.4762	0.5529
12	0.4575	0.5324
13	0.4409	0.5139
14	0.4259	0.4973
15	0.4124	0.4821
16	0.4000	0.4683
17	0.3887	0.4555
18	0.3783	0.4438
19	0.3687	0.4329
20	0.3598	0.4227
25	0.3233	0.3809
30	0.2960	0.3494
35	0.2746	0.3246
40	0.2573	0.3044
45	0.2428	0.2875
50	0.2306	0.2732
60	0.2108	0.2500
70	0.1954	0.2319
80	0.1829	0.2172
90	0.1726	0.2050
100	0.1638	0.1946

Source: Adapted from Table VII of Fisher, R. A. and Yates, F. (1974) *Statistical Tables for Biological, Agricultural and Medical Research* (6th edn), Longman, London, by permission of the publishers

APPENDIX 8: TRANSFORMATION OF PEARSON'S r TO Z_r

r	Z_r	r	Z_r	r	Z_r	r	Z_r	r	Z_r
0.000	0.000	0.200	0.203	0.400	0.424	0.600	0.693	0.800	1.099
0.005	0.005	0.205	0.208	0.405	0.430	0.605	0.701	0.805	1.113
0.010	0.010	0.210	0.213	0.410	0.436	0.610	0.709	0.810	1.127
0.015	0.015	0.215	0.218	0.415	0.442	0.615	0.717	0.815	1.142
0.020	0.020	0.220	0.224	0.420	0.448	0.620	0.725	0.820	1.157
0.025	0.025	0.225	0.229	0.425	0.454	0.625	0.733	0.825	1.172
0.030	0.030	0.230	0.234	0.430	0.460	0.630	0.741	0.830	1.188
0.035	0.035	0.235	0.239	0.435	0.466	0.635	0.750	0.835	1.204
0.040	0.040	0.240	0.245	0.440	0.472	0.640	0.758	0.840	1.221
0.045	0.045	0.245	0.250	0.445	0.478	0.645	0.767	0.845	1.238
0.050	0.050	0.250	0.255	0.450	0.485	0.650	0.775	0.850	1.256
0.055	0.055	0.255	0.261	0.455	0.491	0.655	0.784	0.855	1.274
0.060	0.060	0.260	0.266	0.460	0.497	0.660	0.793	0.860	1.293
0.065	0.065	0.265	0.271	0.465	0.504	0.665	0.802	0.865	1.313
0.070	0.070	0.270	0.277	0.470	0.510	0.670	0.811	0.870	1.333
0.075	0.075	0.275	0.282	0.475	0.517	0.675	0.820	0.875	1.354
0.080	0.080	0.280	0.288	0.480	0.523	0.680	0.829	0.880	1.376
0.085	0.085	0.285	0.293	0.485	0.530	0.685	0.838	0.885	1.398
0.090	0.090	0.290	0.299	0.490	0.536	0.690	0.848	0.890	1.422
0.095	0.095	0.295	0.304	0.495	0.543	0.695	0.858	0.895	1.447
0.100	0.100	0.300	0.310	0.500	0.549	0.700	0.867	0.900	1.472
0.105	0.105	0.305	0.315	0.505	0.556	0.705	0.877	0.905	1.499
0.110	0.110	0.310	0.321	0.510	0.563	0.710	0.887	0.910	1.528
0.115	0.116	0.315	0.326	0.515	0.570	0.715	0.897	0.915	1.557
0.120	0.121	0.320	0.332	0.520	0.576	0.720	0.908	0.920	1.589
0.125	0.126	0.325	0.337	0.525	0.583	0.725	0.918	0.925	1.623
0.130	0.131	0.330	0.343	0.530	0.590	0.730	0.929	0.930	1.658
0.135	0.136	0.335	0.348	0.535	0.597	0.735	0.940	0.935	1.697
0.140	0.141	0.340	0.354	0.540	0.604	0.740	0.950	0.940	1.738
0.145	0.146	0.345	0.360	0.545	0.611	0.745	0.962	0.945	1.783
0.150	0.151	0.350	0.365	0.550	0.618	0.750	0.973	0.950	1.832
0.155	0.156	0.355	0.371	0.555	0.626	0.755	0.984	0.955	1.886
0.160	0.161	0.360	0.377	0.560	0.633	0.760	0.996	0.960	1.946
0.165	0.167	0.365	0.383	0.565	0.640	0.765	1.008	0.965	2.014
0.170	0.172	0.370	0.388	0.570	0.648	0.770	1.020	0.970	2.092
0.175	0.177	0.375	0.394	0.575	0.655	0.775	1.033	0.975	2.185
0.180	0.182	0.380	0.400	0.580	0.662	0.780	1.045	0.980	2.298
0.185	0.187	0.385	0.406	0.585	0.670	0.785	1.058	0.985	2.443
0.190	0.192	0.390	0.412	0.590	0.678	0.790	1.071	0.990	2.647
0.195	0.198	0.395	0.418	0.595	0.685	0.795	1.085	0.995	2.994

Source: Adapted from Edwards, A. L. (1967) *Statistical Methods* (2nd edn), Holt, Rinehart & Winston, New York, by permission of the publishers

APPENDIX 9: TWO-TAILED 0.05 CRITICAL VALUES OF THE BRYANT-PAULSON PROCEDURE

Error df	Number of covariates	Number of groups										
		2	3	4	5	6	7	8	10	12	16	20
3	1	5.42	7.18	8.32	9.17	9.84	10.39	10.86	11.62	12.22	13.14	13.83
	2	6.21	8.27	9.60	10.59	11.37	12.01	12.56	13.44	14.15	15.22	16.02
	3	6.92	9.23	10.73	11.84	12.72	13.44	14.06	15.05	15.84	17.05	17.95
4	1	4.51	5.84	6.69	7.32	7.82	8.23	8.58	9.15	9.61	10.30	10.82
	2	5.04	6.54	7.51	8.23	8.80	9.26	9.66	10.31	10.83	11.61	12.21
	3	5.51	7.18	8.25	9.05	9.67	10.19	10.63	11.35	11.92	12.79	13.45
5	1	4.06	5.17	5.88	6.40	6.82	7.16	7.45	7.93	8.30	8.88	9.32
	2	4.45	5.68	6.48	7.06	7.52	7.90	8.23	8.76	9.18	9.83	10.31
	3	4.81	6.16	7.02	7.66	8.17	8.58	8.94	9.52	9.98	10.69	11.22
6	1	3.79	4.78	5.40	5.86	6.23	6.53	6.78	7.20	7.53	8.04	8.43
	2	4.10	5.18	5.87	6.37	6.77	7.10	7.38	7.84	8.21	8.77	9.20
	3	4.38	5.55	6.30	6.84	7.28	7.64	7.94	8.44	8.83	9.44	9.90
7	1	3.62	4.52	5.09	5.51	5.84	6.11	6.34	6.72	7.03	7.49	7.84
	2	3.87	4.85	5.47	5.92	6.28	6.58	6.83	7.24	7.57	8.08	8.46
	3	4.11	5.16	5.82	6.31	6.70	7.01	7.29	7.73	8.08	8.63	9.03
8	1	3.49	4.34	4.87	5.26	5.57	5.82	6.03	6.39	6.67	7.10	7.43
	2	3.70	4.61	5.19	5.61	5.94	6.21	6.44	6.82	7.12	7.59	7.94
	3	3.91	4.88	5.49	5.93	6.29	6.58	6.83	7.23	7.55	8.05	8.42
10	1	3.32	4.10	4.58	4.93	5.21	5.43	5.63	5.94	6.19	6.58	6.87
	2	3.49	4.31	4.82	5.19	5.49	5.73	5.93	6.27	6.54	6.95	7.26
	3	3.65	4.51	5.05	5.44	5.75	6.01	6.22	6.58	6.86	7.29	7.62
12	1	3.22	3.95	4.40	4.73	4.98	5.19	5.37	5.67	5.90	6.26	6.53
	2	3.35	4.12	4.59	4.93	5.20	5.43	5.62	5.92	6.17	6.55	6.83
	3	3.48	4.28	4.78	5.14	5.42	5.65	5.85	6.17	6.43	6.82	7.12
14	1	3.15	3.85	4.28	4.59	4.83	5.03	5.20	5.48	5.70	6.03	6.29
	2	3.26	3.99	4.44	4.76	5.01	5.22	5.40	5.69	5.92	6.27	6.54

APPENDIX 9: continued

Error df	Number of covariates	Number of groups										
		2	3	4	5	6	7	8	10	12	16	20
	3	3.37	4.13	4.59	4.93	5.19	5.41	5.59	5.89	6.13	6.50	6.78
16	1	3.10	3.77	4.19	4.49	4.72	4.91	5.07	5.34	5.55	5.87	6.12
	2	3.19	3.90	4.32	4.63	4.88	5.07	5.24	5.52	5.74	6.07	6.33
	3	3.29	4.01	4.46	4.78	5.03	5.23	5.41	5.69	5.92	6.27	6.53
18	1	3.06	3.72	4.12	4.41	4.63	4.82	4.98	5.23	5.44	5.75	5.98
	2	3.14	3.82	4.24	4.54	4.77	4.96	5.13	5.39	5.60	5.92	6.17
	3	3.23	3.93	4.35	4.66	4.90	5.10	5.27	5.54	5.76	6.09	6.34
20	1	3.03	3.67	4.07	4.35	4.57	4.75	4.90	5.15	5.35	5.65	5.88
	2	3.10	3.77	4.17	4.46	4.69	4.88	5.03	5.29	5.49	5.81	6.04
	3	3.18	3.86	4.28	4.57	4.81	5.00	5.16	5.42	5.63	5.96	6.20
24	1	2.98	3.61	3.99	4.26	4.47	4.65	4.79	5.03	5.22	5.51	5.73
	2	3.04	3.69	4.08	4.35	4.57	4.75	4.90	5.14	5.34	5.63	5.86
	3	3.11	3.76	4.16	4.44	4.67	4.85	5.00	5.25	5.45	5.75	5.98
30	1	2.94	3.55	3.91	4.18	4.38	4.54	4.69	4.91	5.09	5.37	5.58
	2	2.99	3.61	3.98	4.25	4.46	4.62	4.77	5.00	5.18	5.46	5.68
	3	3.04	3.67	4.05	4.32	4.53	4.70	4.85	5.08	5.27	5.56	5.78
40	1	2.89	3.49	3.84	4.09	4.29	4.45	4.58	4.80	4.97	5.23	5.43
	2	2.93	3.53	3.89	4.15	4.34	4.50	4.64	4.86	5.04	5.30	5.50
	3	2.97	3.57	3.94	4.20	4.40	4.56	4.70	4.92	5.10	5.37	5.57
60	1	2.85	3.43	3.77	4.01	4.20	4.35	4.48	4.69	4.85	5.10	5.29
	2	2.88	3.46	3.80	4.05	4.24	4.39	4.52	4.73	4.89	5.14	5.33
	3	2.90	3.49	3.83	4.08	4.27	4.43	4.56	4.77	4.93	5.19	5.38
120	1	2.81	3.37	3.70	3.93	4.11	4.26	4.38	4.58	4.73	4.97	5.15
	2	2.82	3.38	3.72	3.95	4.13	4.28	4.40	4.60	4.75	4.99	5.17
	3	2.84	3.40	3.73	3.97	4.15	4.30	4.42	4.62	4.77	5.01	5.19

Source: Adapted from Bryant, J. L. and Paulson, A. S. (1976) 'An extension of Tukey's method of multiple comparisons to experimental designs with random concomitant variables', Biometrika 63, 631–8, by permission of the Biometrika Trustees

APPENDIX 10: ONE-TAILED PROBABILITIES OF SMALL OBSERVED VALUES IN THE BINOMIAL TEST

N	n															
	0	1	2	3	4	5	6	7	8	9	10	11	12	13	14	15
1	0.500															
2	0.250	0.750														
3	0.125	0.500	0.875													
4	0.062	0.312	0.687	0.937												
5	0.031	0.188	0.500	0.812	0.969	*										
6	0.016	0.109	0.344	0.656	0.891	0.984	*									
7	0.008	0.062	0.227	0.500	0.773	0.938	0.992	*								
8	0.004	0.035	0.145	0.363	0.637	0.855	0.965	0.996	*							
9	0.002	0.020	0.090	0.254	0.500	0.746	0.910	0.980	0.998	*						
10	0.001	0.011	0.055	0.172	0.377	0.623	0.828	0.945	0.989	0.999	*					
11		0.006	0.033	0.113	0.274	0.500	0.726	0.887	0.967	0.994	*	*				
12		0.003	0.019	0.073	0.194	0.387	0.613	0.806	0.927	0.981	0.997	*	*			
13		0.002	0.011	0.046	0.133	0.291	0.500	0.709	0.867	0.954	0.989	0.998	*	*		
14		0.001	0.006	0.029	0.090	0.212	0.395	0.605	0.788	0.910	0.971	0.994	0.999	*	*	
15			0.004	0.018	0.059	0.151	0.304	0.500	0.696	0.849	0.941	0.982	0.996	*	*	*
16			0.002	0.011	0.038	0.105	0.227	0.402	0.598	0.773	0.895	0.962	0.989	0.998	*	*
17			0.001	0.006	0.025	0.072	0.166	0.315	0.500	0.685	0.834	0.928	0.975	0.994	0.999	*
18			0.001	0.004	0.015	0.048	0.119	0.240	0.407	0.593	0.760	0.881	0.952	0.985	0.996	0.999
19				0.002	0.010	0.032	0.084	0.180	0.324	0.500	0.676	0.820	0.916	0.968	0.990	0.998
20				0.001	0.006	0.021	0.058	0.132	0.252	0.412	0.588	0.748	0.868	0.942	0.979	0.994
21				0.001	0.004	0.013	0.039	0.095	0.192	0.332	0.500	0.668	0.808	0.905	0.961	0.987
22					0.002	0.008	0.026	0.067	0.143	0.262	0.416	0.584	0.738	0.857	0.933	0.974
23					0.001	0.005	0.017	0.047	0.105	0.202	0.339	0.500	0.661	0.798	0.895	0.953
24					0.001	0.003	0.011	0.032	0.076	0.154	0.271	0.419	0.581	0.729	0.846	0.924
25						0.002	0.007	0.022	0.054	0.115	0.212	0.345	0.500	0.655	0.788	0.885

Source: Adapted from Table IV, B of Walker, H. and Lev, J. (1953) *Statistical Inference*, New York: Holt, Rinehart & Winston, by permission of the publishers

APPENDIX 11: TWO-TAILED CRITICAL VALUES OF CHI-SQUARE

df	Level of significance		
	0.10	*0.05*	*0.01*
1	2.71	3.84	6.64
2	4.60	5.99	9.21
3	6.25	7.82	11.34
4	7.78	9.49	13.28
5	9.24	11.07	15.09
6	10.64	12.59	16.81
7	12.02	14.07	18.48
8	13.36	15.51	20.09
9	14.68	16.92	21.67
10	15.99	18.31	23.21
11	17.28	19.68	24.72
12	18.55	21.03	26.22
13	19.81	22.36	27.69
14	21.06	23.68	29.14
15	22.31	25.00	30.58
16	23.54	26.30	32.00
17	24.77	27.59	33.41
18	25.99	28.87	34.80
19	27.20	30.14	36.19
20	28.41	31.41	37.57
21	29.62	32.67	38.93
22	30.81	33.92	40.29
23	32.01	35.17	41.64
24	33.20	36.42	42.98
25	34.38	37.65	44.31
26	35.56	38.88	45.64
27	36.74	40.11	46.96
28	37.92	41.34	48.28
29	39.09	42.69	49.59
30	40.26	43.77	50.89

Source: Adapted from Table IV of Fisher, R.A. and Yates, F. (1974) *Statistical Tables for Biological, Agricultural and Medical Research*, 6th edn, London: Longman, by permission of the publishers

APPENDIX 12: 0.05 CRITICAL VALUES OF THE DUNN MULTIPLE COMPARISON TEST

No. of comparisons	df											
	5	7	10	12	15	20	24	30	40	60	120	∞
2	3.17	2.84	2.64	2.56	2.49	2.42	2.39	2.36	2.33	2.30	2.27	2.24
3	3.54	3.13	2.87	2.78	2.69	2.61	2.58	2.54	2.50	2.47	2.43	2.39
4	3.81	3.34	3.04	2.94	2.84	2.75	2.70	2.66	2.62	2.58	2.54	2.50
5	4.04	3.50	3.17	3.06	2.95	2.85	2.80	2.75	2.71	2.66	2.62	2.58
6	4.22	3.64	3.28	3.15	3.04	2.93	2.88	2.83	2.78	2.73	2.68	2.64
7	4.38	3.76	3.37	3.24	3.11	3.00	2.94	2.89	2.84	2.79	2.74	2.69
8	4.53	3.86	3.45	3.31	3.18	3.06	3.00	2.94	2.89	2.84	2.79	2.74
9	4.66	3.95	3.52	3.37	3.24	3.11	3.05	2.99	2.93	2.88	2.83	2.77
10	4.78	4.03	3.58	3.43	3.29	3.16	3.09	3.03	2.97	2.92	2.86	2.81
15	5.25	4.36	3.83	3.65	3.48	3.33	3.26	3.19	3.12	3.06	2.99	2.94
20	5.60	4.59	4.01	3.80	3.62	3.46	3.38	3.30	3.23	3.16	3.09	3.02
25	5.89	4.78	4.15	3.93	3.74	3.55	3.47	3.39	3.31	3.24	3.16	3.09
30	6.15	4.95	4.27	4.04	3.82	3.63	3.54	3.46	3.38	3.30	3.22	3.15
35	6.36	5.09	4.37	4.13	3.90	3.70	3.61	3.52	3.43	3.34	3.27	3.19
40	6.56	5.21	4.45	4.20	3.97	3.76	3.66	3.57	3.48	3.39	3.31	3.23
45	6.70	5.31	4.53	4.26	4.02	3.80	3.70	3.61	3.51	3.42	3.34	3.26
50	6.86	5.40	4.59	4.32	4.07	3.85	3.74	3.65	3.55	3.46	3.37	3.29
100	8.00	6.08	5.06	4.73	4.42	4.15	4.04	3.90	3.79	3.69	3.58	3.48
250	9.68	7.06	5.70	5.27	4.90	4.56	4.4*	4.2*	4.1*	3.97	3.83	3.72

* Obtained by graphical interpolation

Source: Adapted from Table 1 of Dunn, O. J. (1961) 'Multiple comparisons among means', American Statistical Association Journal 56: 52–64

APPENDIX 13: ONE-TAILED 0.05 CRITICAL VALUES OF *d* (OR *c*) IN FISHER'S TEST WHEN FREQUENCIES OF *b* (OR *a*) ARE ENTERED

Row totals		Cells		Row totals		Cells	
		b	*d*			*b*	*d*
a + *b*	*c* + *d*	(or *a*)	(or *c*)	*a* + *b*	*c* + *d*	(or *a*)	(or *c*)
3	3	3	0	8	8	8	4
						7	2
4	4	4	0			6	1
	3	4	0			5	0
						4	0
5	5	5	1		7	8	3
		4	0			7	2
	4	5	1			6	1
		4	0			5	0
	3	5	0		6	8	2
	2	5	0			7	1
						6	0
6	6	6	2			5	0
		5	1		5	8	2
		4	0			7	1
	5	6	1			6	0
		5	0			5	0
		4	0		4	8	1
	4	6	1			7	0
		5	0			6	0
	3	6	0		3	8	0
		5	0			7	0
	2	6	0		2	8	0
7	7	7	3	9	9	9	5
		6	1			8	3
		5	0			7	2
		4	0			6	1
	6	7	2			5	0
		6	1			4	0
		5	0		8	9	4
		4	0			8	3
	5	7	2			7	2
		6	1			6	1
		5	0			5	0
	4	7	1		7	9	3
		6	0			8	2
		5	0			7	1
	3	7	0			6	0
		6	0			5	0
	2	7	0				

Row totals		Cells		Row totals		Cells	
		b	d			b	d
a + b	c + d	(or a)	(or c)	a + b	c + d	(or a)	(or c)
9	6	9	3	10	6	10	3
		8	2			9	2
		7	1			8	1
		6	0			7	0
		5	0			6	0
	5	9	2		5	10	2
		8	1			9	1
		7	0			8	1
		6	0			7	0
	4	9	1			6	0
		8	0		4	10	1
		7	0			9	1
		6	0			8	0
	3	9	1			7	0
		8	0		3	10	1
		7	0			9	0
	2	9	0			8	0
					2	10	0
						9	0
10	10	10	6				
		9	4	11	11	11	7
		8	3			10	5
		7	2			9	4
		6	1			8	3
		5	0			7	2
		4	0			6	1
	9	10	5			5	0
		9	4			4	0
		8	2		10	11	6
		7	1			10	4
		6	1			9	3
		5	0			8	2
	8	10	4			7	1
		9	3			6	1
		8	2			5	0
		7	1		9	11	5
		6	0			10	4
		5	0			9	3
	7	10	3			8	2
		9	2			7	1
		8	1			6	0
		7	1			5	0
		6	0				
		5	0				

Row totals		Cells		Row totals		Cells	
		b	d			b	d
a + b	c + d	(or a)	(or c)	a + b	c + d	(or a)	(or c)
11	8	11	4	12	11	12	7
		10	3			11	5
		9	2			10	4
		8	1			9	3
		7	1			8	2
		6	0			7	1
		5	0			6	1
	7	11	4			5	0
		10	3		10	12	6
		9	2			11	5
		8	1			10	4
		7	0			9	3
		6	0			8	2
	6	11	3			7	1
		10	2			6	0
		9	1			5	0
		8	1		9	12	5
		7	0			11	4
		6	0			10	3
	5	11	2			9	2
		10	1			8	1
		9	1			7	1
		8	0			6	0
		7	0			5	0
	4	11	1		8	12	5
		10	1			11	3
		9	0			10	2
		8	0			9	2
	3	11	1			8	1
		10	0			7	0
		9	0			6	0
	2	11	0		7	12	4
		10	0			11	3
						10	2
12	12	12	8			9	1
		11	6			8	1
		10	5			7	0
		9	4			6	0
		8	3				
		7	2				
		6	1				
		5	0				
		4	0				

Row totals		Cells		Row totals		Cells	
		b	d			b	d
a + b	c + d	(or a)	(or c)	a + b	c + d	(or a)	(or c)
12	6	12	3	13	11	13	7
		11	2			12	6
		10	1			11	4
		9	1			10	3
		8	0			9	3
		7	0			8	2
		6	0			7	1
	5	12	2			6	0
		11	1			5	0
		10	1		10	13	6
		9	0			12	5
		8	0			11	4
		7	0			10	3
	4	12	2			9	2
		11	1			8	1
		10	0			7	1
		9	0			6	0
		8	0			5	0
	3	12	1		9	13	5
		11	0			12	4
		10	0			11	3
		9	0			10	2
	2	12	0			9	2
		11	0			8	1
13	13	13	9			7	0
		12	7			6	0
		11	6			5	0
		10	4		8	13	5
		9	3			12	4
		8	2			11	3
		7	2			10	2
		6	1			9	1
		5	0			8	1
		4	0			7	0
	12	13	8			6	0
		12	6		7	13	4
		11	5			12	3
		10	4			11	2
		9	3			10	1
		8	2			9	1
		7	1			8	0
		6	1			7	0
		5	0			6	0

Row totals		Cells	
		b	*d*
a + b	*c + d*	*(or a)*	*(or c)*
13	6	13	3
		12	2
		11	2
		10	1
		9	1
		8	0
		7	0
	5	13	2
		12	2
		11	1
		10	1
		9	0
		8	0
	4	13	2
		12	1
		11	0
		10	0
		9	0
	3	13	1
		12	0
		11	0
		10	0
	2	13	0
		12	0
14	14	14	10
		13	8
		12	6
		11	5
		10	4
		9	3
		8	2
		7	1
		6	1
		5	0
		4	0

Row totals		Cells	
		b	*d*
a + b	*c + d*	*(or a)*	*(or c)*
14	13	14	9
		13	7
		12	6
		11	5
		10	4
		9	3
		8	2
		7	1
		6	1
		5	0
	12	14	8
		13	6
		12	5
		11	4
		10	3
		9	2
		8	2
		7	1
		6	0
		5	0
	11	14	7
		13	6
		12	5
		11	4
		10	3
		9	2
		8	1
		7	1
		6	0
		5	0
	10	14	6
		13	5
		12	4
		11	3
		10	2
		9	2
		8	1
		7	0
		6	0
		5	0

Row totals		Cells		Row totals		Cells	
		b	*d*			*b*	*d*
a + b	*c + d*	*(or a)*	*(or c)*	*a + b*	*c + d*	*(or a)*	*(or c)*
14	9	14	6	14	4	14	2
		13	4			13	1
		12	3			12	1
		11	3			11	0
		10	2			10	0
		9	1			9	0
		8	1		3	14	1
		7	0			13	0
		6	0			12	0
	8	14	5			11	0
		13	4		2	14	0
		12	3			13	0
		11	2			12	0
		10	2				
		9	1	15	15	15	11
		8	0			14	9
		7	0			13	7
		6	0			12	6
	7	14	4			11	5
		13	3			10	4
		12	2			9	3
		11	2			8	2
		10	1			7	1
		9	1			6	1
		8	0			5	0
		7	0			4	0
	6	14	3		14	15	10
		13	2			14	8
		12	2			13	7
		11	1			12	6
		10	1			11	5
		9	0			10	4
		8	0			9	3
		7	0			8	2
	5	14	2			7	1
		13	2			6	1
		12	1			5	0
		11	1				
		10	0				
		9	0				
		8	0				

Row totals		Cells		Row totals		Cells	
		b	d			b	d
a + b	c + d	(or a)	(or c)	a + b	c + d	(or a)	(or c)
15	13	15	9	15	9	15	6
		14	7			14	5
		13	6			13	4
		12	5			12	3
		11	4			11	2
		10	3			10	2
		9	2			9	1
		8	2			8	1
		7	1			7	0
		6	0			6	0
		5	0		8	15	5
	12	15	8			14	4
		14	7			13	3
		13	6			12	2
		12	5			11	2
		11	4			10	1
		10	3			9	1
		9	2			8	0
		8	1			7	0
		7	1			6	0
		6	0		7	15	4
		5	0			14	3
	11	15	7			13	2
		14	6			12	2
		13	5			11	1
		12	4			10	1
		11	3			9	0
		10	2			8	0
		9	2			7	0
		8	1		6	15	3
		7	1			14	2
		6	0			13	2
		5	0			12	1
	10	15	6			11	1
		14	5			10	0
		13	4			9	0
		12	3			8	0
		11	3		5	15	2
		10	2			14	2
		9	1			13	1
		8	1			12	1
		7	0			11	0
		6	0			10	0
						9	0

Row totals		Cells	
		b	d
a + b	c + d	(or a)	(or c)
15	4	15	2
		14	1
		13	1
		12	0
		11	0
		10	0
	3	15	1
		14	0
		13	0
		12	0
		11	0
	2	15	0
		14	0
		13	0

APPENDIX 14: TWO-TAILED CRITICAL VALUES OF THE LARGEST DIFFERENCE IN THE KOLMOGOROV-SMIRNOV ONE-SAMPLE TEST

N	0.10	0.05
1	0.950	0.975
2	0.776	0.842
3	0.642	0.708
4	0.564	0.624
5	0.510	0.565
6	0.470	0.521
7	0.438	0.486
8	0.411	0.457
9	0.388	0.432
10	0.368	0.410
11	0.352	0.391
12	0.338	0.375
13	0.325	0.361
14	0.314	0.349
15	0.304	0.338
16	0.295	0.328
17	0.286	0.318
18	0.278	0.309
19	0.272	0.301
20	0.264	0.294
25	0.24	0.27
30	0.22	0.24
35	0.21	0.23
36+	$\dfrac{1.22}{\sqrt{N}}$	$\dfrac{1.36}{\sqrt{N}}$

Source: Adapted from F. J. Massey, Jr. (1951) 'The Kolmogorov-Smirnov test for goodness of fit', *Journal of the American Statistical Association* 46: 70

APPENDIX 15: ONE-TAILED 0.05 CRITICAL VALUES OF THE KOLMOGOROV-SMIRNOV TEST FOR SMALL SAMPLES

n_2 \ n_1	3	4	5	6	7	8	9	10	11	12	13	14	15	16	17	18	19	20	21	22	23	24	25
3	9	10	13	15	16	19	21	22	25	27	28	31	33	34	35	39	40	41	45	46	47	51	52
4	10	16	16	18	21	24	25	28	29	36	33	38	38	44	44	46	49	52	52	56	57	60	61
5	13	16	20	21	24	26	28	35	35	36	40	42	50	46	49	51	56	60	60	62	65	67	75
6	15	18	21	30	25	30	33	36	38	48	43	48	51	54	56	66	61	66	69	70	73	78	78
7	16	21	24	25	35	34	36	40	43	45	50	56	56	58	61	64	68	72	77	77	79	78	85
8	19	24	26	30	34	40	40	44	48	52	53	58	60	72	65	72	73	80	81	84	89	83	85
9	21	25	28	33	36	40	54	46	51	57	57	63	69	68	74	81	80	83	90	91	94	96	95
10	22	28	35	36	40	44	46	60	57	60	62	68	75	76	77	81	85	100	91	98	101	99	101
11	25	29	35	38	43	48	51	57	66	64	67	72	76	80	83	82	92	95	101	110	108	106	110
12	27	36	36	48	45	52	57	60	64	72	71	78	84	88	89	87	98	104	108	110	113	111	116
13	28	33	40	43	50	53	57	62	67	71	91	78	86	90	94	96	102	108	112	117	120	132	120
14	31	38	42	48	56	58	63	68	72	78	78	98	92	96	99	98	108	114	126	124	127	124	131
15	33	38	50	43	56	60	69	75	76	84	86	92	105	101	105	104	113	125	126	130	134	132	136
16	34	44	46	48	58	72	68	76	80	88	90	92	101	112	109	111	120	128	130	136	141	141	145
17	35	44	46	54	61	65	74	77	83	88	94	96	105	109	136	116	125	130	135	141	152	152	148
18	39	46	51	56	64	72	81	82	82	96	98	99	104	116	118	144	127	136	144	148	146	150	156
19	40	49	56	61	68	73	80	85	87	98	102	104	111	120	125	127	152	136	147	151	151	162	161
20	41	52	60	66	72	80	83	100	92	104	108	114	113	128	130	136	144	152	144	160	159	162	168
21	45	52	60	69	77	81	90	91	101	108	112	126	125	130	135	144	147	154	168	163	170	172	180
22	46	56	62	70	77	84	91	98	110	110	117	124	126	130	141	148	151	160	163	198	173	177	182
23	47	57	65	73	79	89	94	101	110	113	120	127	130	136	146	151	159	163	170	173	207	182	188
24	51	60	67	78	83	96	99	106	111	132	124	132	134	140	150	162	162	172	177	182	183	216	194
25	52	61	75	78	85	95	101	110	116	120	131	136	145	148	156	161	168	180	182	188	194	204	225

Source: Adapted from Gail, M. H. and Green, S. B. (1976) 'Critical values for the one-sided two-sample Kolmogorov-Smirnov statistic', Journal of the American Statistical Association 71: 757–60

APPENDIX 16: TWO-TAILED 0.05 CRITICAL VALUES OF THE KOLMOGOROV-SMIRNOV TEST FOR SMALL SAMPLES

n_1

n_2	2	3	4	5	6	7	8	9	10	11	12	13	14	15	16	17	18	19	20	21	22	23	24	25
2							16	18	20	22	24	26	26	28	30	32	34	36	38	38	40	42	44	46
3				15	18	21	21	24	27	30	30	33	36	36	39	42	45	45	48	51	51	54	57	60
4			16	20	20	24	28	28	30	33	36	39	42	44	48	48	50	53	53	59	62	64	68	68
5			20	25	24	28	30	35	40	39	43	45	46	55	54	55	55	61	65	69	69	72	76	80
6			20	25	30	30	34	39	40	43	48	52	54	57	60	62	72	70	72	75	78	80	90	88
7		15	24	28	30	42	40	42	46	48	53	56	63	62	64	68	72	76	79	91	84	89	92	97
8	16	21	28	30	34	40	48	46	48	53	60	62	64	67	80	77	80	82	88	89	94	98	104	104
9	18	24	28	35	39	42	46	54	53	59	63	65	70	75	78	82	90	89	93	99	101	106	111	114
10	20	27	30	40	40	46	48	53	70	60	66	70	74	80	84	89	92	94	107	105	108	114	118	125
11	22	30	33	39	43	48	53	59	60	77	72	75	82	84	89	93	97	102	116	112	121	119	124	129
12	24	30	36	43	48	53	60	63	66	72	84	81	86	93	96	100	108	108	120	120	124	125	144	138
13	26	33	39	45	52	56	62	65	70	75	81	91	89	96	101	105	110	114	126	140	130	135	140	145
14	26	36	42	46	54	63	64	70	74	82	86	89	112	98	106	111	116	121	135	138	138	142	146	150
15	28	36	44	55	57	62	67	75	80	84	93	96	98	120	114	116	123	127	138	145	144	149	156	160
16	30	39	48	54	60	64	80	78	84	89	96	101	106	114	128	124	128	133	140	151	150	157	168	167
17	32	42	48	55	62	68	77	82	89	93	100	105	111	116	124	136	133	141	152	159	157	163	168	173
18	34	45	50	55	72	72	80	90	92	97	108	110	116	123	128	133	162	142	152	159	164	170	180	180
19	36	45	53	61	70	76	82	89	94	102	108	114	121	127	133	141	142	171	160	163	169	177	183	187
20	38	48	53	65	72	79	88	93	107	116	120	126	135	138	140	152	152	160	180	173	176	184	192	200
21	38	51	59	69	75	91	89	99	105	112	120	140	138	145	151	159	159	163	173	189	183	189	198	202
22	40	51	62	69	78	84	94	101	108	121	124	130	138	144	150	157	164	169	176	183	194	194	204	209
23	42	54	64	72	80	89	98	106	114	119	125	135	142	149	157	163	170	177	184	189	194	230	205	216
24	44	57	68	76	90	92	104	111	118	124	144	140	146	156	168	168	180	183	192	198	204	205	240	225
25	46	60	68	80	88	97	104	114	125	129	138	145	150	160	167	173	180	187	200	202	209	216	225	250

Source: Adapted from Table 55 of Pearson, E. S. and Hartley, H. O. (1976) *Biometrika Tables for Statisticians*, vol. 2, Cambridge University Press, London, by permission of the Biometrika Trustees

APPENDIX 17: TWO-TAILED CRITICAL VALUES OF THE KOLMOGOROV-SMIRNOV TEST FOR LARGE SAMPLES

Significance level	D
0.10	$1.22 \sqrt{\dfrac{n_1 + n_2}{n_1 \times n_2}}$
0.05	$1.36 \sqrt{\dfrac{n_1 + n_2}{n_1 \times n_2}}$
0.025	$1.48 \sqrt{\dfrac{n_1 + n_2}{n_1 \times n_2}}$
0.01	$1.63 \sqrt{\dfrac{n_1 + n_2}{n_1 \times n_2}}$
0.005	$1.73 \sqrt{\dfrac{n_1 + n_2}{n_1 \times n_2}}$
0.001	$1.95 \sqrt{\dfrac{n_1 + n_2}{n_1 \times n_2}}$

Source: Adapted from Smirnov, N. (1948) 'Tables for estimating the goodness of fit of empirical distributions', *Annals of Mathematical Statistics* 19: 280–1

APPENDIX 18: CRITICAL VALUES OF U AT 0.05 ONE-TAILED LEVEL AND 0.10 TWO-TAILED LEVEL

n_2

	n_1																			
	1	2	3	4	5	6	7	8	9	10	11	12	13	14	15	16	17	18	19	20
1	—	—	—	—	—	—	—	—	—	—	—	—	—	—	—	—	—	—	0	0
2	—	—	—	—	0	0	0	1	1	1	1	2	2	2	3	3	3	4	4	4
3	—	—	0	0	1	2	2	3	3	4	5	5	6	7	7	8	9	9	10	11
4	—	—	0	1	2	3	4	5	6	7	8	9	10	11	12	14	15	16	17	18
5	—	0	1	2	4	5	6	8	9	11	12	13	15	16	18	19	20	22	23	25
6	—	0	2	3	5	7	8	10	12	14	16	17	19	21	23	25	26	28	30	32
7	—	0	2	4	6	8	11	13	15	17	19	21	24	26	28	30	33	35	37	39
8	—	1	3	5	8	10	13	15	18	20	23	26	28	31	33	36	39	41	44	47
9	—	1	3	6	9	12	15	18	21	24	27	30	33	36	39	42	45	48	51	54
10	—	1	4	7	11	14	17	20	24	27	31	34	37	41	44	48	51	55	58	62
11	—	1	5	8	12	16	19	23	27	31	34	38	42	46	50	54	57	61	65	69
12	—	2	5	9	13	17	21	26	30	34	38	42	47	51	55	60	64	68	72	77
13	—	2	6	10	15	19	24	28	33	37	42	47	51	56	61	65	70	75	80	84
14	—	2	7	11	16	21	26	31	36	41	46	51	56	61	66	71	77	82	87	92
15	—	3	7	12	18	23	28	33	39	44	50	55	61	66	72	77	83	88	94	100
16	—	3	8	14	19	25	30	36	42	48	54	60	65	71	77	83	89	95	101	107
17	—	3	9	15	20	26	33	39	45	51	57	64	70	77	83	89	96	102	109	115
18	—	4	9	16	22	28	35	41	48	55	61	68	75	82	88	95	102	109	116	123
19	0	4	10	17	23	30	37	44	51	58	65	72	80	87	94	101	109	116	123	130
20	0	4	11	18	25	32	39	47	54	62	69	77	84	92	100	107	115	123	130	138

Source: Adapted from Table I of Runyon, R.P. and Haber, A. (1991) *Fundamentals of Behavioral Statistics* (7th edn), McGraw–Hill, New York, by permission of the publishers

APPENDIX 19: CRITICAL VALUES OF U AT 0.025 ONE-TAILED LEVEL AND 0.05 TWO-TAILED LEVEL

n_1

n_2	1	2	3	4	5	6	7	8	9	10	11	12	13	14	15	16	17	18	19	20
1	—	—	—	—	—	—	—	—	—	—	—	—	—	—	—	—	—	—	—	—
2	—	—	—	—	—	—	—	0	0	0	0	1	1	1	1	1	2	2	2	2
3	—	—	—	—	0	1	1	2	2	3	3	4	4	5	5	6	6	7	7	8
4	—	—	—	0	1	2	3	4	4	5	6	7	8	9	10	11	11	12	13	13
5	—	—	0	1	2	3	5	6	7	8	9	11	12	13	14	15	17	18	19	20
6	—	—	1	2	3	5	6	8	10	11	13	14	16	17	19	21	22	24	25	27
7	—	—	1	3	5	6	8	10	12	14	16	18	20	22	24	26	28	30	32	34
8	—	0	2	4	6	8	10	13	15	17	19	22	24	26	29	31	34	36	38	41
9	—	0	2	4	7	10	12	15	17	20	23	26	28	31	34	37	39	42	45	48
10	—	0	3	5	8	11	14	17	20	23	26	29	33	36	39	42	45	48	52	55
11	—	0	3	6	9	13	16	19	23	26	30	33	37	40	44	47	51	55	58	62
12	—	1	4	7	11	14	18	22	26	29	33	37	41	45	49	53	57	61	65	69
13	—	1	4	8	12	16	20	24	28	33	37	41	45	50	54	59	63	67	72	76
14	—	1	5	9	13	17	22	26	31	36	40	45	50	55	59	64	67	74	78	83
15	—	1	5	10	14	19	24	29	34	39	44	49	54	59	64	70	75	80	85	90
16	—	1	6	11	15	21	26	31	37	42	47	53	59	64	70	75	81	86	92	98
17	—	2	6	11	17	22	28	34	39	45	51	57	63	67	75	81	87	93	99	105
18	—	2	7	12	18	24	30	36	42	48	55	61	67	74	80	86	93	99	106	112
19	—	2	7	13	19	25	32	38	45	52	58	65	72	78	85	92	99	106	113	119
20	—	2	8	13	20	27	34	41	48	55	62	69	76	83	90	98	105	112	119	127

Source: Adapted from Table I of Runyon, R.P. and Haber, A. (1991) *Fundamentals of Behavioral Statistics* (7th edn), McGraw-Hill, New York, by permission of the publishers

APPENDIX 20: TWO-TAILED CRITICAL VALUES OF *T* FOR THE WILCOXON TEST

N	Significance level			N	Significance level		
	0.10	0.05	0.02		0.10	0.05	0.02
5	0	—	—	28	130	116	101
6	2	0	—	29	140	126	110
7	3	2	0	30	151	137	120
8	5	3	1	31	163	147	130
9	8	5	3	32	175	159	140
10	10	8	5	33	187	170	151
11	13	10	7	34	200	182	162
12	17	13	9	35	213	195	173
13	21	17	12	36	227	208	185
14	25	21	15	37	241	221	198
15	30	25	19	38	256	235	211
16	35	29	23	39	271	249	224
17	41	34	27	40	286	264	238
18	47	40	32	41	302	279	252
19	53	46	37	42	319	294	266
20	60	52	43	43	336	310	281
21	67	58	49	44	353	327	296
22	75	65	55	45	371	343	312
23	83	73	62	46	389	361	328
24	91	81	69	47	407	378	345
25	100	89	76	48	426	396	362
26	110	98	84	49	446	415	379
27	119	107	92	50	466	434	397

Source: Adapted from Table I of Wilcoxon, F. (1949) *Some Rapid Approximate Statistical Procedures*, American Cyanamid Company, New York, by permission of the publishers

APPENDIX 21: TWO-TAILED CRITICAL VALUES OF SPEARMAN'S rho

N	Significance level	
	0.10	*0.05*
5	0.900	1.000
6	0.829	0.886
7	0.715	0.786
8	0.620	0.715
9	0.600	0.700
10	0.564	0.649
11	0.537	0.619
12	0.504	0.588
13	0.484	0.561
14	0.464	0.539
15	0.447	0.522
16	0.430	0.503
17	0.415	0.488
18	0.402	0.474
19	0.392	0.460
20	0.381	0.447
21	0.371	0.437
22	0.361	0.426
23	0.353	0.417
24	0.345	0.407
25	0.337	0.399
26	0.331	0.391
27	0.325	0.383
28	0.319	0.376
29	0.312	0.369
30	0.307	0.363

Source: Adapted from Glasser, G. J. and Winter, R. F. (1961) 'Critical values of the coefficient of rank correlation for testing the hypothesis of independence', *Biometrika* 48, 444–8, by permission of the Biometrika Trustees

APPENDIX 22: ONE-TAILED CRITICAL VALUES OF KENDALL'S PARTIAL RANK-ORDER CORRELATION

N	0.05	0.025
4	0.707	1.000
5	0.667	0.802
6	0.600	0.667
7	0.527	0.617
8	0.484	0.565
9	0.443	0.515
10	0.413	0.480
11	0.387	0.453
12	0.465	0.430
13	0.347	0.410
14	0.331	0.391
15	0.319	0.377
16	0.305	0.361
17	0.294	0.348
18	0.284	0.336
19	0.275	0.326
20	0.268	0.318
25	0.236	0.279
30	0.213	0.253
35	0.196	0.232
40	0.182	0.216
45	0.171	0.203
50	0.161	0.192
60	0.147	0.174
70	0.135	0.160
80	0.126	0.150
90	0.119	0.141

Source: Adapted from Maghsoodloo, S. (1975) 'Estimates of the quantiles of Kendall's partial rank correlation coefficient', *Journal of Statistical Computing and Simulation*, 4, 155–64; Maghsoodloo, S. and Pallos, L.L. (1981) 'Asymptotic behavior of Kendall's partial rank correlation coefficient and additional quantile estimates', *Journal of Statistical Computing and Simulation*, 13, 41–8

APPENDIX 23: WRITING UP THE RESULTS OF A STATISTICAL TEST IN A RESEARCH PAPER

As space is at a premium in research papers, the results of statistical analyses are written as succinctly as possible. To find out how this is done, it is useful to look at the way such analyses have been presented in journal articles and only a few general guidelines will be offered here. Different journals may have slightly different 'house styles' but these differences are unlikely to be important.

Descriptive statistics such as the mean, standard deviation and correlation should be reported. If there are relatively few such statistics they may be reported in sentences such as in the following examples:

> The mean age in years for women was 21.35 (SD = 1.72) and for men 20.42 (SD = 0.96).

> Mean aggressiveness was significantly higher (t = 1.95, df = 19, one-tailed $p<.05$) in the reward condition (M = 3.13, SD = 1.07) than in the punishment condition (M = 2.21, SD = 1.01).

> Self-reported aggressiveness was significantly positively correlated (r = 0.33, df = 49, one-tailed $p<.01$) with the number of violent television programmes seen over the previous week.

If there are a relatively large number of such statistics then it may be more convenient to present them in a table. Tables are generally preferable to figures such as histograms since the exact values can be more readily presented. The table should have a number and a brief title describing its contents and may have notes at the bottom where this is appropriate. Means and standard deviations should be presented for variables which are correlated. It is not usual to report the distribution of values of variables, although this may be useful.

It is usually necessary to describe the nature of the inferential statistic used for a particular analysis as in the following examples:

> A two-way analysis of variance was carried out with gender and treatment as the two factors.

> Pre-test-post-test changes on the two measures were evaluated with related t tests.

> A stepwise multiple regression was conducted for women and men separately with self-reported aggression as the criterion.

When describing a statistically significant finding, the test statistics which should be presented in the sentence are:

1 The test statistic symbol (e.g. *t*, *r* or *F*) and its value;
2 Its degrees of freedom particularly where these may differ for different analyses;
3 Its probability level and whether this was one-tailed where this is appropriate.

These statistics are placed either within brackets as in the two of the examples above or within commas as in the example below. The degrees of freedom are sometimes alternatively presented as a subscript of the test statistic or in brackets as shown respectively in the two examples below:

The interaction between gender and treatment was significant, $F_{1,20} = 10.95$, $p<.01$.

Test statistics are also sometimes presented for findings which are not significant in which case the significance level is usually reported as *ns*:

The interaction between gender and treatment was not significant, F (1, 20) = 3.27, *ns*.

Answers to exercises

2 MEASUREMENT AND UNIVARIATE ANALYSIS

1 Ordinal
2 Ratio
3 (a) 3 and 4
  (b) 7
  (c) 4.0
  (d) 3.5
  (e) 4.3
  (f) 44.1
  (g) 4.9
  (h) 2.21

3 INTRODUCING SPSS FOR WINDOWS

1 You could assign a single number to each category such as 1 for single and never married, 2 for married, 3 for separated, 4 for divorced and 5 for widowed.
2 With no other information, you could code marital status for this person as missing.
3 →**Transform** →**Compute** . . . →in box entitled **Target Variable:** type **age** →**Numeric Expression:** and type **2000**-year of birth variable name →**OK**
4 (a) Input the information into **Newdata**
  (b) →**Transform** →**Recode** →**Into Different Variables** . . . →first variable to be recoded [e.g. **ci2**] →▶button [puts first variable in **Numeric Variable** −> **Output Variable:** box] →**Name:** box and type name for recoded variable [e.g. **ci2r**] →**Change** →**Old and New Values** . . . Repeat for similarly recoded variables [e.g. **ci4 ci6 ci8 ci10**] →**Range:** in **Old Value** section and type first old value [e.g. **1**] in **Value:** box →**Value:** box in **New Value** section and type first new value [e.g. **2**] →**Add** Repeat for other values [e.g. **2→1**] →**Continue** →**OK**
  (c) →**Transform** →**Compute** . . . →**Target Variable:** box and type new variable name [e.g. **cisum**] →select or type in appropriate expression in **Numeric Expression:** box [e.g. **ci1 + ci2r + ci3 + ci4r + ci5 + ci6r + ci7 + ci8r + ci9 + ci10r**] →**OK**
  (d) →**Transform** →**Compute** . . . →**Target Variable:** box and type new

variable name [e.g.**cimean**] →select or type in appropriate expression in **Numeric Expression:** box [e.g. **cisum/10**] →**OK**

(e) →**Statistics** →**Summarize** →**Descriptives** . . . →**cimean** → ▶ button →**OK**

5 If one or more scores is coded as missing, the total score will be set as missing.

4 STATISTICAL SIGNIFICANCE AND CHOICE OF TEST

1 1 out of 64 ($2 \times 2 \times 2 \times 2 \times 2 \times 2 = 64$) or 0.015625 (1/64 or $0.5 \times 0.5 \times 0.5 \times 0.5 \times 0.5 \times 0.5 = 0.015625$)
2 1 out of 8 ($2 \times 2 \times 2 = 8$) or 0.125 (1/8 or $0.5 \times 0.5 \times 0.5 = 0.125$)
3 0.421875 ($0.75 \times 0.75 \times 0.75 = 0.421875$)
4 25
5 No
6 Two-tailed
7 (a) 0.661
  (b) 0.717
  (c) 0.92
  (d) 0.1788
  (e) 0.3576
  (f) Symmetrical with a nonsignificant tendency of a positive skew
  (g) −0.153
  (h) 1.400
  (i) −0.11
  (j) 0.4562
  (k) 0.9124
  (l) Mesokurtic with a nonsignificant tendency towards platykurtosis
8 (a) about 55.56 (given rounding error)
  (b) 3
  (c) 4
  (d) Less than 0.05
  (e) Yes
  (f) 135.38
  (g) Less than 0.05
  (h) Yes

5 TESTS OF DIFFERENCE FOR INTERVAL/RATIO DATA ON UNRELATED SAMPLES FOR ONE FACTOR

1 (a) 1.41
  (b) 5 in the numerator and 5 in the denominator
  (c) Greater than 0.05
  (d) No
  (e) Yes
  (f) 2.44
  (g) 10
  (h) Less than 0.05
  (i) Yes

2 (a) 5.98
  (b) 1 in the numerator and 10 in the denominator
  (c) Less than 0.05
  (d) Yes
3 (a) 1.1
  (b) 2 in the numerator and 9 in the denominator
  (c) Greater than 0.05
  (d) No
  (e) 4.13
  (f) None

6 TESTS OF ASSOCIATION FOR INTERVAL/RATIO DATA

1 (a) 0.37
  (b) 10
  (c) No
2 (a) z test
  (b) 0.0
  (c) 0.54
  (d) -0.74
  (e) No
3 (a) T_2 test
  (b) 0.35
  (c) 0.16
  (d) 0.05
  (e) 9
  (f) No
4 (a) Z_2^* test
  (b) -0.64
  (c) -0.43
  (d) -0.40
  (e) -2.34
  (f) Yes
5 0.34
6 0.40

7 BIVARIATE AND MULTIPLE REGRESSION

1 (a) 0.39
  (b) 0.37
  (c) 1.81
  (d) 2.59
  (e) 1.03
  (f) 0.31
  (g) 0.81
  (h) 0.14
  (i) 0.05
  (j) 1.56

(k) 1 in the numerator and 10 in the denominator
(l) Greater than 0.05
2 (a) 0.36
  (b) 0.38
  (c) 0.04
  (d) 0.06
  (e) 0.14
  (f) 0
  (g) 0.71
  (h) 2 in the numerator and 9 in the denominator
  (i) Greater than 0.05
  (j) 0.33
  (k) 1.15
  (l) 1 in the numerator and 9 in the denominator
  (m) Greater than 0.05
  (n) 0.03
  (o) 0.01
  (p) 1 in the numerator and 9 in the denominator
  (q) Greater than 0.05

8 TESTS OF DIFFERENCE FOR INTERVAL/RATIO DATA ON RELATED SAMPLES FOR ONE FACTOR

1 (a) −1.58
  (b) 5
  (c) Greater than 0.05
  (d) No
2 (a) 1.86
  (b) 2 in the numerator and 10 in the denominator
  (c) Greater than 0.05
  (d) No

9 TESTS OF DIFFERENCE FOR INTERVAL/RATIO DATA ON UNRELATED SAMPLES FOR TWO FACTORS

1 (a) 1.86
  (b) 2 in the numerator and 6 in the denominator
  (c) Greater than 0.05
  (d) No
  (e) 7.00
  (f) 1 in the numerator and 6 in the denominator
  (g) Less than 0.05
  (h) Yes
  (i) 1.00
  (j) 2 in the numerator and 6 in the denominator
  (k) Greater than 0.05
  (l) No

10 TESTS OF DIFFERENCE FOR INTERVAL/RATIO DATA ON MIXED SAMPLES FOR TWO FACTORS

1 (a) 1.00
  (b) 1 in the numerator and 10 in the denominator
  (c) Greater than 0.05
  (d) No
2 (a) 7.60
  (b) 1 in the numerator and 9 in the denominator
  (c) Less than 0.05
  (d) 0.92
  (e) 1 in the numerator and 8 in the denominator
  (f) Greater than 0.05
  (g) Yes
  (h) 3.00
  (i) 1.83
  (j) Yes

11 TESTS OF DIFFERENCE FOR CATEGORICAL DATA

1 (a) Chi-square. Observed frequencies need to be converted into percentages.
  (b) 10.32
  (c) 3
  (d) Two-tailed
  (e) Less than 0.05
  (f) Yes
2 (a) Chi-square
  (b) 6.95
  (c) 1
  (d) Two-tailed
  (e) Less than 0.05
  (f) Yes
3 (a) McNemar test
  (b) 4.05
  (c) 1
  (d) Two-tailed
  (e) Less than 0.05
  (f) Yes

12 TESTS OF DIFFERENCE FOR ORDINAL DATA

1 (a) 3.09
  (b) 1
  (c) Greater than 0.05
  (d) No
2 (a) $U = 6.0$
  (b) Greater than 0.05
  (c) No

3 (a) 2.51
  (b) 2
  (c) Greater than 0.05
  (d) No
4 (a) Greater than 0.05
  (b) No
5 (a) Greater than 0.05
  (b) No
6 (a) 6.25 (adjusted for ties)
  (b) 2
  (c) Less than 0.05
  (d) Yes

13 TESTS OF ASSOCIATION FOR CATEGORICAL AND ORDINAL DATA

1 (a) 0.21
  (b) 0.20
  (c) 0.15
  (d) 0.00
  (e) 0.02
2 (a) 0.35
  (b) 0.33
  (c) 0.43
  (d) 0.35
  (e) 0.41
  (f) 0.32

14 MEASUREMENT RELIABILITY AND AGREEMENT

1 0.54
2 (a) 0.19
  (b) 0.21
  (c) 0.42
  (d) 0.44
3 (a) 0.42
  (b) 5.5
  (c) 17

Bibliography

Bartlett, M. S. (1937) 'Properties of sufficiency and statistical tests', *Proceedings of the Royal Society* Series A 160: 268–82.

Berenson, M. L. and Levine, D. M. (1992) *Basic Business Statistics: Concepts and Applications*, 5th edn, Englewood Cliffs, NJ: Prentice-Hall.

Bliss, C. I. (1967) *Statistics in Biology, Statistical Methods for Research in the Natural Sciences*, vol. 1, New York: McGraw-Hill.

Boneau, C. A. (1960) 'The effects of violations of assumptions underlying the *t* test', *Psychological Bulletin* 57: 49–64.

Bowley, A. L. (1913) 'Working-class households in Reading', *Journal of the Royal Statistical Society* 76: 672–701.

Box, G. E. P. (1953) 'Non-normality and tests on variances', *Biometrika* 40: 318–35.

Bradley, D. R., Bradley, T. D., McGrath, S. G. and Cutcomb, S. D. (1979) 'Type I error rate of the chi-square test of independence in $R \times C$ tables that have small expected frequencies', *Psychological Bulletin* 86: 1290–7.

Brown, W. (1910) 'Some experimental results in the correlation of mental abilities', *British Journal of Psychology* 3: 296–322.

Camilli, G. and Hopkins, K. D. (1978) 'Applicability of chi-square to 2×2 contingency tables with small expected cell frequencies', *Psychological Bulletin* 85: 163–7.

Camilli, G. and Hopkins, K. D. (1979) 'Testing for association in 2×2 contingency tables with very small sample sizes', *Psychological Bulletin* 86: 1011–14.

Campbell, D. T. and Stanley, J. C. (1966) *Experimental and Quasi-Experimental Designs for Research*, Chicago, IL: Rand McNally.

Cochran, W. G. (1941) 'The distribution of the largest of a set of estimated variances as a fraction of their total', *Annals of Eugenics* 11: 47–52.

Cochran, W. G. (1950) 'The comparison of percentages in matched samples', *Biometrika* 37: 256–66.

Cochran, W. G. (1954) 'Some methods for strengthening the common χ^2 tests', *Biometrics* 10: 417–51.

Cohen, J. (1960) 'A coefficient of agreement for nominal scales', *Educational and Psychological Measurement* 10: 37–46.

Cramer, D. (1994) *Introducing Statistics for Social Research: Step-by-Step Calculations and Computer Techniques Using SPSS*, London: Routledge.

Cramer, D. (1997) *Basic Statistics for Social Research: Step-by-Step Calculations and Computer Techniques Using Minitab*, London: Routledge.

Cramér, H. (1946) *Mathematical Models of Statistics*, Princeton, NJ: Princeton.

Cronbach, L. J. (1951) 'Coefficient alpha and the internal structure of tests', *Psychometrika* 16: 297–334.

Dinneen, L. C. and Blakesley, B. C. (1973) 'Algorithim AS62: A generator for the sampling distribution of the Mann–Whitney *U* Statistic', *Applied Statistics* 22: 269–73.

Dixon, W. J. and Mood, A. M. (1946) 'The statistical sign test', *Journal of the American Statistical Association* 41: 557–66.

Dunn, O. J. and Clark, V. A. (1969) 'Correlation coefficients measured on the same individuals', *Journal of the American Statistical Association* 64: 366–77.

Ebel, R. L. (1951) 'Estimation of the reliability of ratings', *Psychometrika* 16: 407–24.

Fisher, R. A. (1915) 'Frequency distribution of the values of the correlation coefficient in samples from an infinitely large population', *Biometrika* 10, 507–21.

Fisher, R. A. (1918) 'The correlation between relatives on the supposition of Mendelian inheritance', *Transactions of the Royal Society of Edinburgh* 52: 399–433.

Fisher, R. A. (1925a) 'Applications of "Student's" distribution', *Metron* 5: 90–104.

Fisher, R. A. (1925b) *Statistical Methods for Research Workers*, London: Oliver and Boyd.

Fisher, R. A. (1935) *The Design of Experiments,* Edinburgh: Oliver and Boyd.

Fisher, R. A. (1950) 'On a distribution yielding the error functions of several well known statistics', in R.A. Fisher (ed.) *Contributions to Mathematical Statistics*, New York: John Wiley & Sons. (Original work published 1924.)

Fisher, R. A. (1950) 'The arrangement of field experiments', in R.A. Fisher (ed.) *Contributions to Mathematical Statistics*, New York: John Wiley & Sons. (Original work published 1926.)

Fisher, R. A. and MacKenzie, W. A. (1923) 'Studies in crop variation. II. The manurial response of different potato varieties', *Journal of Agricultural Science* 13: 311–20.

Fleiss, J. L. (1971) 'Measuring nominal scale agreement among many raters', *Psychological Bulletin* 76: 378–82.

Friedman, M. (1937) 'The use of ranks to avoid the assumption of normality implicit in the analysis of variance', *Journal of the American Statistical Association* 32: 675–701.

Galton, F. (1886) 'Family likeness in stature, with an appendix by J.D. Hamilton Dickson', *Proceedings of the Royal Society of London* 40: 42–73.

Goodman, L. A. and Kruskal, W. H. (1954) 'Measures of association for cross classifications', *Journal of the American Statistical Association* 49: 732–64.

Goodman, L. A. and Kruskal, W. H. (1972) 'Measures of association for cross classifications, IV: Simplification of asymptotic variances', *Journal of the American Statistical Association* 67: 415–21.

Gosset, W.S. (1908) 'The probable error of a mean', *Biometrika* 6: 1–125.

Gosset, W. S. (1923) 'On testing varieties of cereals', *Biometrika* 15: 271–93.

Hartley, H. O. (1940) 'Testing the homogeneity of a set of variances', *Biometrika* 31: 249–55.

Hays, W. L. (1994) *Statistics*, 5th edn, New York: Harcourt Brace.

Hollander, M. and Wolfe, D. A. (1973) *Nonparametric Statistical Methods*, New York: Wiley.

Kendall, M. G. (1948) *Rank Correlation Methods*, London: Griffin.

Keppel, G. (1991) *Design and Analysis: A Researcher's Handbook*, 3rd edn, Englewood Cliffs, NJ: Prentice-Hall.

Kolmogorov, A. (1933) 'Sulla determinazione empirica di una legge di distribu-tione', *Giornale dell' Istituto Italiano delgi Attuari* 4: 1–11.

Kruskal, W. H. and Wallis, W. A. (1952) 'Use of ranks in one-criterion variance analysis', *Journal of the American Statistical Association* 47: 583–621.

LaPlace, P. S. (1951) *A Philosophical Essay on Probabilities*, New York: Dover. (Original work published 1814.)

Levene, H. (1960) 'Robust tests for equality of variances', in I. Olkin (ed.) *Contributions to Probability and Statistics*, Stanford, CA: Stanford University Press.

Lord, F. M. (1953) 'On the statistical treatment of football numbers', *American Psychologist* 8: 750–1.

Mann, H. B. and Whitney, D. R. (1947) 'On a test of whether one of two random variables is stochastically larger than the other', *Annals of Mathematical Sciences* 18: 50–60.

Mantel, N. and Haenszel, W. (1959) 'Statistical aspects of the analysis of data from retrospective studies of disease', *Journal of the National Cancer Institute* 22: 719–48.

Marascuilo, L. A. and McSweeney, M. M. (1977) *Nonparametric and Distribution-Free Methods for the Social Sciences*, Monterey, CA: Brooks/Cole.

Maxwell, S. E. (1980), 'Pairwise multiple comparisons in repeated measures designs', *Journal of Educational Statistics* 5: 269–87.

McNemar, Q. (1947) 'Note on the sampling error of the differences between correlated proportions of percentages', *Psychometrika* 12: 153–7.

McNemar, Q. (1969) *Psychological Statistics*, 4th edn, New York: Wiley.

Mood, A. M. (1950) *Introduction to the Theory of Statistics*, New York: McGraw-Hill.

Mosteller, F. and Tukey, J. W. (1977) *Data Analysis and Regression*, Reading, MA: Addison-Wesley.

Norusis, M. J./SPSS Inc. (1990a) *SPSS Base System User's Guide*, Chicago, IL: SPSS Inc.

Norusis, M. J./SPSS Inc. (1990b) *SPSS Advanced Statistics User's Guide*, Chicago, IL: SPSS Inc.

Norusis, M. J./SPSS Inc. (1990c) *SPSS/PC+ 4.0 Base Manual*, Chicago, IL: SPSS Inc.

Norusis, M. J./SPSS Inc. (1990d) *SPSS/PC+ Statistics 4.0*, Chicago, IL: SPSS Inc.

Norusis, M. J./SPSS Inc. (1993a), *SPSS for UNIX: Base System User's Guide, Release 5.0*, Chicago, IL: SPSS Inc.

Norusis, M. J./SPSS Inc. (1993b) *SPSS for Windows: Base System User's Guide, Release 6.0*, Chicago, IL: SPSS Inc.

Norusis, M. J./SPSS Inc. (1994a) *SPSS Advanced Statistics 6.1*, Chicago, IL: SPSS Inc.

Norusis, M. J./SPSS Inc. (1994b) *SPSS Professional Statistics 6.1*, Chicago, IL: SPSS Inc.

Overall, J. E. (1980) 'Power of chi-square tests for 2×2 contingency tables with small expected frequencies', *Psychological Bulletin* 87: 132–5.

Pearson, K. (1894) 'Contributions to the mathematical theory of evolution', *Philosophical Transactions of the Royal Society of London* Series A 185: 71–110. (Reprinted in *Karl Pearson's Early Statistical Papers* by E. S. Pearson, ed., 1948, Cambridge: Cambridge University Press.)

Pearson, K. (1895) 'Contributions to the mathematical theory of evolution – II. Skew variations in homogeneous material', *Philosophical Transactions of the Royal Society of London* Series A 186: 343–414. (Reprinted in *Karl Pearson's Early Statistical Papers* by E. S. Pearson, ed., 1948, Cambridge: Cambridge University Press.)

Pearson, K. (1896) 'Mathematical contributions to the theory of evolution – III. Regression, heredity and panmixia', *Philosophical Transactions of the Royal Society of London* Series A 187: 253–318. (Reprinted in *Karl Pearson's Early*

Statistical Papers by E. S. Pearson, ed., 1948, Cambridge: Cambridge University Press.)

Pearson, K. (1900) 'On the criterion that a given system of deviations from the probable in the case of a correlated system of variables is such that it can be reasonably supposed to have arisen from random sampling' *The London, Edinburgh and Dublin Philosophical Magazine and Journal of Science* Series 5 50: 157–75. (Reprinted in *Karl Pearson's Early Statistical Papers* by E. S. Pearson, ed., 1948, Cambridge: Cambridge University Press.)

Pearson, K. (1904) 'Mathematical contributions to the theory of evolution – XIII. On the theory of contingency and its relation to association and normal correlation', *Drapers' Company Research Memoirs* Biometric Series I. (Reprinted in *Karl Pearson's Early Statistical Papers* by E. S. Pearson, ed., 1948, Cambridge: Cambridge University Press.)

Pearson, K. (1905) 'Mathematical contributions to the theory of evolution – XIV. On the general theory of skew correlation and non-linear regression', *Drapers' Company Research Memoirs* Biometric Series II. (Reprinted in *Karl Pearson's Early Statistical Papers* by E. S. Pearson, ed., 1948, Cambridge: Cambridge University Press.)

Rosenthal, R. and Rosnow, R. L. (1991) *Essentials of Behavioral Research: Methods and Data Analysis*, 2nd edn, New York: McGraw-Hill.

Scheffé, H. A. (1953) 'A method for judging all possible contrasts in the analysis of variance', *Biometrika* 40: 87–104.

Scheffé, H. A. (1959) *The Analysis of Variance*, New York: Wiley.

Siegel, S. (1956) *Nonparametric Statistics for the Behavioral Sciences*, 1st edn, New York: McGraw-Hill.

Siegel, S. and Castellan, Jr., N. J. (1988) *Nonparametric Statistics for the Behavioral Sciences*, 2nd edn, New York: McGraw-Hill.

Smirnov, N. V. (1939) 'On the estimation of the discrepancy between empirical distribution curves for two independent samples', *Bulletin de l'Université de Moscou, Série internationale (Mathématiques)* 2: 3–14.

Smirnov, N. V. (1948) 'Table for estimating the goodness of fit of empirical distributions', *Annals of Mathematical Statistics* 19: 279–81.

Snedecor, G. W. (1934) *Calculation and Interpretation of Analysis of Variance and Covariance*, Ames, IA: Collegiate Press.

Somers, R. H. (1962) 'A new asymmetric measure of association for ordinal variables', *American Sociological Review* 27: 799–811.

Spearman, C. (1904) 'The proof and measurement of association between two things', *American Journal of Psychology* 15: 72–101.

Spearman, C. (1910) 'Correlation calculated with faulty data', *British Journal of Psychology* 3: 271–95.

SPSS Inc. (1997a) *SPSS Base 7.5 for Windows User's Guide*, Chicago, IL: SPSS Inc.

SPSS Inc. (1997b) *SPSS Professional Statistics 7.5*, Chicago, IL: SPSS Inc.

SPSS Inc. (1997c) *SPSS Advanced Statistics 7.5*, Chicago, IL: SPSS Inc.

Steiger, J. H. (1980) 'Tests for comparing elements of a correlation matrix', *Psychological Bulletin* 87: 245–51.

Stevens, J. (1992) *Applied Multivariate Statistics for the Social Sciences*, 2nd edn, Hillsdale, NJ: Lawrence Erlbaum.

Stevens, S. S. (1946) 'On the theory of scales of measurement', *Science* 103: 677–80.

Venn, J. (1888) *The Logic of Chance*, 3rd edn, London: Macmillan.

Walker, H. M. (1940) 'Degrees of freedom', *Journal of Educational Psychology* 31: 253–69.

Wilcox, R. R. (1987) 'New designs in analysis of variance', *Annual Review of Psychology*, 38: 29–60.

Wilcoxon, F. (1945) 'Individual comparisons by ranking methods', *Biometrics* 1: 80–3.

Williams, E. J. (1959) 'The comparison of regression variables', *Journal of the Royal Statistical Society* Series B 21: 396–9.

Winer, B. J. (1962) *Statistical Principles in Experimental Design*, New York: McGraw-Hill.

Yates, F. (1934) 'Contingency tables involving small numbers and the χ^2 test', *Journal of the Royal Statistical Society* Supplement 1: 217–35.

Yule. G. U. (1896) 'On the correlation of total pauperism with proportion out-relief. II. Males over sixty-five', *Economic Journal* 6: 613–23.

Index